AMERICAN FARMSTEAD CHEESE

AMERICAN FARMSTEAD CHEESE

The Complete Guide to Making and Selling Artisan Cheeses

Paul Kindstedt *with the*
VERMONT CHEESE COUNCIL

CHELSEA GREEN PUBLISHING / WHITE RIVER JUNCTION, VERMONT

Project Editor: Collette Leonard
Developmental Editor: Ben Watson
Copy Editor: Laura Jorstad
Proofreader: Robin Catalano
Indexer: Peggy Holloway
Designer: Peter Holm, Sterling Hill Productions
Design Assistant: Daria Hoak, Sterling Hill Productions

Printed in the United States on recycled paper
First printing, May 2005

Library of Congress Cataloging-in-Publication Data

Kindstedt, Paul.
American farmstead cheese : the complete guide to making and selling artisan cheeses / Paul Kindstedt ; with the Vermont Cheese Council.
p. cm.
Includes bibliographical references.
ISBN 1-931498-77-6 (pbk.)
1. Cheesemaking—United States. 2. Cheese--United States. I. Vermont
Cheese
Council. II. Title.

SF271.K49 2005
637'.3—dc22

2005002139

Chelsea Green Publishing Company
Post Office Box 428
White River Junction, VT 05001
(800) 639-4099
www.chelseagreen.com

This book is dedicated to Robert and Oletha Bickford in recognition of their steadfast commitment to Vermont agriculture and farmstead cheesemaking. Through their support of Shelburne Farms and the College of Agriculture and Life Sciences at the University of Vermont, Bob and Lee have enriched my journey as a cheese scientist and have helped to make this book possible.

PAUL S. KINDSTEDT

CONTENTS

PREFACE

William Townsend, a dairy farmer and cheesemaker in Vergennes, Vermont, was ahead of his time. In 1839 Townsend, who began producing cheese on his farm in 1828, wrote a book titled *The Dairyman's Manual: Containing Some of the Most Important Processes from the Best Sources for Making Butter and Cheese.* Townsend offered the following explanation for why he wrote his book: "Is it not a fact that successful dairying (that is, cheesemaking and buttermaking) requires more skill, regularity and order, than any other branch of the farming interest? And is it not a fact that our farmers generally are in want of information and rules for every day use and reference on this important subject, and that too, in a condensed form and always at hand. There can scarcely be two opinions upon this question. Therefore, . . . our desire is to diffuse knowledge and elevate the character of our dairies, and our effort has been to merit the favorable notice of the public, and render this little work a necessary inmate of every well regulated farm-house." Townsend understood that quality was key to the future of farmstead cheesemaking in Vermont, and that sound technical knowledge combined with craftsmanship was the key to attaining such quality. In his book Townsend cataloged proven practices that had been developed by successful cheesemakers like himself through years of experience. He also championed the integration of new technologies, such as the routine use of the thermometer, into the craft of cheesemaking.

What Townsend couldn't have foreseen in 1839 was that the factory system of production (the first cheese factory began producing cheese in 1851), combined with rapid advances in technical knowledge, would soon transform cheesemaking in ways unimaginable at the time. Farmstead cheesemaking became a casualty of that transformation and virtually disappeared from the American scene by the end of the 19th century. Industrial cheesemaking was here to stay.

When I joined the faculty at the University of Vermont almost 20 years ago, cheesemaking in my mind occurred in highly automated factories on a large scale. I had little interest in or regard for farmstead cheesemakers or the newly established American Cheese Society, the brainchild of my Ph.D. mentor, Professor Frank Kosikowski. So why have I spearheaded this book? Because I have changed. Years of interacting with farmstead cheesemakers in Vermont and watching them succeed brilliantly, as they demonstrated to the world that there is a place for farmstead artisan cheesemaking in America, slowly but inexorably opened my eyes and profoundly changed my perspective. I have come to understand, appreciate, and embrace Frank Kosikowski's vision for traditional cheesemaking and cheese appreciation in America. This book is a celebration of Kosikowski's vision.

But this book is more than a celebration. The American cheesemaking scene is changing and presenting new challenges to the burgeoning field of American farmstead cheesemakers. The quality expectations of the market and the regulatory requirements are becoming more demanding, and there is an ever growing need for technical resources that are written specifically for farmstead cheesemakers and tailored to their particular needs. Like William Townsend, I see a "want of information and rules for every day use and reference on this important subject." My sincere hope is that this book, like Townsend's manual in his time, earns the right to become "a necessary inmate of every well regulated farm-house."

Paul S. Kindstedt

The Rhyme and Reason of Cheese Diversity: The Old World Origins

1

The more we explore the world of cheese, the more astonishing that world becomes. It is not known precisely how many different cheeses exist, but one thing is certain: The number is dizzying. In the classic handbook titled "Cheese Varieties and Descriptions," the U.S. Department of Agriculture (1953) lists more than 800 cheeses. The World Cheese Exchange, an Internet database maintained by the Wisconsin Center for Dairy Research at the University of Wisconsin (www.cdr.wisc.edu), includes information on more than 1,400 named cheeses! The extraordinary diversity of cheese flavors, textures, aromas, and visual characteristics almost defies the imagination, especially in light of the fact that the starting point for all cheeses is mere milk, a bland, nondescript liquid.

If you are a fledgling farmstead cheesemaker or thinking about starting a farmstead cheese business, this complex world of cheese may seem bewildering at the least, perhaps even intimidating, but it needn't be. There is a rhyme and reason to cheese diversity; it is not as incomprehensible as it might first appear. The primary objective of this chapter is to demystify the origins and development of Old World cheeses by examining some examples of the geographic, climatic, cultural, and economic conditions in Europe that shaped the local cheesemaking technology. The local cheesemaking technology in turn shaped the chemistry and microbiology of the local cheese, which in turn shaped the characteristics and identity of the cheese. Chapter 1 also provides a glimpse into the great technological and cultural debt that American farmstead cheesemakers owe to their European forebears.

When considering the many cheese varieties that originated in Europe, it is important to recognize that local cheeses were often given the name of the town, the locality, or a significant feature of the area in which they were produced. Although the local name created a distinct identity and often served as a source of community pride, it did not necessarily mean that the local cheese was unique. Indeed, it is not uncommon to find cheeses produced in a geographic region that have different local names but are essentially the same cheese, or very closely related (Masui and Yamada, 1996). When we take this into consideration, the number of truly distinct cheese varieties is far fewer than the number of named cheeses. Although it is very difficult to classify all cheeses into distinctly different groups using a single classification scheme, a reasonable estimate is that there are perhaps around 20 truly distinct types of cheese.

How did these 20 or so distinct cheese types originate, and why do they differ so greatly in their characteristics? Perhaps the best way to answer these questions is to consider several specific examples of well-known, distinctive families of cheese. By *family*, I mean a group of cheeses that share a similar manufacturing technology and possess a similar initial chemical composition. As we will see in chapters 4 and 5, cheeses that share key manufacturing conditions *and* key aspects of composition are naturally predisposed to develop distinctive characteristics that differentiate them into the 20 or so distinct types we recognize today.

THE ALPINE CHEESES

Let's first consider the Alpine family of cow's-milk cheeses, among which the so-called Swiss cheeses are best known in the United States. Members of this family are large (typically 88 to 220 pounds/40 to 100 kg in weight), hard, rinded cheeses. They are characterized by a nutty flavor, a smooth, tight-knit, somewhat elastic texture, and usually the presence of holes or eyes, though the extent of eye formation varies considerably and some members of this family may lack eyes completely. The rind may or may not contain reddish brown surface growth depending on the specific cheese. Well-known examples of this family include Emmental, Gruyère (Comté), Appenzeller, and Beaufort.

The fact that this particular family of cheeses originated in the Alpine regions of Switzerland and eastern France makes perfect sense when we consider the conditions under which the cheesemaking methods were perfected. These cheeses originated in remote mountainous regions; farms and villages were situated in isolated valleys surrounded by Alpine meadows that extended high into the mountains. Tillable land in the valleys was quite limited and, therefore, was farmed intensively (Birmingham, 1991). The harsh winters presented an ongoing challenge to the inhabitants to produce enough nonperishable foodstuffs during the summer months to carry through the long winters. Although the Alpine meadows were not suitable for crop production due to the difficult conditions and the short growing season, they did support lush grasses. They also contained abundant water sources that made them suitable for grazing, including grazing by dairy cattle, which are less hardy than goats or sheep but produce more milk. Thus the Alpine meadows represented a valuable agricultural asset, and local peasants began the practice of mountainside grazing and cheesemaking, perhaps as early the first century B.C.E. (Kosikowski and Mistry, 1997).

Initially, grazing and cheesemaking were restricted to the lower meadows that were easily accessed; the cheeses were small in size and made out in the open (Birmingham, 1991). Over time, however, the cattle were allowed to graze higher and higher into the more remote meadows to access untapped grazing at the higher altitudes. Thus began the practice of following the meadows up the mountainside in early summer as the snow receded and then retreating downward at the end of summer in advance of the oncoming snows. *Transhumance,* or the movement of livestock and herders to different grazing grounds with the changing of seasons (generally to the mountains in summer and to the valleys or plains in winter), was widely practiced in mountainous regions throughout Europe (Berman, 1986; Whittaker and Goody, 2001). However, the exceptional remoteness of the Alps formed a distinctive microenvironment that profoundly influenced the local cheesemaking technology. First, it created a need for communal farming and cheesemaking. Because the cows now spent the entire summer on remote Alpine meadows, small-scale farmers, each possessing a few cows, banded together and combined their animals into a single herd of 70 or more cows (Birmingham, 1991). The herding and cheesemaking duties were delegated to a small group of cowmen who lived with the herd and made the cheese throughout the summer. Because cheese now had to be made from the milk of an entire herd rather than from individual cows, dedicated cheesemaking facilities were needed to accommodate the larger scale of production. Therefore, cheesemaking huts (called *chalets* or *byres*) and aging cellars were built at different altitudes to provide for on-site cheesemaking as the cows moved up the mountain and then back down again as summer progressed. An analogous system for sheep's-milk cheesemaking developed in the Pyrenees, where the cheesemaking huts are called *caylors* (Masui and Yamada, 1996). The mountain cheeses of the Pyrenees, such as Ardi-Gasna, can be considered "cousins" to the cow's-milk Alpine cheeses, sharing many similarities, as can several sheep's-milk cheeses such as Fontina and Montasio that originated in the northern Italian Alps. Although Fontina and Montasio are now produced from cow's milk, their origins in the distant past were as sheep's-milk cheeses (Androuët, 1973; Kosikowski and Mistry, 1997).

All the cheesemaking supplies, including the heavy copper cauldron that served as the cheese vat, had to be transported to the chalets up the steep and often grueling mountain paths. Furthermore, the volume of milk that needed to be made into cheese each day was quite large because of the large number of cows in the herd. Under these circumstances, it was not practical to have large-enough cheese vats to allow the evening milk to be stored overnight and then combined with the morning milk before being made into cheese. Therefore, cheesemaking for the most part had to be performed twice daily, immediately after the morning milking and then again following its afternoon counterpart. Salt, the crucial ingredient of all cheeses, which was also needed as a feed supplement for the cows, had to be imported to the village below and then packed up the mountainside to the chalets (Whittaker and Goody, 2001). There was thus a strong incentive to use salt sparingly in the cheesemaking process. Then there was the challenge of getting the cheeses down the mountain to the village below at the end of the season and, later, beyond the local village to the growing population centers and markets such as Vevy on Lake Geneva, and still later to distant export markets (Birmingham, 1991). In those days there were few options for transporting cheese, the most common modes being by human or by packhorse.

Given all these conditions and constraints, the Alpine cheesemaker was quite limited in the type of cheese that he could produce. (The term *he* is used because, unlike the case of many other cheeses where women dominated the craft, Alpine cheesemaking was largely a male profession.) For example, Alpine cheeses had to be hard and somewhat elastic to be durable and to resist fracturing and crumbling during the arduous transport to market. They also had to be large because it was much more practical to transport one large cheese through the mountainous terrain than many small cheeses. And Alpine cheeses had to have a long shelf life that would extend through the winter months when they were needed most, and, later, through distribution systems to increasingly distant export markets (Birmingham, 1991).

The requirements for large size, durability, and long shelf life meant that Alpine cheeses had to be low in moisture content. The higher the moisture, the softer, more fragile, and more short-lived the cheese. Achieving low moisture content presented a real technical challenge for Alpine cheesemakers. Their cheesemilk, being fresh from the cow, did not have time to undergo extensive microbial growth and therefore contained very few of the harmless lactic acid bacteria that are needed to produce lactic acid during cheesemaking. As we will learn in chapter 5, the production of lactic acid during cheesemaking aids in the expulsion of whey from the curd particles. Thus slow acid production makes it more difficult to expel whey and produce cheese with a low moisture content. The sparing use of salt exacerbated the problem because salt also promotes the expulsion of whey. Therefore Alpine cheesemakers had to develop special technological practices to force the moisture out of their curds during cheesemaking so that they would end up with a harder, tighter-knit, more durable, and longer-lived cheese. Undoubtedly through trial and error, they discovered three key practices that enabled them to accomplish this: (1) cutting the curd into tiny rice-sized particles (which vastly increased the surface area available for whey expulsion); (2) cooking the curds to very high temperatures (122 to 129°F/50 to 54°C) for extended time with vigorous stirring (which greatly enhanced curd shrinkage and whey expulsion); and (3) pressing with external pressure (which further enhanced the removal of whey and created a tight-knit structure and closed rind).

In summary, the following manufacturing practices, which were shaped by the local cheesemaking conditions and adapted to the peculiar needs of the Alpine cheesemaker, came to characterize the Alpine family of cheeses: (1) slow, delayed acid production during manufacture; (2) small cut size; (3) vigorous high-temperature cooking; (4) pressing with external pressure; (5) sparing use of salt. This common cheesemaking technology in turn shaped the chemistry and microbiology of the Alpine cheeses. For example, slow acid production during cheesemaking ensures that the final cheese will have a high mineral (specifically, calcium phosphate) content. High mineral content in turn produces a "sweet" cheese (that is, a cheese with low acidity or high pH); this, along with the sparing use of salt, creates a chemical environment within the cheese that has the potential to support the growth of a specific bacterium called *Propionibacterium shermanii*, which is naturally present in milk and cheese as a harmless contaminant. Cheeses that contain higher salt content and/or lower pH cannot support the growth of this organism. *P. shermanii* is essential to Alpine cheeses because it produces flavor compounds that contribute to the characteristic Swiss-like flavor and the carbon dioxide gas that results in the formation of round holes, or eyes. The low acidity (high pH) of Alpine cheeses also renders them potentially able to support the growth of aerobic bacteria (bacteria that require oxygen), such as the reddish *Brevibacterium linens* and other coryneform bacteria at the cheese surface. These organisms, which are unable to grow on the surfaces of more acidic cheeses, play an important role in the ripening of some Alpine cheeses such as Gruyère. Finally, the high mineral content and high pH of Alpine cheeses gives the curd a degree of elasticity that enables it to expand under pressure from accumulating carbon dioxide gas into spherical eyes rather than to fracture into unsightly slits. And so it is evident that the Alpine cheeses, because of the way that they are made and the chemical composition that results, are predisposed to develop the distinctive characteristics that we associate with this family of cheeses.

One final note about the Alpine cheeses. Although all the members of this family have the potential to support the growth of *Propionibacterium shermanii* and *Brevibacterium linens*, the extent to which these organisms flourish during aging and their influence on the final character of the cheese will depend on the specific conditions during aging and the actions of the cheesemaker or *affineur* (cheese finisher or ager). For example, gas production by *P. shermanii* requires warm temperatures; thus the Alpine cheeses that are aged at cooler temperatures, such as Beaufort, tend to have fewer and smaller eyes than those like Emmental that are held at warmer temperatures for extended periods. Similarly, the prolific growth of aerobic coryneform bacteria such as *B. linens* on the surface of Gruyère cheese requires a higher atmospheric humidity and a nurturing of the bacterial surface flora by the cheesemaker. In contrast, Emmental, with its clean, smooth rind, is aged at a lower humidity and requires more abrasive surface scraping and cleaning on the part of the cheesemaker.

Thus although the Alpine cheeses start out with a common initial chemistry and microbiological potential, they may diverge in character depending on the conditions during aging, thereby creating diversity within the family. The process of aging and the art of *affinage*, or finishing, will be the subjects of later chapters.

THE SOFT RIPENED CHEESES

Let's now turn our attention to the opposite end of the cheese spectrum and consider the soft ripened cheeses, among which two great families are renowned: the bloomy-rind (white-mold-ripened) cheeses, and the soft smear-ripened and washed-rind (aerobic-bacteria-ripened) cheeses. Characteristically these are smaller, softer, shorter-lived cheeses that ripen quickly through the action of microorganisms that grow at the cheese surface. The most familiar members of the bloomy-rind family are Camembert and Brie. Well-known examples of the soft smear-ripened and washed-rind cheeses include Muenster and Limburger.

The bloomy-rind cheeses originated chiefly in the plains of northern France (Normandy and Ile de France), where small villages surrounded by tiny peasant farms dotted the countryside. Cheesemakers in this region of France, usually women, produced their cheeses either for home consumption or for sale at the ubiquitous local village market. Therefore, in contrast to the Alpine cheeses, the cheeses of Normandy did not need to withstand the rigors of transport and extended storage and thus did not need to be large, hard, or long-lived (and therefore did not need to be low in moisture content). What these peasant women cheesemakers needed most were cheeses that could be easily and conveniently made during time carved out of their busy domestic schedules, that were enjoyable to eat, and that were sized appropriately for family use and for retail sale at the local market. Through trial and error, cheesemakers in Normandy discovered that such cheese could be made by a very simple, practical technology: coagulate the milk with rennet, drain the curd in small molds to form the cheese, apply salt to the cheese surface, and then store the bland fresh cheese briefly in a cool, damp cellar until white mold grew on the surface and the cheese developed desirable eating characteristics. This simple technology, which was perfectly adapted to the cool, damp climate of Normandy, would have been completely impractical in the high Alps. Conversely, there was little incentive for cheesemakers in Normandy to explore the cumbersome, though useful, technologies that were perfected by their Alpine cheesemaker counterparts, such as cooking at high temperatures and pressing with external pressure.

With respect to the smear-ripened cheeses, many, if not most, of them had their distant origins in the monasteries of Europe (Widcombe, 1978). In the sixth century A.D., Benedict of Nursia, founder of the most influential monastic order in Europe, unknowingly encouraged cheese to become a central element of the Benedictine diet when he formulated his monastic code, known as the Rule of St. Benedict. The Rule formed the basis for

European monastic practice for 1,000 years and profoundly shaped the agricultural and cultural development of Europe. Concerning mealtimes, the Rule specified that "there be at all seasons of the year two cooked dishes, so that he who cannot eat of the one may make his meal of the other" (Benedict, 1966). However, "All, save the very weak and sick, are to abstain wholly from eating the flesh of quadrupeds" (Benedict, 1966). Thus the Rule represented a balance between the spiritual ideal of self-denial and discipline and the human longing for variety and need for adequate nutrition. Variety in meal preparation was encouraged by requiring that there be two cooked dishes, but the prohibition of meat placed significant constraints on types of dishes that could be served, and greatly increased the risk of protein deficiency in the diet, a common problem in the Middle Ages. Thus the ban on eating meat made the eating of cheese all the more attractive from the standpoint of variety and all the more important as a protein source, and cheese was destined to become a common element of monastery life in Europe (Knowles, 1963). The importance of cheese in the monastic diet can be gauged by efforts in later years during the Cistercian reform to tighten up the Rule with respect to the observance of Lent. The Rule originally instructed each brother to "deny his body in food, drink, sleep, talking or laughter, and with spiritual joy await the holy feast of Easter" (Anonymous, 1966). Later, this general prohibition was revised to specifically prohibit the eating of cheese (and also eggs and imported spices) during Lent (Knowles, 1963). Evidently cheese had become such a common and pleasurable part of monastic life that it had to be explicitly banned during the Lenten season of abstinence.

The Benedictine monastery was organized as a self-contained and self-sufficient unit with its own agricultural and food-processing capability (Knowles, 1963). Thus it was logical for the Benedictines and other monastic orders such as the Cistercians, which sprang out of the Benedictine movement, to develop their own in-house cheesemaking practice. The monks probably borrowed existing cheesemaking techniques from the local peasants and then perfected the methods according to their circumstances and needs. Initially monasteries produced cheese primarily for consumption at the monastery, so unlike their Alpine counterparts, monastic cheeses generally did not need to be large, hard, or long-lived. Like the peasant cheesemaker in Normandy, monastic cheesemakers could produce cheese suitable for their needs using a very simple, practical technology: coagulate the milk with rennet, drain the curd in small molds to form the cheese, apply salt to the cheese surface, and store the bland fresh cheeses briefly in a damp, cool cellar until they developed a surface growth and desirable eating characteristics. Later, as cheesemaking became an important source of income for the abbey, some monasteries incorporated low-temperature cooking and light pressing into their cheesemaking practices. This enabled them to produce lower-moisture washed-rind cheeses that were close cousins to the soft smear-ripened cheeses

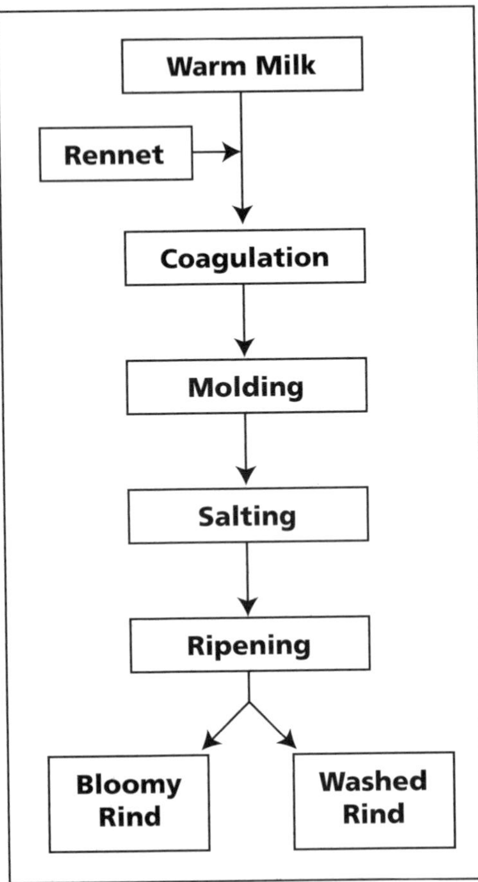

Figure 1.1. Basic steps used in the manufacture of bloomy-rind and washed-rind cheeses. Although the two cheeses follow a similar manufacturing procedure, upon ripening they differ dramatically in flavor, aroma, texture, and appearance.

but were firmer and had a longer shelf life, and thus were better suited for external sale.

And so it was that the technologies for bloomy-rind and soft smear-ripened cheeses developed along a simple and amazingly similar pattern, illustrated schematically in figure 1.1. Why then are these two families of cheese so different in character? The bloomy-rind cheeses, with their luxuriant coat of white mold, develop earthy mushroom flavor notes, whereas the soft smear-ripened cheeses, with their reddish bacterial surface growth, progress to a sulfury, pungent character. The answer relates to one critical cheesemaking parameter not evident in figure 1.1, but clearly illustrated in figure 1.2. The graph in figure 1.2 compares the typical patterns of acidity development (specifically the pH profiles) during the manufacture of bloomy-rind versus smear-ripened cheeses. For bloomy-rind cheeses, acid develops quickly and the cheese pH drops to very low levels within the first 24 hours (to around pH 4.6; very acidic). In contrast, in smear-ripened cheeses the acid develops slowly and the cheese pH remains relatively high after 24 hours (around pH 5.2; not very acidic). This difference in the acidity of the curd at the start of ripening predisposes these two cheese families to develop microbiologically along different pathways. The acidic curd of bloomy-rind cheese strongly favors the growth of acid-tolerant molds at the cheese surface but prevents the growth of aerobic coryneform bacteria, such as the reddish *Brevibacterium linens,* during the early stages of ripening. The particular species of mold that comes to dominate the cheese surface will depend on environmental conditions and the chemical composition of the cheese. When the moisture and salt contents of the curd and the atmospheric humidity and temperature of the environment are just right, the white mold *Penicillium camemberti* is favored and has the potential to grow prolifically at the cheese surface. Such is the fate of Brie and Camembert.

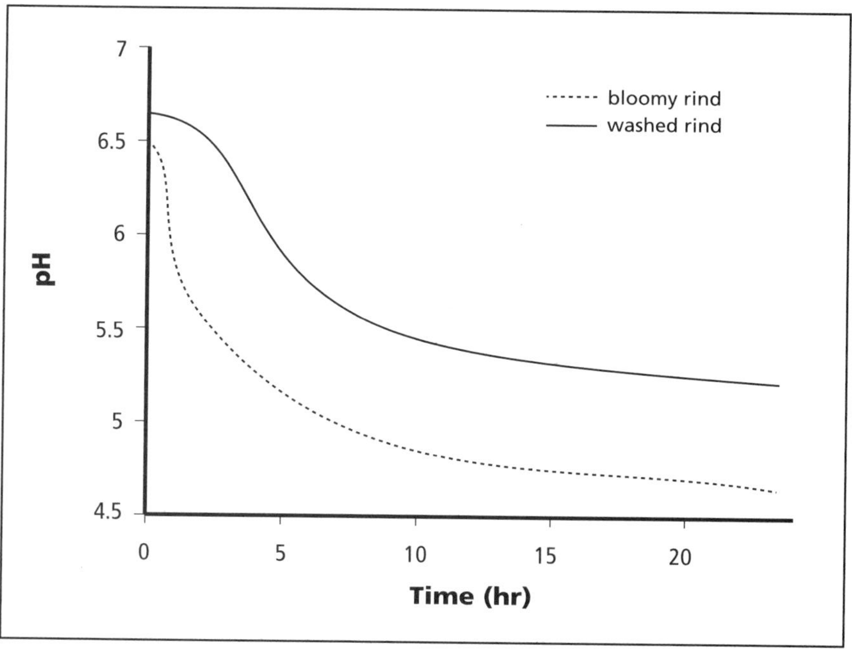

Figure 1.2. Typical acidity development (pH changes) during the manufacture of bloomy-rind and washed-rind cheeses. The pH decreases much more quickly during the manufacture of bloomy-rind than washed-rind cheeses, which creates a different chemical environment and ripening potential in the newly made cheeses.

Contrast this with the smear-ripened cheeses, which start out at a higher pH (lower acidity) and quickly increase to even higher pH values at the surface due to action of naturally present yeasts. High pH at the cheese surface strongly favors the growth of coryneform bacteria such as *Brevibacterium linens,* which have the potential to grow prolifically provided that the moisture content of the curd and the atmospheric humidity and temperature of the environment are in proper balance. Both the bloomy-rind and the smear-ripened cheeses rely on the skill of the cheesemaker or affineur to nurture the cheeses during aging to ensure good growth of the surface flora. However, the microbiological makeup of the surface flora is strongly predetermined by the schedule of acidification during the first 24 hours of cheesemaking (figure 1.2). Thus the smear-ripened cheeses and the bloomy-rind cheeses, like the Alpine cheeses, are predisposed to develop their distinctive characteristics because of the way they are made and the chemical composition of the cheese that results. The same can be said for all the major families of cheeses, the reasons for which will be examined in more detail in chapter 6.

Although the above discussion explains the why the bloomy-rind and smear-ripened cheeses develop remarkably different characteristics during aging, it also raises an intriguing question. Why did monastic cheesemakers use a slow process of acidification, which enabled the smear-ripened cheeses to be developed, in contrast with peasant cheesemakers in Normandy who used a faster schedule of acidification, which led to the development of bloomy-rind cheeses? The answer undoubtedly relates to differences in the amount of time that elapsed between the harvesting of the milk and the making of the cheese. Slow acidification meant that the milk used for cheesemaking contained very few of the harmless lactic acid bacteria that the cheesemaker relies on to produce lactic acid during cheesemaking. Therefore monastic cheesemakers, like their Alpine counterparts, must have made cheese shortly after harvesting the milk.

It is not difficult to imagine how this practice may have developed. Unlike the peasant farms of Normandy, which typically had one or two cows, monasteries kept large flocks or herds to supply the monastic community, and thus the monastic cheesemaker had daily access to large amounts of milk. There was no need to combine multiple milkings in order to accumulate enough milk for cheesemaking. Cheese could be made every day from freshly harvested milk. Furthermore, the monastic life was one of discipline, predictability, and formalized routine (which is why the monks made such great cheesemakers). The Rule specified that the monk be engaged in work from the hours of around 6:00 to 10:00 A.M. and again from about 2:00 to 6:00 P.M. during summer, which extended from Easter to the end of October (Butler, 1919). The work of the monks was largely artisan in nature, whereas much of the manual agricultural labor on the monastery's farm was carried out by peasants who were essentially employed by the monastery (Daly, 1965; Knowles, 1963) or, later, by lay brothers (Berman, 1986). Thus the culture of the monastery gave rise to a specialized calling: the artisan cheesemaker who practiced his craft according to the rigid schedule defined by the Rule. Typically, the routine milking of the monastic flock or herd was carried out by peasant workers (Daly, 1965) or lay brothers, who milked the animals in the fields and then carried the milk in wooden pails to the place where cheese was made. Although it is difficult to say for certain due to the scarcity of records, it is likely that the monastic cheesemaker had fresh, warm milk ready and waiting when he assumed his duties at around 6:30 A.M. Under such a scenario, the fresh milk would be bound to acidify slowly during cheesemaking, and the general procedure for making smear-ripened cheeses would fit well into the monastic schedule. As for the milk from the afternoon milking, perhaps the monks, like their Alpine counterparts, made cheese twice daily from the fresh milk, which their work schedule would have permitted, or perhaps they used the evening milk for other purposes. Either way, the milk that they used for cheesemaking would have been newly harvested and perfectly suited for soft smear-ripened cheeses.

Contrast this with the small peasant farm in Normandy, which possessed only one or two cows. In order to accumulate enough volume to make it worth her while, the cheesemaker had to combine the milk from the previous evening with the morning milk before making cheese.

In the absence of refrigeration, warm milk from the cow (or goat, or sheep) cooled slowly, and the growth of lactic acid bacteria was a natural consequence of any delay between the harvesting of the milk and the making of the cheese. Thus milk from the previous evening would have become enriched with lactic acid bacteria and would have served the same function as a starter culture when combined with the fresh morning milk. This preripening process was later refined as the technique known as *pied de cuvée,* or "bottom of the vat." According to this process, the cheesemaker retained a small portion of the milk from the previous day and held it at the temperature of the cheesemaking room (around 63°F/20°C) until the next morning (Le Jaouen, 1990). When added to the fresh morning milk, this small preripened portion of milk provided the large population of lactic acid bacteria that were needed to kick-start the acid production for this type of cheesemaking.

Another factor that would have contributed to the proliferation of lactic acid bacteria in the cheesemilk was the practice of using partly skimmed milk for cheesemaking. Normandy had become a major butter-producing region, and it was common practice to let fresh, warm milk sit in shallow pans to allow the cream to rise for subsequent skimming (Pirtle, 1926). During creaming, the population of lactic acid bacteria would increase. When the partly skimmed milk, now rich in lactic acid bacteria, was combined with fresh milk from the next milking, it essentially served as a starter culture, ensuring that the production of lactic acid would proceed rapidly during cheesemaking. Thus the milk of the peasant cheesemaker in Normandy was bound to produce a more acidic cheese than that of the monastery.

And so it was that two great families of cheese, the smear-ripened and the bloomy-rind cheeses, came into being because two groups of cheesemakers, who had similar objectives and employed similar technologies, differed in the time that they allowed to elapse between the harvesting of milk and the making of cheese.

Although we don't have time here to consider each of the 20 or so distinct cheese varieties, each has its own story of the geographic, climatic, economic, and cultural forces that shaped its development. You may rest assured that each has a rhyme and reason that makes for fascinating study and that ultimately makes perfect sense.

CHEESEMAKING IN ENGLAND

Before leaving our discussion of the origins of the Old World cheeses, it is necessary to turn our attention across the Channel and consider the cheesemaking of Old England. We cannot fully understand the rise, decline, and subsequent rebirth of farmstead cheesemaking in America, the focus of chapter 2, without first considering the English roots that run so deep. As fate would have it, the extraordinary changes that took place in English society and English cheesemaking during the period leading up to and encompassing the great colonization of the New

World would profoundly shape and dominate the cheesemaking practices of America for the next 300 years.

During the Middle Ages agriculture in England and other parts of Europe was dominated by feudalism. In feudal societies the ownership of land was concentrated in the hands of the nobility, a few medieval lords who built and maintained self-sufficient manors, and in the monasteries, which were often associated symbiotically with the local manor. The manor lord or the monastery in turn granted peasant farmers secure land tenure in the form of smallholdings for growing crops, typically 10 acres/4 hectares or less, and access to common lands for raising livestock. In return, the peasant serfs paid rent to the landlord or monastery from the proceeds of their agricultural produce. In essence, the landlord retained the right to receive revenue from the land, whereas the peasant farmer and his heirs were guaranteed the right to farm on the landholdings they had been granted. Guaranteed access to common lands was a vital part of the peasant's economic compensation package because the peasant farmer could not support his family on the small landholdings alone. The raising of livestock on communal land provided supplemental income and filled a critical economic need (Kulikoff, 2000).

The practice of communal grazing of livestock limited peasant dairying to a few cows because it precluded a mechanism for the individual farm to increase its herd size. Any significant attempt by peasants to expand their herds would jeopardize the sustainability of the entire peasant farm community through overgrazing of the commons upon which all relied. Milk production on peasant farms was thus marginal, and cheese was produced in small batches for home use, for payment to the landlord, and, later, for sale at the local market as manorial communities grew into villages. As in France, soft farmstead cheeses made by methods similar to those represented in figures 1.1 and 1.2 were common fare in England during this period (Cheke, 1959).

However, things began to change in the 15th century. The bubonic plague, or Black Death, decimated England in the mid-14th century, reducing the population by at least a third, and possibly even by half. This created an acute labor shortage within the manorial agricultural system while simultaneously freeing up vast quantities of land, the tenant rights to which could now be purchased by peasants who had survived and had managed to accumulate a little extra cash. Add to this the vast monastic landholdings that became available as monasteries throughout England (578 in all) were dissolved under Henry VIII (Durant, 1957). Many of these former monastic holdings were turned over to sheep raising—with one important exception. In East Anglia, already known by that time for its dairying, monastic lands reverted mostly to dairying, establishing East Anglia as England's premier region for production of cow's milk (Kulikoff, 2000).

As the 15th century progressed, some of the richer peasants accumulated considerable property, up to 50 acres/20 hectares, and began to employ other peasants as farm laborers, often under terms more favorable than those offered by the noble landlords. This competition for labor fundamentally changed the relationship between lord and peasant. Peasants could now demand greater freedom and a greater share of the agricultural profits from their landlord, for if denied they could now move elsewhere where the employment terms were more favorable. The stable, almost familial relationship that had existed between lord and peasant family for hundreds of years crumbled in the 15th century as the English peasantry became more assertive, demanding, and mobile. Landlords began to view the peasantry as a necessary evil, even the enemy, rather than as loyal subjects of the manorial community.

During the 16th and early 17th centuries feudalism in England collapsed completely and was replaced by agricultural capitalism. Wealthy peasants began to enclose their fields, setting a precedent for private ownership. Landlords, fed up with the demands of the small peasantry, then began to enclose what for centuries had been common lands, making the rights to the commons available for purchase by wealthy peasants. The relatively few rich peasants, now possessing 50 to 100 acres/20 to 40 hectares, became the yeomen, the landlord's chief tenants, whereas the many small peasants, unable to feed their families and pay the rent without access to the commons, were evicted from the land. Lacking the means of survival, they streamed from the countryside into the towns and cities, especially London, in search of work. A population explosion further accelerated the growth of urban areas during this period (Kulikoff, 2000).

Back in the countryside, landlords replaced land tenure with short-term leases, thereby reducing the security of the yeoman and enabling the landlords to raise the rent according to what the market would bear. Consequently, the comparatively wealthy yeoman farmers came under capitalistic pressure to become more efficient, entrepreneurial, and profitable. In response they acquired more land, consolidated their holdings, and became specialized and market oriented. During this period the concept of competency began to take root in yeoman agricultural practice. Like the self-sufficiency of the feudal peasant, competency called upon the yeoman farmer to produce many of the basic needs of the family on the farm. However, it also called for a strong emphasis on improving agricultural efficiency and on the production of cash crops to generate income to pay for a growing list of goods and services that were becoming increasingly important in the new capitalistic economy (Kulikoff, 2000). For yeoman dairy farmers, competency meant a dramatic movement away from cheeses produced for home and local consumption in favor of those destined for the rapidly growing and profitable but more distant urban markets, especially London. London became the primary market for East Anglia, which by this time had become England's most concentrated cheesemaking region, and a complex distribution system was created by the cheesemongers of London to transport cheese from country to city over newly built networks of roads (Stern, 1979). Cheeses that were made in the East Anglian counties of Suffolk and Essex for the London market had to be large, durable, and long-lived for purposes of transport and distribution. Therefore the cheesemaking emphasis shifted away from the many soft, high-moisture cheeses that had been made from time immemorial to a few hard, low-moisture, aged types. A similar process occurred later during the 18th century in the counties of Cheshire and Somerset, which eventually surpassed East Anglia as the primary suppliers to the London market (Foster, 1998; Cheke, 1959). Thus cheesemaking in England took a dramatically different path from that of France. In France small peasant farming with its diversity of soft cheeses persisted well into the 20th century; vestiges are still evident today, though they are now under siege by the forces of free trade and globalization. In stark contrast, cheesemaking in England during the 16th and early 17th centuries was fundamentally reoriented by the emerging capitalistic economy toward the production of relatively few hard cheeses that were suitable for sale in distant urban markets.

Because the English not only loved cheese but also had an even greater appetite for butter, it was more profitable to make butter than to make whole-milk cheeses. Therefore, most of the cheeses in the 16th and early 17th centuries were made from milk that was skimmed of its cream to varying degrees (Cheke, 1959). Today we would call these reduced-fat cheeses. Production of whole-milk cheeses was very limited, and such cheeses were enjoyed only by the wealthy, whereas reduced-fat and skim-milk cheeses were the standard fare for the common man (Cheke, 1959). The practice of letting the fresh milk set in shallow pans at room temperature for purposes of skimming ensured that the remaining partly skimmed milk contained large numbers of lactic acid bacteria by the time that it was used alone or in combination with fresh milk for cheesemaking. Furthermore, it was normal practice in England to combine the milks from two or even three milkings, or "meals," before making them into cheese (Cheke, 1959).

Consequently, the hard English cheeses, first developed on a large scale in East Anglia and later refined and improved in Cheshire and Somerset, came to be characterized by moderate to rapid acid production during manufacture. Furthermore, these cheeses needed to be low in moisture content to attain the necessary hardness and durability for transport and distribution. Like their Alpine counterparts, then, English cheesemakers turned to scalding (cooking at elevated temperatures) and pressing at high pressure to produce a drier-rinded cheese. Unlike their Alpine counterparts, however, English cheesemakers could count on moderate to vigorous production of lactic acid during cheesemaking, which aided in the expulsion of whey. Also, salt was plentiful and could be applied liberally, which further aided in whey expulsion. Consequently English cheesemakers did not need to cut the curd into tiny particles or cook at the extremely high temperatures that Alpine cheesemakers found so necessary under their peculiar set of conditions. In short, although the English cheeses were hard and low in moisture like the Alpine cheeses, they possessed a fundamentally different chemistry (acidity, mineral, and salt contents), microbiology (due in part to less severe heating), and structure, all of which predisposed them to develop along very different pathways during aging. This characteristic technology would soon make its way to the New World and would define American cheesemaking for the next three centuries.

Finally, there is one more development in 16th- and early 17th-century England that is key to our understanding of cheesemaking in America. During this watershed period England witnessed an almost catastrophic meltdown of society. Crime skyrocketed and the moral fabric of the poorer segments of society crumbled as dispossessed peasants, stripped of their land, their centuries-old community life, and their dignity, wandered the countryside in search of work (Kulikoff, 2000). Eventually most of them found their way into the slums of the teeming urban areas, especially London.

The obvious breakdown of society, moral decay, and rampant economic injustice were decisive factors that prompted the Puritan reformers, who were strongly concentrated in the cheesemaking region of East Anglia, to look to the New World for a fresh start. As fate—or, in my view, Providence—would have it, the East Anglian Puritans chose New England to become their promised land. They came to view New England as a land where they could practice their religious convictions free from the growing repression by the royal government and the Church of England, free from the appalling economic injustices that had accompanied the English transition from feudalism to capitalism, and free from the moral decay that had ensued. The Puritan emigration to New England resulted in a regional demographic profile that was unique to the new colonies because, unlike the southern colonies, which heavily recruited their immigrants from the urban poor, the Puritan immigrants represented a cross-section of English society (Kulikoff, 2000). They included craftsmen and artisans, servants and laborers, yeoman farmers and farmhands, and even merchants and gentlemen. Moreover, many emigrated as families and even as entire communities. Thus New England became a microcosm of Old England, more so than in any other region of the New World. The fact that the Puritans were heavily concentrated in East Anglia, England's most important cheesemaking region at the time, ensured that the state-of-the-art (that is, market-oriented) technology of English cheesemaking and the concept of agricultural competency were transferred directly to New England. And so New England was destined to become the epicenter of cheesemaking in America, and the English hard cheeses were destined to dominate American cheesemaking for the next 300 years.

CHAPTER 1 REFERENCES

Androuët, P. 1973. *Guide du Fromage: The Complete Encylopedia of French Cheese.* Harper's Magazine Press, New York.

Benedict, Saint. 1966. *The Rule of Saint Benedict.* Translated and with an introduction by Cardinal Gasquet. Cooper Square Publishers, Inc., New York.

Berman, C. H. 1986. "Medieval Agriculture, the Southern French Countryside and the Early Cistercians: A Study of Forty-three Monasteries." *Transactions of the American Philosophical Society* 76(5), American Philosophical Society, Philadelphia.

Birmingham, D. 1991. "Gruyère's Cheesemakers." *History Today* 41(Feb.): 21.

Burton, J. 1994. *Monastic and Religious Orders in Britain, 1000–1300.* Cambridge University Press, Cambridge.

Butler, C. 1919. *Benedictine Monachism: Studies in Bendictine Life and Rule.* Longmans, Green and Co., London.

Cheke, V. 1959. *The Story of Cheese-Making in Britain.* Routledge & Kegan Paul, London.

Daly, L. J. 1965. *Benedictine Monasticism: Its Formation and Development through the 12th Century.* Sheed and Ward, Inc., New York.

Durant, W. 1957. *The Story of Civilization,* Vol. VI: *The Reformation.* Simon & Schuster, Inc., New York.

Foster, C. F. 1998. *Cheshire Cheese and Farming in the North West in the 17th and 18th Centuries.* Arley Hall Press, Northwich, Cheshire.

Knowles, D. M. 1963. *The Monastic Order in England: A History of Its Development from the Times of St. Dunstan to the Fourth Lateran Council 940–1216.* Cambridge University Press, Cambridge.

Kosikowski, F. V., and V. V. Mistry. 1997. *Cheese and Femented Milk Foods,* Vol. 1: *Origins and Principles.* F. V. Kosikowski, LLC, Great Falls, Va.

Kulikoff, A. 2000. *From British Peasants to Colonial American Farmers.* University of North Carolina Press, Chapel Hill.

Le Jaouen, J.-C. 1990. *The Fabrication of Farmstead Goat Cheese,* 2nd ed. Cheesemakers' Journal, Ashfield, Mass.

Masui, K., and T. Yamada. 1996. *French Cheeses.* DK Publishing, Inc., New York.

McManis, D. R. 1975. *Colonial New England: A Historical Geography.* Oxford University Presss, London.

Pirtle, T. R. 1926. *History of the Dairy Industry.* Mojonnier Bros. Co., Chicago.

Stern, W. M. 1979. "Where, Oh Where Are the Cheesemongers of London?" *London Journal* 5(2): 228.

U.S. Department of Agriculture. 1953. "Cheese Varieties and Descriptions." U.S. Department of Agriculture, Handbook No. 54, Washington, D.C.

Whittaker, D., and J. Goody. 2001. "Rural Manufacturing in the Rouergue from Antiquity to the Present: The Examples of Pottery and Cheese." *Comparative Studies in Society and History* 43(2): 225.

Widcombe, R. 1978. *The Complete Book of Cheese.* Ure Smith, Sydney.

Cheesemaking in the New World: The American Experience

2

During the past two decades farmstead cheesemaking in the United States, and especially in Vermont and the Northeast, has experienced an astonishing rebirth. Farmstead cheesemaking is hardly new to America. Indeed, cheeses and cheesemaking were part of the culture and economy of colonial America from the beginning. What is new, however, is that this current generation of farmstead cheesemakers has embraced the rich heritage of European cheesemaking in all its diversity. In Vermont alone more than 100 different and very diverse farmstead cheeses are produced, the origins of which can be traced to Belgium, England, France, Germany, Greece, Italy, the Netherlands, Switzerland, and beyond (Tewksbury, 2002). A sample of the diversity of Vermont cheeses is shown in figure 2.1. Such diversity was not always part of the American cheesemaking scene. In fact, cheesemaking in the early colonies quickly became characterized by English-style hard cheeses, which set the stage for an almost monolithic production of Cheddar-type cheese throughout the United States until the early part of the 20th century. This dominance of Cheddar cheesemaking profoundly contributed to the near extinction of American farmstead cheesemaking in the second half of the 19th and early part of the 20th centuries.

How did Cheddar come to be America's preeminent cheese, how did it contribute to the decline of farmstead cheesemaking, and why is this new generation of American farmstead cheesemakers so enamored with the great European heritage of cheesemaking in all its diversity? The answers to such questions help to define the unique identity of today's American farmstead cheesemaker. The objective of chapter 2 is to provide an overview of the rise, decline, and renaissance of farmstead cheesemaking in America so that the current generation of farmstead cheesemakers can better appreciate and celebrate its singular American heritage and identity.

Figure 2.1. A sample of the diversity of cheeses made in Vermont. Most of the cheeses shown are produced on the farm. Such diversity is a recent phenomenon in Vermont and the United States, and represents a renaissance in American farmstead cheesemaking. (Photo courtesy of the Vermont Cheese Council.)

CHEESEMAKING IN THE COLONIES

To understand the development of cheesemaking in America, we must first consider the demographics of the newly formed colonies. The southern colonies were established by English mercantile companies with the goal of developing large plantations dedicated to the production of profitable cash crops such as tobacco (Virginia), indigo and rice (South Carolina, Georgia), and later cotton for export to England. The southern plantations were designed not to be self-sufficient but rather as moneymaking enterprises, relying on the importation of food staples from England and the other colonies. The immigrants who worked the southern plantations initially were recruited as indentured servants, primarily from among the urban poor of London and other major cities (later to be replaced by black slaves), and they were disproportionately male. Thus the southern colonies attracted comparatively few experienced farmers and farm families in the early years, and southern agriculture quickly became dominated by the plantation system and a few profitable cash crops. Small family farms, each raising a few milk cows to provide milk, butter, and cheese, were the exception rather than the norm in the early southern colonies.

Consequently, cheesemaking never really gained a foothold in the South (Kulikoff, 2000).

The New England colonies developed along a very different track. By the end of the 16th century English explorers had determined that the climate of the North Atlantic coastal region (present-day New England) could not support the cultivation of the cash crops of the day. The best hope for a profitable colony in this part of the New World resided in fishing and the fur trade. Although explorers had observed evidence of an extensive Native civilization in this area, there was considerable uncertainty in the early 1600s as to whether an English settlement could survive and flourish in the harsh and perilous environment of the North Atlantic coast. It took a group of religious separatists, motivated primarily by personal religious conviction and backed financially by a mercantile company with interest in fishing and fur trading, to demonstrate the potential of English colonization in the North. The Plymouth Colony, established in 1620 by the Pilgrims, became the catalyst for what was to become, literally, a "new England." The Pilgrims came mostly from East Anglia, but they were not farmers and they struggled terribly for the first few years. Nevertheless, they managed to adapt and thereby showed the English world that colonization in New England was possible (McManis, 1975).

The Plymouth Colony began to import dairy cattle in 1623 and was producing cheese and butter in small amounts soon thereafter. However, it was not the Pilgrims who kick-started cheesemaking in the New World, but rather the better-prepared and better-funded Puritans of the Massachusetts Bay Colony. Like the Pilgrims, the Puritans came primarily from East Anglia, an area that was renowned for its dairying and cheesemaking; it was also a stronghold of Puritanism in early 17th-century England. As the moral and social fabric of England crumbled around them (see chapter 1), and as they came under increasing civil and ecclesiastical oppression because of their criticism of the Church of England, the Puritans began to look to the New World as their promised land (Kulikoff, 2000). The success of the Plymouth Colony confirmed to Puritan leaders that the hand of Providence was leading them to New England. And so, with the backing of powerful Puritan merchants and business leaders, the Massachusetts Bay Colony was established in 1629 (McManis, 1975).

Unlike other English colonies, the Massachusetts Bay Colony was specifically established as a religious settlement rather than a mercantile venture. Furthermore, a group of influential East Anglian Puritan leaders headed by John Winthrop convinced the English authorities to grant the new colony complete legal authority, so as to be free from interference from the royal government and the Church of England (McManis, 1975). Thus the seeds of independence were sown in the Massachusetts Bay Colony from its inception, a strategic political error that would come back to haunt England more than a century later. Also unlike other English colonies, the Massachusetts Bay Colony essentially reflected a cross-section of English society and professions, included entire families, and had a strong emphasis on traditional family farming (Kulikoff, 2000). A flood of immigration from East Anglia occurred between 1630 and 1640, sometimes involving the movement of entire communities to the "new England." Dairy farmers and cheesemakers were included among the Puritan immigrants, and dairy cattle were imported from the beginning. Immigrants in the early years were warned to bring with them a year's supply of food, including "a hundred or two old cheeses." They were also warned to bring their own rennet stomachs for cheesemaking, because of the limited availability of cattle stomachs (Booth, 1971). Every new farm kept a milk cow or two, and it wasn't long before farmstead cheesemaking and buttermaking became ubiquitous throughout the new colony (Bidwell and Falconer, 1941).

Within a decade of the founding of the Plymouth Colony, it had become evident that the supply of furs in the area was dwindling. By 1627 Plymouth fur traders were coming into conflict with their Dutch counterparts to the south based in New Netherland, now New York (McManis, 1975). Thus fur trading was never a major enterprise for the Massachusetts Bay Colony, and there was strong incentive to develop other exports that could be used to purchase or barter for a growing spectrum of the essential and nonessential imported goods then becoming available through global trade. Massachusetts cheesemakers and merchants recognized an opportunity. Before immigrating to New England, these Puritan dairy farmers had been schooled in the agricultural concept of competency, with its emphasis on near self-sufficiency combined with the efficient production of products for external sale. Their grandfathers' and fathers' generations had witnessed the transformation of farmstead cheesemaking in England from the small-scale production of diverse, mostly fresh cheeses intended for home use or for sale at the local market to a specialized, export-oriented industry aimed at supplying hard cheese to the London market (Kulikoff, 2000). Thus Puritan cheesemakers brought to the New World a working knowledge of market-oriented cheesemaking and the technology to produce hard cheeses that could withstand the rigors of time and transportation. In short, they knew how to produce cheese for export and they understood that there was money to be made by doing so, provided that they had access to a stable and profitable market.

The West Indies sugar plantations in the Caribbean became an ideal export market for Massachusetts cheese, along with butter, beef, pork, and wheat. The production of sugar on West Indies plantations was so profitable that the plantation owners elected to import food staples rather than to utilize the land to grow enough food for self-sufficiency. The plantations were very labor intensive, and thus there was a pressing and ongoing need to import food. By 1650 a bustling trade had developed between Boston and the West Indies, with Boston exporting cheese, butter, beef, pork, and wheat and importing molasses and rum in return (Bidwell and Falconer, 1941). A distribution and marketing network for cheese became established around the local agricultural market, where farmers could sell their products to merchants and purchase imported goods from the West Indies and England. As time went on these markets developed into the ubiquitous local shop or country store. The country store became an indispensable element of the marketing network, providing farmers with imported goods and taking cheese and butter in exchange, to be resold to merchants on the seacoast for export (Bidwell and Falconer, 1941; Kulikoff, 2001). Thus cheesemaking in the Massachusetts Bay Colony quickly became centered on exportable cheese. This meant English hard cheese, later to be known as Cheddar cheese. Of course, farm wives (who were the cheesemakers of the family) continued to make a variety of traditional English cheeses for home use and for the local market, but the real profit in cheesemaking, as early as 1650, was in the making of English hard cheese for export.

Ironically, the Puritans, who had left England in large part because of dissatisfaction with the Church of England, almost immediately experienced religious dissatisfaction within their own ranks. Between 1630 and 1640 groups of dissenters led by Roger Williams, Anne Hutchinson, John Wheelwright, Thomas Hooker, John Davenport, and Theophilus Eaton, among others, left Massachusetts and settled in Rhode Island, Connecticut, and New Hampshire. Thus English Puritan culture, and English cheesemaking, quickly expanded into what would become separate New England colonies (McManis, 1975). By 1660 Connecticut was exporting butter and probably cheese to the West Indies (Bidwell and Falconer, 1941). Wheat also was grown extensively throughout southern New England for export; by 1680, however, the soil was becoming exhausted through unsustainable agricultural practices. About this time, the production of wheat began to move westward to more fertile lands in eastern Pennsylvania and the Hudson River Valley in New York. Dairying gradually replaced wheat production in southern New England as wheat moved west, a pattern that would repeat itself again and again over the next two centuries (Bidwell and Falconer, 1941).

During the first half of the 18th century, parts of Massachusetts, Rhode Island, and Connecticut became specialized in dairying and became major producers and exporters of cheese (Bidwell and Falconer, 1941). Cheese was standard fare in the ubiquitous taverns of the time, and there was always a local demand for it. More importantly, the West Indies market for cheese continued to expand, and cheese would remain among New England's top exports to the West Indies for more than a century. Indeed, by the start of the 19th century New England was shipping close to a million pounds/450,000 kg of cheese annually to the West Indies, according to one estimate (Bidwell, 1972). Furthermore, cheese exports to the southern American colonies grew steadily during the 1700s, providing New England cheesemakers with new markets and new incentives to produce English hard cheese for export (Bidwell, 1972). Closer to home, the growing East Coast cities of Boston, Providence, Hartford, New York, Philadelphia, and others also created new demand for New

England cheese during this period (Bidwell and Falconer, 1941).

By the time of the American Revolution, then, New England had become the undisputed center of cheesemaking in America. When the Massachusetts patriot John Adams, a fifth-generation descendant of the Massachusetts Bay Colony Puritans, became the second president of the United States, his wife, Abigail, arranged to have Adams's favorite cheeses (undoubtedly English hard cheeses) sent special delivery to their residence in Philadelphia (McCullough, 2001). Cheesemaking was also on the rise in New York State, primarily due to the recent migration of New England cheesemakers into that state. New England cheesemakers had become quite prosperous, with some farms producing as much as 8,000 to 13,000 pounds/3,600 to 5,900 kg of cheese annually by end of the 18th century (Bidwell and Falconer, 1941). The stage was thus set for English hard cheese (Cheddar) to preoccupy American cheesemakers for yet another century.

But what about other European nationals, such as the Dutch, Germans, and Swedes, who emigrated to America during the early years? Didn't they bring their own cheesemaking traditions and technology with them? Why did these other cheesemaking traditions sink into obscurity? The answer lies in the overwhelming dominance of English immigration to America during the 17th century, accounting for almost 90 percent of the total during this period. Although other ethnic groups immigrated to America during the early years, their influx was not sustained as in the case of the English. The Dutch, for example, established a fur-trading colony on Long Island in 1623, and aggressively recruited dairy farmers from Holland to emigrate to the New World and establish farms. Some Dutch farmers heeded the call and emigrated to New York in the early and mid-17th century, settling along the Hudson River Valley (Stamm, 1991). They also imported dairy cattle, and by the middle of the 17th century they had developed an excellent reputation for their fresh and aged Dutch cheeses. But unlike England, which was in a state of social and economic upheaval, Holland at the time was stable and prosperous; few farmers were willing to leave (Kulikoff, 2000). Dutch immigration never amounted to more than a trickle. The same can be said of other non-English immigrant groups during this period. Furthermore, restrictions on citizenship that were applied to Europeans from the Continent, especially Catholics, discouraged non-English immigration. Contrast this with the English, who flooded into New England and the other colonies seeking a better life. By the mid-1600s the English from New England were spilling over into Dutch-occupied Long Island in search of new land, and by 1664 they constituted a majority in that region (Kulikoff, 2000). Although the Hudson River Valley remained a stronghold of Dutch culture and cheesemaking until the American Revolution, the decades that immediately followed the Revolution witnessed the movement into New York State of a flood of New Englanders, who infiltrated and ultimately overwhelmed the remnants of Dutch culture (Stamm, 1991).

As the 18th century progressed, immigration from England slowed substantially while non-English immigrants, primarily from Scotland, Northern Ireland, Germany, and Switzerland, streamed in at a collective rate four times that of the English (Kulikoff, 2000). Nevertheless, the English continued to dominate the population throughout the 18th century, as reflected in the census of 1790, when a national census was first conducted. In that year an estimated 84 percent of the U.S. white population was of English descent; for New England the figure was around 95 percent (McManis, 1975). The English dominated both the population and the culture of America in 1790, and overwhelmingly dominated its cheese industry: Almost all the cheesemakers of that time were Yankees who lived in New England or had recently relocated to New York State, and who for the most part specialized in producing hard English cheese.

By the second half of the 18th century, farmers in southern New England were looking northward and westward for new land. During the waning years of the 18th century and early years of the 19th, southern New England would send her English farmers and English cheesemakers en masse to the rugged north country of Vermont and the fertile valleys of central and western New York. Soon to follow would be a relentless migration farther westward to the vast open expanses stretching from western New York to Wisconsin. English cheesemaking was soon to be transplanted into what would become one of the world's largest milk-producing regions.

THE NORTHWARD MIGRATION

By the middle of the 18th century, population growth in southern New England in general and the growth of the coastal cities in particular began to create a shortage of land for farming. Farmers who wanted to pass on their way of life to their children did not own enough land to support all of their sons and sons' families. Land for purchase in southern New England had become scarce and expensive, making it impossible for many of the next generation to remain in the area and remain in farming. Rather than abandon their way of life, farmers in Massachusetts, Rhode Island, and especially Connecticut began to move northward in search of new land along two major paths of migration. To the east they followed the Connecticut River Valley into Vermont and New Hampshire; to the west, the Hudson River Valley into the Champlain Valley of Vermont (Kulikoff, 2000). Sometimes entire communities moved as a group. Seventy-four towns were settled in Vermont between 1760 and 1764, many in the Connecticut River Valley (Bidwell, 1972). By the time of the American Revolution cheese was beginning to be made in a few areas in southern Vermont, including Bennington (Kulikoff, 2000). Only after the war ended, however, did Vermont experience a major influx of immigration. The demand for new land had been building for decades under the pressure of population growth, but migration had been strongly suppressed by the uncertainties of the French and Indian Wars and then the Revolutionary War. By the end of the Revolution, the demand could no longer be contained, and the floodgates of northward migration were opened (Kulikoff, 2000). Consequently, the population of Vermont surged from an estimated 7,000 in 1772 to 85,425 in 1790, the first year of the census. By 1810 the figure had jumped to 217,895 (Lamson, 1922).

The majority of these newcomers were from Connecticut, with significant numbers also coming from Massachusetts, Rhode Island, and New Hampshire (Stilwell, 1937). The transformation that took place in Vermont during this period was dramatic. Nathan Perkins, a Connecticut pastor who traveled the length of western Vermont in 1789 to preach the Gospel and plant new churches, found mostly primitive settlements and subsistence farmers who lived in grinding poverty (yet who were content and cheerful, much to his astonishment and personal shame). After having traveled to within 30 miles of the Canadian border, Perkins commented in his diary, "No cheese anywhere—no beef—no butter—I pine for home—for my own table" (Perkins, 1920). By the early 1800s the picture had changed considerably, as reflected in the writings of later travelers to Vermont. Winslow Watson, a New York native who traveled the Champlain Valley northward to Canada in 1807, wrote that his route "led through a range of excellent farms occupied by substantial houses; every appearance announcing abodes of high-minded, intelligent, republican farmers. A few elegant seats exhibited the presence of affluence and taste" (Watson, 1968). The Englishman John Lambert, traveling in northern Vermont during November 1807, was pleasantly surprised by both the hospitality and the prosperity of a Shelburne farmer who invited Lambert and his companions into his home at around 4:00 A.M. after learning of their harrowing experience on Lake Champlain when their sloop ran aground on rocks. Lambert wrote of "the pleasure of sitting down to a substantial American breakfast, consisting of eggs, fried pork, beefstakes, apple-tarts, pickles, cheese, cider, tea, and toast dipped in melted butter and milk. We were surprised at seeing such a variety of eatables, as it was not a tavern; but the farmer was a man of property, and carried on the farming business to a considerable extent. He showed us a great number of cheeses of his own making" (Lambert, 1810).

Cheesemaking had indeed progressed to the northernmost reaches of Vermont by this time. John Melish, an English businessman who traveled widely in America during 1806 and 1807, and whose assignment was to accurately and thoroughly characterize the commerce and other relevant features of the United States, concluded of Vermont that "The great business of the state is agriculture . . . . They raise great stores of beef and pork, with excellent butter and cheese for market" (Melish, 1970). Melish went on to write that the principal markets for Vermont products were Canada (that is, Montreal), New York, Hartford, and Boston. Thus cheesemaking in Vermont oriented itself toward distant markets very early on, which meant that English hard cheese—or Yankee cheese, or American cheese, as it was now being called—was becoming the preeminent cheese in the state, as it had been in southern New England for more than a century. This is hardly surprising given that the fact that the lion's share of recent immigrants had come from Connecticut, where, as Melish observed, "vast quantities of cheese and butter are made" (Melish, 1970). It was only logical that transplanted Connecticut cheesemakers (and likewise those transplanted from Rhode Island, New Hampshire, and Massachusetts) who had produced English hard cheese for distant markets in the West Indies, southern states, and eastern cities quickly established markets for their Vermont cheese. They understood that there was money to be made in market-oriented cheesemaking.

Farmers in northeastern Vermont began to export cheese to Montreal in the early 1800s. Butter and cheese were transported overland along a trade route that started in Wells River on the upper Connecticut River and followed in part one of the old Indian trails (Lamson, 1922). Most of the hauling was carried out during winter using sleds because the roads were in such poor condition as to be almost impassable at any other time of the year (Crockett, 1921a; Rozwenc, 1949). By 1820 the transport of butter and cheese along this route had become so considerable that the Vermont legislature appointed a committee to lay out and establish a market road from Wells River to the Canadian border at Berkshire (Lamson, 1922).

To the south, cheese produced in southeastern Vermont was transported by barge down the Connecticut River to Hartford and New Haven, or hauled by four-horse teams overland to Boston, often during winter on sleds (Kirkland, 1961). The local country store served as the marketing and distribution system for cheese and other farm products. Storekeepers during the early 1800s accepted a wide range of agricultural goods from the local farmers in exchange for imported and manufactured goods, but cheese was one of the most highly sought-after items because the market for it was stable and profitable (Sloat, 1985). Storekeepers would accept almost any quantity of cheese, no matter how small, in trade. They would store the cheese until the next team was sent to Boston, which in prosperous times and productive seasons could occur as often as monthly. One Dummerston storekeeper hauled more than 6,000 pounds/2,700 kg of cheese to Boston during a single trip in September 1830 (Sloat, 1985).

Cheese produced in the Champlain Valley was transported northward by boat to Montreal or southward down the lake and then overland to Albany on the Hudson River en route to New York City. The opening of the Lake Champlain Canal in 1823, which linked Lake Champlain with the Hudson River at Troy, shifted the Champlain Valley trade to New York, where the greatest profit was to be made (Crockett, 1921b; Stilwell, 1937). Cheesemaking and buttermaking in the Champlain Valley flourished, and by 1829 almost a million pounds of cheese and butter were shipped south through Whitehall via the canal en route to New York City (Stilwell, 1937). Vermont was becoming a cheesemaking juggernaut. The coming of the railroad to the northwestern part of the state around 1850 opened up still-greater opportunities for new markets, and cheese and butter production in the Champlain Valley surged ahead during the next decade (Bassett, 1981).

One of the factors that contributed to the rapid growth of dairying in Vermont during the first half of the 19th century was the widespread failure of wheat production in the state. Wheat had been Vermont's premier cash crop in the early years of her settlement. But as had occurred in southern New England a century earlier, wheat production began to fail in Vermont within a generation due to unsustainable growing practices that left the soil depleted of nutrients (Stilwell, 1937). Soil exhaustion, outbreaks of disease and pests, and increased competition from New York, Pennsylvania, and eventually Ohio wheat brought on the demise of wheat growing in Vermont (Bidwell and Falconer, 1941). Dairying proved to be an ecologically sustainable and profitable alternative. However, dairying had not yet achieved the status of being Vermont's premier agricultural enterprise.

The raising of sheep for wool dominated the Vermont landscape for the first half of the 19th century (Balivet, 1965; Stilwell, 1937). Wool was in high demand, with its price kept at artificially high levels by the federal government through the imposition of a high tariff that protected domestic producers from foreign competition. Although the sheep industry experienced periodic downturns, overall the times were good; by 1840 Vermont was second in the nation in wool production. Such prosperity hung on the thread of trade policy, however, and when the protective tariff rates were lowered and then abolished completely in the late 1840s, the industry collapsed (Balivet, 1965). Vermont lost one quarter of her sheep population during the next decade, and dairying moved in to fill the void, with butter- and cheesemaking becoming the main industry of the state. By 1850 Vermont was producing some 8.7 million pounds/3.9 million kg of cheese annually—third in the nation, behind New York (49.7 million pounds/22.6 million kg) and Ohio (20.8 million pounds/9.4 million kg). Massachusetts (7.1 million pounds/3.2 million kg) and Connecticut (5.4 million pounds/2.5 million kg) rounded out the top five cheese-producing states (Bidwell and Falconer, 1941). But Vermont's, and indeed New England's, glory days as a major cheesemaking region were already past. Cheesemaking was moving west, and Vermont would fall lower and lower in the state rankings for cheese production in the years to come (Bidwell and Falconer, 1941). Her future glory would reside not in quantity of cheese produced but in a tenacious commitment to quality and craftsmanship in an era when much of the industry succumbed to an unhealthy preoccupation with cost, efficiency, and standardization.

THE WESTWARD MIGRATION

New Englanders began moving into southeastern New York in the middle of the 17th century and gradually pushed northward and westward. Yankee cheesemakers were among the first New England transplants; by 1758 English cheese was being produced as far north and west as Otsego County (Stamm, 1991). But it wasn't until the end of the Revolutionary War that New Englanders would move west in great waves, bringing with them their Yankee culture and a strong orientation toward the making of English hard cheese for market. During this period, speculators who had bought vast tracts of land in New York aggressively promoted land sales to Yankee farmers in the crowded southern New England states, offering them a variety of financing packages and economic incentives (Gates, 1960). The lure of cheap land and new opportunity unleashed an unprecedented surge of migration out of New England. Between 1790 and 1820 the population of upstate New York counties increased by an astonishing 800,000, mostly due to transplanted New Englanders (Gates, 1960). Even Vermont, which experienced her own wave of immigration after the Revolution, began to hemorrhage by 1820 when Vermonters commenced a mass exodus westward (Stilwell, 1937).

The movement of wheat production westward characterized this period. Initially wheat was grown intensively in the Hudson and Mohawk River valleys and beyond into Oneida County in central New York. Within a few decades the unsustainable growing practices of the time had once again taken their toll, however, and the soil was worn out. By the 1820s wheat crops were failing, and wheat production moved into western New York (Stilwell and Falconer, 1941). The opening of the Erie Canal in 1825 created a direct transportation link between New York City and western New York and beyond, further accelerating the movement westward (McMurry, 1995). New England dairy farmers with a strong bent toward English cheesemaking moved rapidly into the Hudson and Mohawk River lands vacated by the wheat growers, and then pushed farther north and west along the track of the Erie Canal. As with the western wheat growers, the canal afforded cheesemakers direct access to New York City. Cheese production surged, and by 1844 New York State was producing some 37 million pounds/17 million kg of cheese, which increased to 50 million pounds/23 million kg by 1849 and, by 1864, better than 100 million pounds/45 million kg (Stamm, 1991).

The pattern of a westward march of wheat production, followed by soil depletion, followed by still farther movement west and, in its wake, replacement by dairying and cheesemaking, did not stop at the New York State border. By 1840 Ohio led the nation in wheat production. By 1850 dairying had moved into Ohio on a large scale, and Ohio ranked number two in cheese production in the nation, behind New York. Wheat farmers, meanwhile, moved still farther west in search of virgin soil. By 1860 the top three wheat-producing states were Illinois, Indiana, and Wisconsin, in that order (Stilwell and Falconer, 1941). Dairying and cheesemaking then continued their westward march in the wake of wheat production.

Dairy farmers and their children who had moved from southern New England to Vermont or south-central New York State at the end of the 18th century once again left everything behind for still-greener pastures in the Midwest. Milo Jones, a native of Richmond, Vermont, was reportedly the first person to make cheese in Wisconsin in 1839 (O'Brien, 1948). The coming of the railroad to the Midwest by midcentury opened up the vast heartland of America to the almost unlimited markets of the East Coast, and there would be no turning back for American agriculture. Wisconsin would decisively displace New York as the nation's leading cheese producer during the 1890s. By the end of the 19th century the United States was producing an astounding 299 million pounds/136 million kg of cheese annually, up from about 100 million pounds a year at the century's midpoint (Pirtle, 1926).

Why did cheesemaking in New York State, and later the Midwest, experience such explosive growth during the 19th century? First, the demand for English hard cheese skyrocketed. The U.S. population surged as a result of very high birthrates coupled with new waves of immigration from Europe. The demand for cheese in the East Coast cities and the southern states grew rapidly. The West Indies continued to import large amounts of cheese. And toward the middle of the century, England, which was undergoing a population explosion of her own, reduced tariffs on cheese imports and threw open her vast market to America. Exports of cheese from New York to England increased from 723,713 pounds/328,566 kg in 1840 to 40 million pounds/18.2 million kg in 1861 (Gates, 1960). It was during this period that the name *Cheddar* came to be applied to Yankee or American cheese, because it offered a marketing advantage. Genuine Cheddar cheese, a hard cheese that originated in Somerset County, England, was in high demand in England by this time. Cheddar cheesemaking was a lucrative business, and American cheesemakers—the vast majority of whom were of New England origin or descent—were well equipped to take advantage. After all, New England cheesemakers had specialized in the production of English hard cheese for distant markets for 200 years.

Not only were there more farms producing cheese, but the scale of production on the average farm also increased dramatically. Whereas in the early and mid-18th century a typical cheese-producing farm had at most 5 milk cows, by the start of the 19th century farms with 6 to 10 cows were common, and over the next few decades farms with 40 or more cows were rife (Stamm, 1991). Dairy farms were becoming larger and more specialized. One factor that enabled these farms to produce more cheese was the onset of the Industrial Revolution and, specifically, the development of the textile industry, which brought about an end to the homespun age. Farm women no longer needed to spend endless hours spinning wool and making clothes for the family, giving them more time to dedicate to dairying and cheesemaking (McMurry,

1995). Because the market for cheese was so profitable, farm families could also afford to hire outside help and to build separate facilities specifically designed for cheese production (Stamm, 1991). Though still taking place on the farm, cheesemaking began to move out of the kitchen and into the cheese house. Moreover, the Industrial Revolution encouraged the development and commercialization of dedicated cheesemaking equipment, including the first cheese vats in the 1830s, new curd-cutting knives, and better cheese presses (McMurry, 1995). These new devices significantly reduced the backbreaking labor involved in cheesemaking and allowed much larger batches to be made.

THE DECLINE

Until 1850 all the cheese produced in America was made on the farm. But in 1851 cheesemaking would be forever changed when a dairy farmer named Jesse Williams and his son George resolved to make cheese on a larger scale. The Industrial Revolution had given rise to the concept of factory production, but the idea had not yet been applied to cheesemaking. Williams and his son constructed dedicated factory buildings for the manufacture and aging of Cheddar cheese that were separate from the farm and were designed to accommodate the combined milk of both their herds, along with that from a number of neighboring farms. Because Cheddar is a relatively simple cheese to manufacture and age, scaling up the process in a factory setting proved to be very feasible. During their first season the Williamses' factory produced more than 100,000 pounds/45,000 kg of cheese, about a fivefold increase over the amount produced by large farmstead operations (around 30 cows) of the time (Stamm, 1991). The resulting economies of scale, destined to drive future cheesemaking relentlessly toward larger and larger scales of manufacture, were immediately evident. A striking reduction in labor was achieved by producing cheese centrally. Moreover, large amounts could now be made by a single cheesemaker, resulting in cheese of more uniform quality. Bulk purchase of supplies at wholesale costs provided a further advantage.

The Williamses' experiment soon attracted attention, and others began to copy the factory concept. By 1860, 38 cheese factories had been erected in New York State (Pirtle, 1926). The onset of the Civil War greatly accelerated the transition from farmstead to factory cheesemaking. In response to the loss of markets in the southern states, northern cheesemakers redirected their exports to the growing market in England. Exporting to England offered a distinct advantage because English importers paid for cheese in gold, thereby providing hard currency and security at a time when the American currency was badly inflated due to the war (McMurry, 1995). Thus there was enormous economic incentive to export more cheese to England, and, indeed, exports rose from 5 million pounds/2.3 million kg in 1859 to 50 million pounds/22.7 million kg in 1863 (McMurry, 1995). At the same time, an acute shortage of farm labor occurred because men had left the northern farms en masse to fight for the Union, leaving behind the women, who now had responsibility for the entire farm and far less time for cheesemaking (McMurry, 1995). The cheese factory offered welcome relief to weary dairy farm families from the grueling and time-consuming task of cheesemaking and enabled the farm to concentrate on producing milk for sale. Thus the times encouraged a major structural change in the cheesemaking industry, and the factory system prevailed. By 1866 some 500 cheese factories were in operation in New York State (Stamm, 1991). The effect of the factory on farmstead cheesemaking was dramatic, as reflected in the production figures of farmstead versus factory cheese during the second half of the 19th century, shown in figure 2.2. By 1869 two-thirds of all U.S. cheese was produced in factories; by the end of the century the value had increased to 95 percent (Pirtle, 1926).

Farmstead cheesemaking all but disappeared during the second half of the 19th century. In the meantime, American factory cheesemaking would become increasingly preoccupied with efficiency and cost. By the late 1870s the rise of the factory system had created a glut of cheese; prices dropped precipitously. Cheese factories responded by cutting costs at the expense of quality, not to mention integrity. The practice of skimming cream from the milk before making cheese in order to produce butter for extra income became commonplace. The resulting skim cheese, abnormally low in fat and of poor quality, was shipped to England and sold as full-cream Cheddar (Stamm, 1991). Astonishingly, factories then began adding lard to skim milk in order to produce "filled" cheese. Large amounts of filled cheese were deliberately mislabeled and shipped to England. Such cheese appeared to be normal when very young, but turned rancid and foul over time (Stamm, 1991). By the end of the 19th century the vast export trade in cheese with England, totaling 148 million pounds/67 million kg in 1881, collapsed as English importers turned their back on America in disgust and in favor of higher-quality cheese from Canada, New Zealand, and Australia (Pirtle, 1926). America would never regain the English market.

Along with an unhealthy preoccupation with efficiency and cost, and sometimes wanton disregard for quality and integrity, the factory system brought about other, more subtle changes in the American attitude toward cheesemaking. During the first half of the 19th century the geographic area of cheesemaking had expanded greatly, and it soon became evident that the cheese made in one region differed from the cheese made in another. One writer of the time contended that "the cheeses of the granite hills and valleys of New England differ from those of the secondary soils of Herkimer, Oneida, and northern New York, while the latter differ from those produced on the shales of the 'southern tier' and northern Pennsylvania; and they again are a different article from the cheeses made on the slaty clays of the Ohio Western Reserve" (McMurry, 1995).

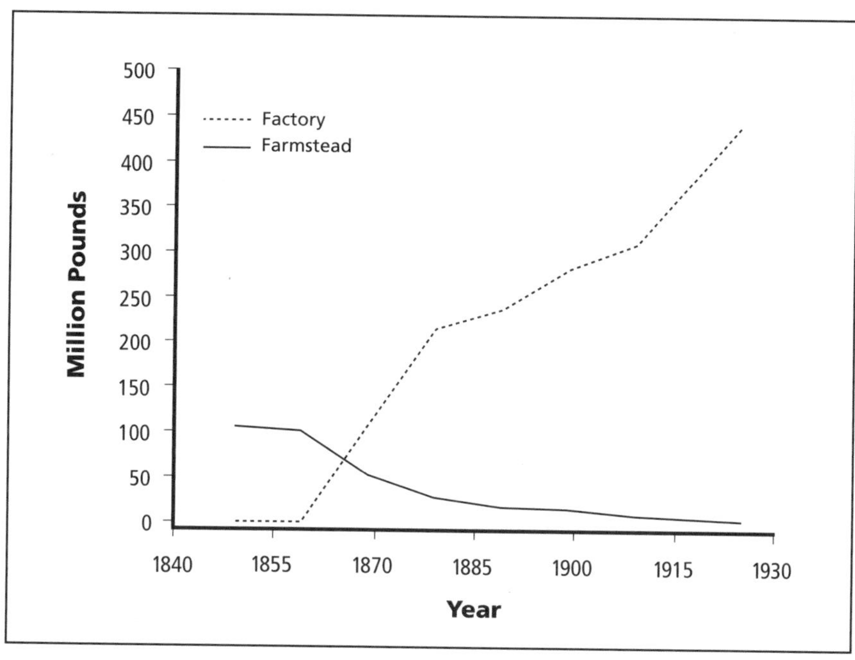

Figure 2.2. Annual production of farmstead and factory cheeses in the United States from 1848 to 1925. The factory system for cheesemaking was introduced in 1851 and quickly came to dominate the U.S. cheese industry. Farmstead cheesemaking in America all but disappeared by the beginning of the 20th century. (Adapted from Pirtle, 1926.)

Cheesemakers and buyers had come to embrace the concept of *terroir,* the notion that place, for a variety of reasons, shapes the quality and character of a cheese. Such ideas were already deeply etched in the hearts and minds of European cheesemakers. However, the explosive growth of factory cheesemaking brought about a new emphasis on standardization, on using the tools of science and new and better equipment to control the process of cheesemaking, to control cheese quality, and to root out variation. The informed opinion of the time shifted toward the view that the scientific knowledge and skill of the cheesemaker and the sophistication of the equipment, not the place, determined the quality and character of the cheese. The factory was viewed as an example of "progress," and farmstead cheesemakers lost respect and even became the object of ridicule (McMurry, 1995). By the end of the 19th century the science of cheesemaking, as represented by the factory system, had triumphed in America over the art of cheesemaking. Sadly, art and science were seen by many as being incompatible, even mutually exclusive. American farmstead cheesemaking had all but disappeared as the new century dawned.

THE RENAISSANCE

The time was early 1983. The place was Stocking Hall on the campus of Cornell University in Ithaca, New York. Professor Frank Kosikowski, eminent cheese scientist and author of *Cheese and Fermented Milk Foods* (or "the Bible," as his graduate students referred to it), had scheduled a regular meeting of his research group. Our group included a dozen or so graduate students from around the globe, laboratory technicians, postdoctoral researchers, and visiting foreign scholars. After Kosi (the nickname that we always used with affection, though never in his presence) had opened the customary bottle of wine and as we sampled several cheeses, he handed out an announcement that he asked us to read. It was a press release proclaiming the formation of the American Cheese Society, a grassroots organization whose mission was to encourage cheesemaking and cheese appreciation in this country. Kosi's vision was to create a forum for the dissemination of technical information that would be aimed particularly at the needs of home and farmstead cheesemakers. Kosi dreamed of a safe haven in America for traditional cheesemaking, a place where the history and traditions of cheesemaking worldwide would be preserved, shared, and encouraged, a place where Americans could taste and experience and ultimately strive to conserve the dizzying array of traditional cheeses that he correctly understood were rapidly disappearing from the world.

"Well, what do you think?" he asked. There was silence. I nearly broke out laughing, thinking that this was some kind of a joke. But the look on his face spoke volumes, and this was no joke. Kosi was planning to host a conference in June, the First Annual Meeting of the American Cheese Society. We politely offered words of mild support, but as graduate students we knew that Kosi would look to us to execute the logistics of this conference and that it would rob us of a fair amount of our time over the next several months. I for one was not enthusiastic.

At the time I was a third-year Ph.D. student heavily involved in my dissertation research. My approach to cheese science was to deconstruct the processes that led to the development of cheese characteristics, understand the fundamental science that governs those processes, and then use that knowledge to reconstruct the cheese in my own image. That is, to make it be what I wanted it to be—more efficient in manufacture, more uniform in quality, and more tailored to the demands of the market. Cheesemaking in my mind occurred in factories on a large scale. I had heard about farmstead cheesemakers, whom I glibly concluded were leftover hippies from the 1960s who had taken a shine to raising goats. I viewed farmstead cheesemaking as an anachronism, a naive attempt to return to an era that had long since disappeared. With a degree of arrogance to which I now look back in shame, I asked myself why I should waste my precious time orchestrating a conference for these idiosyncratic nonconformists.

Kosi knew better. He had traveled the world and had observed and experienced cheesemaking in all its fullness. He understood that traditional cheesemaking was not simply about food, or even about gastronomic delight, but rather carried with it the weight of the culture and local identity that are so essential for providing context and meaning to our lives. Kosi's vision was about enriching our lives as Americans, and he sensed that America could be on the threshold of a renaissance in traditional cheesemaking if only this tiny, fragmented, but growing group of cheesemakers and cheese lovers could come together, encourage one another, and forge a common dream.

The conference went on as planned (see figure 2.3) and, much to my amazement, was an unqualified success, attended by 150 cheese enthusiasts (Carroll, 1999). Following the meeting, Kosi "suggested" that I volunteer to serve as the new society's first vice president, to which I grudgingly agreed. I was convinced that the ACS was a happening that would fade away when Kosi, who was near retirement, stepped back from leadership. Of course, the ACS didn't fade away. It grew . . . and grew. Kosi's timing had been impeccable. In the years that followed that first ACS meeting, the American public would develop a growing level of discomfort with conventional foods. Genetically engineered bovine somatotropin, or bST, came into use on dairy farms. Consumers learned that hormones and antibiotics were being used in the raising of beef and poultry. Genetically modified organisms, or GMOs, became increasingly commonplace across the agricultural landscape. Massive outbreaks of foodborne illness associated with mass-produced foods drew international attention. And small family farms were disappearing in droves while enormous factory farms seemed to thrive and proliferate. All these developments raised questions in the minds of many Americans about our country's

Figure 2.3. Professor Frank V. Kosikowski, founder of the American Cheese Society, evaluates a cheese sample at the First Annual Meeting of the American Cheese Society in 1983. Twenty years after Professor Kosikowski first shared his dream of a safe haven for traditional cheesemaking and appreciation in America, that dream has become a reality through the outstanding efforts of the American Cheese Society.

approach to growing and processing food. Farmstead cheesemaking, like organic foods, tapped into an undercurrent of sentiment among some Americans that all was not well in conventional agriculture.

At the same time, America was enjoying unprecedented prosperity, giving rise to a new generation of upscale, educated consumers who were widely traveled, adventurous in their food-buying habits, and willing and able to pay a premium for foods that were more in line with their values and concerns. Many had experienced life and food in Europe, and they returned to America with a new appreciation of European culture and an appetite for traditional European cheeses. New farmstead cheesemakers, some of whom had traveled to Europe to learn their craft, began springing up in the Northeast, the West Coast, the Midwest, and many places in between. Farmstead cheesemaking had returned to America, no longer dominated by Cheddar (though some superb traditional Cheddars have been rediscovered) but now reflecting the full range of cheese traditions in all their diversity. Vermont, my home state, has led the way in many respects (Tewksbury, 2002). And the American Cheese Society has matured to the point that it is no longer preoccupied with survival and indeed is thriving. Incredibly, two decades after Frank Kosikowski first shared his dream of a safe haven for traditional cheesemaking and appreciation in America, that dream has become a reality.

And so here we are, in the midst of what is truly a renaissance of American farmstead cheesemaking.

CHAPTER 2 REFERENCES

Balivet, R. F. 1965. "The Vermont Sheep Industry: 1811–1880." Vermont History 33(1): 243.

Bassett, T. D. 1956. "A Case Study of Urban Impact on Rural Society: Vermont, 1840–80." *Agricultural History* 30(1): 28.

———. 1981. "500 Miles of Trouble and Excitement: Vermont Railroads, 1848–1861." *Vermont History* 49(3): 133.

Bidwell, P. W. 1972. *Rural Economy in New England at the Beginning of the 19th Century.* August M. Kelley Publishers, Clifton, N.J.

Bidwell, P. W., and J. I. Falconer. 1941. *History of Agriculture in the Northern United States 1620–1860.* Carnegie Institution of Washington, Peter Smith, New York.

Booth, S. S. 1971. *Hung, Strung, & Potted: A History of Eating in Colonial America.* Clarkson N. Potter, Inc., New York.

Carroll, R. 1999. "The American Cheese Society: A History." The American Cheese Society Newsletter (Oct.).

Cheke, V. 1959. *The Story of Cheese-Making in Britain.* Routledge & Kegan Paul, London.

Coolidge, A. J., and J. B. Mansfield. 1860. *History and Description of New England.* Austin J. Coolidge, Boston.

Crockett, W. H. 1921a. *History of Vermont,* Vol. 2. The Century History Company Inc., New York.

———. 1921b. *History of Vermont*, Vol. 3. The Century History Company Inc., New York.
Eckles, C. H., W. Barnes Combs, and H. Macy. 1951. *Milk and Milk Products*, 4th ed. McGraw-Hill Book Co., New York.
Everest, A. S. 1969. "Early Roads and Taverns of the Champlain Valley." *Vermont History* 37(4): 247.
Foster, C. F. 1998. *Cheshire Cheese and Farming in the North West in the 17th and 18th Centuries*. Arley Hall Press, Northwich, Cheshire.
Gates, P. W. 1960. *The Economic History of the United States*, Vol. III: *The Farmer's Age: Agriculture 1815–1860*. Holt, Rinehart and Winston, New York.
Kirkland, E. C. 1961. "Life and Livelihood in the Middle Gants, 1850–1950." *Vermont History* 29(4): 185.
Klyza, C. M., and S. C. Trombulak. 1999. *The Story of Vermont: A Natural and Cultural History*. University Press of New England, Hanover, N.H.
Kulikoff, A. 2000. *From British Peasants to Colonial American Farmers*. University of North Carolina Press, Chapel Hill.
Lambert, J. 1810. *Travels through Lower Canada and the United States in the Years 1806, 1807 and 1808*, Vol. 2. London.
Lamson, G. 1922. "Geographic Influences in the Early History of Vermont." *Vermont Historical Society Proceedings:* 75.
McCullough, D. 2001. *John Adams*. Simon & Schuster, New York.
McManis, D. R. 1975. *Colonial New England: A Historical Geography*. Oxford University Presss, London.
McMurry, S. 1995. *Transforming Rural Life: Dairying Families and Agricultural Change, 1820–1885*. Johns Hopkins University Press, Baltimore.
Melish, J. 1970. *Travels through the United States of America in the Years 1806 & 1807, and 1809, 1810 & 1811*. Johnson Reprint Corp., New York.
O'Brien, J. 1948. "Vermont Fathers of Wisconsin." *Vermont Quarterly* 16(2): 74.
Perkins, N. 1920. *A Narrative of a Tour through the State of Vermont from April 27 to June 12, 1789*. The Elm Tree Press, Woodstock, Vt.
Pirtle, T. R. 1926. *History of the Dairy Industry*. Mojonnier Bros. Co., Chicago.
Rozwenc, E. C. 1949. "Agriculture and Politics in the Vermont Tradition." *Vermont Quarterly* 17(4): 81.
Sloat, C. F. 1985. "The Center of Local Commerce: The Asa Knight Store of Dummerston, Vermont 1827–1851." *Vermont History* 53(4): 205.
Stamm, E. R. 1991. *The History of Cheese Making in New York State*. E. R. Stamm, Publishing Agencies, Endicott, N.Y.
Stern, W. M. 1973. "Cheese Shipped Coastwise to London towards the Middle of the Eighteenth Century." *Guildhall Miscellany* 4(4): 207.
——— 1979. "Where, Oh Where Are the Cheesemongers of London?" *London Journal* 5(2): 228.
Stilwell, L. D. 1937. "Migration from Vermont (1760–1860)." *Proceedings of the Vermont Historical Society* 5(2): 63.
Tewksbury, H. 2002. *The Cheeses of Vermont*. The Countryman Press, Woodstock, Vt.
Watson, E. 1968. *Men and Times of the Revolution*. Crown Point Press, Elizabethtown, N.Y.
Wilson, H. F. 1947. *The Hill Country of Northern New England: Its Social and Economic History in the Nineteenth and Twentieth Centuries*. Vermont Historical Society, Montpelier, Vt.

Milk: The Beginning of All Cheesemaking

3

If you think about it, it is pretty amazing that a bland raw material such as milk can give rise to the diversity of flavors, aromas, colors, and textures we find in cheese. This suggests that milk is far more complex than first meets the eye, a conclusion amply borne out by more than a century of scientific research. Milk is indeed a complex biological material. Although it is not necessary to become an expert in dairy science to make good cheese, it is important to understand certain key aspects of milk chemistry in order to make good cheese (and safe cheese) day in and day out, and to be able to diagnose and correct problems quickly when they arise, as they inevitably will. The objective of chapter 3 is to introduce the essential aspects of milk chemistry, which will serve as a foundation for the next few chapters. This information will help to illuminate what cheese actually is, and what happens during its manufacture and subsequent ripening.

This is the first of several chapters that focus on the science of cheesemaking. Some farmstead cheesemakers may feel uncomfortable with the scientific approach to cheesemaking, viewing it as unnecessary or perhaps even incompatible with their art. If you fall into this camp, please be assured that the science presented in this book is not meant to replace the art of cheesemaking but rather to augment and strengthen it. After all, the art of cheesemaking is really about working with, shaping, and to some extent controlling the forces of nature. The science of cheesemaking offers a complementary set of tools for shaping and controlling those forces more effectively. In today's unforgiving marketplace, where retailers and consumers demand cheeses with consistently good quality and absolute safety, effective control is a prerequisite to successful cheesemaking at any scale. The challenge for the farmstead cheesemaker is to strike the right balance between art and science. The goal should be to achieve the appropriate level of control to ensure safety and consistently high quality while at the same time giving nature enough free rein to encourage the diversity and uniqueness of character that make artisanal cheeses special. When viewed from this perspective, the art and science of cheesemaking go hand in hand; both are essential to achieving the difficult balance of making truly special artisanal cheeses while maintaining the high level of safety and quality that is demanded in 21st-century America.

THE COMPOSITION OF MILK: COW, GOAT, AND SHEEP

In addition to water, milk contains four major constituents: fat, protein, lactose, and minerals. Before we examine the characteristics of these constituents as they relate to cheesemaking, it is important to recognize that the composition of milk, particularly the fat and protein contents, varies greatly regardless of whether the milk comes from a cow, goat, or sheep. Among the major factors that cause milk composition to vary are the breed and genetic history of the animal, its health status (the incidence of mastitis, for instance), plane of nutrition (quality of the diet), stage of lactation (time from giving birth), and season of the year. We will consider the importance of compositional variation later in this chapter. Because milk composition is so variable, the values for milk components that we find in various reference texts may seem inconsistent, and sometimes even contradictory. For example, some texts indicate that goat's milk contains more fat than cow's milk, while other references state the opposite. It all depends on the particular group of animals being examined. Clearly it is difficult to make broad generalizations about milk composition, given the high degree of variability.

The data presented in table 3.1 provide a comparison of the gross compositions of cow's, goat's, and sheep's milk. These data represent average values obtained from various research studies and may not reflect the average value of any individual animal, breed, herd or flock, geographic region, and so forth. Nevertheless, the data do provide a general picture of how the three types of milk compare in gross composition. Sheep's milk almost always contains much higher levels of fat, protein, and ash (that is, minerals) than cow's or goat's milk. The high solids content of sheep's milk strongly affects its coagulation and acidification properties, and its cheese-yielding potential, as will be discussed later in this chapter. The fat and protein contents of cow's and goat's milk are generally fairly similar, and this seems particularly true in Vermont. However, that does not mean that cow's and goat's

	SPECIES		
Constituent	**Cow[1]**	**Goat[2]**	**Sheep[1]**
Fat	3.7	3.6	7.4
Total Protein	3.4	3.5	4.5
Casein	2.6	2.6	3.9
Lactose	4.8	4.5	4.8
Ash	0.7	0.8	1.0
Total Solids	12.7	12.4	19.3

1. Data taken from Fox et al., 2000.
2. Data taken from Guo et al., 2001.

Table 3.1. Chemical composition of cow's, goat's, and sheep's milk. The data represent average values obtained from various research studies and may not reflect the average value of any individual animal, breed, herd or flock, geographic region, and so forth.

milk are the same. In fact, there are significant differences, such as in the specific makeup of fat and protein, that have important implications for cheesemaking, as we will discuss shortly. But first, let's review the major constituents in milk and some of their key characteristics.

Water

Water is by far the most abundant constituent in milk. The water molecule is made up of two hydrogen atoms bonded to a single oxygen atom. What makes this molecule so special is that it contains four separate regions of weak electrical charge, two positively charged and two negatively charged regions, as illustrated in figure 3.1. Molecules such as water that possess separate regions of negative and positive charge are called *polar molecules*. Each charged region of a polar molecule is attracted to oppositely charged regions of other polar molecules or ions (ions are either positively charged, as in sodium, or negatively charged, as in chloride) that happen to be in the vicinity. Because of

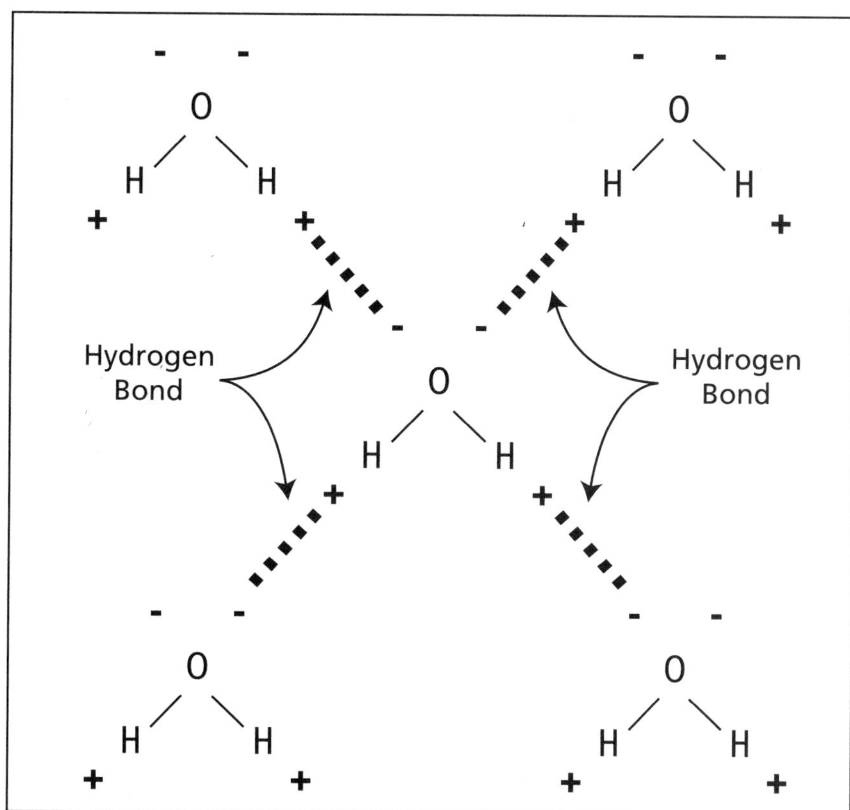

Figure 3.1. Structure of the water molecule. Each water molecule possesses two regions of positive charge and two regions of negative charge. Each charged region is attracted to, and capable of bonding (via hydrogen bonds) with, an oppositely charged region of another water molecule, a different polar molecule, or an ion.

this, water molecules preferentially and instantaneously form, break, and re-form weak attractive bonds with other water molecules (see figure 3.1), and with other polar molecules and ions. This is important because it means that polar molecules such as lactose and ions such as sodium and chloride are attracted to, mix intimately with, and remain uniformly dispersed in water. Consequently, they do not separate out from water under normal conditions. In contrast, nonpolar molecules such as fat do not mix with water because the water molecules preferentially interact with each other and effectively push the fat molecules out of the way, causing them to coalesce as a separate phase of liquid or solid fat, depending on the temperature. The only way fat can remain suspended in water is if it exists as an emulsion—that is, as small droplets that are surrounded by a surface layer or membrane that is polar in nature. Milkfat globules are essentially packaged in a polar surface membrane known as the milkfat globule membrane. This polar surface membrane enables milkfat globules to behave as though they were completely polar in nature, even though right below the surface the actual fat droplet is nonpolar. If milkfat globules lose their polar surface layer—as occurs in the making of butter, for example—the exposed nonpolar fat droplets lose their ability to interact with water and quickly coalesce and separate as a distinct fat phase.

The process of cheesemaking is somewhat analogous to buttermaking in the sense that casein, the major protein in milk, is essentially converted from a polar form that interacts well with water to a nonpolar form. This transformation, which is accomplished through either acidification (for acid-coagulated cheeses) or the action of rennet enzymes (for rennet-coagulated cheeses), causes the casein to separate from the water phase of milk in the form of a coagulum. The casein coagulum entraps most of the fat, a large share of the minerals, and various other milk constituents, which gives rise to the curd from whence cometh cheese.

Fat

About 98 percent of the fat in milk consists of triglycerides, which are molecules formed from two separate components: glycerol and fatty acids (figure 3.2). Glycerol is a molecule made up of three carbon atoms, with each carbon serving as a point of attachment for a fatty acid. Fatty acids consist of chains of carbon atoms to which are bonded hydrogen atoms. For milkfat, most of the fatty acid chains range in length from 4 to 18 carbons. These carbon–hydrogen chains are nonpolar in nature; the longer the fatty acid chain length, the more readily it separates from water. Animal fats (such as lard) and vegetable fats (such as corn oil and olive oil) consist mostly of fatty acids with 16 to 18 carbons. In contrast, milkfat is somewhat unusual in that it contains relatively high proportions of short-chain fatty acids. The term *short-chain* refers to fatty acids with only 4, 6, 8, or 10 carbons in the chain. These short-chain fatty acids are important to cheesemaking because they have very strong aromas and flavors if they become

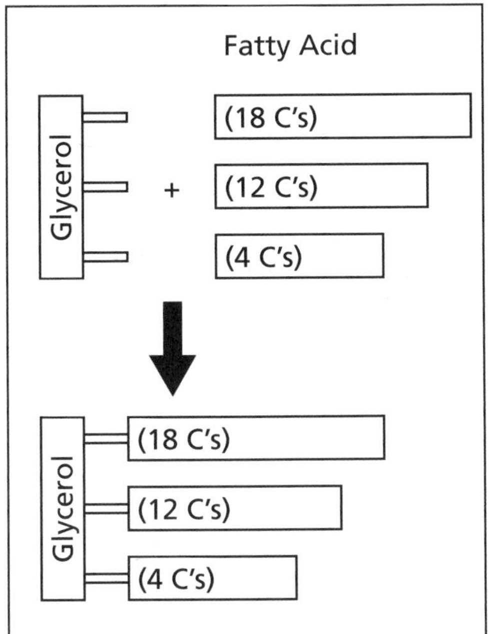

Figure 3.2. The triglycerides of milkfat consist of three fatty acid molecules bonded to a glycerol molecule. Fatty acids consist of chains of carbon (C) atoms of varying length. Most fatty acids in milkfat range from 4 to 18 carbon atoms. Milkfat is unusual in that it contains a high proportion of short-chain fatty acids—that is, fatty acids containing 10 carbon atoms or fewer.

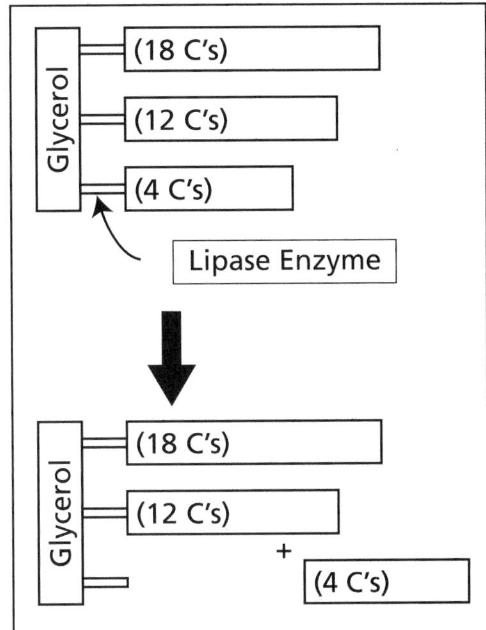

Figure 3.3. Breakdown of a triglyceride by lipase enzyme to form a diglyceride plus a free fatty acid. Free fatty acids with ten or fewer carbon (C) atoms have powerful piquant flavors and aromas that contribute to cheese flavor, but may also cause rancidity if they occur in high concentrations or in the wrong proportions.

separated from glycerol to form free fatty acids (figure 3.3). Short-chain free fatty acids are essential sources of desirable piquant flavor and aroma in many cheeses, but they can also be sources of rancid defects if they occur at excessively high concentrations or in the wrong proportions. The fat in sheep's milk and goat's milk contains higher concentrations of short-chain fatty acids than that in cow's milk. Because of this, some sheep and goat cheeses attain a more peppery, piquant flavor and aroma profile than their cow's-milk counterparts.

The nonpolar triglycerides in milk are packaged in the form of droplets or globules. Each milkfat globule contains thousands of triglyceride molecules that coalesce to form a droplet surrounded by a polar surface membrane. The milkfat globule membrane is derived primarily from the cell membrane of the mammary cell that produced the globule and is applied to the surface of the fat droplet during milk secretion. This milkfat globule membrane, being polar in nature, interacts well with water and prevents the fat globules from coalescing with each other and separating out as a distinct fat phase. As alluded to earlier, the objective of buttermaking is to disrupt and dislodge the milkfat globule membrane by violent agitation so that the nonpolar fat droplets, stripped of their polar surface membrane, coalesce and separate out as butter granules. The same process, known as churning, may occur to varying degrees in your cheesemilk if the milk is subjected to excessive agitation and foaming, in which case you may observe butter granules floating on the surface of the milk or, at higher temperatures, an oily layer. Freeze–thaw cycles also disrupt the milkfat globule membrane and can lead to fat destabilization.

It is important to understand that fat destabilization and its separation as a distinct phase caused by churning or freezing is not the same thing as creaming. Creaming occurs very quickly in freshly harvested cow's milk as fat globules spontaneously rise and form a cream layer on the surface. Rapid creaming occurs because cow's milk contains a "sticky" whey protein known as cryoglobulin, which attaches to the surface of milkfat globules as the milk cools and causes globules to stick together as clusters. The resulting clusters quickly rise to the surface and form a cream layer, due to their large size and low density. Goat's and sheep's milk do not contain cryoglobulin; consequently, their fat globules do not cluster and creaming occurs much more slowly than in cow's milk (over several days versus several hours for cow's milk). Creaming does not damage the milkfat globule membrane. The clusters that make up the cream layer can be easily broken up and the milkfat globules redispersed by warming and stirring the milk. In contrast, churning or freezing causes permanent damage to the fat globule membrane, and the destabilized fat cannot be reincorporated into the milk by simple means.

Churning and freezing should be avoided in milk for cheesemaking, especially in cow's and goat's milk, for at least two reasons. First, destabilized fat that is present as floating butter granules or as an oily layer, depending on temperature, will be lost to the whey instead of being incorporated into the curd. The result is lost cheese yield, therefore lost profit. Second, fat globules with damaged surface membranes are very vulnerable to the action of lipase enzymes that may be present in the milk. Lipase enzymes attack vulnerable triglycerides and preferentially snip off the short-chain fatty acids, converting them into free fatty acids (figure 3.3). As noted earlier, short-chain free fatty acids have powerful flavors and aromas. For many cheeses, the formation of short-chain free fatty acids *in the cheese* during ripening is necessary to obtain desirable flavor and aroma. However, the formation of free fatty acids *in the milk* before cheesemaking is never desirable, because free fatty acids can inhibit the starter culture and cause slower acidification during cheesemaking; as we will see in later chapters, this may affect cheese quality. Furthermore, disruption of the milkfat globule membrane through agitation or freezing may lead to the formation of excessive or unbalanced amounts of short-chain free fatty acids in the cheese during ripening, and ultimately to rancid defects.

Cow's and goat's milk are particularly susceptible to rancid defects because they contain indigenous lipase enzymes that originate from the animal herself, which she secretes in her milk. In normal cow's and goat's milk, the milkfat globule membrane protects the triglyercides against these indigenous lipase enzymes. However, if the membrane becomes damaged through freezing or churning, lipase is able to gain access to the triglycerides and release free fatty acids into the milk. Furthermore, around 80 percent of the indigenous lipase enzymes preferentially attach to the casein micelles (see figure 3.5). Consequently, when the milk is coagulated and made into cheese, the lipase enzymes from the milk are carried by the casein micelles into the cheese, where they become concentrated in an active form and able to attack milkfat globules with damaged membranes. This greatly increases the risk of rancidity development during aging. Sheep's milk is more forgiving in this respect because it has very little indigenous lipase activity; it is much less vulnerable to rancidity, even when the milk experiences churning or freezing. Consequently, freezing is sometimes used as a means to store sheep's milk for use in winter when the supply of fresh milk is limited. Even sheep's milk, however, may develop rancid defects if stored frozen for long periods of time at temperatures near the freezing point. Ideally sheep's milk should be stored frozen at temperatures of -17°F/-27°C or lower to minimize problems with rancidity (Wendorff, 2000).

The bottom line is that it is wise for the cheesemaker, especially of cow's- or goat's-milk cheese, to avoid situations that lead to excessive agitation, foaming, or freezing of the cheesemilk. This is even more important if the milk is from animals that are near the end of their lactation cycle and/or have a high incidence of mastitis. Both conditions trigger an increase in lipase activity in milk, thereby rendering milkfat globules especially vulnerable to lipolysis and the production of free fatty acids. Thus cheesemakers who produce milk and cheese seasonally should be particularly gentle with their milk in autumn as their animals approach the end of their lactation cycle. Cheesemakers should also be very cognizant of the health status of each animal that they milk and minimize the incidence of mastitis in the herd or flock.

Even if milkfat is not subject to abuse such as freezing and churning, it is still vulnerable to the action of lipases that are produced by bacteria in the milk, if the bacteria are allowed to reach high populations. *Psychrotrophic* bacteria—that is, bacteria that grow at refrigeration temperatures—are particularly troublesome because many of the psychrotrophes secrete lipases that can penetrate even undamaged milkfat globules and cause rancidity. Furthermore, these psychrotrophic bacteria and their lipase enzymes become concentrated in the cheese and remain active during ripening, thus increasing the potential for rancid defects. Consequently, the longer that milk is held in refrigerated storage before being made into cheese, the higher the population of psychrotrophic bacteria in the milk, the greater the concentration of bacterial lipase in the cheese, and the greater the potential for rancidity. Likewise, storing milk at higher temperature (for example, 45°F/7°C, as allowed in some states) versus lower temperature (40°F/4°C) leads to accelerated growth of psychrotrophes, greater secretion of bacterial lipases, and greater potential for rancidity in the cheese. Incidentally, these same psychrotrophic bacteria also secrete enzymes that attack casein, which can lead to poor coagulation and cause bitterness to develop in the cheese. Thus the cheesemaker has strong incentives to keep contaminating psychrotrophic bacteria out of the cheesemilk (through proper cleaning and sanitation practices—the topic of chapter 7), and to prevent the psychrotrophes from growing (by holding the milk at no higher than 40°F and using the milk as quickly after harvest as possible, preferably within 24 hours). These practices will also enhance safety.

Before leaving our discussion of milkfat, one other feature deserves mention. The fat in cow's milk tends to be yellow in color, and the intensity varies with season, especially if the cows are pasture fed. The origin of the yellow color is a pigment called beta-carotene that is derived from green forages. Beta-carotene is fat soluble, which means that it is carried by the fat in milk and thus gives the fat its characteristic yellow color. Sheep's and goat's milk lack beta-carotene because the beta-carotene that the animal consumes in her feed is converted into vitamin A, which is not pigmented. Therefore, the fat in sheep's and goat's milk is white, and cheeses made from these milks are much whiter than those made from cow's milk.

Protein

The proteins in milk are divided into two major families: the caseins and the whey proteins. The caseins make up about 80 percent of the total protein in cow's milk on average; slightly more (about 82 percent) in sheep's milk, and slightly less (about 75 percent) in goat's milk. The whey proteins, as their name implies, are lost to the whey during cheesemaking and are of limited relevance to this book. They will be discussed only with respect to their role in cheesemaking. Whey proteins are polar in their native folded state and therefore remain uniformly dispersed in the water phase of milk unless they are denatured (that is, unfolded) by high temperature, which can cause problems with weak coagulation and poor syneresis.

The caseins are a group of proteins that are designated by Greek letters: There are alpha-, beta-, and kappa-caseins. Actually, there are two distinctly different alpha-caseins and many slight variations on all the caseins; thus they form a complex group of proteins. Sheep's milk contains much higher levels of total protein and, therefore, casein than does cow's or goat's milk. Because casein coagulates to form the structural backbone of cheese curd, sheep's milk coagulates more rapidly to a much firmer curd and yields about twice the amount of cheese per unit of milk as cow's or goat's milk. The casein in goat's milk is different from that in cow's or sheep's milk in that it contains much lower proportions of the alpha-caseins and much higher proportions of beta-casein. The specific casein makeup in milk can affect its coagulation properties.

For example, the unique makeup of goat's-milk casein results in a more fragile coagulum than that obtained with cow's milk and gives a lower yield of cheese, even though goat's and cow's milk contain about the same amount of casein and fat (table 3.1).

Like all proteins, casein molecules consist of long chains of amino acids, ranging in length from 169 to 209 amino acids (figure 3.4). An important feature of the caseins is that several of the amino acids along the amino acid backbone have a negatively charged phosphate group attached to them as a side chain. This is important because each negatively charged phosphate group is able to bind a positively charged calcium ion; these ions are abundantly present in milk. Thus caseins readily bind calcium ions (figure 3.4).

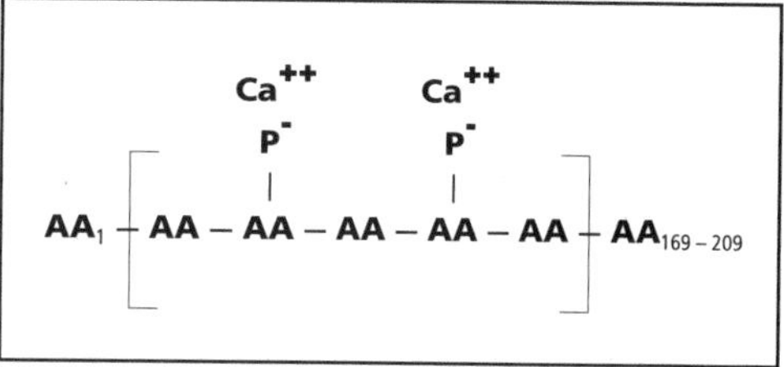

Figure 3.4. A simplified representation of the casein molecule. Casein molecules consist of long chains of amino acids (AA). Most casein molecules range in length from 169 to 209 amino acids, and most have from 1 to 13 negatively charged phosphate (P) ions attached to the amino acid backbone at specific locations. The phosphate ions readily bind calcium ions. Therefore, casein serves as an excellent carrier of calcium to the newborn. Casein-bound calcium also contributes to the colloidal calcium phosphate in the casein micelle (see figure 3.5).

Most of the casein molecules in milk do not exist as isolated molecules but instead aggregate together to form a complex structure known as the casein micelle. The general structure of the casein micelle is illustrated in figure 3.5. The exact micellar structure remains the subject of scientific debate, but the model shown in figure 3.5 depicts the important characteristics from a cheesemaking perspective. According to this model, the micelle is made up of many submicelles that aggregate together to form the spherical micellar structure. Each submicelle consists of many casein molecules that coalesce to form a spherical submicelle. The casein molecules that make up the submicelle are oriented in such a way that their phosphate groups are concentrated at the submicelle surface. Consequently, each submicelle is able to bind calcium at its surface. Because each calcium ion possesses two positive charges, the calcium ions that are bound to the surfaces of the submicelles are also able to bind negatively charged free phosphate ions that are also present in milk, which in turn bind more calcium ions, and so forth. These calcium and phosphate ions form what is known as colloidal calcium phosphate, which acts as a sort of glue that binds the submicelles together and allows them to form a stable complex structure known as the casein micelle (figure 3.5). In nature, the casein micelle serves as a delivery system for calcium phosphate to the newborn lamb, kid, or calf. Newborns require substantial intakes of calcium phosphate to support growth, and casein micelles allow far more calcium phosphate to be packaged into milk than would otherwise be possible.

From a cheesemaking standpoint, the

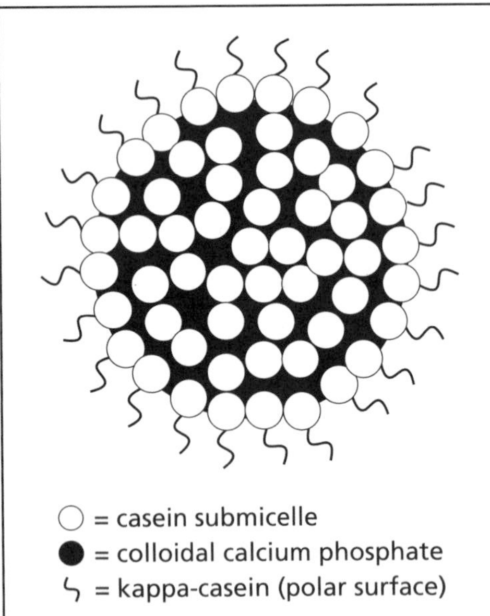

Figure 3.5. A simplified representation of the casein micelle. The micelle consists of casein submicelles that are held together through colloidal calcium phosphate bonding to form the micelle. Each submicelle is made up of many casein molecules that form a spherical aggregate. Polar kappa-casein molecules protrude from the micelle surface, thus creating a "hairy" polar surface layer that enables the micelle to remain dispersed in water.

casein micelle has three critically important features. First, the micelles are very polar at their surface, so they mix well with water and do not aggregate and separate out under normal conditions. Casein micelles are polar at their surface because kappa-casein, which is very polar at one end of its amino acid chain, is concentrated at the micelle surface, where it forms a sort of protective coating (figure 3.5). Basically, the polar ends of the kappa-casein molecules protrude from the micelle surface, forming a "hairy" polar covering that attracts a layer of water molecules and prevents the micelles from aggregating and separating out. However, casein micelles will aggregate in an unusual manner known as coagulation under the right conditions of acidification or enzymatic modification by rennet. Because of this unusual coagulation behavior, casein is able to form a curd, which becomes the foundation for cheese structure. If caseins were unable to coagulate, there would be no cheese as we know it.

A second critical feature of casein micelles is that their high calcium phosphate content enables them to act like a sponge for acid. Basically, during cheesemaking the coagulated casein micelles absorb some of the lactic acid (or, more correctly, some of the hydrogen ions that are released by the lactic acid molecules) as it is produced by the starter culture. (Chapter 4 contains a detailed explanation of acidity and pH measurement. You cannot fully understand cheese and cheesemaking unless you understand acidity and pH.) The casein micelles in turn release some of their calcium phosphate to the whey in response to the hydrogen ions. The greater the amount of lactic acid produced by the starter during cheesemaking, the greater the absorption of hydrogen ions by the casein micelles and the greater the release of calcium phosphate to the whey. Therefore, the rate of acidification during cheesemaking determines the mineral (that is, calcium phosphate) content of the final cheese. As we will see in chapter 6, the mineral content profoundly infuences cheese flavor and texture development. One of the keys to making consistent-quality cheese is to produce cheese with consistent mineral content. This process of absorbing hydrogen ions, known as *buffering,* and releasing calcium phosphate to the whey will be explained more fully in chapters 5 and 6.

Milk with high casein (and therefore high calcium phosphate) content has much greater buffering capacity (the capacity to absorb hydrogen ions) than milk with low casein content. Therefore, when the casein content of milk changes —seasonally, for example—the buffering capacity of the milk changes and the amount of starter culture needed to produce cheese with the same mineral content will change. The higher the casein content, the more starter culture will be needed to attain similar mineral content in the final cheese, all else being equal. As we will see later, the cheesemaker is often faced with the need to make adjustments in the cheesemaking process, such as with the starter culture, as milk composition changes in order to make cheese of consistent quality.

A final noteworthy feature of casein is that it is susceptible to breakdown by enzymes, leading to desirable or undesirable consequences. The enzymes in milk and cheese that break down casein, known as *proteolytic enzymes* or *proteases,* may originate from several different sources. The most obvious source is the rennet used to coagulate the milk. For many (but not all) cheeses, about 5 to 10 percent of the rennet enzymes added to the milk are retained in the cheese in active form. During ripening, these enzymes attack the amino acid backbones of the casein molecules, cutting the long chains into smaller fragments called *peptides.* The production of peptides by rennet is the first step in a complex process that leads to the development of desirable flavor and texture in many aged cheeses such as Cheddar.

Milk also contains a proteolytic enzyme known as *plasmin* that originates from the animal herself, as well as proteolytic enzymes that originate from bacteria present in the milk. The starter bacteria, as well as nonstarter bacteria present in the milk as contaminants, display varying degrees of proteolytic activity. When high-quality milk is used in cheesemaking, these milk- and bacterial-derived proteolytic enzymes often contribute to the development of desirable flavor and texture. When cheese is made from poor-quality milk, however, excessive proteolysis may occur in both the milk and the final cheese, which is never desirable. For example, milk from animals that suffer from mastitis contains elevated levels of the plasmin and other proteolytic enzymes. The same is true for animals that are at the end of their lactation cycle. Consequently, mastitic and late-lactation milks may undergo considerable proteolysis before the milk is made into cheese, resulting in damage to the casein micelles. Milk with damaged casein micelles coagulates to form a weak curd that loses more solids to the whey, resulting in lower cheese yield. The fragile curd also retains more water, resulting in cheese with abnormally high moisture content that is susceptible to excessive proteolysis and the development of bitterness. Thus mastitic and late-lactation milks are quite problematic for the cheesemaker due in part to the proteolytic damage that is inflicted on the casein micelles.

Psychrotrophic bacteria represent another important source of excessive proteolysis in milk. Many of the psychrotrophic bacteria secrete proteolytic enzymes that attack casein and damage the casein micelles. The proteolytic damage caused by psychrotrophic growth results in poor coagulation, lower cheese yield, higher-moisture cheese, and increased risk of bitterness development during ripening. Thus, as highlighted earlier, it behooves the cheesemaker to keep psychrotrophic bacteria out of the cheesemilk and to prevent them from growing.

Minerals

Milk contains about 30 different minerals, but only a few of them are present in greater than trace amounts. The two most abundant are calcium and phosphorus. Calcium constitutes about 30 percent of the total minerals in milk. In turn, about 30 percent of the total calcium is soluble (that is, dispersed throughout the water phase of the milk), with 20 percent of that being bound to citrate and 10 percent existing as free ions. The other two-thirds are associated with the casein micelles in the form of colloidal calcium phosphate. Phosphorus constitutes about 15 percent of the total minerals in milk, and about 50 percent of the total phosphorus is associated with the casein micelles. Thus casein micelles serve as a major carrier for calcium and phosphorus in milk, as discussed earlier. Other major minerals in milk include sodium, chlorine, and potassium, which, in contrast to calcium and phosphorus, exist almost exclusively as free ions in milk's water phase.

The total mineral content of milk is often estimated by incinerating a sample at an extremely high temperature (1,022°F/550°C) and then measuring the amount of ash that remains. The ash content is not exactly the same thing as the total mineral content, but it gives a reasonable estimate. Sheep's milk has a much higher ash content than cow's and goat's milk because sheep's milk is also much higher in casein (see table 3.1) and, therefore, has many more casein micelles that serve as carriers for calcium phosphate. Thus the higher ash content in sheep's milk reflects the higher calcium phosphate content associated with the casein micelles.

Lactose

Lactose, the structure of which is shown in figure 3.6, is a sugar made up of the same atoms as those in sucrose (table sugar), arranged in much the same way, but with some important differences. Lactose consists of two simple sugars, glucose and galactose, bonded together. An important feature of lactose is that it contains eight -OH groups—that is, eight hydrogen atoms bonded to an oxygen atom. As noted earlier with respect to the water molecule, the bonding of hydrogen

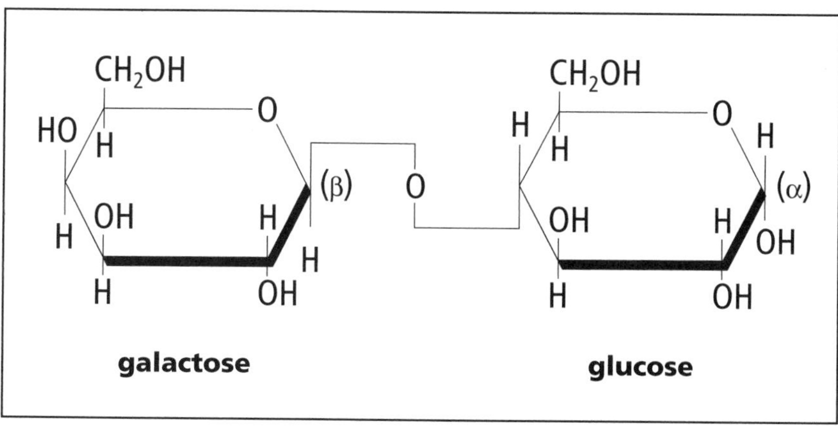

Figure 3.6. Chemical structure of lactose. Notice the -OH groups that surround the ring structures of galactose and glucose. Each -OH group forms a polar region along the ring. Lactose is therefore very polar in nature and disperses well in water.

with oxygen creates separate regions of positive and negative charge that render the -OH group polar in nature. Therefore, the carbon rings that make up the glucose and galactose components of the lactose molecule are surrounded by polar -OH groups, which enable lactose to mix well with water.

The most important feature of lactose with respect to cheesemaking is that it serves as an energy source (in other words, food) for the starter culture and other bacteria that may be present in the milk as contaminants. The primary function of the starter culture is to ferment the lactose to lactic acid, which we will examine in more detail later. Although most of the lactose is either lost to the whey or fermented by the starter culture during cheesemaking, a small amount is carried over into the cheese. This residual lactose is very important because it serves as an energy source for bacteria present in the cheese, both desirable and undesirable, and thus can influence desirable and undesirable fermentations during ripening. Consequently, proper control over residual lactose levels is very important, and some of the manufacturing steps in the making of certain cheeses, such the addition of water to curds and whey or to the drained curd, specifically serve to control the amount of residual lactose in the final cheese.

One of the nutritional concerns presented by some dairy products is that a sizable proportion of the human population is lactose intolerant, or unable to digest lactose, which results in gastrointestinal upset when such individuals consume lactose. Although fresh cheeses typically contain some residual lactose that may be problematic to lactose-intolerant individuals, properly aged cheeses generally do not present a problem because the residual lactose is fermented to negligible levels during ripening.

COMPOSITIONAL VARIATION IN CHEESEMILK

As noted earlier, many factors influence the composition of milk and cause it to vary. Some, like mastitis, breed, and the genetic history of the animals, can be controlled through good management practices. Others, such as seasonal changes, are largely beyond the control of the cheesemaker. Seasonality is probably the single most important source of variation for farmstead cheesemakers because seasonal changes can be large in magnitude and cannot be eliminated completely. To produce cheese of consistent quality farmstead cheesemakers must therefore adapt their manufacturing practices as the season progresses to accommodate changes in milk composition. This is especially true for farms that practice both pasture feeding and seasonal milk production—that is, farms where all the animals give birth in spring, dry off in fall, and are sustained wholly or mostly on pasture, as is sometimes the case in farmstead cheesemaking. Under these conditions, the effects of season (caused by changes in temperature, quality of the feed, and so forth) and lactation stage (caused by changes in the physiology of the animal) are synchronized and become superimposed. This creates larger swings in composition than occur in nonseasonal milk where breeding is staggered and milk is produced year-round.

The fat and casein contents of milk undergo especially large variation across seasons as illustrated in figure 3.7. The data in figure 3.7 represent weekly analyses of bulk tank samples obtained from Shelburne Farms' seasonal herd of Brown Swiss cows in Shelburne, Vermont, starting in May and ending in December. It is readily apparent that fat and casein followed the same general pattern of variation, with both falling to their lowest levels in summer and then peaking in late autumn. Consequently, the cheese-yielding potential of the milk was lowest in summer and highest in late fall; the actual measured yields of Cheddar cheese produced from this milk, shown in figure 3.8, followed the same trend across season as the fat and casein contents in the milk. In quantitative terms, the highest levels of fat and casein in the milk and highest yield of cheese, which occurred during November, were 39, 39, and 41 percent greater, respectively, than their lowest levels, which occurred during July. This clearly illustrates the direct influence of fat and casein contents in the milk on cheese yield.

Large fluctuations in the casein content of milk across seasons, such as shown in figure 3.7, are accompanied by large changes in the buffering capacity of the milk, being lowest in summer when casein is lowest, and peaking in fall. Thus in order to keep the acidification schedule during cheesemaking constant across season, the cheesemaker must adjust for the changes in buffering capacity by adjusting the starter culture usage, generally by using less starter in summer and more in fall.

Another, more subtle change that occurred across seasons in the data shown in figure 3.7 was in the ratio of casein to fat in the milk. During summer, casein levels were high relative to fat; the casein:fat ratio peaked in August at 0.78:1. In contrast, during autumn fat

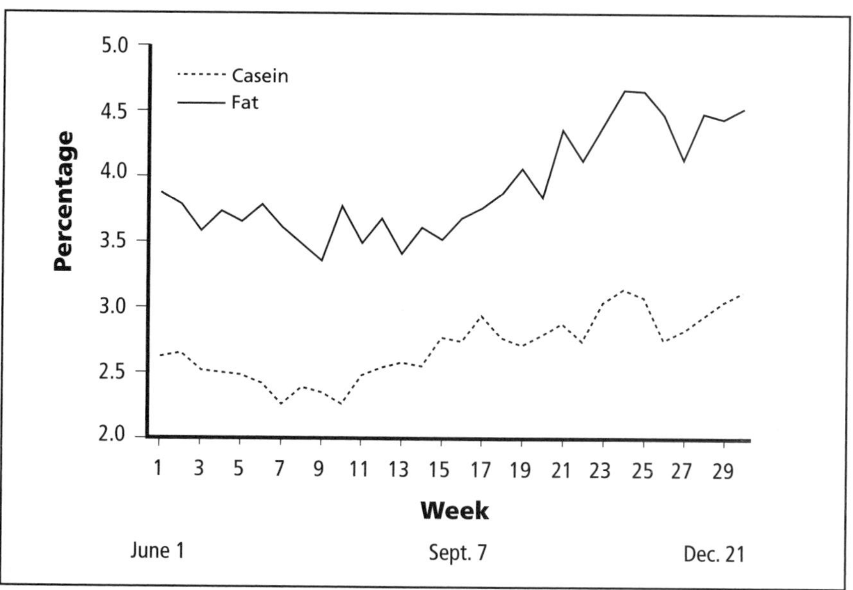

Figure 3.7. Seasonal variation in the fat and casein contents of milk produced by Shelburne Farms' spring-calving herd of Brown Swiss cows in Shelburne, Vermont. The herd commenced milk production in May and was dried off in December. (Source: Dixon, 1999.)

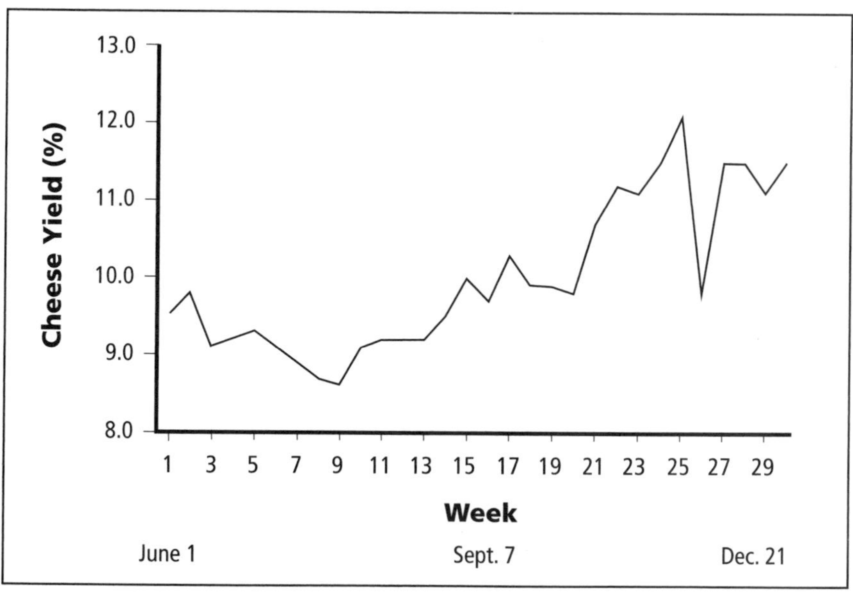

Figure 3.8. Seasonal variation in the yield (unadjusted) of Cheddar cheese produced from the milk of Shelburne Farms' spring-calving herd of Brown Swiss cows. The herd commenced milk production in May and was dried off in December. (Source: Dixon, 1999.)

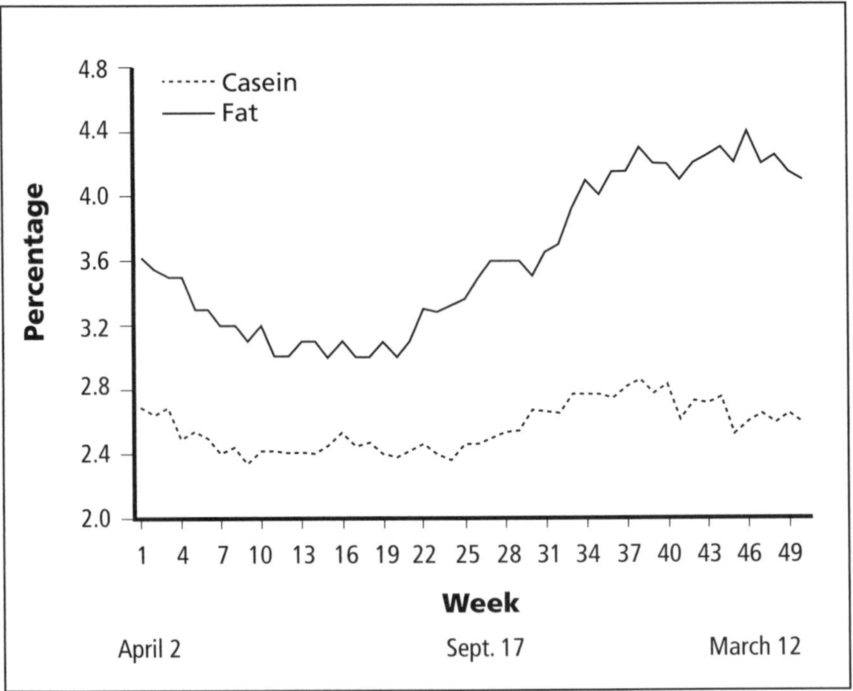

Figure 3.9. Seasonal variation in the fat and casein contents of commingled goat's milk produced in New Hampshire and Vermont. Bulk milk samples were collected weekly from the same group of 12 goat farms for one year. The milk production cycle was strongly seasonal, with majority of the animals giving birth in spring and drying off in late autumn. (Adapted from Guo et al., 2001.)

increased to a greater extent than casein, with a concomitant decrease in the casein:fat ratio, to a low of 0.62:1 in November. This is important because fat interferes with the ability of the curd to shrink and expel whey during cheesemaking, and also tends to reduce the uptake of salt by the curd during salting. Therefore, milk with higher fat content relative to casein tends to produce cheese with higher moisture and lower salt contents, all else held constant. Large industrial cheese plants usually standardize the casein:fat ratio in their milk so that it remains constant year-round. However, standardization is usually not feasible at the farmstead level and is generally incompatible with the philosophy of most artisanal cheesemakers. Therefore, farmstead cheesemakers must learn to work with the natural variation in milk composition and adapt their manufacturing practices to control for moisture and salt contents in the cheese across season. For example, when milk contains a low casein:fat ratio, as in autumn, cheesemakers may need to work harder to expel whey from and incorporate salt into the curd in order to avoid making cheese with undesirably high moisture or low salt content.

Data in figure 3.9 demonstrate that goat's milk undergoes much the same seasonal changes in composition that we observe in cow's milk. Casein and fat levels in these weekly milk samples, which were collected for an entire year from commingled milk obtained from 12 farms in Vermont and New Hampshire, bottomed out in summer and then peaked in late fall. The take-home message is that milk composition changes with the season, and you, the cheesemaker, must learn to adapt your manufacturing practices, especially with respect to starter culture usage and moisture control, to adjust to those changes. This applies to all cheesemaking, whether it involves the milk of cows, goats, or sheep, although some cheeses are more forgiving and require fewer manufacturing adjustments across seasons than others. The manufacturing process and the controls needed to produce cheese of consistent composition and quality will be examined in the following chapters.

FROM MILK TO CHEESE: SELECTIVE CONCENTRATION

Cheesemaking is a process of selective concentration, whereby some of the components in milk become concentrated in the form of cheese curd and others are separated out in the form of whey. The data presented in table 3.2 illustrate the selective concentration that takes place during the making of Cheddar cheese from cow's milk. Although the exact values for other types of cheese will differ from those in table 3.2, all cheeses undergo basically the same partitioning of components between curd and whey.

The example in table 3.2 starts with 100 pounds of cow's milk of typical composition. Water makes up 87 pounds of the total. During cheesemaking, 96 percent of the water is separated out as whey, leaving

Lost to Whey			Concentrated in Cheese	
%	Lb	Milk (100 Lb)	Lb	%
95.5	83.1	water - 87 lb	3.9	4.5
96.0	4.9	lactose - 5.1	0.2	4.0
7.5	0.3	fat - 4.0	3.7	92.5
4.0	0.1	casein - 2.5	2.4	96.0
92.9	0.65	whey prot. - 0.7	0.05	7.1
50.0	0.35	salts - 0.7	0.35	50.0
40.0	0.048	Ca - 0.12	0.072	60.0
45.0	0.045	P - 0.010	0.055	55.0
96.0		Na - 0.06	4.0	
	89.4	Total = 100 lb	10.6	

Table 3.2. The selective concentration of milk components during the manufacture of Cheddar cheese. This example starts with 100 pounds of cow's milk of typical composition. During cheesemaking, some of the components in milk become concentrated in the form of cheese (such as fat and casein), while others are separated out in the form of whey (lactose and whey protein).

only 4 percent of the original cow water retained in the final cheese. Solids components such as lactose, whey proteins, and sodium ions that are polar or charged in nature remain uniformly dispersed in the water throughout cheesemaking and, therefore, separate along with the water at about the same percentages (93 to 96 percent). This means that the amount of lactose retained in the cheese is directly influenced by the amount of moisture retained: The higher the moisture content of the cheese, the higher the residual lactose content unless measures are taken during cheesemaking to reduce lactose levels. Therefore, high-moisture cheeses generally contain high residual lactose, which renders them vulnerable to unwanted fermentations during aging and is one of the reasons why high-moisture cheeses have shorter shelf lives.

In contrast to lactose, casein and fat become concentrated during cheesemaking and collectively constitute about 90 percent of the total milk solids in the final cheese—hence their direct impact on cheese yield (see figures 3.7 and 3.8). About 96 percent of the casein in the milk becomes selectively concentrated in the cheese through the process of coagulation and subsequent separation of the whey from the coagulum, known as *syneresis*. During coagulation, fat globules become physically entrapped within the porous network formed by the coagulated casein micelles. Under ideal conditions, about 93 percent of the fat in milk is retained in Cheddar cheese curd, but fat retention will vary for different types of cheese and will be affected by the skill of the cheesemaker. In general, the more gently the curd is handled throughout cheesemaking, the greater the retention of fat in the cheese and the greater the cheese yield. Conversely, rough treatment leads to higher fat loss and decreased cheese yield.

Calcium and phosphorus are also concentrated in the cheese, though to a lesser extent (60 percent and 55 percent, respectively) than casein and fat. The retention of these minerals is largely determined by the amount of acid produced during cheesemaking and the schedule of acidification; that is, whether the acid is produced early in the process or only toward the end of cheesemaking. Remember, casein micelles act as a sponge for acid, absorbing hydrogen ions and releasing calcium phosphate in response. Therefore, the acidification process defines how much calcium and phosphorus are retained in the final cheese.

In summary, the data in table 3.2 indicate that at the end of the day, milk that contained 87 percent water, 4.0 percent fat, 2.5 percent casein, 5.1 percent lactose, and 0.12 percent calcium was selectively concentrated into Cheddar cheese containing about 37 percent water, 35 percent fat, 23 percent casein, 1.9 percent lactose (theoretically, although the residual lactose will be fermented by the starter culture during cheesemaking to less than 1 percent in the final cheese), and 0.7 percent calcium.

CHAPTER 3 REFERENCES

Dixon, P. 1999. "The Effect of Seasonal Milk Production on Cheddar Cheese Composition, Quality and Yield." M.S. thesis, University of Vermont, Burlington.

Fox, P. F., T. P. Guinee, T. M. Cogan, and P. L. H. McSweeney. 2000. "Chemistry of Milk Constituents." Chapter 3 in *Fundamentals of Cheese Science*. Aspen Publishers, Inc., Gaithersburg, Md.

Guo, M. R., P. H. Dixon, Y. W. Park, J. A. Gilmore, and P. S. Kindstedt. 2001. "Seasonal Changes in the Chemical Composition of Goat Milk." *Journal of Dairy Science* 84(E. Suppl.): 79–83.

Wendorff, W. L. 2000. "Freezing Qualities of Raw Sheep Milk for Further Processing." *Journal of Dairy Science* 83(Suppl. 1): 9.

Starter Culture: The Heart of Cheesemaking

4

It is often said that the starter culture is the heart of cheesemaking, and with good reason. The identity, quality, and safety of almost all cheeses are profoundly shaped by the starter culture. Starter cultures consist of harmless bacteria that occur ubiquitously in raw milk and milk environments as natural inhabitants. They are well adapted to grow in milk because they are able to ferment lactose to lactic acid and can withstand high concentrations of the latter; thus they are known as lactic acid bacteria. Up until about 100 years ago, cheesemakers relied on lactic acid bacteria naturally present in the raw milk used for cheesemaking that day, or in small quantities of milk or whey that were saved from the previous day, to accomplish the fermentation during cheesemaking. During the early part of the 20th century, however, microbiologists began to isolate lactic acid bacteria from batches of fermented milk and whey at commercial cheese factories that produced good-quality cheese. This led to the development of pure cultures that had proven track records for producing good-quality cheese, and that could be continuously maintained in pure form and made available to cheesemakers on an ongoing basis. Soon commercial companies began to specialize in producing and maintaining pure bacterial cultures that were specifically selected for use in cheesemaking. Cheesemakers in turn used these commercially produced pure cultures as seed stock to prepare the much larger quantities of starter culture that were needed each day to inoculate their cheese vats. By adding pure active starter culture to the milk at the start of cheesemaking, the cheesemaker essentially gained control over the amounts and types of lactic acid bacteria that would dominate during cheesemaking, rather than relying solely on the indigenous microflora present in the current or previous day's milk.

Today starter-culture supply companies maintain large collections of defined-strain cultures that have been characterized extensively and screened for important properties such as rate of acid production, salt tolerance, and ability to produce good cheese flavor. In addition, some companies continue to maintain undefined mixed cultures that consist of complex mixtures of various bacteria that have not been characterized but have been used successfully by cheesemakers for many years and continue to be popular.

FUNCTIONS OF THE STARTER CULTURE

Starter cultures generally perform several different functions during cheesemaking and cheese ripening, although the precise contributions of the starter will vary to some extent depending on the type of cheese.

Production of Lactic Acid

The preeminent function of the starter culture is to provide a uniform, predictable, reproducible rate of acid production during cheese manufacture. The starter culture initiates, or starts, the production of lactic acid through its fermentation of lactose—hence the name *starter*.

Why is acid production so important to cheesemaking? Because the schedule of acidification (that is, how quickly acid is produced, and, particularly, how much acid is produced early in cheesemaking when the whey is being released from the curd versus later when most of the whey has already been expelled) directly influences three critical aspects of cheese composition: the initial pH, moisture content, and mineral (calcium phosphate) content. These in turn profoundly shape the ripening pathways and quality characteristics of the final cheese (see chapter 6). For virtually all cheeses, the primary role of the starter is to produce lactic acid according to a specific schedule, but the optimum rate of acidification varies considerably depending on the type of cheese being made. As noted earlier, for example, mold-ripened cheeses require much more rapid acidification than do smear-ripened cheeses (see chapter 1, figure 1.2).

Suppression of Undesirable Microorganisms

Milk is a very rich growth medium, and is thus able to support the growth of a wide range of microorganisms. Furthermore, the temperature conditions that are used in the making of cheese are ideal for microbiological activity. Consequently, milk used in cheesemaking is extremely vulnerable to a wide range of microbial growth, including the growth of spoilage and pathogenic (disease-producing) microorganisms, should they happen to gain entrance to the milk as contaminants. To make matters worse, the environment in which milk is produced and harvested (the dairy farm) is home to an abundance of spoilage and pathogenic microorganisms, and there are almost limitless opportunities for contamination to occur. Thus contamination of the cheesemilk by spoilage organisms or pathogenic bacteria that have the potential to gain a foothold during cheesemaking, proliferate in the cheese, and ultimately produce quality defects or foodborne illness is a constant risk that cheesemakers face. There are a number of effective risk-reduction measures, such as strict observance of Good Manufacturing Practices and Standard Operating Procedures, meticulous sanitation and hygiene, HACCP-type programs (Hazard Analysis Critical Control Point), and pasteurization, that can reduce the risk substantially, as will be covered later in chapters 7 and 9, but the risk can never be eliminated completely.

Fortunately, an active starter culture during cheesemaking represents an important second line of defense against spoilage bacteria and pathogens that may evade even the best defensive measures and gain entrance into the cheesemilk. The starter culture helps to suppress unwanted microorganisms by several different means. First, some starter bacteria produce antimicrobial proteins called bacteriocins that inhibit the growth of other bacteria. For example, some strains of *Lactococcus lactis* ssp. *lactis* produce nicin, a protein that inhibits *Bacillus, Clostridium, Staphylococcus, Listeria*, and *Streptococcus*. Second, and more importantly, lactic acid is inhibitory toward many microorganisms; therefore, vigorous production of lactic acid by the starter bacteria acts as a strong deterrent to unwanted microbial growth. Furthermore, the rate of acid production by the starter is directly proportional to starter population growth (that is, rapid acidification corresponds with rapid increase in starter population). Therefore, vigorous lactic acid production also means that the starter bacteria are reproducing rapidly and are thus well positioned to outcompete any contaminating microorganisms for lactose and other nutrients needed for growth. Conversely, abnormally slow acid production during cheesemaking should always be viewed as a red flag: Slow acidification means there is less lactic acid present to inhibit unwanted contaminants and fewer starter bacteria to compete for lactose and nutrients. Consequently, the resulting cheese will be at greater risk for unwanted microbial growth, including the growth of pathogens. Therefore, if the rate of acidification during cheesemaking is slightly slower than normal, the resulting cheese should be segregated, monitored closely during ripening, and withheld from sale if it fails to ripen normally. *If the rate of acidification is extremely slow during cheesemaking, the cheese should not be offered for sale under any circumstances.* To do so could be considered negligent. The risk is too great.

Enzymatic Contribution to Ripening

Starter bacteria contain *proteolytic* (protein-degrading), *lipolytic* (fat-degrading), and other enzymes that are believed to contribute to cheese ripening. Some of these enzymes are located in the cell walls of the bacteria and contribute to ripening while the starter bacteria are still alive. Most are contained inside the cells and do not participate in ripening until the starter cells die and burst open, thereby releasing the intracellular enzymes into the water phase of the cheese, where they remain catalytically active. Over the years, starter-culture companies have isolated and selected specific strains of starter bacteria that produce superior cheese flavor. Others strains that have been shown to produce a high incidence of defects in cheese, such as bitterness, have been deliberately eliminated from commercial culture collections. Whether a particular strain produces superior cheese flavor or defects such as bitterness will depend, in part, on the specific profile of enzymes that are found in the starter cells.

Production of Gas, Flavor, and Aroma

Some cheeses require the production of carbon dioxide gas during ripening in order to form eyes (such as Gouda and Swiss) or an open texture (including Havarti and blue) in the cheese. The gas is produced by special gas-producing starter cultures or secondary cultures that simultaneously produce carbon dioxide gas and specific flavor and aroma compounds that contribute to the characteristic flavor and aroma of these cheeses.

IMPORTANT CHEESE STARTERS

There are seven different types of bacteria, shown in table 4.1, used as starter cultures for cheesemaking. Over the years the names of some of the bacteria have changed as a result of newer research that furnished more accurate classifications based on genetic relatedness. Starter cultures are divided into two broad categories, *mesophilic* and *thermophilic* starters, according to their optimum growth temperatures. The two principal mesophilic starter bacteria, *Lactococcus lactis* ssp. *lactis* and *L. l.* ssp. *cremoris,* grow best at around 77 to 86°F/25 to 30°C, are inhibited by cooking temperatures of around 102°F/39°C (ssp. *cremoris*) to 104°F/40°C (ssp. *lactis*) or higher, and are used alone or in combination with one another. In addition, there are two specialized mesophilic starters—Cit^{+} *Lactococcus lactis* ssp. *lactis,* often referred to as diacetylactis, and *Leuconostoc mesenteroides* ssp. *cremoris*—that are able ferment naturally occurring citrate in milk and produce carbon dioxide gas and diacetyl, a pleasant buttery aroma compound, as by-products. These aroma- and gas-producing mesophiles are used in certain eye-forming cheeses (such as Gouda) and cheeses that require an open texture (such as Havarti and blue mold types). Cit^{+} *Lactococcus* vigorously ferments lactose to lactic acid and produces a high amount of carbon dioxide gas. In contrast, *Leuconostoc* produces carbon dioxide gas more slowly and grows poorly in milk; therefore it is always used in combination with a non-citrate-fermenting *Lactococcus lactis* culture.

Thermophilic starter bacteria, which include *Streptococcus thermophilis, Lactobacillus delbrueckii* ssp. *bulgaricus*, and *L. helveticus*, prefer warmer temperatures, growing optimally in the range of around 95 to 105°F/35 to 41°C. They are able to survive at temperatures as high as 130 to 140°F/54 to 60°C. The thermophilic streptococci and lactobacilli are often used in combination with one another because they share a complex synergy that enables them to produce lactic acid much more rapidly when they are combined than when used individually. Not surprisingly, cheeses that are uncooked (including

Current Name	Previous Name(s)	Type	Fermentation Products
Lactococcus lactis ssp. *lactis*	*Streptococcus lactis*	mesophilic	Lactic acid
Lactococcus lactis ssp. *cremoris*	*Streptococcus cremoris*	mesophilic	Lactic acid
(Cit+) *Lactococcus lactis* ssp. *lactis*	*Lactococcus lactis* ssp. *lactis* biovar. *diacetylactis* *Streptococcus lactis* ssp. *diacetylactis*	mesophilic	Lactic acid, CO_2, diacetyl
Leuconostoc mesenteroides ssp. *cremoris*	*Leuconostoc cremoris*	mesophilic	CO_2, diacetyl
Streptococcus thermophilus	*Streptococcus salivarius* ssp. *thermophilus*	thermophilic	Lactic acid
Lactobacillus delbrueckii ssp. *bulgaricus*	*Lactobacillus bulgaricus*	thermophilic	Lactic acid
Lactobacillus helveticus		thermophilic	Lactic acid

Table 4.1. There are seven major types of bacteria used as starter cultures for cheesemaking. Over the years the names of some of the bacteria have changed due to reclassification.

fresh, bloomy-rind, and smear-ripened cheeses) or cooked to moderate temperatures (Cheddar types, Dutch types, feta, Havarti, and washed-rind cheeses) are made with mesophilic starters, whereas those cooked to higher temperatures (Swiss types and hard Italian types) require thermophilic cultures.

FORMS OF STARTER CULTURE

Three different forms of starter culture are used by cheesemakers: the mother culture, the bulk-set culture, and the direct-set culture. The mother culture is a traditional system that is rarely used in the United States these days. Bulk-set cultures are used mostly by large industrial cheesemakers, while farmstead cheesemakers generally prefer direct-set cultures.

Mother Culture

Mother cultures were commonly used by small cheese factories in the United States in the first half of the 20th century. The mother culture is a seed culture used daily to prepare the so-called bulk starter culture (the culture that is added directly to the cheese vat). The mother culture is maintained continuously by the cheesemaker by transferring a small portion of the culture each day to fresh, virtually sterile milk. This may be either fresh milk from the farm or skim milk obtained by reconstituting nonfat dry milk powder with water to a specific solids level, usually around 9 to 11 percent solids. In either case, the milk must be virtually sterilized by heating to 185°F/85°C for one hour in a suitable glass container with loose-fitting cap (such as a glass quart Mason jar with the cap partly unscrewed, or a glass Erlenmeyer flask that is plugged with cotton). After heating, the milk is cooled to the incubation temperature before it is inoculated with the mother culture. The inoculated milk is incubated under suitable temperature conditions (usually around 70°F/21°C for mesophilic starters, and around 108°F/42°C for thermophilic starters) to allow the starter bacteria to multiply and ferment lactose to lactic acid until the milk coagulates, in around 14 to 16 hours (with mesophilic starters) or 4 to 8 hours (with thermophilic starters). The fresh mother culture then serves as the seed stock to inoculate a new bottle of virtually sterile milk, which upon incubation becomes the mother culture the following day, and so forth. In addition, the mother culture is used to inoculate a larger quantity of heated (185°F/85°C for 30 minutes) milk, usually equal to about 1 to 3 percent of the milk that will be made into cheese on the following day (depending on the rate of inoculation), which will become the bulk starter. The inoculated milk is incubated overnight until the milk coagulates and then is used the next morning as bulk starter for cheesemaking. Thus the mother culture system involves daily transfer and incubation of the mother culture to prepare fresh mother culture and fresh bulk starter for use in cheesemaking.

Although the mother culture system was used widely in the past, it has several disadvantages that have prompted cheesemakers to switch to other alternatives. The biggest disadvantages include the following:

1. **Very labor intensive.** Bottles of virtually sterile milk must be prepared regularly for the daily transfers of the mother culture. At least two bottles are needed each day, one for acidity testing and the other for inoculating fresh mother culture and fresh bulk starter. The milk used for the bulk starter also must be heat treated before inoculation. Inoculations must be performed using aseptic (sterile) techniques. The amount of mother culture inoculated into fresh milk (usually 1 percent) should be measured, not estimated, using sterile measuring utensils (such as a pipette and graduated cylinder). The mother culture and bulk culture should be monitored for acidity development and cooled immediately upon the onset of coagulation to prevent acid injury and decreased starter activity. All of this adds up to a lot of work on a daily basis.
2. **High risk of contamination.** The mother culture is easily contaminated unless careful aseptic techniques are used, such as flaming the opening of the Mason jar using a Bunsen burner before transferring the culture, proper sterilizing and handling of utensils, and so on.

Farmstead cheesemakers should not attempt the mother culture system for commercial cheese production unless they have had formal training in basic microbiological techniques.

3. **Variation in starter activity.** During the fermentation of the bulk starter, lactic acid accumulates to high concentrations, which causes the pH to decrease. Cow's milk begins to coagulate at around pH 5.2 and is complete at pH 4.6. The coagulation first becomes noticeable at around pH 5.0. If permitted, the starter culture will continue to ferment lactose to lactic acid well beyond the point when coagulation first becomes evident at around pH 5.0. The pH will continue to decrease until the concentration of lactic acid becomes toxic to the starter bacteria and they become injured and begin to die off. If acid injury is severe, the bulk starter will show reduced activity during cheesemaking.

   Mesophiles begin to experience acid injury at around pH 5.0; therefore, the bulk starter should be cooled at the first sign of coagulation to halt the acid production so that the final pH does not fall below about 4.9 to 4.8. If the cheesemaker fails to cool the culture, the pH will continue to decrease to around 4.4 or lower, resulting in significant acid injury and culture inactivation. In practice, it is difficult for farmstead cheesemakers to cool the starter to just the right point to achieve a consistent final pH of around 4.8. Consequently, the amount of acid injury and thus the activity of the starter in the cheese vat are likely to vary from one day to the next, which may lead to variation in cheese composition and quality. (Thermophiles are more forgiving with respect to acid injury because they can tolerate much lower pH levels before injury sets in.)

4. **Equipment requirements.** Precise control over temperature (say, 70±1°F/21±0.5°C) during the preparation of the mother culture and bulk culture is necessary to ensure consistent starter activity. Therefore, a thermostatically controlled system (such as an incubator, water bath, or well-controlled ambient room temperature) is needed to maintain the incubation temperature of the mother culture and bulk culture.

For these reasons, I do not recommend the mother culture system for farmstead cheesemakers unless they are properly trained in microbiological techniques and willing and able to monitor and control the fermentation of the mother culture and bulk starter to prevent uncontrolled acid injury. If despite these disadvantages you still wish to learn more about the mother culture system, detailed practical guidelines can be found in Kosikowski and Mistry (1997), Van Slyke and Price (1992), and Wilster (1977).

Bulk-Set Culture

A bulk-set culture is a seed culture purchased from a culture supply company that essentially serves as a replacement for the mother culture. Bulk-set culture is usually obtained as a frozen liquid concentrate packaged in aluminum cans. The culture is partially thawed and added directly to the heat-treated milk that will serve as the growth medium for the bulk culture. The inoculated milk is incubated overnight in the usual way to produce the bulk culture, which is added to the cheese vat(s) the following day. Bulk-set cultures eliminate the need for daily sterile transfers of the mother culture. The frozen concentrated cultures are shipped in insulated containers containing dry ice and must be stored in a special deep freezer able to maintain extremely low temperature, ranging from -40 to -94°F/-40 to -70°C, depending on the culture.

Direct-Set Culture

Most farmstead cheesemakers in the United States use direct-set cultures, also called direct-vat set or direct-vat inoculation, because they offer the ultimate in convenience. Direct-set cultures are added directly to the cheese vat, so there is no need for a mother culture or bulk starter. The cultures are produced in either liquid frozen concentrate or powdered freeze-dried form. Freeze-dried cultures are packaged in aluminum foil pouches, while frozen concentrated cultures are available as pellets that can be poured directly from the container without thawing or as a liquid packaged in aluminum cans, which must be partially thawed before the culture can be removed from the can. Frozen concentrated cultures generally need to be stored in a special deep freezer at -40°F/-40°C or lower, whereas some freeze-dried cultures can be stored for up to several months in a domestic refrigerator with no loss of activity, making them exceptionally convenient.

Direct-set cultures differ from traditional bulk starter in two important ways. First, they are extremely concentrated and active; therefore the amount of direct-set culture that is added to the cheese vat is far smaller than that of traditional bulk culture. Consequently, whereas the addition of bulk starter to cheesemilk—typically at a rate of around 1 to 2 percent—causes the pH of the milk to decrease immediately by about 0.1 pH unit or greater due to the acidity of the starter, the addition of direct-set starter causes no immediate change to the milk pH. Second, bulk-set cultures begin to produce lactic acid shortly after addition to the cheesemilk, while direct-set cultures tend to experience a lag period of an hour or more before they begin to produce acid. Consequently, milk inoculated with direct-set culture typically shows little or no change in acidity through renneting, and the resulting coagulum tends to be weaker due to the unchanged pH. Once they commence acid production, however, direct-set cultures often produce acid more rapidly than traditional bulk culture. Consequently, the overall profile of acidification that occurs when cheese is made with direct-set culture is somewhat different from that obtained when the same culture is used in the form of a traditional bulk starter. Traditional cheesemaking recipes that assume the use of traditional bulk starter therefore often need to be modified somewhat when direct-set cultures are used. Some farmstead cheesemakers prefer to use traditional bulk starter rather than direct-vat cultures for this reason. If you fall into this camp, you may want consider using either bulk-set or direct-set culture as the seed culture to prepare your bulk starter, rather than maintaining your own mother culture. This approach represents a compromise that enables you to use bulk starter in traditional manufacturing procedures without having to confront all the challenges of maintaining a mother culture system.

SOURCES OF STARTER INCONSISTENCY AND FAILURE

At the risk of being redundant, let me emphasize again that a key prerequisite to successful cheesemaking is using a starter culture that consistently produces lactic acid at the optimum rate for your particular cheese variety. A number of factors can lead to variation in starter activity and even, in extreme cases, complete failure.

Factors Involving the Starter Culture

Commercial culture suppliers offer many different strains of the same starter organisms. Some strains are faster at producing acid; others are slower. Therefore, changing to a different culture strain may result in a significant change in the rate of acidification during cheesemaking. Furthermore, the activity of a particular direct-set or a bulk starter culture may decrease if the concentration of viable bacteria in the culture decreases (for example, due to improper storage and handling), or if the bacteria's metabolic state becomes altered (for example, due to injury).

Direct-Set Starter: Storage and Handling

Direct-set cultures are standardized precisely for activity by the manufacturer, and their activities are very consistent from batch to batch provided that the culture is stored and handled properly. Always follow the manufacturer's instructions for storage and handling. Some cultures are designed to be stored at -40°F/-40°C for no more than six weeks; others may be stored in a domestic refrigerator for several months with no loss of activity. Make sure that your freezer is providing the correct storage temperature, and that you use the culture before the expiration date. Follow the recommended procedures for thawing and inoculation. Some frozen liquid direct-set cultures are added directly to the cheesemilk with no thawing, while others are thawed slightly and then added to milk. Freeze-dried powders are usually first dispersed in a small portion of cheesemilk, which is then added to the cheese vat. In all cases direct-set starters should be used immediately after they are removed from frozen or refrigerated storage and never allowed to sit around at room temperature for an extended period before being added to the milk. Never thaw and then refreeze a frozen liquid direct-set culture for future use. Freeze–thaw cycles result in activity loss. Self-defrosting freezers should never be used to store frozen cultures; their temperature fluctuates too widely during defrosting.

Bulk Starter: Preparation and Storage

As noted earlier, the activity of bulk starter will be influenced by the extent of acid injury that has occurred during preparation and storage, which in turn is determined by how far the pH declines before the culture is used. The culture should be cooled promptly at the first sign of coagulation so that the final acidity does not increase to a level that causes injury and reduces starter activity. Injury will also set in if bulk culture is stored for an extended period before use. Therefore, bulk starter should be prepared fresh daily.

Other factors that affect the activity of bulk starter include overheating the milk before inoculation and variation in the solids content of the milk. Starter activity will be lower if the milk is overheated to the point where it turns a light brown color. Also, starter activity will be higher if prepared with milk containing higher solids (specifically casein) content because casein acts as a buffer against acid injury and allows the starter bacteria to reach a larger population with greater activity.

Bacteriophage

Bacteriophage are virus particles that infect starter bacterial cells, reproduce inside the bacteria, and then cause the cells to burst open, thereby releasing upward of 50 to 150 new virus particles—which then infect new starter cells and repeat the cycle. Each cycle may take only about 30 minutes to complete, resulting in an explosive increase in bacteriophage population and precipitous declines in the population of viable starter cells and lactic acid production by the starter. Acid-coagulated cheeses are especially vulnerable to bacteriophage because their long coagulation times provide ample opportunity for the virus to complete many reproduction cycles and attain astronomical populations before coagulation is complete. In severe cases the milk may fail to reach pH 5.3 to 5.0 and show no signs of coagulation. In other cases the milk pH may decrease to 5.3 to 5.0 and then stop, causing partial coagulation, which sediments as a sludge on the bottom of the vat. Milk from the farm is a major source of bacteriophage; therefore, phage is a far greater problem for large industrial cheesemakers that process commingled milks from many different farms, which act as multiple sources of phage, than for farmstead cheesemakers who produce cheese from the milk of a single farm.

Bacteriophage are found in raw milk and milk environments, and they thrive in whey and wet environments that contain residues of whey. Therefore, it is important to segregate whey far from the cheese room, avoid spillage, and follow meticulous cleaning and sanitizing practices. Bacteriophage are highly strain specific: A specific phage is able to infect only a specific strain of bacteria, while other strains are immune to that particular phage. Culture supply companies offer many different cultures that have different phage sensitivities. If you succumb to a phage infection, therefore, you can overcome the problem by replacing your infected culture with one that is not sensitive to the same phage.

Factors Involving the Milk

The chemical composition and microbiological characteristics of milk can vary substantially for a variety of reasons. Some of these changes can greatly affect the rate of acidification by the starter culture during cheesemaking.

Mastitic and Late-Lactation Milk

Milk produced by animals that have mastitis or are in late lactation contains substances that inhibit starter-culture activity, resulting in abnormally slow acidification during cheesemaking. Reduced starter activity during the early stages of late lactation can be counteracted by increasing the amount of starter added to the vat, but eventually severe inhibition of the starter is unavoidable. Milk from animals in very late lactation thus should not be used for cheesemaking.

Elevated Free Fatty Acid Levels

Free fatty acids, which cause rancidity at high concentrations, inhibit starter activity. Animals that have mastitis or are in late lactation secrete milk that contains elevated levels of free fatty acids, which can inhibit the starter. Also, freezing–thawing or excessive foaming and churning—which all disrupt the milkfat globule membrane and render milkfat susceptible to lipase enzymes—or excessive growth of lipase-secreting psychrotrophic bacteria may result in high levels of free fatty acids.

Protein Content of the Cheesemilk

Casein micelles act like a sponge for acid, mopping up the hydrogen ions that accumulate when lactic acid is produced by the starter culture. Therefore, the hydrogen ion concentration will increase more slowly during cheesemaking when milk with a high protein content is used. To compensate, the amount of starter culture should be increased to maintain the same rate of acidification during cheesemaking. This is particularly challenging when cheese is made from seasonally produced milk, which undergoes large changes in casein content across the seasons (see chapter 3, figures 3.7 and 3.9). Consequently, the cheesemaker must adjust starter usage periodically to maintain a consistent rate of acidification.

Agglutination

It has been observed that some strains of starter-culture bacteria are sensitive to naturally occurring antibodies, or immunoglobulins, in cow's milk. The immunoglobulins bind to the cell walls of sensitive strains and cause the starter cells to clump together. Being denser than water, the bacterial clumps sediment to the bottom of the vat; therefore, the starter becomes more concentrated and produces more acid at the bottom of the vat than at the top. The pH of the milk at the bottom of the vat decreases more quickly, and casein micelles then coagulate locally around the bacterial clumps, forming a gelatinous sludge, whereas the top of the vat coagulates slowly or sometimes not at all. This *agglutination* occurs very slowly, so it is not a problem in rennet-coagulated cheeses, which coagulate very rapidly; it can be quite severe in acid-coagulated cheeses, however, which take many hours to coagulate. The problem can be remedied by switching to a different strain of starter bacteria that is not sensitive to the immunoglobulins in your milk. As far as I am aware, the agglutination phenomenon is restricted to cow's milk and has not been reported in goat's or sheep's milk.

Antibiotic Residue

Antibiotics that are used to treat mastitis in dairy animals readily pass into the animals' milk. Starter-culture bacteria are extremely sensitive to and inhibited by these antibiotics; it is essential that the milk from a treated animal not be used for cheesemaking until the antibiotics have completely cleared from the animal's system. Follow the manufacturer's instructions meticulously for withholding milk after antibiotic treatment for the required period of time. Do not allow tainted milk from a single animal into your bulk tank.

Excessive Aeration

In general, starter cultures are *microaerophilic*, meaning that they are most active when the level of dissolved oxygen in the milk is low, and are inhibited by high oxygen levels. Avoid careless milk-handling practices such as splashing, foaming, and leaky seals in pipelines, which can introduce air into the cheesemilk and inhibit the starter in severe cases. Shallow vats of milk are especially vulnerable to air incorporation because of the large surface area exposed to the atmosphere relative to the total volume of milk.

Indigenous Microflora

Runaway acid production can occur during cheesemaking if the milk contains high populations of nonstarter acid-producing bacteria. Slow cooling of milk after harvesting can lead to high numbers of indigenous bacteria that will produce lactic acid along with the starter bacteria during cheesemaking. Poor sanitation can lead to a high population of coliform bacteria that vigorously ferment lactose to lactic acid. In extreme cases, fast acid production may be accompanied by curds that float and whey that effervesces because coliforms also produce large amounts of carbon dioxide.

SECONDARY (RIPENING) CULTURES

Some culture supply companies offer a range of secondary cultures that are used to perform various specialized functions during ripening. Secondary cultures include not only bacteria but also yeasts and molds that participate in the ripening of certain cheeses. These organisms were originally isolated from various traditional cheeses. Their abilities to perform desirable functions at the surface or in the body of cheese during ripening have been characterized, and specific organisms that are deemed important to ripening are now produced in pure culture and made available to cheesemakers to add directly to the milk or cheese. The major secondary cultures that are currently used in cheesemaking are listed in table 4.2.

Propionibacterium freudenreichii ssp. *shermanii* is a bacterium commonly found in milk that ferments lactic acid and produces carbon dioxide and propionic and acetic acids as by-products. The carbon dioxide gas produced by this organism is responsible for the formation

Type	Function	Application
Propionibacterium freudenreichii ssp. *shermanii*	CO2, propionic and acetic acid production for eye and flavor development	Swiss-type cheeses
Geotrichum candidum	Modulation of white mold growth, deacidification of cheese surface, flavor development	Bloomy-rind, smear-ripened cheeses
Penicillium camemberti album; candidum	Surface white mold growth, deacidification, texture and flavor development	Bloomy-rind, white mold cheeses
Penicillium roqueforti	blue-green mold growth, deacidification, texture and flavor development	Blue mold cheeses
Brevibacteriu linens cornyneform bacteria	Red smear surface flora, flavor and texture development	Smear-ripened, washed-rind cheeses
Surface yeasts	Deacidification of cheese surface, enhancement of *B. linens,* flavor development	Smear-ripened, washed-rind cheeses, tommes
Micrococci	Surface growth, aroma development	Washed-rind cheeses, tommes
Nonstarter lactobacilli	Flavor and texture development	Hard aged cheeses

Table 4.2. The major types of yeasts, molds, and bacteria that are used as secondary cultures for cheese ripening. These organisms were originally isolated from various cheeses based on their ability to perform desirable functions at the surface or within the body of the cheese during ripening.

of eyes in Swiss-type cheeses, and propionic and acetic acids contribute directly to typical Swiss-like flavor and aroma. The fermentation of lactic acid results in a partial deacidification of the cheese; therefore, the pH of Swiss cheese generally increases during ripening from an initial level of about 5.2 to around 5.6 to 5.8 at the end of ripening.

Geotrichum candidum is classified as a mold, but it possesses yeastlike characteristics, as well. It is sometimes referred to as "dairy mold" and is believed to be naturally present on the surfaces of most mold and bacterial surface-ripened cheeses. It is used as a secondary culture in the production of bloomy-rind cheeses, where it colonizes the cheese surface before the white mold growth commences and contributes to flavor development. *Geotrichum* helps to control the growth of the white mold *(Penicillium camemberti),* prevents the white mold from being overly proteolytic, which could lead to bitterness defect, and appears to inhibit the growth of certain foreign molds that may contaminate the cheese. *Geotrichum* is also used in the making of smear-ripened cheeses, where it serves to deacidify the curd at the cheese surface and thus pave the way for reddish bacterial surface growth.

Penicillium camemberti, also known as *P. album,* is a white mold that changes to a grayish color after several days. It is the traditional bloomy-rind mold. However, a particular variant of *P. camemberti* exists that remains white in color rather than changing to gray. Up until the 1970s the white variant was classified as a separate mold species known as *Penicillium caseicolum*. More recently, however, the species *P. caseicolum* was eliminated from the official taxonomy and reclassified as a white variant of *P. camemberti,* which is now sold under the trade name *P. candidum. P. candidum* is widely used in the making of bloomy-rind cheeses where a permanent white surface is desired. Given the right conditions of temperature and humidity, and cheese containing the correct salt and moisture contents, *P. candidum* will flourish, dominating the microflora at the cheese surface and inhibiting foreign molds. *P. camemberti* is mostly used in goat's-milk and traditional natural-rind cheeses where grayish mold growth is desired.

Penicillium roqueforti is the blue-green mold used in blue-veined cheeses such as Roquefort, Stilton, and Gorgonzola. This robust mold grows rapidly and will outcompete most other foreign molds under proper conditions of temperature and humidity. *P. roqueforti* causes extensive breakdown of the fat in cheese, resulting in the formation of free fatty acids and concomitant development of piquant flavor and aroma. Furthermore, this mold converts free fatty acids to methyl ketones, which are responsible for the characteristic blue cheese flavor and aroma. The mold also deacidifies the curd, which raises the pH, and is very proteolytic, which promotes a softening of the texture.

Brevibacterium linens and other coryneform bacteria are bacteria that form the red smear flora on smear-ripened and washed-rind cheeses. They require a high pH (greater than 5.8) to grow; thus it is necessary for other microorganisms (such as *Geotrichum candidum* and surface yeasts) to first colonize and deacidify the cheese before the red smear flora can proliferate. This bacterium is very proteolytic and produces ammonia, which causes the pH at the cheese surface to increase, and readily degrades the amino acid methionine, which leads to production of strong sulfur-based flavors and aromas.

Surface yeasts are used in combination with *Brevibacterium linens* as deacidifying agents that raise the surface pH of the cheese and thereby initiate the growth of the red smear flora on smear-ripened and washed-rind cheeses. The yeasts also contribute to the flavor and are used in cheeses with natural rinds such as tommes.

Micrococci are commonly found on the surfaces of smear-ripened and washed-rind cheeses. They are used to promote surface growth and aroma in washed-rind and natural-rind cheeses.

Finally, nonstarter lactobacilli such as *Lactobacillus casei* ssp. *casei* are believed to be important to the development of flavor and texture in long-aged cheeses such as Cheddar.

MONITORING STARTER ACTIVITY: ACIDITY MEASUREMENT

Because acid production by the starter culture is so important to cheese quality and safety, all commercial cheesemakers, including farmstead cheesemakers, should routinely monitor acidity at critical points during cheesemaking. Two different tests are commonly used to measure acidity: titratable acidity (TA) and pH. Although both tests measure acidity, they do not measure precisely the same thing because acids exist in two different forms, which are measured differently by TA and pH. An acid by definition is a molecule that is capable of releasing a positively charged hydrogen ion (H^+) to the surrounding environment in the presence of water. Thus when an acid is placed in water it spontaneously releases hydrogen ions. The hydrogen ion represents the working end of the acid molecule because hydrogen ions are highly reactive with other atoms and molecules. The high reactivity of hydrogen ions is the reason why acids are corrosive in nature. The greater the concentration of hydrogen ions, the more corrosive they become. For example, lactic acid that accumulates during cheesemaking releases hydrogen ions that react with and essentially "corrode" the casein micelles, causing calcium phosphate in the micelles to dissolve into the whey.

Acids are classified as being either strong or weak. An acid is considered strong if every single molecule releases its hydrogen ion(s) when placed in water. In contrast, when a weak acid is placed in water, some of the acid molecules release their hydrogen ions while others do not. The greater the tendency to hold on to and not release their hydrogen ions, the weaker the acid. The difference between a strong acid and a weak acid can be illustrated as follows. Let's assume that we have 10 molecules of a strong acid and 10 molecules of a weak acid. When the strong acid is placed in water, all 10 of the molecules spontaneously release their hydrogen ions into the water.

STRONG ACID: 10 $ACID^-H^+$ + water $\rightarrow$ 10 $ACID^-$ + 10 H^+ + water

Where: $ACID^-H^+$ = acid molecule with hydrogen ion intact

$ACID^-$ = negatively charged acid molecule after releasing hydrogen ion

H^+ = positively charged free (released) hydrogen ion

In contrast, when 10 molecules of a weak acid are placed in water, perhaps only 5 of the molecules release their hydrogen ions; the other 5 hold on to their hydrogen ions.

WEAK ACID: 10 $ACID^-H^+$ + water $\rightarrow$ 5 $ACID^-$ + 5 H^+ + 5 $ACID^-H^+$ + water

Thus the strong acid in this example is twice as strong as the weak acid with respect to the hydrogen ion concentration that occurs when the acid is placed in water. Essentially, the difference between titratable acidity and pH is that titratable acidity measures all acid molecules in the sample, both those that have released their hydrogen ions and, in the case of weak acids, those that have not. Titratable acidity is sometimes referred to as total acidity because it is a measure of all acids, both strong and weak, contained within the sample. In contrast, the pH is a direct measurement of free hydrogen ions in water and thus measures only those acid molecules that have released their hydrogen ion(s).

Measurement of Titratable Acidity (TA)

The measurement of TA is based upon the principle that free hydroxyl ions (OH^-) have an overwhelming attraction to hydrogen ions. If free hydroxyl ions are added to a sample of water containing weak and strong acids, the hydroxyl ions will first seek out and combine with the free hydrogen ions that have been released by the strong and weak acids to the water. After the free hydrogen ions are depleted, the hydroxyl ions will seek out and strip off any hydrogen ions that remain complexed to weak acids, and combine with them to form water. In other words, hydroxyl ions will neutralize both the strong and weak acids in an acidic solution by combining with all available hydrogen ions, at which point the sample reaches neutrality. Pure water is defined as being neutral. If the hydrogen ion concentration is greater than that which occurs in pure water due to the presence of acids, the solution is said to be acidic. Conversely, if the hydrogen ion concentration is less than that of pure water, the solution is considered basic or alkaline. Once an acidic sample is neutralized, any further addition of hydroxyl ions causes the solution to become basic.

In practice, the measurement of titratable acidity works like this. An indicator compound (phenolphthalein) that is colorless in acidic solution but turns bright pink in basic (alkaline) solution is added to the acidic sample that is to be measured. Then a known amount of sodium hydroxide (NaOH) is added to neutralize the sample. Sodium hydroxide completely dissociates in water to form free hydroxyl ions (OH^-), which immediately seek out and complex with available hydrogen ions (from strong and weak acids) to form water. The sodium hydroxide is added incrementally until the indicator compound changes from colorless to a faint but stable pink color. The color change indicates that all the acid has been neutralized; the final addition of sodium hydroxide that causes the indicator to change from colorless to pink corresponds to when the sample becomes alkaline after all the available hydrogen ions originating from acids have been neutralized. Because each hydroxyl ion combines with one hydrogen ion to form water, the number of hydroxyl ions required to neutralize the sample (in other words, the amount of sodium hydroxide that is needed to cause the indicator to change color) is equivalent to the number of acid molecules in the sample. In summary, the measurement of titratable acidity essentially involves counting out the number of hydroxyl ions (in the form of sodium hydroxide) needed to neutralize the sample, which is equivalent to the number of acid molecules in the sample.

The measurement of TA can be illustrated as follows. Let's assume that we have 10 molecules of a strong acid and 10 molecules of a weak acid in our sample, and that they release their hydrogen ions as follows:

STRONG ACID: 10 $ACID^{-}H^{+}$ + water⟶10 $ACID^{-}$ + 10 H^{+}

WEAK ACID: 10 $ACID^{-}H^{+}$ + water ⟶5 $ACID^{-}$ + 5 H^{+} + 5 $ACID^{-}H^{+}$

TOTAL ACIDS: 20 $ACID^{-}H^{+}$ + water⟶ 15 $ACID^{-}$ + 15H^{+} + 5 $ACID^{-}H^{+}$

When sodium hydroxide is added incrementally to the sample, each NaOH molecule immediately dissociates into sodium and hydroxyl ions. The first 15 molecules of sodium hydroxide added dissociate into 15 hydroxyl ions that immediately combine with the 15 free hydrogen ions to form water:

15 NaOH + water⟶15 Na^{+} + 15 OH^{-}

15 OH^{-} + 15H^{+} + 15 $ACID^{-}$ + 5$ACID^{-}H^{+}$⟶15 H_2O + 15 $ACID^{-}$ + 5$ACID^{-}H^{+}$

The next five sodium hydroxide molecules added dissociate into five hydroxyl ions. These strip off the hydrogen ions that remain complexed to the five weak acid molecules, and combine with them to form water.

5 NaOH + water ⟶ 5 Na^{+} + 5 OH^{-}

5 OH^{-} + 5 $ACID^{-}H^{+}$ + 15 H_2O + 15 $ACID^{-}$ ⟶ 5 H_2O + 5 $ACID^{-}$ + 15 H_2O + 15 $ACID^{-}$ ⟶ 20 H_2O + 20 $ACID^{-}$

At this point all the acid in the sample has been neutralized to form water. Any further addition of sodium hydroxide will cause the sample to become basic (alkaline), which will cause the indicator to change from colorless to pink, alerting the analyst that the titration is complete. Since it took 20 molecules of sodium hydroxide to completely neutralize all acid in the sample, the sample must have contained 20 acid molecules. The TA measurement does not reveal the type(s) of acid present in the sample—lactic, acetic, citric, what have you—only that the equivalent of 20 acid molecules are present.

When you measure the TA of a sample by titration, you basically count out sodium hydroxide molecules until the sample is neutralized and then mathematically convert the amount of sodium hydroxide added to the equivalent amount of acid. For calculation purposes, it is assumed that all the acid in the milk or whey sample consists of lactic acid; thus titratable acidity measurements are expressed as percent of lactic acid. In reality, this is not the case. For example, high-quality fresh milk contains no lactic acid, yet the titratable acidity of fresh cow's milk is typically around 0.16 percent expressed as lactic acid. Why? Because milk contains various weak acids such as citric (citrate) and phosphoric (phosphate), which are measured as titratable acidity but expressed as though they were lactic acid. During the making of Cheddar cheese, the TA increases from about 0.16 percent in the starting milk to around 0.6 percent in the final whey that is expelled from the curd at the end of cheesemaking, due to the production of lactic acid by the starter culture.

Procedure for Measuring Titratable Acidity

1. Measure exactly 9 milliliters (ml) of milk or whey into a clean white porcelain cup or a clear beaker or flask using a pipette.

(Ideally, exactly 9 grams of sample should be used, but 9 ml is close enough to 9 g for cheesemaking purposes.)

2. Add 4 drops of phenolphthalein indicator solution (1 percent phenolphthalein in 95 percent alcohol).
3. Fill a 10 ml burette (graduated to read to 0.1 ml) with 0.1 Normal NaOH solution so that the bottom on the curved meniscus is aligned with the zero graduation. Slowly add 0.1 Normal NaOH to the test sample and swirl the sample as each drop is added. (*Normal* is a unit of concentration. The concentration of the sodium hydroxide must be known so that you can determine the amount of hydroxyl ions it takes to neutralize the sample, from which you can calculate the amount of acid in the sample. In the United States 0.1 Normal NaOH is usually used, whereas 1/9 Normal NaOH is commonly used in Europe. The principle of the test is the same regardless of the concentration used.)
4. Slowly and deliberately, continue to add NaOH until the first discernible and stable shade of pink is attained.
5. Read the burette (the milliliters of NaOH added to the sample) at the bottom of the curved meniscus and multiply the reading by a factor of 0.1 to calculate the acidity value, expressed as percent of lactic acid. For example, if it takes 1.6 ml of NaOH to reach the first stable pink end point, the titratable acidity value will be 0.16 percent, expressed as lactic acid.

Cheesemakers often use an automatic acidity tester to perform the titration for TA measurements. The acidity tester contains a 10 ml burette that can be read directly as percent TA (the burette is graduated in milliliters but the numerical scale reads in ml/10, thus the percent TA can be read directly from the burette). The burette can be filled automatically from an attached reservoir containing 0.1 Normal sodium hydroxide. It is a very convenient way to measure titratable acidity. Burettes, pipettes, acidity testers, indicator and sodium hydroxide solutions, and laboratory glassware and plasticware can be obtained from scientific supply companies and companies that specialize in supplying the dairy industry.

Measurement of pH

The pH is a measure of the concentration of hydrogen ions contained within the water phase of the test sample, expressed according to a logarithmic scale (that is, a scale based on tenfold differences between units). Thus, a 1.0 pH unit difference corresponds to a tenfold difference in hydrogen ion concentration. Pure water has a pH of 7.0, which corresponds to neutrality. Values below pH 7.0 indicate that the sample has a concentration of hydrogen ions greater than that of pure water and is therefore acidic; the lower the pH value, the higher the acidity. For example, at pH 6.0 the concentration of hydrogen ions is 10 times greater (more acidic) than at 7.0. At pH 5.0, the concentration of hydrogen ions is 10 times greater than at 6.0, or 100 times greater than at 7.0. Values above pH 7.0 indicate that the sample has a concentration of hydrogen ions less than that of pure water and is therefore basic. Thus at pH 8.0 the hydrogen ion concentration is 10 times lower (more basic) than at 7.0, and so forth. During Cheddar cheesemaking, the pH decreases from nearly pH 7.0 in the starting milk to around 5.0 in the final cheese, representing about a hundredfold increase in hydrogen ion concentration due to the production of lactic acid by the starter culture. It is this increase in hydrogen ions that becomes "corrosive" to the casein micelles, causing calcium phosphate in the micelles to dissolve into the whey. During ripening, the concentration of hydrogen ions in the water phase of the cheese strongly influences microbial and enzymatic activity, as discussed in chapter 6.

The measurement of pH is based upon the principle that a hydrogen ion possesses a positive electrical charge. Therefore, the greater the concentration of hydrogen ions in a sample, the greater the total positive electrical charge that is collectively carried by the hydrogen ions. A pH meter is an instrument that measures the positive electrical charge collectively carried by the hydrogen ions in the test sample and translates the positive charge into hydrogen ion concentration. To accomplish this, the pH meter requires four components, as illustrated in figure 4.1: a hydrogen-ion-sensing (that is, pH-sensing) electrode; a reference electrode; a voltmeter; and a test sample with a continuous water phase. Often the pH and reference electrodes are packaged together as a single unit, referred to as a combination electrode.

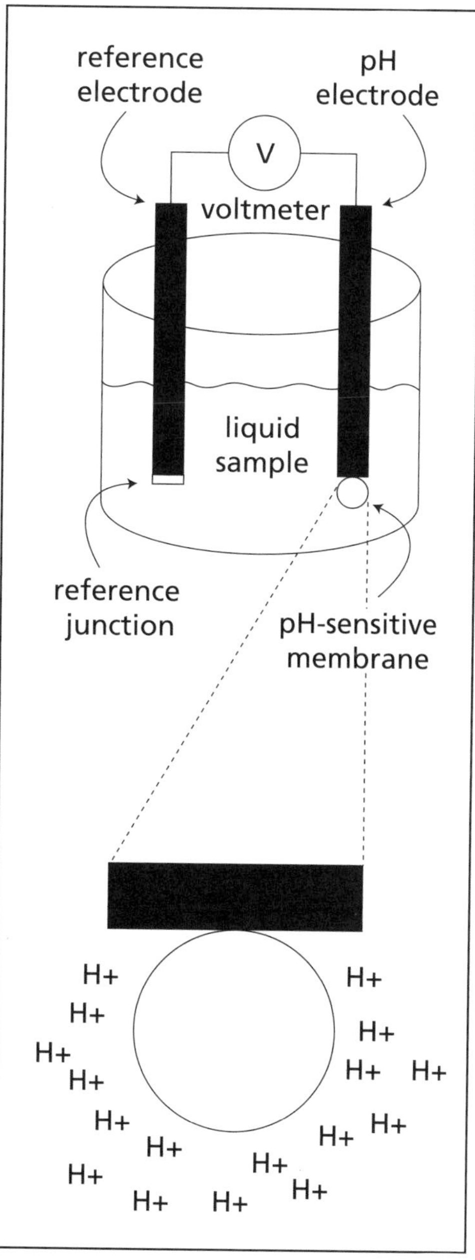

Figure 4.1. A pH meter requires four components: a pH electrode, a reference electrode, a voltmeter, and a test sample that contains a water phase. The pH electrode is equipped with a glass membrane that is sensitive to the hydrogen ion concentration in the sample.

The pH electrode contains a special glass membrane that allows positively charged hydrogen ions present in the test sample to migrate into the membrane. The greater the concentration of hydrogen ions in the sample, the greater their migration into and accumulation in the exposed surface of the glass membrane of the pH electrode; therefore the greater the difference in electrical charge (referred to as the *electrical potential*) that develops across the glass membrane. In contrast, the reference electrode is designed to possess a constant electrical potential. The reference and pH electrodes are manufactured such that when the two electrodes are placed in a sample having a pH value of 7.0, the electrical potential of the pH electrode will be equal to that of the reference electrode. In other words, the difference in electrical potential between the two electrodes will be zero.

In pH measurement systems, the two electrodes are coupled to one other through a voltmeter, which is able to measure any difference in the electrical potentials of the two electrodes. If the test sample has a pH of 7.0, the voltmeter detects no difference in electrical potential. However, it is a basic law of nature that for every tenfold change in the hydrogen ion concentration of a test sample, the electrical potential of an ideal pH electrode will theoretically change by 59 millivolts (millivolts, or mv, is a measure of electrical potential) at 68°F/20°C. Therefore, if the pH of the test sample is changed by 1.0 pH unit (for example, a change from pH 7.0 to 6.0, which represents a tenfold increase in hydrogen ion concentration), there will be an accompanying increase in the electrical potential of the pH electrode equal to +59 mv. Thus the pH electrode will possess an electrical potential that is 59 mv larger than that of the reference electrode. The voltmeter measures the +59 mv potential difference. If the sample has a pH of 5.0, the potential difference between the pH and reference electrodes will be +118 mv. If the sample has a pH of 8.0, the potential difference between the pH and reference electrodes will be -59 mv. Thus there is logarithmic relationship between the hydrogen ion concentration in the sample and the difference in electrical potential that occurs between the pH and reference electrodes. The job of the voltmeter is to measure the potential difference between the pH and reference electrodes and then translate that difference into a sample pH value (e.g., +59 mv = pH 6.0; +118 mv = pH 5.0; -59 mv = pH 8.0; and so forth).

Procedure for Measuring pH

There are many different pH meter and electrode designs; the proper use and maintenance of pH equipment will vary somewhat from one model to the next. Make sure you follow the recommended procedures for your equipment. Every pH meter and electrode comes with a set of operating instructions from the manufacturer. The following guidelines generally apply to pH measurement regardless of the specific equipment used:

1. **Calibration.** The pH meter must be calibrated before it can provide accurate measurements. Calibration essentially teaches the voltmeter to translate elec-

trical potential differences accurately into pH units. You will need at least one, preferably two, buffer solutions manufactured to have precisely known pH values, such as 7.0 and 4.0. A two-point calibration, performed according to the manufacturer's instructions using pH 7.0 and pH 4.0 buffer solutions, is much more accurate than a one-point calibration using a single buffer. The pH 7.0 buffer is used to adjust the system so that the potential difference between the pH and reference electrodes equals zero when both are placed in a pH 7.0 solution. Brand-new electrodes should generate a potential difference that is close to zero in pH 7.0 buffer, but as the electrodes age they tend to drift and need to be reset to zero through calibration. The pH 4.0 buffer is used along with the 7.0 buffer to adjust the system so that each 1.0-unit change in sample pH corresponds to a 59-mv change in electrical potential. Brand-new pH electrodes should show a potential difference close to 58 mv for each 1.0-unit change in sample pH (that is, about 98 percent of the theoretical ideal difference), but as electrodes age the potential difference will decrease. For example, instead of changing by 59 mv per 1.0-pH-unit change (referred to as the slope of the electrode response), the pH electrode may only show only a 53 mv change (about 90 percent of the ideal theoretical difference). This deterioration in the slope of the electrode response is part of the normal aging process, and it must be offset through proper calibration. When the slope of the electrode's response falls below 90 percent of the theoretical ideal (that is, below 53 mv), it's time to get a new pH electrode.

2. **Electrode maintenance.** Electrode performance will deteriorate quickly if the electrodes are not stored and maintained properly. Most electrode manufacturers recommend storing electrodes in a specific ionic solution (say, potassium chloride) when they are not in use. Make sure you use the correct solution for storage, which is usually similar to but not exactly the same as the solution used to fill the reference electrode. The reference electrode must be kept filled with the proper filling solution, and the filling solution should be free of crystals inside the electrode. The hole used to fill the reference electrode with filling solution should be kept open during pH measurements but sealed at other times to prevent the solution from evaporating and crystallizing.

The pH electrode must be kept meticulously clean to prevent the pH-sensitive membrane from becoming clogged with organic matter, especially fat and protein, that tends to accumulate from the test samples. A clogged pH electrode results in slow electrode response times and readings that drift. Likewise, the reference electrode contains a permeable opening or junction (see figure 4.1) that allows ions to slowly migrate from the inside of the electrode to the test sample and vice versa, thereby completing the electrical circuit between the two electrodes. If this junction becomes obstructed, the electrodes will experience slow response times and readings that drift. Thus both electrodes should be cleaned regularly. Consult the electrode manufacturer's instructions for recommended cleaning procedures. Some manufacturers recommend periodic soaking in dilute acid (for example, 0.1 M hydrochloric or nitric acid) or in 1 percent pepsin in 0.1 M hydrochloric acid. I find that the electrodes generally remain clean and maintain a good response time if they are periodically immersed in a warm solution of a mild household dishwashing detergent for about 10 seconds followed by thorough rinsing. When measuring milk or whey, a mild detergent wash may be needed after every 10 measurements. When measuring cheeses, especially high-fat cheeses, more frequent washes may be needed. When frequent detergent washes are needed, such as when measuring many cheeses samples, the filling solution should be periodically drained from the reference electrode and replaced with new filling solution to prevent the solution from becoming contaminated with detergent components that may diffuse through the junction.

3. **Temperature control.** The temperature of the sample being measured influences the relationship between hydrogen ion concentration and electrical potential difference (that is, the slope of the electrode response). For example, at 68°F/20°C the theoretical change in the electrode response of an ideal pH electrode is 59.15 mv per unit change in pH. At 104°F/40°C the theoretical change is 62.17 mv. Therefore, the two buffers must be at the same temperature when the calibration is performed in order to achieve an accurate calibration. Furthermore, test samples must be measured at the same temperature as the buffers that were used to calibrate the pH meter to avoid temperature effects. In other words, if the buffers were at 70°F/21°C during calibration, the samples should be within 2°F/1°C of that temperature for maximum accuracy. Many pH meters come equipped with an automatic temperature compensator that electronically or mathematically adjusts the pH measurement to account for temperature differences between the calibration buffers and test samples. Temperature compensators are probably sufficiently accurate for most cheesemaking applications, but the ideal is to have all samples adjusted to the same temperature as the buffers used in the calibration.

CHAPTER 4 REFERENCES

Kosikowski, F. V., and V. V. Mistry. 1997. *Cheese and Femented Milk Foods,* Vol. 1: *Origins and Principles.* F. V. Kosikowski, LLC, Great Falls, Va.

Van Slyke, L. L., and W. V. Price. 1992. *Cheese.* Ridgeview Publishing Co., Atascadero, Calif.

Wilster, G. 1977. *Practical Cheesemaking,* 12th ed. Oregon State University Book Stores, Inc., Corvallis.

The Eight Basic Steps of Cheesemaking

5

In chapter 3 we learned that the transformation from milk to cheese involves the process of selective concentration. We will now examine how that process is accomplished. To use a local analogy, making cheese is something like traveling from east to west in the state of Vermont. "You can't get there from here" is the classic Vermont response, at least not by a direct route. Indeed, you usually find yourself making many twists and turns as you work your way across mountain passes and through winding river valleys. And it is easy to go astray and end up lost unless you have a detailed road map and can recognize key landmarks along the way. So it is with cheesemaking. The route that leads from milk to cheese, this process of selective concentration, involves many twists and turns, and it is easy to go astray. The objective of chapter 5 is to examine the road map for cheesemaking and the major technological landmarks that we must pass along the journey. Because each distinct family of cheese represents a unique destination, the exact route that we follow from milk to cheese will differ from one cheese family to the next, but the road map and the major technological landmarks will be the same.

Almost 40 years ago the late Professor Frank Kosikowski published his classic book *Cheese and Fermented Milk Foods,* which is now coauthored by his former graduate student Professor Vikram Mistry and remains an invaluable and highly recommended addition to every cheesemaker's library. Kosikowski proposed that most cheeses are made by the same fundamental process involving eight basic steps, or eight technological landmarks if we think in terms of our analogy to a journey. Although most cheeses share this basic manufacturing scheme, according to Kosikowski, the various cheese families become differentiated from one another during manufacture based on the specific conditions that the cheesemaker employs at each of the eight steps. Thus changing the emphasis at one key cheesemaking step may result in a distinctly different cheese. Scientific research over the past century, and especially during the past 30 years, has largely validated Kosikowski's model for explaining both unity and diversity among cheeses. We now know that each of the eight basic steps of cheesemaking influences the chemical, microbiological, and enzymatic characteristics of newly made cheese, which in turn shape the ripening process and, ultimately, the identity and quality of the final cheese. Substantial changes at any of the eight basic steps will likely result in a very different cheese, for better or for worse. Consequently, it is essential for the cheesemaker to understand what happens at each of these eight steps and the overall effect that each step has on the final cheese.

As we explore Kosikowski's eight basic steps from the perspective of farmstead cheesemaking, it is important to bear in mind that if you produce cheese in the United States for commercial sale, your practices, equipment, and facilities must conform to U.S. regulatory standards. Milk handling and cheesemaking practices that may have been used for centuries in Europe may not be permissible in today's regulatory environment. Older equipment and utensils may not satisfy current sanitary standards. Aging cellars and caves must now be constructed and maintained according to stricter hygienic standards than in earlier times. In short, today's farmstead cheesemaker is constantly faced with the need to adapt traditional artisanal cheesemaking practices to today's realities. To succeed, you will need to work closely with your local regulatory authority (for instance, in Vermont, the Vermont Department of Agriculture, Food & Markets) at every step of the way. Get to know the inspectors and other regulatory personnel and go out of your way to establish a constructive working relationship with them. They want you to succeed, and although their primary mission is to protect public health, in the process they are also protecting you, the cheesemaker, from mishaps that could be very costly indeed.

STEP ONE: SETTING THE MILK

Setting involves the preparation of the cheesemilk for coagulation and the actual coagulation process. Coagulation is the first step toward selective concentration because it creates the conditions that allow the casein and fat in milk to separate from the water and water-soluble components. You'll recall from the previous chapter that native casein micelles are polar in nature at the surface and, therefore, attract a layer of water molecules around their periphery (see figure 3.5). This surface layer of weakly bound water acts as a cushion that prevents the micelles from sticking together when they collide with one another, thereby enabling them to remain uniformly dispersed in the water phase of the milk. During coagulation the casein micelles are altered in such a way as to become nonpolar at the surface; consequently, they lose their weakly held peripheral layer of water. No longer cushioned by a layer of water, these nonpolar micelles quickly collide with one another due to their natural motion and stick together. As more micelles collide, they form growing chains that branch out in all directions. Soon the chains interlock with one another, establishing a spongelike, three-dimensional casein matrix that encompasses the entire water phase of the milk. Fat droplets, which on average are about 10 times greater in diameter than casein micelles, become physically entrapped within the casein matrix. The process of coagulation, as illustrated in figure 5.1, occurs through two different mechanisms—rennet coagulation and acid coagulation—which result in two distinctly different families of cheese.

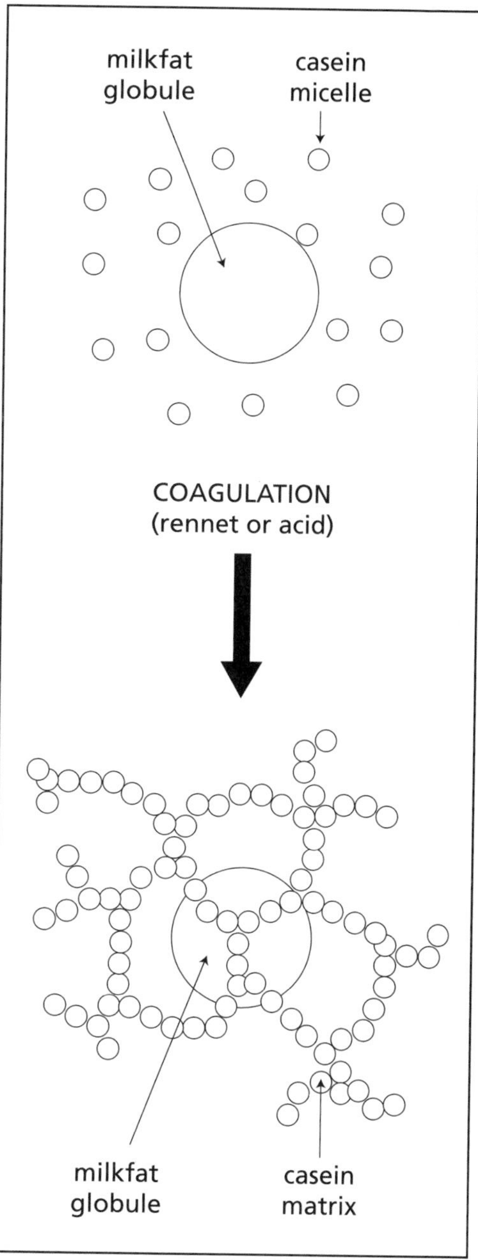

Figure 5.1. Coagulation of milk may occur through the action of rennet enzymes added to the milk (rennet coagulation) or lactic acid produced by the starter culture (acid coagulation). Casein micelles aggregate to form a three-dimensional, spongelike matrix that entraps fat globules and the water phase of the milk.

Rennet Coagulation

The large majority of cheeses, and virtually all hard aged cheeses, are made by rennet coagulation. Technically, *rennet* refers to enzyme preparations that are used to coagulate milk and that are derived exclusively from the *abomasa,* or true stomachs, of ruminants. However, the term is often used generically in reference to any enzymatic agent that is used to coagulate milk, whether of animal, plant, or microbial origin. Originally, rennet enzymes were obtained from the stomach linings of the calf, kid, or lamb. Before weaning, these ruminants contain high concentrations of the milk-coagulating enzyme called chymosin in their stomach linings. After weaning, and as the animal matures, chymosin in the stomach lining is replaced by another milk-coagulating enzyme known as pepsin. Both chymosin and pepsin are proteolytic enzymes that readily attack casein and coagulate milk, but the specific manner in which they break down casein is not the same.

Because of this, chymosin is a better cheesemaking enzyme than pepsin, hence the use of stomachs from young animals came to be preferred early on in the history of cheesemaking. By Roman times it was well known that an excellent coagulant for cheesemaking could be obtained by drying the stomach of the young animal and adding a portion of this to the milk. Later, rennet coagulants were refined by working macerated stomach into a rennet paste, or combining macerated stomach with salt brine to produce a liquid extract.

Today a variety of milk coagulants from animal and microbial sources are commercially available. Commercial calf rennet, which is extracted from the stomach linings of milk-fed calves, typically contains 80 to 90 percent chymosin and 10 to 20 percent pepsin in highly purified liquid form. Calf rennet is considered by many to be the standard against which all other coagulants are compared and is generally recognized to produce superior aged cheeses. However, although calf rennet produces excellent cheese, it is not perfect for all applications. It is generally more expensive relative to other coagulants, does not qualify for use in vegetarian cheeses, and may present animal welfare concerns for some.

Rennet paste, prepared from the macerated stomach linings of milk-fed calves, is also available commercially. Because the stomach lining contains not only chymosin and pepsin but also lipase enzymes that break down fat, rennet paste is rich in both chymosin and lipase. The lipase enzymes readily migrate from the rennet paste into the milk during setting and become incorporated in active form into the resulting cheese. Rennet paste is used in place of liquid rennet extract in the making of certain cheeses that are very piquant in favor, such as Romano and provolone. You'll recall that piquant flavor and aroma originate from short-chain free fatty acids that are liberated from milkfat through the action of lipase enzymes. The use of rennet paste ensures that the cheese becomes enriched with desirable lipase enzymes that produce the right amount and correct balance of free fatty acids. Alternatively, purified liquid extracts of lipase are available commercially, which can be used in combination liquid rennet as a substitute for rennet paste.

Several milk coagulants are available commercially that are derived from microbial (fungal) sources. The most widely used microbial rennets are derived from the mold *Rhizomucor miehei,* formerly called *Mucor miehei,* which produces a proteolytic enzyme that coagulates milk. The mold is grown in large fermentation vats where it produces the coagulant enzymes, which are then recovered and purified into a liquid extract. Another commercially available microbial rennet is derived from the mold *Cryophonectria parasitica,* formerly *Endothia parasitica.* Because they are not derived from animal sources, microbial rennets are often the coagulants of choice for those who have concerns about the use of calf rennet. A certified organic microbial rennet recently became available commercially.

Although all commercial coagulants perform well at coagulating the milk, they are not all equal in their ability to contribute to desirable ripening in aged cheeses. Chymosin is ideal for aged cheeses because it has a potent ability to coagulate milk, but once inside the cheese its proteolytic activity is relatively slow paced and proceeds along a pathway that is particularly well suited for the development of desirable flavor and texture. In contrast, *Cryophonectria parasitica* coagulant is much more proteolytic and proceeds along pathways that are detrimental to flavor and texture development. Therefore, this particular coagulant should only be used in cheeses that are cooked at very high temperatures, such as Swiss types, if at all. In highly cooked cheeses, the high cooking temperature inactivates the coagulant enzymes of *C. parasitica,* and thus excessive proteolysis is avoided in the cheese during ripening. Coagulants derived from *Rhizomucor miehei* are much less proteolytic than those from *C. parasitica* and can be used with success in the making of any rennet-coagulated cheese. As noted above, however, it is generally recognized that calf rennet produces superior aged cheeses.

During the last decade a new generation of coagulants has come on the market that essentially represents a genetic merging of calf rennet with microbial synthesis. These genetically engineered coagulants, known as fermentation-produced chymosin, were created by taking the gene that codes for the chymosin enzyme from the cow and transferring it in active form to a host microorganism, such as the mold *Aspergillus niger,* the yeast *Saccharomyces cerevisiae,* or the bacterium *Escherichia coli*. The genetically modified organism (GMO) then obediently produces the chymosin enzyme, which can be recovered and purified into the liquid coagulant known as fermentation-produced chymosin. Most fermentation-produced chymosin coagulants contain pure (100 percent) chymosin. However, some manufacturers now offer coagulants that are a blend of about 90 percent fermentation-produced chymosin and about 10 percent pepsin in order to more closely approximate the mix of enzymes in calf rennet.

To some, fermentation-produced chymosin represents the best of both worlds. . . . A cost-effective coagulant that delivers the superior performance of calf rennet but does not require the slaughter of young animals. To others, it is an offensive and chilling assault of biotechnology on nature, one of many assaults that are occurring all across the agricultural landscape. It is sometimes argued that fermentation-produced chymosin is not genetically engineered because the amino acid sequence of the chymosin enzyme that is produced by the transformed microorganism is identical to that produced by the cow. Since the enzyme is not changed, it is technically not genetically engineered. Although this may be an important distinction for scientists and regulatory authorities, consumers who are concerned about genetic engineering and GMOs in the food supply are unlikely to make such a distinction. For you as a cheesemaker, the bottom line is that you want a coagulant that works well, is compatible with your own philosophy, and is a good fit for your market.

Regardless of the type of rennet used, several preparatory steps normally precede the addition of rennet to the milk. First, the milk may be pasteurized depending on the type of cheese being made. Current U.S. standards of identity for cheese specify that certain cheeses must be made from pasteurized milk. For example, Camembert, Limburger, mozzarella, and Monterey Jack cheeses, along with a number of others, must be made from pasteurized milk. Furthermore, any cheese that is aged for less than 60 days after manufacture must be made from pasteurized milk. On the other hand, most cheeses that are aged for more than 60 days at a temperature of not less than 35°F/2°C may be made from either pasteurized or raw milk. Pasteurization will be considered in more detail in chapter 9.

Whether raw or pasteurized, the milk is first adjusted to an optimum setting temperature that depends on the specific cheese, but generally ranges from 86 to 96°F/30 to 36°C. The higher the setting temperature, the shorter the coagulation time, up to temperatures of around 110°F/43°C. At higher temperatures rennet enzymes become heat inactivated and the milk will coagulate more slowly or not at all. Lower temperatures such as 86 to 96°F/30 to 36°C are mostly used in cheesemaking to accommodate the growth requirements of the starter culture and to avoid the formation of a tough and rubbery curd that occurs readily at higher temperatures. If the milk temperature drops too low, however, the coagulation time is greatly extended; at 65°F/18°C or lower coagulation will fail to even occur.

The starter culture must be added to the milk before renneting so that the starter bacteria become entrapped and concentrated within the curd. Starter bacteria are roughly the same size as milkfat globules, and as with fat globules about 95 percent of the starter bacteria become physically entrapped within the porous casein matrix upon coagulation and are retained in the curd. These entrapped starter cells play a critical role during cheesemaking by producing lactic acid inside the curd particles, which then diffuses out into the whey. They also play an important role in aged cheeses during ripening. Ideally, the starter culture is added to the milk as soon as the milk has been warmed to the setting temperature in preparation for renneting. Many cheeses require a ripening period of up to 60 minutes between the time that the starter is added and renneting to allow the culture to become acclimated, begin to produce lactic acid, and reproduce. The length of the ripening period is important because it affects the rate of acid production by the starter throughout the remainder of cheesemaking. The longer the ripening time, all else being equal, the more opportunity the starter bacteria have to reproduce during the earliest stages of cheesemaking, and thus the higher the starter population and the faster the acid production at each subsequent step of the cheesemaking process. Because bacteria reproduce exponentially, a relatively small difference in starter population early on can have a surprisingly large effect on acid production throughout the remainder of cheesemaking. Therefore, the cheesemaker should establish the optimum time and temperature conditions for ripening and then hold those conditions consistent from vat to vat.

A general word of caution about temperature control is in order before we proceed. In order to save time, some cheesemakers add starter to the milk before the milk has reached the setting temperature. If this is your practice, you will want to standardize these conditions by adding the starter when the milk reaches a specific target temperature and by keeping the time that elapses from adding the starter to adding the rennet consistent from vat to vat. The goal is to keep the time–temperature profile that the starter experiences during ripening consistent from one day to the next. In fact, this rule applies to the entire cheesemaking process. Times and temperatures should be carefully defined, routinely monitored, and closely controlled at every step of the way. A few degrees of difference from one vat to the next at any stage in cheesemaking can change the resulting cheese, for better or for worse. (The important exception to this rule is when the cheesemaker *intentionally* changes the conditions in order to compensate for changes in starter-culture activity or milk composition, which we will consider in more detail in chapter 8.)

To ensure that you obtain reliable temperature measurements, the thermometers that you use in day-to-day operation should be checked regularly against an accurate standard thermometer, such as a standard mercury glass model. *Don't fool around when it comes to measuring and controlling temperature.* Furthermore, keep meticulous records with respect to times and temperatures (and acidity, which we will consider later) throughout cheesemaking. When problems arise, as they inevitably will, this information may prove helpful toward identifying the cause and formulating a remedy. Moreover, from the standpoint of legal liability—always a concern in the litigious age in which we live—comprehensive records of times, temperatures, and acidity may furnish valuable documentation that your cheeses were made with due diligence and in a manner that was not negligent.

Rennet coagulation is a two-stage process, involving an initial enzymatic phase followed by a nonenzymatic phase. During the enzymatic phase, the coagulant enzyme (for example, chymosin if the coagulant is calf rennet) attacks the casein micelles and specifically snips off the polar end of kappa-casein molecules. This is important because, as noted earlier, kappa-casein is primarily concentrated at the surface of the casein micelle, where it forms a hairy protective polar covering that enables the micelle to remain dispersed in water (see figure 3.5). The coagulant essentially shaves off the polar hairy layer with its weakly bound water, leaving the micelle surface exposed. This enzymatic phase typically occurs during the first 10 minutes or so following the addition of rennet to the milk, at which point the nonenzymatic phase commences.

The nonenzymatic phase is set into motion when about 85 percent of the kappa-casein has been attacked by the coagulant enzymes. By that time, the casein micelles, stripped of their protective coating of polar kappa-casein and its cushioning layer of weakly bound water, collide with one another and stick together, forming chains that eventually interlock as a three-dimensional matrix (see figure 5.1). This process occurs spontaneously and very quickly, provided that the milk is within the right temperature range (around 86 to 96°F/30 to 36°C for most manufacturing procedures) and contains adequate levels of free calcium ions in the water phase. Free calcium ions act as a sort of glue that enables micelles to stick together upon collision. You'll recall that about 10 percent of the total calcium in milk on average is present as free ions. However, the concentration of free calcium ions can vary considerably, and if the concentration is too low, the nonenzymatic phase of coagulation will be impeded, coagulation will occur slowly, and the resulting coagulum will be weak and fragile.

The goal of setting is to consistently produce a coagulum of optimum firmness in a defined period of time (usually about 25 to 30 minutes) from renneting to cutting. Obtaining the right *firmness* at cutting is important because cutting the curd when it is too soft results in greater fat and casein losses to the whey and lower cheese yield. On the other hand, curd that is too firm is difficult to cut and may tear into pieces of widely ranging sizes rather than cutting cleanly into particles of uniform size. Cutting firmness also influences curd particle size and whey expulsion. A low curd firmness at cutting generally results in smaller curd particles and lower moisture in the cheese, all else held constant. Achieving a consistent *coagulation time* is important because, as with the ripening time, large variations in the coagulation time can influence the rate of acid production by the starter throughout the rest of cheesemaking. For example, an increase in coagulation time from 30 to 60 minutes may lead to faster acidification throughout the rest of the cheesemaking process, because the starter has more time to reproduce and attain a higher population. A number of different factors may influence the coagulation process, at both the enzymatic and the nonenzymatic phases. If you are experiencing problems with rennet coagulation, the cause is probably related to one or more of the following factors.

Coagulant Strength

Determining the right amount and right strength of coagulant to use can be a source of confusion for farmstead cheesemakers. Coagulants are standardized by the manufacturer to a specific milk-clotting strength. In the United States liquid coagulants are generally standardized on a 1:15,000 basis. This means that 1 unit of rennet (for instance, 1 gram) will coagulate 15,000 units (in this example, 15,000 grams) of milk in 40 minutes at 95°F/35°C. Liquid rennet that is standardized on a 1:15,000 basis is traditionally called single-strength rennet in the U.S. Cheesemaking procedures in the U.S. typically call for around 70 to 100 ml of single-strength rennet per 1,000 pounds/454 kg of milk. Rennet is also available in more concentrated forms, such as double and triple strength. Double-strength rennet is twice as concentrated as single strength; therefore, only half as much double-strength rennet gives the same milk-clotting result as single-strength rennet. Likewise, triple-strength rennet is three times more concentrated than single strength.

To complicate matters further, rennets

in Europe are usually standardized on a 1:10,000 basis rather than a 1:15,000 basis. Thus U.S. rennet is 1.5 times more concentrated than European rennet. If you use a European cheesemaking procedure, chances are you will need to adjust your rennet usage to account for this difference in strength. It is therefore important to know the amount and strength of the rennet called for by your cheesemaking procedure, and the strength of the rennet that you are using, then adjust your usage appropriately. For example, if a cheesemaking procedure from France specifies the addition of 30 ml of rennet (1:10,000) per 100 liters of milk, the equivalent amount of U.S. single-strength rennet (1:15,000 strength) would be 20 ml per 100 liters of milk/88 ml per 1,000 pounds of milk. The amount of double-strength rennet would be half that, or 10 ml per 100 liters of milk/44 ml per 1,000 pounds of milk.

Recently a new system for measuring coagulant strength, based on international milk-clotting units (IMCU/ml), was adopted by the scientific community and is now being used by commercial coagulant suppliers. For farmstead cheesemakers, this new system is likely to increase rather than decrease the level of confusion. If you are unsure about the strength of your coagulant or the amount to use, consult with your coagulant supplier on the appropriate usage rate for your particular application. Rennet usage can be varied to some extent without adversely affecting the cheese. However, the use of too much rennet can result in unusually rapid coagulation; an overly firm, rubbery coagulum that is difficult to cut and may retain more moisture than normal; and the development of bitterness during aging due to excessive proteolysis. Too little rennet may give the opposite: long coagulation time, a weak set, and slow flavor development during aging due to too little proteolysis.

Although the milk-clotting abilities of all commercial coagulants are precisely standardized by the manufacturer, several factors can cause a coagulant to lose strength, resulting in longer coagulation time and a weaker set:

1. **Dilution.** Coagulants are quite potent: Very small amounts are used to set very large amounts of milk. In order to obtain a uniform distribution of the coagulant enzymes throughout the vat of milk, which is necessary for uniform coagulation, the coagulant is diluted in cold potable water according to the manufacturer's instructions, typically at a ratio of 1:40 for single-strength rennet (1:15,000). For example, 10 ml of single-strength rennet would be diluted in 400 ml of water. The dilution factor should be increased proportionally for more concentrated rennets. Thus double-strength rennet should be diluted 1:80 because it is twice as concentrated. However, the coagulant enzymes become unstable in the diluted state, and if there is a delay between diluting the coagulant and adding it to the milk the coagulant may lose strength. Once diluted, therefore, the coagulant should be immediately added to the milk. As an aside, make sure that you accurately measure the coagulant using an appropriately sized pipette or

graduated cylinder, depending on the amount. For example, if your procedure calls for 40 ml of single-strength rennet and you are using double-strength rennet, measure out exactly 20 ml. . . . *Don't guesstimate!*

2. **Alkaline pH.** Coagulants are very pH sensitive and are rapidly inactivated if they are exposed to an alkaline pH—7.0 or higher. Such exposure can occur if the dilution water is alkaline or if the vessel used to dilute the coagulant contains residues of alkaline detergent, chlorine sanitizer, or annatto coloring (if used in cheesemaking), which are very alkaline. Make sure that your dilution vessel is thoroughly cleaned and rinsed before use, and that your water supply is not alkaline. The pH of your water supply can be tested with a pH meter (see chapter 4) or with pH-sensitive paper strips that change color in response to the pH of the liquid being measured.
3. **Ultraviolet light.** Coagulant enzymes are inactivated by exposure to UV light. Rennet should thus be stored in an opaque container; direct exposure to sunlight should be completely avoided.
4. **Storage temperature.** Rennet should be stored at refrigeration temperature when not being used. Prolonged exposure to higher temperatures can lead to loss of coagulant strength.
5. **Rough treatment.** Enzymes may become inactivated if exposed to excessive agitation and especially foaming. Be gentle with liquid rennet and avoid foaming at all costs.

Milk Chemistry

Coagulation behavior is profoundly influenced by the chemistry of the milk. Therefore, it is not surprising that coagulation properties vary considerably from one species to the next (cow, goat, sheep), within a species due to breed (Holstein versus Jersey cow's milk, for instance), and over time, especially with season and lactation stage. Both the enzymatic and nonenzymatic phases of coagulation are affected by milk chemistry. The chemical characteristics of milk that have the greatest effect on coagulation include the following:

1. **Casein content.** Casein micelles form the structural elements of the coagulum. Thus the amount of casein in milk will directly influence coagulation time and curd firmness. Milk with high casein content, such as sheep's milk, coagulates rapidly to a very firm curd, whereas low-casein milk, like that from a Holstein cow, coagulates more slowly to form a weaker curd. As the casein content of milk changes across season, so, too, will the coagulation properties. During summer, when casein is typically at its lowest level, the coagulum is generally weaker than in autumn when casein levels increase (see chapter 3, figures 3.7 and 3.9). An exception occurs in late-lactation milk, which may have a relatively high casein content yet coagulate poorly due to other chemical changes that occur at the end of lactation.
2. **Ionic calcium.** You'll recall that free calcium ions are needed to initiate the nonenzymatic phase of coagulation. If the concentration of calcium ions is too

low, coagulation time may be increased and the resulting coagulum may be abnormally weak and fragile. Low calcium ion concentration seems to be particularly problematic for milk with low casein content, such as Holstein or Ayrshire cow's milk during summer. The cheesemaker can compensate for inadequate ionic calcium by adding food-grade calcium chloride to the milk. Calcium chloride, which can be legally added to cheesemilk up to a maximum rate of 0.02 percent (0.02 pound of calcium chloride per 100 pounds of milk, for example), contributes free calcium ions that will help to shorten the coagulation time and increase the setting firmness. Also, the addition of calcium chloride causes a slight decrease in milk pH, which further improves coagulation. Industrial cow's-milk cheesemakers often add calcium chloride to improve coagulation. Farmstead cow's- and goat's-milk cheesemakers may want to consider adding calcium chloride if coagulation becomes problematic at certain times of year. How much calcium chloride should be added is a matter of debate. The maximum allowed by law (0.02 percent) is probably overkill and may even cause undesirable changes in texture in some cheeses. You may want to start with the addition of 0.01 percent and then modify the level based on experience. Food-grade calcium chloride can be purchased in liquid form, in which case the amount added to the milk will need to be adjusted according to the concentration of the liquid product. For example, if the liquid product contains 34 percent calcium chloride, then the amount to add to 100 pounds of milk to attain a 0.01 percent concentration is calculated as follows:

100 lbs. x 0.0001 x 1/.34 = .029 lb.
(13.4 g) calcium chloride solution per
100 lbs. milk

3. **Milk pH.** The pH of the milk at the time of renneting strongly affects both the enzymatic and nonenzymatic phases of coagulation. You'll recall that pH is a measure of acidity or, more specifically, hydrogen ion concentration. The lower the pH value, the more acidic the sample. Neutrality occurs at pH 7.0. Increases in the pH value above 7.0 indicate an increase in alkalinity, whereas decreases below 7.0 indicate increasing acidity. When milk leaves the udder, the pH is normally around 6.5; it will increase slightly to between 6.6 and 6.7 upon cooling. Both the enzymatic and nonenzymatic phases of coagulation are accelerated as milk pH decreases in the range of 6.7 to 6.0, resulting in progressively shorter coagulation times and increasing curd firmness. At the other extreme, the pH of milk may increase to 7.0 or higher for animals that are near the end of their lactation cycle, or for animals that develop mastitis. The addition of large amounts of water to milk may also cause the pH to increase. High pH wreaks havoc with the enzymatic phase of coagulation because rennet enzymes are very sensitive to alkaline pH and progressively lose activity when the pH exceeds 6.6, resulting in long coagulation times. To make matters worse, high pH reduces the level of ionic calcium, which impedes the nonenzymatic

phase and further contributes to slow coagulation and a weak and fragile set. Some improvement can be gained by adding calcium chloride to milk with high pH, because calcium chloride both lowers the pH slightly and contributes calcium ions.

The pH of milk at renneting is influenced by the type of starter culture used —for example, bulk-set versus direct-set starter. (Starter cultures are examined in more detail in chapter 4.) In earlier times so-called bulk-set starter was prepared by the cheesemaker using milk or sometimes whey as the growth medium. The cheesemaker inoculated sterilized milk with starter bacteria from a mother culture and then held the milk at a good growth temperature. The starter bacteria then reproduced to a maximum concentration of around 10^9 viable bacteria per milliliter of milk and, in the process, fermented lactose to lactic acid until the pH decreased to around 4.6. The resulting bulk-set culture was thus quite acidic and rich in calcium ions (due to the low pH). When added to the cheesemilk at rates typically ranging from around 1 to 2 percent of the weight of the milk, the acidic culture caused the milk's pH to immediately decrease by around 0.1 to 0.2 units. The combination of decreased milk pH and increased calcium ion concentration virtually guaranteed a short coagulation time and firm coagulum.

Today, however, traditional bulk-set cultures have been replaced by newer, more concentrated cultures that are far more active. For farmstead cheesemakers the most common forms of starter now used are the direct-set cultures. These are commercially available as a frozen liquid concentrate or freeze-dried powder, and are added directly to the cheesemilk, making them extremely convenient. Direct-set cultures are hundreds, even thousands, of times more concentrated than the traditional bulk-set culture; the amount added to the cheesemilk is extremely small. Consequently, the pH of the cheesemilk does not decrease and the level of free calcium ions does not increase when direct-set starter is added. Furthermore, direct-set cultures have a longer lag period between the time they are added to the milk and the time they begin to produce lactic acid. When direct-set cultures are used, then, it is not unusual for the pH of the cheesemilk to remain unchanged (around pH 6.6 to 6.7) at renneting, resulting in longer coagulation times and weaker sets than occur with traditional bulk-set starter. Thus minor problems with slow coagulation and weak set are probably more commonplace for farmstead cheesemakers now than in the heyday of the traditional bulk-set starter. Again, the addition of calcium chloride may help to compensate for poor coagulation when necessary.

4. **Proteolysis in the milk** before renneting causes damage to casein micelles, which in turn contributes to poor coagulation properties. Proteolytic degradation of casein can be caused by high populations of psychrotrophic bacteria. As noted earlier, the presence of these highly destructive bacteria should be minimized through proper cleaning and sanitation practices, storing the milk at 40°F/4°C or lower,

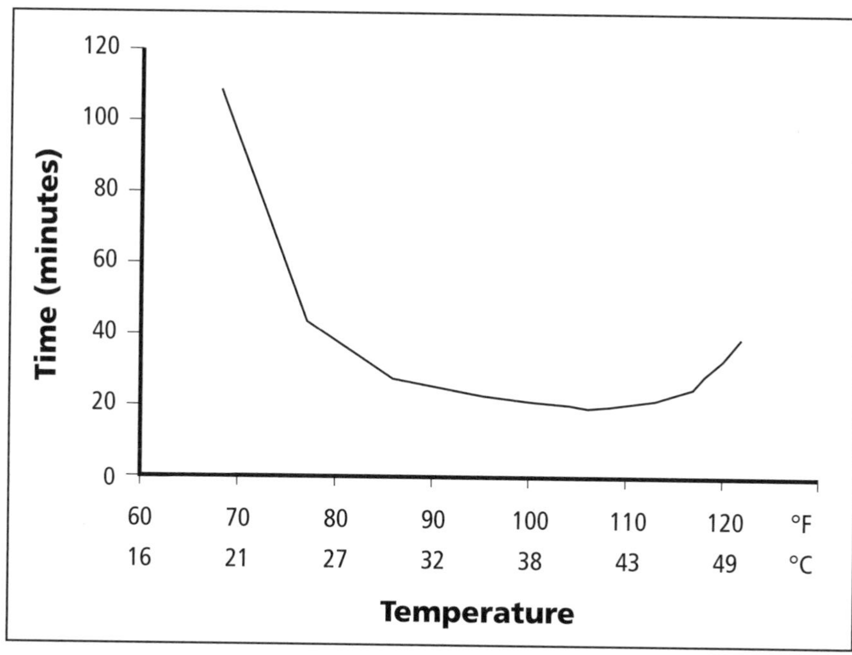

Figure 5.2. An example of how the setting temperature may affect the time required to coagulate cow's milk—cutting time—during Cheddar cheesemaking. Coagulation occurs most rapidly at around 106°F/41°C. (Adapted from Sammis, 1946.)

and limiting the time between milking and cheesemaking, ideally to one day or less. Considerable proteolysis may also occur in milk from animals that are in late lactation or that have mastitis, because such milk contains higher levels of plasmin and other proteolytic enzymes. Thus late-lactation and mastitic milks tend to suffer from exceptionally poor coagulation properties due to the combination of proteolytic damage to the casein, abnormally high pH, and low calcium ion concentration.

Milk Temperature

As noted earlier, coagulation time is directly affected by temperature. The higher the temperature (up to around 110°F/43°C), the faster the coagulation, whereas milk loses the ability to coagulate at temperatures less than about 65°F/18°C (see figure 5.2). Sometimes a slightly higher setting temperature can be used to remedy minor problems with slow coagulation, whereas lower setting temperature will exacerbate such problems. Uneven temperature in the vat caused by surface cooling during renneting can also prove problematic. If severe enough, surface cooling may result in slow coagulation at the milk surface, although coagulation may proceed normally in the middle and bottom of the same vat where the temperature is higher. Thus by the time the cool surface has formed a curd suitable for cutting, if at all, the curd beneath the surface has become tough, rubbery, and difficult to cut. This is particularly troublesome when open vats are used and when the room temperature is substantially lower than the milk temperature, as may occur during colder weather. Surface cooling can be reduced by increasing the temperature of the cheese room and by covering the vat during renneting with a suitable cover made from an approved material.

Hot spots in the vat can be another source of temperature-related problems. Temperature uniformity within a vat may vary depending on the type of heating (steam-heated water versus direct steam in the vat jacket, for instance) and the type of system used to circulate the water in the jacket. This is less of a problem when the milk is being stirred, but during coagulation, when the milk is motionless, localized regions of higher temperature can develop, which results in faster coagulation and the formation of zones of tough, rubbery curd. Most modern vats are designed to give reasonably uniform temperature in the milk, but older vats may suffer from a certain degree of temperature variation, particularly if steam or water valves become leaky.

Pasteurization Temperature

Severe heat treatment causes the whey proteins in milk to bind to the surfaces of the casein micelles, thereby altering the coagulation properties of the casein. The resulting coagulum is weak and fragile and resists syneresis, resulting in cheese with abnormally high moisture content. Avoid overheating the cheesemilk during pasteurization. Don't allow the milk temperature and holding time to substantially exceed the minimum times and temperatures required by law: 145°F/63°C for 30 minutes or 161°F/72°C for 15 seconds. Pasteurization will be examined in more detail in chapter 9.

Movement or Physical Disruption

As soon as the nonenzymatic phase of milk coagulation commences (about 10 minutes after adding the rennet), any movement of the milk due to stirring, vibrations, or the like will cause the casein to aggregate as flocs rather than as a gel, resulting in a poor coagulum. After the rennet is added, therefore, the milk should be stirred for no longer than three minutes to allow the enzymes to become uniformly distributed throughout the milk and to distribute any cream that may have risen to the milk surface. Then stirring should be halted and the milk should remain perfectly still until cutting.

After coagulation has occurred, the rest of the cheesemaking process is designed first and foremost to accomplish three interrelated goals:

1. To progressively expel whey from the coagulum (curd) at an optimum rate so as to attain the correct (optimum) initial moisture content in the final cheese.
2. To enable the starter culture bacteria to reproduce and produce lactic acid at optimum rates.
3. To progressively remove calcium phosphate from the coagulum (curd) at an optimum rate so as to attain the correct (optimum) mineral content and initial pH in the final cheese.

In chapter 6 we will examine why the control of moisture content, calcium phosphate content, and pH are critical in the making of rennet-coagulated cheeses.

Acid Coagulation

A number of soft fresh cheeses are made by acid coagulation. Familiar examples include cottage cheese, cream cheese, and quark. As the name implies, acid coagulation occurs in response to the production of lactic acid by the starter culture and does not depend on the action of rennet enzymes. Thus many manufacturing procedures for acid-coagulated cheeses do not call for any rennet to be added to the milk. On the other hand, some manufacturing procedures may include the addition of a small amount of rennet, which serves not to coagulate the milk but rather to improve curd firmness and syneresis (whey separation). For example, some cottage cheese manufacturing procedures call for the addition of 0.8 to 1.0 ml of single-strength rennet (1:15,000) per 1,000 pounds/454 kg of milk; this is only about 1 percent of the amount used for rennet-coagulated cheese.

In the United States acid-coagulated cheeses are always made from pasteurized milk because they are fresh cheeses that are aged for less than 60 days after manufacture. Most cow's-milk acid-coagulated cheeses are made from skim milk because whole cow's milk undergoes creaming during the long incubation time leading up to coagulation. Thus when coagulation finally occurs, the resulting coagulum is heterogeneous and somewhat difficult to handle, with coagulated cream at the top of the vat and coagulated skim at the bottom. The resulting curds must be worked together in order to obtain a smooth homogeneous paste. During the early 20th century, makers of cream and Neufchâtel cheeses in the United States sometimes added between 30 and 60 ml of single-strength rennet per 1,000 pounds/454 kg of milk so that the milk would thicken before the cream had a chance to separate. The resulting cheese was essentially a hybrid involving both rennet and acid coagulation. Today, however, whole cow's milk is usually homogenized before it is made into acid-coagulated cheeses such as cream and Neufchâtel to prevent the fat globules from creaming.

In contrast to cow's milk, goat's and sheep's milk lack the cryoglobulin protein responsible for rapid creaming. Therefore, acid-coagulated cheeses can be made from whole goat's and sheep's milk without having to resort to adding rennet or homogenizing the milk to prevent creaming. Nevertheless, some fresh goat's-milk cheeses combine rennet and acid coagulation. For example, the procedure for making Sainte-Maure calls for the equivalent of about 29 ml of single-strength rennet (1:15,000) per 1,000 pounds/454 kg of milk; this is about one-third of the amount used for most rennet-coagulated cheeses. Upon renneting, the milk is held at about 70°F/21°C, which is the normal setting temperature for acid-coagulated cheeses but is much lower than that used in rennet-coagulated cheesemaking. The lower setting temperature allows the enzymatic phase of rennet coagulation to occur but essentially prevents the nonenzymatic phase from proceeding. Thus coagulation does not take place until the starter culture lowers the pH to around

4.6 (which occurs about 24 hours later), resulting in acid coagulation. This unusual combination of renneting and acid coagulation presumably produces a desirable body and texture in fresh goat's-milk cheese. A comprehensive description of these cheeses and their manufacture can be found in *The Fabrication of Farmstead Goat Cheese* by Jean-Claude Le Jaouen (1990).

Acid coagulation occurs by a different mechanism than rennet coagulation, resulting in a different curd structure and a final cheese with very different characteristics. Setting is accomplished by adding a specific amount of starter culture to the milk at a specific setting temperature, which is usually around 70°F/21°C, though it can be as high as 90°F/32°C for some procedures, depending on how quickly the milk is to be coagulated. Acid coagulation takes place over a long period of time—5 hours to more than 24 hours—depending on the activity of the starter culture. Procedures that involve shorter coagulation times require the addition of more starter culture and higher setting temperatures (90°F/32°C), which stimulate the starter to produce lactic acid more rapidly, whereas less starter and lower setting temperatures (70°F/21°C) are used for overnight coagulation.

Once added to the cheesemilk, the starter ferments lactose to lactic acid and the milk pH begins to decrease. As lactic acid is produced and hydrogen ions accumulate (hydrogen ions represent the business end of the lactic acid molecule), the casein micelles absorb some of the hydrogen ions and, in response, release calcium phosphate into the water phase of the milk. As acidification proceeds, then, the casein micelles become more and more depleted of calcium phosphate. The absorption of hydrogen ions and loss of calcium phosphate cause the casein micelles to become less and less polar in nature. By the time the pH of the milk decreases to around 5.3, the micelles retain so little of their polar nature that they begin to stick together upon collision. This process continues until the pH reaches 4.6, at which stage the micelles are completely aggregated in the form of a three-dimensional matrix of interlocking casein chains (see figure 5.1). The characteristics of this acid coagulum are quite different from those of a rennet curd. Because rennet coagulation occurs at high pH, the casein micelles that form the rennet curd are rich in calcium phosphate, which acts as a sort of glue holding the casein matrix together. Consequently, rennet curd is relatively firm and elastic, and readily shrinks and expels whey during subsequent steps of the cheesemaking process. In contrast, the aggregated casein micelles that make up the acid coagulum are almost completely depleted of calcium phosphate; consequently, the "glue" that holds the casein matrix together is much weaker, and the curd strongly resists shrinkage. The result is a much weaker coagulum that requires much more effort to expel whey during the rest of the cheesemaking process. The end result is a softer, more fragile, and higher-moisture cheese.

Acid coagulation is affected by several of the same factors that affect rennet coagulation, including the casein content of the milk, the severity of heat treatment during pasteurization, and movement of the milk during coagulation, especially at pH values of 5.3 or lower. In addition, several problems may occur with acid coagulation that arise from the inhibition or failure of the starter culture. The most common causes of starter inhibition, including mastitic and late-lactation milk, elevated free fatty acid levels, bacteriophage, agglutination, and antibiotic residues, are discussed in chapter 4. In addition, acid coagulation is particularly sensitive to the temperature during setting. Acid coagulation requires setting times ranging from 5 hours to more than 24. During this long incubation period there is ample opportunity for the temperature of the milk to change if it differs substantially from the room temperature, especially if an open cheese vat is used. A chilly cheese room can cause the milk to cool off in the vat, particularly at the surface, resulting in slower acidification and longer coagulation time, whereas a higher room temperature may lead to warming, faster acid production, and shorter coagulation time. Ideally, you want the coagulation time to be consistent and predictable from one vat to the next so that the curd is always cut at its optimum firmness, which occurs in the pH range of 4.6 to 4.7. Thus it is particularly important with acid-coagulated cheeses to maintain the temperature of the cheese room at or near the setting temperature and to cover the vat during setting with an appropriate cover when possible.

For acid-coagulated cheeses, once the milk has coagulated at pH 4.6 to 4.7, the rest of the cheesemaking process is carried out with one fundamental goal in mind: to progressively expel whey from the coagulum and firm up the curd so as to attain the optimum moisture content and firmness in the resulting cheese. Controlled removal of calcium phosphate from the curd—critical in the making of rennet-coagulated cheeses—is not a concern in acid-coagulated cheesemaking, because the curd is essentially depleted of calcium phosphate at the time of coagulation.

STEP TWO: CUTTING OR BREAKING THE CURD

When milk first coagulates, all the water and water-soluble components are contained within the coagulum. There is, however, a natural tendency for the cut curd to contract and expel whey over time. The rate of contraction and whey expulsion, or syneresis as it's called, depends among other things on the amount of surface area through which the whey may escape from the coagulum. The greater the surface area, the greater the expulsion of whey. The primary purpose of cutting or breaking the coagulum is to increase its surface area and thereby enhance the expulsion of whey, so that the water content of the curd can be reduced to a specific target level in the final cheese.

Rennet-Coagulated Cheeses

For rennet-coagulated cheeses, cutting should generally take place when the curd is firm enough to cut cleanly into uniformly sized particles with little or no shattering. If the curd is too weak at cutting it may shatter excessively into fines, resulting in fat and casein losses to the whey, lower moisture content, and decreased yield of cheese. On the other hand, if the curd is too firm it may resist cutting, bunch up around the knives, and tear into pieces of widely ranging size. Furthermore, very tough and rubbery curd tends to resist syneresis and favors higher moisture content in the final cheese. Rennet coagulums are almost always cut into discrete particles, but the size and shape of the cut particles vary depending on the type of cheese being made. For example, in Cheddar cheesemaking the curd is typically cut into ⅜-inch/1 cm cubes, whereas in Swiss cheesemaking it is cut into much smaller rice-sized particles. The traditional cutting patterns for different cheeses were developed over the centuries through trial and error and are essentially designed to allow the right amount of whey to be expelled during cheesemaking to achieve the correct moisture content in the final cheese. For cheeses that are not pressed, the size and shape of the cut particles may also influence the texture of the final cheese.

Ideally, every curd particle after cutting should have exactly the same dimensions as every other particle, because particle size and shape directly influence whey expulsion during the rest of cheesemaking. The smaller the curd particle, all else being equal, the greater the whey expulsion and the lower the final moisture content. Thus when cutting results in a wide range of curd particle sizes, the smaller particles will become drier as cheesemaking progresses, whereas larger particles will retain more moisture. If the moisture differences among particles are very large when the particles are combined to form the final cheese, the body of the cheese may not develop uniformly due to pockets of abnormally high or low moisture. Of particular concern are pockets of high moisture, which can lead to sour and fermented defects.

A second reason why you should strive to achieve uniform particle size during cutting—particularly if the curd is to be cooked to elevated temperature—is to promote uniform temperature throughout the curd mass. During heating, the internal temperatures of smaller curd particles will increase more rapidly than those of larger particles, which in turn may influence both the rate of whey expulsion and the rate of acid production by the starter culture entrapped within the particles. Thus the more uniform the particle size, the more uniform the rate of whey expulsion and acidification among particles, and the less likely the finished cheese will suffer from defects related to pockets of abnormal composition within its body.

So how do you determine when the curd is ready for cutting? Several approaches may be used. The simplest method is to always begin cutting at a constant time after adding the rennet—say, 30 minutes after renneting. This is not recommended, however, because milk coagulation properties may vary considerably from one day to the next, especially in milk produced seasonally at the farmstead level. A better alternative is to evaluate the curd firmness as coagulation proceeds and attempt to cut each vat at the same level. Firmness can be evaluated by inserting a small sanitized spatula into the coagulum at a 45-degree angle, gently lifting the spatula straight up, and observing the curd as it splits open. For most cheeses a sharp, clean split with the accumulation of green whey at the base of the cleavage indicates that the curd is ready for cutting. In contrast, a mushy, ragged split with milky whey and shorn bits of coagulum indicates that the curd is not yet ready for cutting. However, the ideal cutting firmness will vary depending on the type of milk and the type of cheese being made. For example, the coagulum of Roquefort cheese (made from sheep's milk) will always be firmer at cutting than that of blue cheese (made from cow's milk), because the casein content of sheep's milk is much higher than that of cow's milk. The coagulum of Emmental cheese made from cow's milk will characteristically be weaker at cutting than that of Cheddar cheese made from cow's milk, because it is difficult to obtain rice-sized particles when the curd is too firm at cutting. Thus there is no substitute for experience in learning to recognize the optimum cutting firmness for any particular cheese. The art of cheesemaking is perfected through practice.

A third method used to determine cutting time is to observe the onset of flocculation, which represents the first visible signs of the nonenzymatic phase of coagulation; it usually occurs around 10 minutes after renneting. The time from adding rennet to the first sign of flocculation is then multiplied by a mathematical factor to calculate the cutting time. This approach is based on what appears to be a reasonably sound assumption, that the optimum cutting time is proportional to the flocculation time; the longer the milk takes to flocculate, the longer the time to optimum cutting firmness. In practice, the cheesemaker can determine flocculation time by inserting a sanitized spatula into the milk, withdrawing it, and observing the film of milk as it flows off the spatula. The flocculation time corresponds to the first evidence of tiny white flecks in the film of milk. The mathematical factor used to calculate the cutting time will vary depending on the specific cheese. A factor of 2.5 (or 3) is used for Cheddar cheese made from cow's milk, for instance. Thus if flocculation occurs at 10 minutes after the rennet is added in Cheddar cheesemaking, the recommended cutting time is 10 × 2.5, or 25 minutes. Other cheeses have recommended factors ranging from 2 to 6 (see chapter 10 for further discussion of the flocculation test). Again, experience is probably the best guide for any particular farmstead operation.

Several different utensils are used for cutting. By far the most common cutting utensil used in the United States consists of rectangular stainless-steel frames on which are strung evenly spaced wires (¼ inch/0.6 cm or ⅜ inch/1.0 cm, for instance) that are oriented either horizontally or vertically (see figure 5.3). The curd is cut first with the horizontal knife by swinging the knife into the curd at one end of the vat and drawing it through the curd lengthwise to the vat's other end. This action is repeated once or twice in slightly overlapping passes until the entire curd mass has been cut. Then the vertical knife is drawn lengthwise through the vat in the same manner and finally crosswise through the vat in a series of slightly overlapping passes. If done

Figure 5.3. Curd knives consist of rectangular stainless-steel frames on which are strung evenly spaced (1/4 inch/0.6 cm or 3/8 inch/1.0 cm, for instance) wires that are oriented either vertically (left) or horizontally (right).

properly, this results in cubic particles of nearly uniform dimensions.

Cutting should be performed carefully but expeditiously because the curd continues to increase in firmness during cutting; if too much time elapses, the curd may become difficult to cut and subject to bunching and tearing before cutting is completed. The size of the curd particles will depend on the spacing of the wires, which may range from ¼ inch to ¾ inch/ 0.6 cm to 1.9 cm. Very small rice-sized particles can be attained by cutting in the usual way with ¼-inch wire knives and then using the vertical knife to further reduce the particle size. For some cheeses such as Camembert, the curd may be cut and crosscut with a vertical wire knife or sword only, the horizontal cut being made by a ladle at the time of dipping, as in figure 5.4. Other cutting knives that are used in traditional practice include the harp, a rounded, vertically strung wire knife used in Swiss cheesemaking; the spino, a horizontally strung, three-dimensional, egg-shaped cutting device used in Italian cheesemaking; and a variety of long knives and swords. As with all cheesemaking equipment and utensils, make sure ahead of time that the cutting device that you intend to use meets regulatory approval.

Acid-Coagulated Cheeses

For some acid-coagulated cheeses the curd is cut with wire knives in a manner similar to rennet curds, whereas for others the curd is simply broken up by stirring.

Figure 5.4. In the making of traditional Brie and Camembert cheeses, the coagulated milk is cut vertically into strips and then crosscut vertically with a long knife (top). Later, the horizontal cut is made using a ladle at the time of dipping (bottom).

In either case the most consistent results are obtained by cutting or breaking the curd when the coagulum reaches the optimum cutting pH, generally between 4.6 and 4.7. Below pH 4.6 the curd becomes brittle and shatters more easily; above pH 4.7 it is firmer but more rubbery and clumps together, making it more difficult to expel moisture. Cutting with wire knives is mostly used for cheeses that contain discrete curd particles, such as cottage cheese. Breaking the curd by stirring is more commonly used for cheeses such as quark that have a smooth homogeneous body and lack discrete curd particles. Some traditional acid-coagulated cheeses are simply ladled out of the vat without being cut or broken ahead of time.

STEP THREE: COOKING AND HOLDING THE CURDS

Immediately after cutting, the curd particles are very fragile and can easily shatter into fines, and fat globules can easily be dislodged from the newly cut surfaces and lost to the whey if the curd is handled roughly. Therefore, the cut curd is generally left undisturbed for at least 3 to 5 minutes and up to 10 or 15 minutes after cutting, depending on the cheese type. During this time the curd is allowed to firm up slightly and develop a thin film at the particle surface in a process known as *healing*. After healing the curds may be cooked at elevated temperatures or may remain uncooked, meaning that they are held without heating until draining or dipping, depending on the type of cheese.

Rennet-Coagulated Cooked Cheeses

For most rennet-coagulated cooked cheeses the healing time should not be extended too long because the curd has a strong tendency to clump and mat together. The length of healing will largely depend on the moisture content of the final cheese. For lower-moisture aged cheeses that are cooked to higher temperatures, such as Cheddar and Swiss, it is important to prevent matting and clumping during cooking so that the whey can be expelled freely and uniformly from the curd particles during this critical stage. Large clumps of curd retain more moisture than smaller discrete particles, which can result in undesirable pockets of high moisture and sour and fermented defects within the body of the final cheese. Thus for lower-moisture cheeses stirring usually begins within three to five minutes of cutting, starting out slowly and then continuing throughout cooking, either continuously or intermittently. Stirring is maintained at a rate vigorous enough to keep the particles from clumping, but not so vigorous as to cause the curd particles to shatter into fines. On the other hand, for higher-moisture cheeses that are cooked to lower temperatures, such as the washed-rind cheeses, matting and uneven whey expulsion are less of a concern; the curd may heal for 15 minutes or more before gentle stirring is initiated. Some uncooked cheeses such as Brie and Camembert may receive no stirring at all.

Before the start of cooking, the inside walls of the cheese vat should be freed of adhering curds using a sanitized plastic knife or other utensil that will not scratch the walls. Curd that remains stuck to the sides of the vat during cooking will be heated more severely than the other curds and become overcooked, which is never desirable and can be particularly troublesome in certain cheeses, such as Swiss types.

Cooking involves heating the curd–whey mixture at a *specific* rate to a *specific* final target temperature, and then holding the mixture at the final temperature for a *specific* period of time before initiating draining or dipping. Thus cooking represents a time–temperature program that should be carefully followed from one vat to the next. The goal is to keep the time–temperature profile that the curd particles experience consistent from vat to vat. Why? Because the primary purpose of cooking is to expel whey from the curds in a controlled manner, so that the moisture content of the final cheese will fall within the narrow range that is optimum for the specific type of cheese being made. Control over syneresis is achieved through the systematic and consistent application of heat and stirring during cooking (see figure 5.5). The more consistent the application of heat and stirring, the more consistent the moisture content of the final cheese, and the more consistent the quality of the cheese.

The amount of whey that is expelled from the curd during cooking is mostly determined by four key parameters:

1. **Curd particle size.** As noted earlier, smaller curd particles have more surface area available for whey expulsion and therefore will lose more moisture than larger curd particles. Also, the internal temperature of small curd particles will increase more quickly and uniformly during cooking than that of large curd particles, further enhancing curd shrinkage and whey expulsion. Therefore, the smaller the curd particle, all else being equal, the greater the expulsion of whey during cooking and the lower the moisture content in the final cheese.

Figure 5.5. Cooking involves the stirring and heating of the curd–whey mixture at a specific rate to a specific final temperature, and then holding at the final temperature for a specific period of time. Control over syneresis (curd shrinkage and whey expulsion) is achieved through the systematic and consistent application of heat and stirring.

2. **Stirring rate.** Stirring keeps the curd particles from matting together and thus maximizes the surface area through which whey can be expelled from the particles. Continuous stirring that prevents particles from clumping will enhance syneresis and uniform moisture content, then, whereas intermittent stirring that allows substantial clumping to occur will favor greater moisture retention overall and greater variation in moisture content among curd particles. Stirring also creates localized pressure on the curd as the curd particles collide with one another and with the walls of the vat. The resulting applied force helps to squeeze whey out of the particles. The greater the stirring, the greater the applied force, the greater the expulsion of whey, and the lower the moisture content in the final cheese, all else being equal. A variation on this theme is the practice of partially draining the whey during cooking. Less whey means that the curd particles collide more frequently and thus undergo greater syneresis, leading to lower moisture content in the final cheese.
3. **Time–temperature profile.** The rate at which the temperature is increased at the start of cooking is important. If the temperature increases too quickly too soon, a dense skin may form at the surface of the curd particles that can impede subsequent syneresis and result in abnormally high moisture content in the final

cheese. Heating too rapidly at first also favors increased matting and clumping. For these reasons, cooking schedules generally call for the temperature to be raised very gradually at the start of cooking and then more quickly as the final temperature is approached. In general, the higher the final cooking temperature, the greater the expulsion of whey from the curd particles and the lower the moisture content in the final cheese. Furthermore, the longer the curd remains at elevated temperature, the greater the expulsion of whey.

4. **Acidity profile.** Curd particles shrink and expel whey more readily at any given temperature as the acidity increases (in other words, as the pH decreases). The lower the pH of the curd during cooking, all else being equal, the greater the syneresis and the lower the moisture content in the final cheese. The acidity profile during cooking is determined by the activity of starter culture, which in turn is influenced by the temperature. Therefore, if the temperature profile during cooking varies from vat to vat, the starter activity and acidity profile will probably also vary, as will the syneresis rate and the moisture content of the final cheese. Maintaining consistent starter activity and acidification rate is still another reason why the cheesemaker should ruthlessly hold the time–temperature conditions during cooking constant from vat to vat.

In summary, the conditions during cooking that favor higher moisture in the final cheese include larger cut size, less stirring, lower cooking temperature, shorter cooking time, and higher curd pH. Conversely, smaller cut size, continuous stirring, higher cooking temperature, longer cooking time, and lower curd pH favor a lower-moisture cheese. Thus it is not surprising to find that cooking conditions vary greatly from one cheese type to the next, depending on the moisture content desired in the final cheese and the level of acidity that occurs during cooking. At one extreme, high-moisture types such as the smear-ripened cheeses are cooked only slightly, if at all, the temperature increasing by only 2 to 4°F/1 to 2°C (for example, from 90 to 92 or 94°F/32 to 33 or 34°C). Furthermore, the time between cutting and draining or dipping is generally less than one hour with minimal stirring. At the other extreme, the lower-moisture Swiss-type cheeses may be cooked to as high as 130°F/54°C, and the time from cutting to draining/dipping may be as long as two and a half hours with continuous stirring. The cooking temperatures for Swiss-type cheeses are particularly severe because the pH remains quite high during cooking (whey pH around 6.4 at the end of cooking); thus the curds do not readily contract and expel whey. In contrast, Cheddar cheese, which has a final moisture content similar to that of Swiss, requires a much lower cooking temperature—around 100°F/38°C—because the pH is lower during cooking (whey pH around 6.2 at the end of cooking); the curds shrink and expel whey much more readily. Thus much less heat is needed in Cheddar cheesemaking to achieve a final moisture content similar to that of Swiss.

Rennet-Coagulated Uncooked Cheeses

Some rennet-coagulated cheeses, invariably high in moisture, are not cooked at all, meaning that the curds are simply held without heating during the time from coagulation until dipping. In some cases, such as in traditional Brie and Camembert cheesemaking, the temperature in the vat may actually decrease as the contents cool down from the setting temperature toward room temperature. The curd may be cut and then remain undisturbed until dipping (as with some bloomy-rind cheeses such as Brie and Camembert), or cut and then gently stirred (as with some smear-ripened cheeses). As with cooked cheeses, the moisture content of the final cheese will be influenced by the time–temperature conditions, the amount of stirring, and the acidity, all of which should be kept consistent from one vat to the next.

Acidification during Cooking and Holding

Although the primary function of cooking and holding is to expel whey from the curd in a controlled manner, an equally important function is to regulate the loss of calcium phosphate from the curd to the whey. The amount of calcium phosphate that is lost from the curd to the whey will depend on the partitioning of the total curd calcium phosphate between the soluble and casein-associated states *during the period when whey is being released from the curd.* When the acidity of the curd is low (in other words, the pH is high) during cooking, most of the calcium phosphate remains complexed to the casein matrix rather than being dissolved in the water phase of the curd. Consequently, the whey that is released from high-pH curd during cooking contains relatively little calcium phosphate, while the final cheese retains higher amounts of these crucial minerals. On the other hand, if the acidity increases (the curd pH decreases) during cooking, calcium phosphate will shift to the soluble form as hydrogen ions from lactic acid are absorbed by the casein matrix and calcium phosphate is released into the water phase. (Remember, casein acts like a sponge for hydrogen ions by absorbing them and releasing calcium phosphate in return.) The lower the pH, the greater the movement of calcium phosphate from the casein matrix to the water phase of the curd. Therefore, whey that is released from low-pH curd during cooking will be rich in calcium phosphate and, conversely, the final cheese will be depleted.

As alluded to earlier, this is important because calcium phosphate strongly influences the characteristics of the final cheese, for reasons that we will examine in chapter 6. The take-home message is that acidity (pH), along with times, temperatures, and stirring rate, must be carefully controlled during cooking and holding and maintained within narrow parameters that will depend of the specific type of cheese. If the pH profile during cooking varies substantially from one vat to the next, you can be certain that the final cheese will be affected, for better or for worse.

Washing during Cooking and Holding

Some cheeses call for a washing step at the beginning of cooking, Gouda and Havarti being well-known examples. Likewise, Swiss-type cheeses are also often washed. During washing, a portion of the whey may be drained from the vat at the beginning of cooking and replaced with water at a higher temperature. The added water raises the temperature of the vat to the final cooking temperature and reduces the concentration of lactose and lactic acid in the whey, which has the effect of drawing lactose and lactic acid out of the curd particles. Consequently, the washed curd contains less lactose for the starter culture to ferment throughout the rest of the cheesemaking process, resulting in a less acidic, higher-pH final cheese. In general, the greater the amount of water added to the vat, the higher the pH of the final cheese. Thus the purpose of washing at the start of cooking is to heat the contents of the vat to the final cooking temperature and to elevate the pH of the final cheese.

A different version of washing, used in the making of certain cheeses such as Colby and Monterey Jack, occurs at the end of cooking instead of at the beginning. In this case, cool water is added to the warm whey at the end of cooking, thereby diluting the whey and lowering the temperature in the vat. Warm cheese curd has a natural ability to absorb water that is at a lower temperature; therefore, the warm curd particles absorb water from the cooler diluted whey. The lower the temperature that the whey is diluted to, the greater the uptake of moisture by the curd and the higher the moisture content in the final cheese. At the same time, lactose moves in the opposite direction, out of the curd particles and into the diluted whey. The end result is a cheese curd that is higher in moisture and lower in lactose. Thus washing the curd with cool water at the end of cooking is the means by which the moisture content of the final cheese can be increased while decreasing its lactose content, preventing the pH from dropping too low and the cheese from developing sour and fermented defects.

If you employ a washing step, at either the beginning or the end of cooking, you will want to be certain that your water is microbiologically clean. A potable water supply, as described in the Pasteurized Milk Ordinance of the U.S. Food and Drug Administration (http://www.cfsan.fda.gov/~ear/pmo01-2.html), that is bacteriologically safe and practically free of any type of bacterial contamination, as well as free of chemical impurities and off-flavors, is essential. You will also want to be sure that the temperature conditions during washing are consistent from vat to vat.

Acid-Coagulated Cheeses

Most acid-coagulated cheeses are not cooked. The curd is broken up at the optimum pH (4.6 to 4.7) by stirring and then dipped into cloth draining bags. Cottage cheese, which is cut into cubes and cooked to high temperature (around 125°F/52°C) to firm up the curd particles, is an exception. Despite the severe heating, the moisture content of the cottage cheese curd decreases by only a small amount during cooking because acid curd strongly resists contraction and whey expulsion. Cottage cheese curd is washed extensively with cold water at the end of cooking to cool the curds and wash out residual lactose and lactic acid, giving it a very bland flavor.

STEP FOUR: DRAINING THE WHEY; DIPPING THE CURDS

Draining the whey and/or dipping the curds initiates the permanent separation of whey from the curds and allows the curd particles to coalesce and fuse together into a continuous curd mass that will ultimately form the body of the final cheese. Draining consists of removing most or all of the free whey from the curd, usually by placing a screen over the exit valve of the cheese vat and allowing the whey to drain out while the curd is retained by the screen. Thus the curd remains in the vat upon draining, at least in farmstead practice (see figure 5.6A). The partially or fully drained curds are transferred, either immediately or after a period of curd knitting, to special forms, known as hoops or molds, for pressing into the final size and shape of the cheese. In contrast, dipping involves the transfer of both curds and whey, usually by ladling or scooping, from the cheese vat to special draining forms, also called hoops or molds (see figure 5.6B). The draining hoops rest on mats that allow the whey to exit freely through the bottom, and the hoops may or may not be perforated to facilitate draining through the sides, depending on the type of cheese

Figure 5.6. Draining (top) consists of removing most or all of the free whey from the curd, usually by placing a screen over the exit valve of the cheese vat and allowing the whey to drain out while the curds are retained. Dipping (bottom) involves the transfer of both curds and whey, usually by ladling or scooping, from the cheese vat to special draining forms, called hoops or molds.

being made. As the whey drains from the hoops, the curd particles settle, coalesce, and fuse to form the cheese. Thus draining occurs in the hoops rather than in the vat for dipped cheeses, and the size and shape of the draining hoop determines the size and shape of the final cheese.

Draining is generally employed in the making of lower-moisture cheeses that are cooked at moderate to high temperatures. By the end of cooking, a large fraction of the total whey has been expelled from the curd, the curds have firmed up, and the large volume of free whey can be easily drained from the firm curds. For example, in the making of Cheddar cheese, which is cooked to a moderate temperature of about 100°F/38°C, more than three-quarters of the total whey is expelled from the curd by the time of draining. Thus the volume of free whey is large, the curds are dry and firm, and draining proceeds rapidly, typically taking about 15 to 30 minutes in farmstead practice depending on the size of the vat, with relatively little whey expelled thereafter.

In contrast, dipping is used when the curd particles still contain large amounts of whey at the end of cooking and holding, as in the case of high-moisture, lightly cooked cheeses, such as the smear-ripened cheeses, and uncooked cheeses like Brie and Camembert. When these fragile, moisture-laden curds are scooped into the draining hoops, the modest amount of free whey present with the curds drains first; then the curds continue to contract and expel large amounts of whey in a steady stream for several hours as they settle and fuse. Thus the expulsion of whey from dipped curds occurs much more gradually over a much longer period of time than that from the lower-moisture, more highly cooked drained cheeses. During this extended draining, the hoops should be flipped over periodically to promote uniform release of whey throughout the curds as they fuse to form the cheese. Draining may proceed solely under the force of gravity, or a lid constructed of an approved material, known as a *follower*, may be placed on top of the curd along with a weight to enhance draining and knitting.

Some moderately and highly cooked cheeses combine draining and dipping in their manufacture. Swiss-type cheeses, for example, are highly cooked, and the expulsion of whey is nearly complete by the end of cooking/holding. Nevertheless, in traditional practice both curds and whey are dipped out of the copper kettle that serves as the vat and transferred directly into the pressing hoop. The purpose of dipping in this case is to allow the curd particles to coalesce and fuse together during the early stages of pressing while they are still surrounded by and bathed in whey. This process, known as pressing under the whey, ensures that the curds are not honeycombed with air pockets during pressing, as occurs when fully drained curds are pressed. This enables the curd particles to fuse tightly into a continuous mass devoid of the small fissures and mechanical openings that normally occur when air pockets are present during pressing. A tight, uninterrupted structure is necessary for the formation of uniform round eyes later on during ripening. Other eye-forming cheeses, such as Gouda, are also pressed under the whey for similar reasons.

Draining and/or dipping accomplishes not only the permanent separation of whey from the curd but also the permanent removal of calcium phosphate. In fact, the amount of calcium phosphate retained in the final cheese—which greatly affects its characteristics and quality—is chiefly determined by the extent of losses to the whey up to and during draining. For moderately to highly cooked cheeses, more than 75 percent of the total whey is expelled, and up to 90 percent of the total calcium phosphate loss to the whey occurs by the time of draining or dipping. Therefore, the level of calcium phosphate in the final cheese is largely determined by the draining stage. For example, if the curd manages to hold on to its calcium phosphate through the end of draining, the resulting cheese will be rich in these crucial minerals regardless of what happens after draining. If the curd fails to do so, the resulting cheese will be low in calcium phosphate. Whether or not the curd holds on to its calcium phosphate is determined by the acidity (that is, pH) profile up to the time of draining, as alluded to earlier. When the pH at draining is high, for example, in the making of Swiss-type cheeses (whey pH around 6.5 to 6.4), very little of the total calcium phosphate in the curd is lost to the whey. The final cheese, therefore, remains rich in calcium phosphate. As the draining pH decreases, an increasingly larger proportion of the total curd calcium phosphate is lost to the whey, and so the resulting cheese is progressively lower in calcium phosphate. The bottom line is that the pH at the start of draining is a critical control parameter for the low-moisture cheeses that are cooked at moderate to high temperature. Therefore, the draining pH should be optimized for the type of cheese being made and held constant from one vat to the next. Inconsistent pH at draining time is a definite no-no, and is likely to contribute to inconsistent cheese quality.

For high-moisture cheeses that are uncooked or only slightly cooked, both the pH at the start of dipping and the pH profile throughout the long, gradual draining process will determine the calcium phosphate losses to the whey. If the pH changes little before dipping and remains high throughout the gradual draining, the resulting cheese will be rich in calcium phosphate, as in the case of washed-rind cheeses. In contrast, if the pH decreases before dipping and continues to decrease after dipping, *while the whey is still draining from the curds,* the calcium phosphate losses to the whey will be extremely high and the final cheese will be highly depleted of minerals. The bloomy-rind cheeses typify this pattern. Again, the take-home message is that acidity matters. Acidity should change according to a defined schedule throughout cheesemaking, and the period leading up to and during draining is especially critical. Indeed, an essential requirement of the starter culture is that it produce acid according to the correct schedule, day in and day out.

Acid-Coagulated Cheeses

For most acid-coagulated cheeses, the curd is dipped out of the vat and transferred to draining bags made of muslin cloth or synthetic material. The bags may be hung from hooks so that the whey drains from the bottom of the bag by gravity, or they can be tied and piled in the vat to drain under their own weight. Either way, draining occurs slowly and usually continues overnight. The rate of draining decreases with decreasing temperature; therefore the temperature of the draining room should not be allowed to fluctuate widely. The draining bags can become a major source of microbial contamination if they are not meticulously cleaned and sanitized. They should be thoroughly washed and then sanitized by soaking in chlorine sanitizer (100 ppm) or in boiling water after each use.

STEP FIVE: KNITTING THE CURDS

Curd knitting involves the coalescence and fusion of curd particles into a homogeneous mass. During knitting, additional whey is expelled from the curd to a greater or lesser extent depending on the cheese type, and the pH continues to decrease as the starter culture ferments lactose to lactic acid. For rennet-coagulated cheeses, curd knitting may occur in three different ways: (1) in the cheese vat, (2) in the cheese press, or (3) in the draining hoop.

Knitting in the Cheese Vat

For some low-moisture cheeses that are moderately to highly cooked, such as Cheddar and low-moisture pasta-filata types, knitting occurs in the cheese vat after draining. The drained curd particles are banked to the sides of the vat and allowed to fuse together. The mass of fused curd is then cut into slabs, which are turned regularly (every 15 minutes, say) in a practice known as cheddaring (see figure 5.7). During cheddaring, a modest but critical amount of whey is released from the curd. If too much whey is expelled during cheddaring, the resulting cheese will be too dry and ripen very slowly. If too little is expelled, the cheese will be too high in moisture, abnormally low in pH, and likely to develop defects such as (in the case of Cheddar) a weak and pasty body and acid and bitter flavors.

As with cooking, factors governing the amount of whey that is expelled during cheddaring include the amount of surface area through which the whey is released, especially the surface area in direct contact with the warm bottom on the cheese vat, and the temperature and pH of the curd. The greater the surface area of the curd slabs relative to their volume or weight, the greater the expulsion of whey. This principle can be used to regulate the expulsion of whey by controlling the thickness of the slabs and by piling the slabs on top of one another to a greater or lesser extent. Thicker slabs have less surface area per unit of volume overall, and less surface area in direct contact with the warm vat bottom, through which most of the whey will drain. Likewise, piling the slabs reduces the surface area and thus slows the expulsion of whey. The more the slabs are piled (three high versus two high versus one high), the slower the whey is expelled.

The higher the curd temperature and more time that elapses during cheddaring, the greater the release of whey and the

Figure 5.7. Curd knitting involves the coalescence and fusion of curd particles into a homogeneous mass. For some cheeses such as Cheddar, knitting occurs in the cheese vat. The drained curds are banked to the sides of the vat and allowed to fuse together (left). The mass of fused curd is then cut into slabs that are turned regularly in a practice known as cheddaring (right).

lower the moisture content of the final cheese, all else being equal. Furthermore, the expulsion of whey at any given temperature will increase as the acidity of the curd increases (that is, as the pH decreases). Of course, the acidity of the curd during cheddaring is determined by the activity of starter culture, which in turn is influenced by the temperature. Therefore, it is important to keep the temperature among the curd slabs as uniform as possible and to keep the overall curd temperature during cheddaring at a specific target level (for example, about 98°F/37°C for Cheddar cheese) and as consistent as possible from one day to the next.

The curd slabs should be turned and repiled every 15 minutes during cheddaring to achieve better temperature uniformity, and their positions within the pile should be rotated systematically. Each slab should be held at the bottom (directly exposed to the warm bottom of the vat), middle (if piled three high), and top (directly exposed to the ambient air, which is usually cooler than the curd temperature) of the pile for the same amount of time as every other slab. If some slabs are held longer at the bottom of the pile and others longer at the top, the former will be warmer while the latter will cool off.

The overall curd temperature during cheddaring will be determined primarily by two parameters: the temperature of the walls (bottom) of the cheese vat and the temperature of the air above the curd slabs. Ideally, both should be maintained within narrow limits from vat to vat and day to day. The temperature of the bottom of the cheese vat can usually be precisely controlled by careful regulation of the steam or hot water in the jacket of the vat. Control over the room temperature may prove more challenging for some farmstead cheesemakers. If at all possible, cover the vat during cheddaring with a suitable cover to hold in the heat, especially if you are unable to control the temperature of your cheese room very precisely. You may need to make other adjustments depending on conditions. For example, if the temperature of the cheese room becomes chilly during those bitter January mornings in Vermont (or Wisconsin, or Minnesota . . .), the vat jacket temperature may need to be increased and the slabs turned and repiled more frequently (for instance, every 10 rather than every 15 minutes) in order to keep the curd at the optimum target temperature. The bottom line is that times, temperatures, and acidity (pH) during cheddaring should be closely monitored and maintained within narrow limits that will depend on the specific type of cheese. If the curd temperature and pH profiles during cheddaring vary substantially from one vat to the next, the characteristics of the final cheese are likely to vary, for better or for worse.

Finally, it should be mentioned that several variants of Cheddar-type cheeses, such as Colby, Jack, and stirred-curd Cheddar, are not actually cheddared. Instead, the curds are stirred continuously after draining and deliberately kept from matting together. This vastly increases the surface area available for whey to drain from the curd; draining therefore proceeds much more quickly, resulting in a shorter manufacturing time.

Knitting in the Press

For many moderately to highly cooked lower-moisture cheeses, knitting occurs not in the cheese vat but in the cheese press. For these cheeses, at the end of cooking either the curds and whey are dipped from the vat en masse and transferred directly to the pressing hoop (as with traditional Swiss-type cheeses), or else the whey is drained partially or completely and the drained curds are then transferred to the pressing hoop (as with some hard Italian cheese types). The free whey quickly drains from the pressing hoop, and as pressure is gradually applied, some additional whey is squeezed out as the curds knit together. If the pressure is applied too quickly at the beginning of pressing, the cheese surface may close up and form a rind that hinders subsequent draining, leaving pockets of whey within the cheese that may cause problems later. Curd knitting may continue in the press for several hours to several days, depending on the cheese type. During this time a small amount of whey continues to drain from the cheese, the starter culture continues to ferment lactose to lactic acid, and the pH decreases. In traditional practice the cheese is usually pressed in a vertical cheese press

Figure 5.8. In the making of Brie cheese, knitting takes place gradually in the draining molds as the whey drains through the mats at the bottom (left). Eventually the top half of the draining mold can be removed as the curd settles and fuses into a compact wheel about 1 inch/2.5 cm in thickness (right).

and the block or wheel must be turned during pressing, more frequently at the beginning, to allow the whey to drain uniformly. If the block or wheel is not turned the whey tends to accumulate in the lower side of the cheese, resulting in a gradient of moisture within the body of the final cheese. The drainage of whey from the block, the production of lactic acid by the starter culture, and the extent to which the curd particles fuse together to form a tight body and close-knit rind that resists infiltration by mold are all influenced by the temperature of curd. Therefore, the temperature of the room during pressing should be maintained at an optimum level that is consistent from day to day, usually around 75°F/24°C.

Knitting in the Draining Hoop

Knitting in the draining hoop can occur in two different formats, depending on whether both curd and whey are transferred to the draining hoop or the curds are drained before the transfer. For lightly cooked and uncooked high-moisture cheeses, such as the washed-rind and bloomy-rind types, both curds and whey are dipped into draining hoops as described earlier. Knitting takes place as the whey gradually drains and the curd particles settle and fuse under the force of gravity (see figure 5.8). The presence of whey during curd fusion prevents air pockets from forming among the curd particles and thus gives a closer-knit texture. In some cases, curd knitting proceeds solely by gravity; in others, a lid and weight are placed on top of the draining curd. In either case the hoops are turned regularly to promote uniform whey drainage.

The drainage of whey, the production of lactic acid by the starter, and the extent of curd fusion are strongly influenced by the temperature of curd and therefore the temperature of the cheese room. Cooler temperatures in the cheese room result in slower acid development (a slower decrease in the curd pH) during knitting, slower drainage of the whey (hence higher moisture in the final cheese), and less fusion of the curd particles (hence more small mechanical openings in the body of the final cheese). Higher room temperature encourages the opposite: faster acidification, accelerated whey drainage, lower-moisture cheese, and greater curd fusion. These types of cheeses (including washed-rind and bloomy-rind) are particularly unforgiving with respect to fluctuations in the temperature of the cheese room from day to day; maintaining this temperature within an optimum range is a high priority. Furthermore, some manufacturing procedures require changing the room temperature (generally from warmer to cooler) as cheesemaking progresses. If you decide to make these types of cheeses, you would do well to invest in a reliable climate control system for your cheese room if at all possible.

Some moderately cooked cheeses, such as the Havarti and blue types, are drained completely after cooking. The dry curds, with or without added salt, are then transferred to draining hoops for curd knitting. Under these conditions, the drained curd particles become honeycombed with small air pockets that give rise to a very open texture. The particles are allowed to settle and fuse together in the draining hoop under the force of gravity or light pressure, which may be applied by placing a lid and a weight on top of the curd. Again, it is important to control the temperature of the room during knitting in order to obtain proper acid development by the starter and proper knitting of the curd.

Acid-Coagulated Cheeses

Acid curds are very limited in their ability to knit together because of their low pH and highly depleted state with respect to calcium phosphate. Upon draining, the acid curd is usually allowed to compress under its own weight to form an amorphous, weak, and spreadable texture.

STEP SIX: PRESSING THE CURDS

Pressing involves the compacting of the curd into a final solid form, such as a block, cylinder, or wheel. The purpose of pressing is threefold: (1) to expel some whey from the curd; (2) to hasten the knitting of the curd; and (3) to impart a desirable shape and texture to the cheese. For slightly cooked or uncooked high-moisture cheeses such as smear-ripened and bloomy-rind types, draining, knitting, and pressing occur more or less simultaneously in the draining hoop, as described earlier. Pressing for these cheeses may occur solely under the force of gravity, or light pressure may be applied by placing a lid and weight on top of the curd as it settles and compacts. The limited pressure during pressing gives the newly made cheese a somewhat open texture. As noted earlier, a very open texture is achieved when the free whey is drained completely before the curds are transferred to the draining hoop, as in the making of Havarti- and blue-type cheeses.

In contrast, moderately to highly cooked, lower-moisture cheeses that are pressed under higher pressure have a more

Figure 5.9. A rectangular cheese hoop filled with Cheddar curds ready for pressing. The curds will be pressed overnight at 40 psi (water gauge reading) to form a 40-pound/18 kg block.

closed texture (see figure 5.9). Few or no mechanical openings can be achieved by pressing under the whey, as noted earlier, whereas a slightly open texture is obtained when the curds are drained completely before pressing. The fusion of the curd particles during pressing is influenced by the temperature and acidity of the curd. If the temperature is too low during pressing, the curds may fail to fuse properly, resulting in mechanical openings in the cheese body and an open rind that is vulnerable to infiltration by mold. Likewise, if the acidity fails to increase during pressing, curd fusion is hindered and openness may occur. For very highly cooked cheeses such as Swiss and hard Italian types, rapid cooling at the surface of the cheese during pressing may stimulate the starter bacteria to produce lactic acid too quickly. This can result in excessive surface curd fusion that acts as a barrier to proper drainage of the whey during the remainder of pressing. For cheeses made from whole milk and thus relatively high in fat content, pressing when the curd temperature is too high can cause the release of excessive free fat from the curd particles and a greasy, seamy finish. In summary, the message once again is that temperature is important. Temperature needs to be controlled and optimized during pressing, as elsewhere in cheesemaking.

STEP SEVEN: SALTING THE CURDS

Salt (sodium chloride) is almost always applied to the cheese near or at the end of the cheesemaking process. Salt has both immediate effects when applied and effects that occur over time during ripening. Indeed, salt performs an amazing number of different functions in cheese.

Functions of Salt

The amount of salt that is used in cheesemaking and the roles that it plays in shaping the identity and quality of cheese vary considerably from one variety to the next, but virtually all cheeses require some level of salt for normal function. The most important functions of salt include the following.

Whey Expulsion/Moisture Control

Immediately upon its application, salt begins to dissolve into the water phase of the curd at the surface of the cheese or curd chip or particle, depending on the method of salting, and moisture is drawn osmotically to the surface, where it accumulates as the salt diffuses inward. The free moisture at the surface may be released as a steady stream of whey, as in the making of Cheddar cheese; it may diffuse into the brine, as in the making of brine-salted cheeses; or it may evaporate from the cheese surface, as in surface dry-salted cheeses. Thus the application of salt almost always results in a lower-moisture cheese than would otherwise be attained if the cheese remained unsalted. For example, in the making of Cheddar cheese the lowest moisture content that can be attained without salting is around 38 to 39 percent, which is too high for Cheddar meant to be aged. Moisture content is a critical determinant of the enzymatic and microbiological properties of the cheese during aging, and every cheese type has a narrow range within which it must fall in order to ripen normally. Thus salting plays an essential role in Cheddar cheesemaking by lowering the moisture content to a desired range of about 35 to 37 percent. Furthermore, as whey is lost from the cheese during salting, lactose is also removed. This is an important function in some cheeses, because the retention of excessive lactose can lead to abnormally low pH and abnormal fermentations during ripening.

Surface Dehydration/Rind Formation

As moisture diffuses or evaporates from the cheese surface during brining or surface dry-salting, respectively, a layer of dehydrated cheese, or rind, is formed. The thickness and density (toughness) of the rind can be controlled by manipulating the brining conditions and the humidity and temperature conditions during and after dry-salting. The use of salting to dehydrate the cheese surface results in a rind that is both low in moisture and high in salt, which acts as a selective environment that strongly influences the microbial ecology that develops on the rind. Thus for surface-ripened cheeses, salt plays an important role in promoting the growth of the right mix of microorganisms at the cheese surface that are needed to perform the desired ripening function.

Inhibition of Lactose Fermentation/pH Control

For some cheeses, such as Cheddar, the addition of salt temporarily disrupts the fermentation of lactose to lactic acid by the starter culture, thereby preventing the pH from dropping too low during pressing and the early stages of ripening. Inadequate salting often results in abnormally low pH in the young cheese, which may detrimentally affect the ripening process and ultimate cheese quality.

Textural Improvement/Physicochemical Changes

During the first weeks of aging, salt promotes physicochemical interactions between the casein matrix and the water phase of the cheese. Consequently, loosely held water that is abundantly present within the body of the newly made cheese becomes absorbed by the casein, and the cheese texture is transformed from a moist and curdy state to one that is drier, softer, and more mellow.

Regulation of Microbiological and Enzymatic Characteristics

Salt strongly influences the activities of proteolytic enzymes and microorganisms in the cheese that shape the ripening process. In general, abnormally high salt content, all else held constant, results in slower breakdown of casein by proteolytic enzymes during aging and, consequently, slower development of cheese flavor and texture. Furthermore, as salt content increases, the chemical environment within the cheese becomes more microbiologically restrictive. Therefore, high salt content greatly restricts the types of microorganisms that can survive in the cheese, whereas low salt content opens the door to a wider range of organisms that can grow, for better or for worse. Thus salting to the correct level is essential to control proteolytic and microbiological activity during ripening. Consequently, most ripened cheeses have a fairly narrow range within which the salt content must fall in order for ripening to proceed normally. For some cheeses, salt also inhibits the survival and growth of pathogenic (food-poisoning) microorganisms that could be present as contaminants and thus has important implications for food safety.

Flavor Development and Enhancement

As in other foods, salt has a seasoning effect in cheese. That is, it enhances the flavor present in the cheese by increasing our perception of cheese flavor. However, salt's contribution to flavor is more than simply a seasoning effect. Because salt influences both microbiological and enzymatic activity during ripening, it directly affects the formation of flavor compounds that contribute to typical cheese flavor. If the salt content is too high or too low, key flavor compounds may not be produced in the right amount or in the right balance, resulting in the lack of typical flavor and/or abnormal flavors. In some highly salted cheeses such as feta and blue types, the high salt content enhances flavor development by stimulating the action of lipase enzymes, which produce free fatty acids responsible for piquant flavor and aroma.

Methods of Salting

Salt may be applied to the cheese in three different ways depending on the cheese type: (1) dry-salting before pressing, (2) dry-salting after pressing, and (3) brine salting. Often more than one approach is used.

Dry-Salting before Pressing

Examples of cheeses that use this approach included milled-curd (such as Cheddar), stirred-curd (such as Colby), and some blue-type cheeses. In the case of Cheddar, the curd slabs are milled into chips or "fingers" approximately 2 inches/5 cm long and ⅝ inch/1.6 cm square. Milling serves several functions. First, it increases the surface area of the curd for more efficient and uniform salt uptake and whey expulsion. Furthermore, by exposing the warm interior of the curd slabs to the ambient atmosphere, milling also enables the curd to cool down to a more suitable temperature before the salt is applied.

In order for salt at the particle surface to be absorbed into the curd, it must first dissolve in the water that is initially present at the cheese surface to create a brine. Once dissolved, the salt then diffuses inward; concurrently, moisture inside the curd is drawn osmotically in the opposite direction to the surface of the particle, where it accumulates and allows additional salt to dissolve and diffuse inward. The uptake of salt by the curd particles is governed by several parameters:

1. **Particle dimensions.** Ideally, you want all of the milled-curd or stirred-curd particles to have the same dimensions because smaller particles will absorb more salt and lose more moisture than larger particles. If the salt and moisture differences among particles are large enough, the body of the cheese may not develop uniformly due to pockets of abnormally low salt and high moisture or, conversely, high salt and low moisture. Of particular concern are pockets of low salt and high moisture, which can lead to sour and fermented defects.
2. **Type of salt.** Coarse rather than fine salt should generally be used, because it is better for the salt to dissolve gradually rather than quickly. Fine salt tends to dissolve too quickly, which promotes a flush of whey out of the curd that can wash away the undissolved salt at the particle surface, resulting in less efficient salt uptake. The flush of whey can also carry fat along with it, resulting in greater fat losses.
3. **Method of application.** Generally dry salt should be added in several equal increments, with stirring in between, rather than as one single application. Adding all the salt at once tends to create a flush of whey that can wash away salt and fat from the particle surfaces. Addition of salt in three increments allows it to dissolve gradually, thereby minimizing the whey flush. After each addition the curd particles should be stirred *very* gently (rough stirring causes shattered particles and fines) to distribute the salty whey around the particles and promote uniform salt uptake. Then the salted curds should be left undisturbed for a brief period, usually around 10 minutes, to allow the salt to be absorbed before adding the next increment. The amount of stirring and the amount of time between each addition of new salt should be consistent from one vat to the next.
4. **Curd temperature.** The curd temperature during salting should be around 87 to 92°F/31 to 33°C. The higher the curd temperature at salting, the greater the flush of whey and the more liquid the fat becomes. Therefore, more salt and liquid fat are washed away when salt is added at high temperature (say, 95 to 100°F/35 to 38°C), and the resulting cheese will tend have a greasy, seamy appearance because of the excess fat losses. On the other hand, salting when the curd temperature is too low results in a limited flush of whey and thus limited brine forming at the surface of the particles. Consequently, more of the salt remains undissolved and less salt is absorbed into the cheese. Thus it is important to control the salting temperature within a fairly narrow range.

Figure 5.10. For some cheese varieties, such as Camembert, dry salt is sprinkled onto the surface of the newly made cheese. As the salt dissolves in the available moisture at the surface and begins to diffuse into the body of the cheese, water is drawn osmotically to the cheese surface, where it accumulates and enables the remaining salt to dissolve and form a brine.

Dry-Salting after Pressing

For some cheese varieties, dry salt is sprinkled or rubbed onto the surface of the finished cheese (see figure 5.10). As the salt dissolves into the available moisture at the surface, water is drawn osmotically to the cheese surface, where it accumulates and enables the remaining salt to dissolve and form a brine. Coarse salt, which dissolves slowly, works best. Once dissolved, the salt gradually migrates into the cheese. In the case of hard-rinded cheeses, the ambient relative humidity is kept low (usually around 85 percent, but always less than 90 percent) during and after salting. Consequently, the moisture that is drawn to the cheese surface evaporates quickly, leaving behind a dehydrated layer or rind. Repeated applications of dry salt will draw additional moisture out of the cheese and thus increase the density and toughness of the rind. Once a dense, hard rind has formed, very little additional moisture can diffuse to the cheese surface upon application of additional dry salt. Consequently, the newly added salt is unable to dissolve and migrate readily from the surface to the interior of the cheese. For large, rinded cheeses, it is difficult to incorporate the required amount of salt into the body of the cheese through dry-salting alone before the rind impedes further uptake of salt. Large, rinded cheeses, therefore, are usually brine-salted first to incorporate adequate salt into the body of the cheese, and then dry-salted to create the hard rind. When rubbed onto the surface of some hard-rinded cheeses, undissolved coarse salt acts as an abrasive that is used to etch off microbial growth, creating a smooth, clean rind surface.

In the case of soft-rind cheeses such as some of the bloomy-rind and washed-rind cheeses, the cheeses are stored in a high-humidity (around 95 percent) environment after dry-salting. The humidity prevents excessive evaporation of moisture from the cheese surface, thereby preventing the formation of a dense, tough rind. These cheeses must remain high in moisture at the surface in order for the ripening process, which is driven by the surface growth of yeasts and molds or bacteria, to progress inward into the body of the cheese.

Brine-Salting

For many cheeses, some or all of the salt is incorporated by soaking the cheese in a concentrated brine solution for an appropriate period of time, which may range from a few hours to several days depending on the size and salt content of the cheese. During brining, salt diffuses into the surface of the cheese while moisture migrates in the opposite direction and is released into the brine. Therefore, the concentration of salt in the brine is constantly decreasing and must be replenished with new salt on a regular basis. In addition to water, the water-soluble components of the cheese (lactose, lactic acid, soluble minerals such as calcium, and so forth) also diffuse into the brine; therefore, the soluble-component makeup of the brine changes over time. The uptake of salt by and loss of moisture from the cheese during brining, as well as the surface properties of the cheese, are strongly influenced by the conditions employed during brining. It is particularly important to optimize and control the following parameters:

1. **Brine concentration.** Most cheesemaking procedures call for brine concentrations ranging from 18 to 23 percent salt concentration, expressed on a weight-to-weight basis (18 to 23 pounds salt per 100 pounds brine), which corresponds to a range of approximately 70 to 88 percent saturation. Brine with less than 16 percent salt is never used because the range of microorganisms that can survive and proliferate in the brine, including spoilage organisms and pathogens, increases dramatically as brine concentration falls below 16 percent. Weak brines are notorious sources of contamination and should be avoided at all costs. Weak brines also result in greater moisture retention at the cheese surface, resulting in a soft, swollen, slimy rind. At the other extreme, brine that contains greater than 23 percent salt increases the risk that moisture will be lost from the cheese surface too quickly. Rapid moisture loss may result in the formation of a dehydrated layer that may impede further uptake of salt before adequate salt has penetrated into the body of the cheese, resulting in

decreased salt content in the final cheese. Thus it is important to prepare brine at the proper concentration and then to monitor the brine concentration and replenish the salt regularly, maintaining the correct concentration within a narrow range over time. The brine will need to be replenished more frequently if the amount of cheese that is brined increases, because the salt taken up by and moisture released from the cheese will increase, resulting in more rapid dilution.

Brine concentration can be measured easily and inexpensively using a float device called a salometer (see figure 5.11). The salometer contains a graduated neck calibrated to indicate the percentage of salt, or the percent saturation of the brine, at 60°F/14°C, depending on the type of salometer. The salometer actually measures the density of the brine, which is directly proportionate to the salt concentration. (However, because brines contain soluble solids from the cheese such as lactose and minerals, which also contribute to the density, salometer readings slightly overestimate the true salt concentration.) At 60°F/14°C brine theoretically becomes saturated at around 26 percent salt, meaning that 26 percent is the maximum salt concentration possible; any further salt added to the brine will fail to dissolve and will settle to the bottom of the brine tank. To obtain a salometer reading, a sample of well-mixed brine, which should be adjusted to 60°F/14°C to give the most accurate measurement, is transferred to a glass cylinder, and the salometer is carefully placed in the brine and allowed to float freely. The measurement is taken at the position on the calibrated neck where it emerges from the brine.

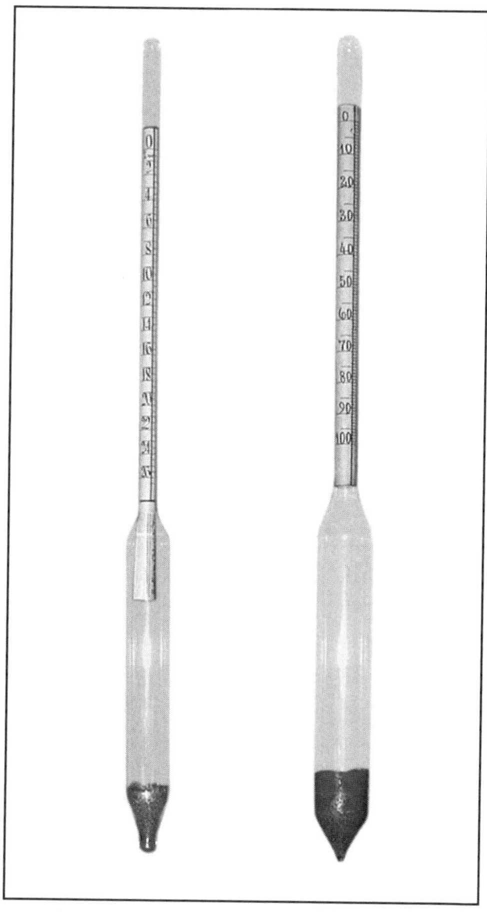

Figure 5.11. Brine concentration can be measured easily and inexpensively using a float device called a salometer. The salometer measures the density of the brine, which is directly proportionate to the brine concentration. The brine concentration may be expressed as either percentage of salt in the brine (0–26 percent, left) or percentage of salt saturation (0–100 percent, right).

2. **Uniform exposure to brine.** Ideally, every surface of every cheese that is being brined should be exposed to the same brine concentration for the same length of time. In reality, as salt is taken up by

Figure 5.12. Example of a brine tank overpacked with cheese. A general rule of thumb is that the volume of brine should be at least five times the volume of cheese. Furthermore, cheeses should never be allowed to remain in contact with one another for long periods during brining: Little or no salt can be absorbed by, nor moisture removed from, the cheeses at the points of contact.

and moisture is released from the cheese, the concentration of salt in the layer of brine immediately adjacent to the cheese surface decreases. The closer the cheeses are packed together in the brine, the more diluted the brine becomes in the narrow spaces that separate the cheeses. This localized dilution slows down further uptake of salt by and release of moisture from the exposed cheese surfaces, thereby contributing to variation in the salt and moisture content of the final cheeses, and variation in the rind characteristics. A general rule of thumb is that the volume of brine should be at least five times the volume of cheese to prevent overpacking. Also, the brine should be stirred regularly to minimize localized zones of dilution from forming at the cheese surfaces. Furthermore, adjacent cheeses should never be allowed to touch one another for long periods during brining (see figure 5.12): Little or no salt can be absorbed by, nor moisture removed from, the cheeses at the points of contact. Typically, prolonged contact results in the formation of high-moisture, low-salt patches on the cheese surface that may later develop into rind rot. When cheeses must be packed tightly during brining, they should be turned frequently to limit prolonged contact.

Another challenge is presented because cheese is less dense than brine and therefore floats about ½ inch/1.3 cm above the brine. If the cheese is left unattended, the exposed surface will remain unsalted and will dry out and form a hard skin due to evaporation. Therefore, most brining procedures call for cheeses to be turned daily and for dry salt to be sprinkled onto the exposed surface to promote more uniform salt uptake. Failure to turn the cheeses daily tends to result in excessive evaporation at the exposed surface, giving a dry rind that may wrinkle and crack during ripening. The amount of evaporation that occurs at the exposed surface will be influenced by the relative humidity in the brining room, which normally should be around 80 to 85 percent. If the brining room has very low humidity, the exposed surfaces will dry out more quickly, and it may become necessary to turn the cheese more than once daily.

3. **Brine temperature.** Ideally, the temperature of brine should remain constant and for most cheeses should fall within the range of 50 to 60°F/10 to 14°C. The brining room should thus be kept constant at, and cheeses cooled to, this temperature before being placed in the brine. Increasing the brining temperature results in an increase in salt uptake and an even larger increase in moisture loss. Therefore, wide fluctuations in brining temperature can cause the salt and especially the moisture content in the final cheese to vary. Brining should not be performed at temperatures higher than 60°F/14°C, because a wider range of microorganisms, including spoilage organisms and pathogens, can survive and proliferate in the brine at higher temperatures. Brining at temperatures below 50°F/10°C is also problematic for rinded cheeses, because less moisture is lost from the surface of the cheese, rendering it difficult to develop a suitable rind. Unripened pasta-filata cheeses such as mozzarella are an exception to this rule. Cold brining of these cheeses is essential to achieve rapid cooling and to avoid excessive moisture loss.
4. **Calcium concentration and pH.** When cheese first enters a newly prepared brine, calcium ions and hydrogen ions present in the water phase of the cheese at its surface migrate into the brine until their concentrations reach equilibrium with the water phase of the cheese. This leaching process leaves the cheese surface depleted of calcium and hydrogen ions, which causes the casein at the surface to absorb water and swell, resulting in the formation of a soft, slimy layer that leads to rind rot during ripening. This can be prevented by acidifying newly made brine with food-grade lactic acid or vinegar to approximately the same pH as that of the cheese, and by adding 0.1 percent food-grade calcium chloride to the brine.

STEP EIGHT: SPECIAL APPLICATIONS

Special applications is a broad category of cheesemaking practices that are specific to a particular class or group of cheeses and essential to their quality and character. Well-known examples include: plasticization and stretching of curd in hot water during the making of pasta-filata cheeses; spraying mold spores onto the surface of bloomy-rind cheeses before ripening; holding Swiss-type cheeses in a warm room during ripening to promote eye formation; needling blue cheese wheels before ripening to allow air to penetrate and support the growth of blue mold; and rubbing the surface of washed-rind cheeses with dilute salt brine to create a bacterial smear. Special applications encompass the various practices of the affineur, which will be considered in more detail later.

FINAL THOUGHTS

The eight basic steps described in chapter 5 represent the road map for making cheese. Almost all cheeses follow this road map, although the exact route taken will vary from one cheese type to the next. It is not possible in this book to give detailed directions for making all the different types of cheeses you may be interested in. Such recipes can be acquired from a variety of sources, including those cited at the end of this book under Further Reading. From my perspective, the most important goal of this chapter is that you understand the principles underpinning these eight basic steps. Once you do, you will be better equipped to make sense of cheesemaking recipes that lack detail and appear confusing to the untrained eye; to modify recipes to meet your needs; and in general to gain control over the process. Cheesemaking will never be easy, but the right knowledge can help smooth the way and prevent you from being driven to distraction, indeed madness.

CHAPTER 5 REFERENCES

Kosikowski, F. V., and V. V. Mistry. 1997. *Cheese and Femented Milk Foods*, Vol. 1: *Origins and Principles*. F. V. Kosikowski, LLC, Great Falls, Va.

Le Jaouen, J.-C. 1990. *The Fabrication of Farmstead Goat Cheese,* 2nd ed. *Cheesemakers' Journal,* Ashfield, Mass.

Sammis, J. L. 1946. *Cheese Making.* The Cheese Maker Book Co., Madison, Wis.

Chemical Composition: How It Shapes Cheese Identity and Quality

6

In chapter 5 we learned that almost all cheeses are made by the same eight basic steps. Furthermore, all cheeses start out immediately after manufacture as rather bland, largely undifferentiated curd. They do not, of course, all end up at the same destination. Indeed, bland young cheese curd has the potential to ripen into a stunning diversity of distinctly different cheeses. How is it that different cheeses ripen so differently to produce such diverse results?

The previous chapters have touched on some of the factors that lead to diversity and differentiation. We will now examine those factors in more detail. Cheese ripening is largely governed by three sets of factors, namely: (1) the quality of the milk and level of hygiene and sanitation throughout cheesemaking and ripening, (2) the initial chemical composition of the cheese (specifically, the pH and calcium phosphate content, as well as the salt and moisture contents), and (3) the technological and artisanal conditions that are applied to the cheese after manufacture (during ripening). Milk quality and hygiene and sanitation are discussed in chapter 7. Affinage, or finishing, is touched on in chapter 10. The goal of this chapter is to explain how key aspects of chemical composition shape the character and quality of all cheeses. My hope is that this information will encourage all farmstead cheesemakers to implement systems to monitor and control the initial composition of their cheeses. In chapter 8 we will examine practical approaches that farmstead cheesemakers can use to gain control over key aspects of composition in order to consistently produce high-quality cheese.

CALCIUM CONTENT AND PH

The pH of a cheese immediately after manufacture and its calcium phosphate content go hand in hand; thus we will consider them together. Cheese that contains a high level of calcium phosphate naturally starts out at a higher initial pH than cheese with low calcium phosphate content, all else being equal. Why? Because as you'll recall, the casein micelles that make up the protein matrix of the cheese act like a sponge for acid, absorbing hydrogen ions (the business end of the acid molecule) and releasing calcium phosphate in response. By mopping up the free hydrogen ions present in the cheese, the casein prevents the pH from dropping too low. However, if casein micelles lose most of their calcium phosphate to the whey during cheesemaking—as, for example, in the making of bloomy-rind and blue mold cheeses—the mineral-depleted casein cannot absorb hydrogen ions that the starter produces in the curd toward the end of cheesemaking. Consequently, hydrogen ions accumulate and the pH of the newly made cheese declines sharply, to around pH 4.6. On the other hand, if the casein micelles retain most of their calcium phosphate during cheesemaking, as in the making of Swiss-type and washed-rind cheeses, the mineral-rich casein is able to absorb a significant share of these ions. Consequently, hydrogen ions do not accumulate to such high concentrations, and the pH of the newly made cheese remains high, at around 5.0 to 5.4. The final cheese pH will depend on both the calcium phosphate and moisture contents. The high-moisture, calcium phosphate–rich cheeses such as the washed-rind cheeses tend to fall in the lower end of the pH range (around pH 5.0 to 5.2) because they contain more whey and residual lactose, which results in more lactic acid produced at the end of cheesemaking. The low-moisture, calcium phosphate–rich cheeses such as the Swiss types have less whey and residual lactose and typically remain at the high end of the pH range (around pH 5.2 to 5.4). Overall, cheeses tend to be differentiated into broad overlapping categories that are defined by calcium phosphate content and initial pH. Examples include:

1. High–calcium phosphate, high–initial pH (5.0 to 5.4) cheeses such as Swiss, smear-ripened, and washed-rind types.
2. Moderate–calcium phosphate, moderate–initial pH (4.95 to 5.2) cheeses such as Cheddar, Colby, Jack, and mozzarella.
3. Low–calcium phosphate, low–initial pH (4.6 to 4.9) cheeses such as bloomy-rind, Cheshire, feta, and blue mold.

The closer two cheeses fall with respect to initial pH and total calcium phosphate content, the more closely related they are from a chemical standpoint and the more similar will be their microbiological and enzymatic potentials during ripening.

As touched on in chapter 5, the calcium phosphate content and initial pH of cheese are primarily determined by the rate at which the starter culture produces lactic acid during cheesemaking. If acid is produced rapidly during the early stages of manufacture (during the period when most of the whey is being expelled from the curd), the whey will contain much dissolved calcium phosphate (released from the casein matrix) as it exits the curd. Consequently, the resulting cheese will be depleted of calcium phosphate and, therefore, predisposed to having a low initial pH. Conversely, when acid production is delayed until after most of the whey has been expelled (for example, when acid production occurs primarily during overnight pressing), the whey will contain very little dissolved calcium phosphate as it exits the curd. Consequently, the curd will remain rich in calcium phosphate and the initial cheese pH will remain high. Thus control over starter performance (that is, the rate of acidification) is key to controlling the calcium phosphate content and initial pH and, therefore, the character and quality of the cheese. Ideally, the pH during cheesemaking should change according to the same (optimum) schedule from one vat to the next. Thus the cheesemaker should know the optimum acidity schedule for the type of cheese being made and how to monitor and control acid development from one vat to the next. These topics will be considered in more detail in chapter 8.

Importance of Initial pH

All cheeses must fall within a fairly narrow pH range immediately after manufacture in order to ripen normally and develop typical flavor and texture. If the pH of your newly made cheese deviates significantly from its optimum range, your cheese is in trouble, perhaps beyond repair. Why? Because pH, along with salt and moisture contents, shapes the chemical environment within the cheese that governs the microbiological and enzymatic processes that are responsible for changes during ripening. Moreover, the pH directly affects the structure of the cheese and therefore its texture.

Effect on Microbiological Potential

Microorganisms (yeasts, molds, bacteria) vary greatly in their sensitivities to pH. All microorganisms possess an optimum range of pH values within which they grow most readily and outside of which their growth is suppressed. Yeasts and molds generally thrive at low pH (high acidity) levels that are inhibitory to most bacteria; therefore, their growth is favored in cheese that has low pH (say, 4.6). In contrast, some bacteria require quite high pH levels in order to survive and grow. Therefore, the initial pH of the cheese serves as a powerful selective agent for microbiological activity. In general, as the pH of cheese decreases, the chemical environment within the cheese becomes more hostile to microbial growth, and the range of organisms that can survive and proliferate becomes increasingly limited. Conversely, as the pH increases, the chemical environment becomes more hospitable, and the door is opened for a much wider range of microbiological growth, for better or for worse. Thus the initial pH of any cheese sets the stage for the microbial ecology that is to develop during ripening. If the cheese starts out at a pH level outside its optimum range, the microorganisms that normally participate in ripening may fail to grow, and/or the microorganisms that are normally kept in check during ripening may gain a foothold, proliferate, and produce undesirable results.

A couple of examples will illustrate the importance of the initial pH on the microbial ecology and ripening of cheese. Let's first consider Emmental or Swiss-type cheese, which relies upon the bacterium *Propionibacterium freudenreichii* ssp. *shermanii* to produce carbon dioxide (necessary to form the eyes) and propionic and acetic acids (necessary for typical Swiss-like flavor). This organism grows best at about pH 6.0 or higher and decreases steeply in activity with decreasing pH at values below 5.5. Ideally, the initial pH of Swiss-type cheeses should fall between about 5.2 and 5.3, because small deviations outside this range can have a large effect on the activity of *Propionibacterium.* For example, cheese with a day one pH of 5.0 is more likely to develop few if any eyes and to lack typical Swiss flavor due to the strong pH-suppression effect on *Propionibacterium*. In contrast, cheese with a day one pH of 5.5 will be more likely to develop an overabundance of eyes and to experience fracturing due to excessive gas production by *Propionibacterium*.

An experience that my undergraduate students had some years ago during a Cheddar cheesemaking exercise offers a particularly vivid illustration of the impact of initial pH on ripening. The class was divided into two groups, each making Cheddar cheese from 220 pounds/100 kg of fresh pasteurized whole milk. On this particular occasion the starter culture for both vats was very slow, and the two groups were forced to drain the whey at the abnormally high pH of around 6.4 (Cheddar should normally be drained at a whey pH of around 6.2). Furthermore, the cheddaring time had to be lengthened significantly, and the curd never quite reached the target milling pH of about 5.4. The resulting cheeses ended up with an abnormally high day one pH of around 5.4 (the day one pH of Cheddar should normally fall around 5.0 to 5.2). In addition, it happened that the salt content of both cheeses ended up being on the low side for Cheddar cheese, about 1.0 to 1.2 percent salt rather than the target of around 1.5 to 1.8 percent (we'll consider the importance of salt content later). Upon aging, lo and behold, both groups' cheeses developed a few small eyes and the distinct Swiss flavor notes of propionic and acetic acids. Thus even though the students intended to produce Cheddar cheese, the high initial pH (along with abnormally low salt content) enabled *Propionibacterium,* present in the milk and cheese as a natural contaminant, to grow and produce enough carbon dioxide and propionic and acetic acids to give their Cheddar cheeses a Swiss-like character. The moral of this story is that your day one pH (along with salt and moisture contents) matters, because the initial pH predisposes your cheese to develop microbiologically along a specific pathway that influences the ultimate quality and character of the cheese.

Effect on Enzymatic Potential

Enzymes, like microorganisms, vary greatly in their sensitivities to pH, having optimum ranges within which they are most active and outside of which their activity decreases. Although the precise effects of pH on enzymatic activity during cheese ripening are less well understood than are the effects of pH on microorganisms, a couple of examples involving proteolytic enzymes will help to illustrate the importance of pH on enzymatic changes. Proteolysis, or the breakdown of protein, plays an important role in the development of flavor and texture in virtually all aged cheeses. There are five general sources of proteolytic enzymes in cheese: (1) residual rennet, (2) plasmin originating from the milk, (3) enzymes from the starter culture, (4) enzymes from secondary or adjuct cultures (blue or white molds, *Brevibacterium linens,* and so on), and (5) enzymes from nonstarter bacteria present as contaminants. Thus a ripening cheese represents a very complex proteolytic system. Optimum ripening requires that the various proteolytic enzymes perform in the proper balance and at the correct rates, which will differ depending on the type of cheese. Attaining the proper pH helps to control and optimize the proteolytic changes during ripening.

For example, during Cheddar cheese ripening, casein molecules, primarily alpha-caseins, are cleaved into large protein fragments, or peptides, by the residual rennet. The large peptides are then broken down into progressively smaller peptides and free amino acids by various starter culture enzymes. This complex cascade of protein degradation, which is critical to both texture and flavor development, proceeds along the most desirable pathway when the cheese pH starts out at around 5.0 to 5.2 and increases only modestly during ripening. At this relatively low pH range, plasmin, which is most active at around pH 7.5, has limited activity and contributes minimally to Cheddar cheese proteolysis, whereas residual rennet is quite active and dominates the first steps in the proteolytic cascade. In contrast, the high cooking temperatures used in the making of Swiss-type cheeses result in the complete inactivation of rennet; therefore, rennet plays little or no role in the ripening of Swiss-type cheeses. However, plasmin survives high cooking temperatures and plays a key role in Swiss ripening. Plasmin is proteolytically active because Swiss-type cheeses start out at a higher initial pH (5.2 to 5.4) and undergo considerable pH increases during ripening (to around 5.6 to 5.8). The higher pH levels stimulate plasmin activity, which contributes to the development of desirable texture and flavor. In the case of Gruyère cheese, higher pH at the surface also allows *Brevibacterium linens* and other coryneform bacteria to grow; these in turn produce proteolytic enzymes that contribute to the distinctive flavor profile of that cheese. In short, pH is one of several key parameters that influence enzymatic activity during cheese ripening, both directly, by affecting specific enzymes, and indirectly, by affecting the growth of microorganisms, which in turn produce enzymes that participate in the ripening process.

Effect on Cheese Structure

The bonds that hold the casein matrix of cheese together are directly influenced by the pH. Therefore, the initial cheese pH profoundly affects the structure and therefore body and texture of the cheese. A critical dividing point occurs around pH 5.0, at least for cow's milk. For cheeses that have an initial pH above 5.0, the casein matrix is held together largely through calcium phosphate crosslinking, and the casein strongly interacts with water. This enables the curd to have a relatively springy, elastic structure, as can be readily observed in newly made Swiss, Dutch, Cheddar, and other cheeses that have an initial pH greater than 5.0. As the initial pH decreases below 5.0, the casein matrix loses its ability to interact with water, and calcium phosphate crosslinking is progressively replaced by a different type of protein–protein bonding. This results in a harder, more brittle structure that fractures readily and is unable to melt and flow upon application of heat. Thus cheeses that fall significantly below pH 5.0 (such as Cheshire, feta, and blue and white mold cheeses initially) characteristically have relatively hard and brittle textures. Indeed, as my undergraduate students have observed over the years during Cheddar cheesemaking exercises, if acidification proceeds too rapidly and the curd loses too much calcium to the whey, the day one pH will likely fall well below 5.0. The resulting texture will be brittle and crumbly, much more like that of Cheshire than Cheddar cheese.

If you are making a pasta-filata cheese such as mozzarella, controlling the pH to within a narrow optimum range is critical to achieving a curd that can be plasticized and stretched. Like texture, melting characteristics are governed by the nature of the bonding that holds the casein matrix together. We can appreciate the profound effect that pH has on cheese structure by observing the melting characteristics of mozzarella with different pH values, as illustrated in figure 6.1. The four cheese samples (A through D) shown in this figure were from the same batch of low-moisture mozzarella cheese having a pH of 5.24. Sample A was the original cheese at pH 5.24. The pH values of samples B, C, and D were changed to 6.15 (B), 4.95 (C), and 4.83 (D) using an experimental method that permits the pH to be manipulated without changing other aspects of cheese composition. The pH-modified samples were melted at 140°F/60°C and then "stretched." The results were dramatic. As the pH was increased from 5.24 to 6.15, the cheese retained its abilty to melt and stretch but became substantially more elastic, fibrous, and chewy because the calcium phosphate–type bonding of the casein structure was essentially strengthened at the higher pH. In contrast, as pH declined from 5.24 to 4.83, the cheese lost its ability to melt and stretch and assumed a brittle, granular consistency that failed to flow. This occurred because calcium phosphate–type bonding was replaced by a different type of bonding. Again, the take-home message is that the initial (and subsequent) pH of your cheese profoundly affects its structure and, therefore, texture and related characteristics.

SALT CONTENT

As with the initial pH of your cheese, the initial salt content exerts a strong influence

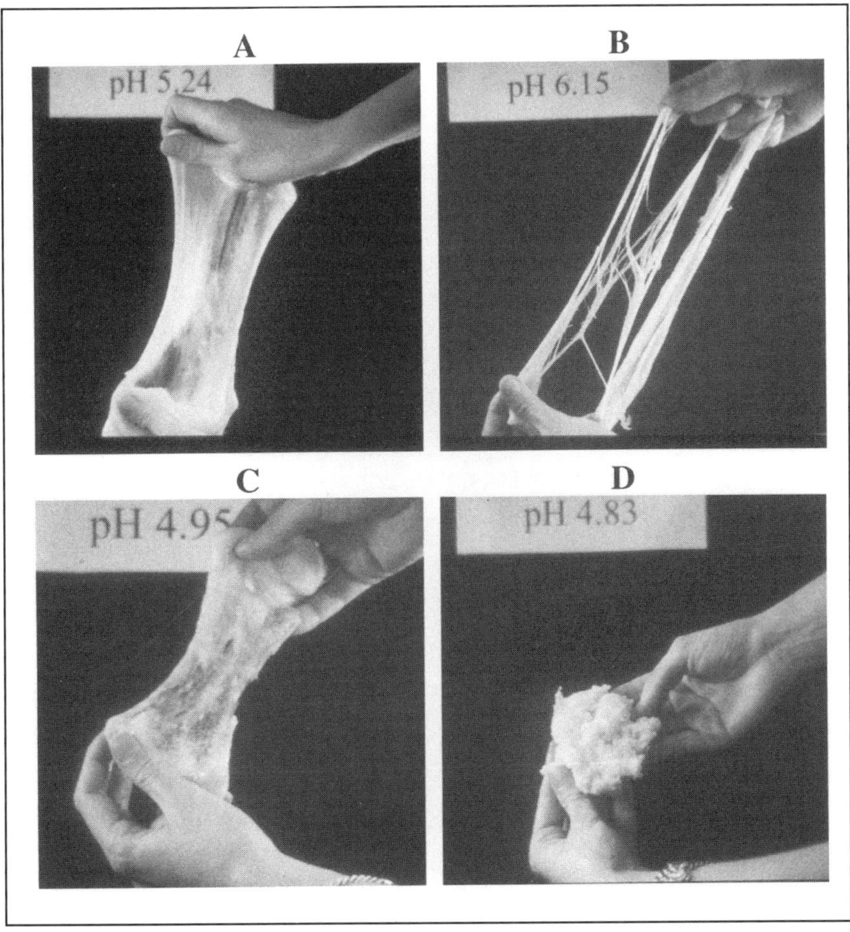

Figure 6.1. Appearance of a commercial low-moisture part-skim cheese at four different pH levels when melted at 140°F/60°C. The cheese melted to a more tough and fibrous consistency when the pH was increased to above 5.2. In contrast, the cheese lost the ability to melt and flow when the pH was decreased to below 5.0. (From Kindstedt et al., 2001; used with permission.)

on the changes that occur during ripening. Salt may be applied to cheese through dry-salting or brining. In either case, the added salt becomes dissolved in the water phase of the cheese and essentially forms an internal brine solution. The concentration of the brine within the cheese strongly impacts microbiological and enzymatic changes during ripening, as well as directly affecting cheese texture. Therefore, the initial salt content of most cheeses must fall within a fairly narrow range in order for flavor and texture to develop in the characteristic desired fashion.

Effect on Microbiological Potential

Microorganisms (yeasts, molds, and bacteria) vary greatly in their sensitivities to salt concentration, much the same as they vary in sensitivity to pH. All microorganisms possess an optimum range of salt concentrations within which they grow most readily and above which their growth is suppressed. Some yeasts, molds, and bacteria thrive at very high salt levels, whereas others are strongly inhibited by relatively low concentrations. Therefore, like pH, the salt content of cheese serves as a powerful selective agent for microbiological activity. In general, as the salt content increases, the chemical environment within the cheese becomes more hostile to microbial growth, and the range of organisms that can survive and proliferate becomes increasingly limited. Conversely, as the salt content decreases, the chemical environment becomes more hospitable, and the door is opened for a much wider range of microbiological growth, for better or for worse. Thus the salt content of any cheese sets the stage for the microbial ecology that is to develop during ripening. If the salt content deviates substantially from the optimum range for a particular cheese type, the microorganisms that normally participate in ripening may fail to grow, and/or the microorganisms that are normally kept in check during ripening may gain a foothold, proliferate, and produce undesirable results.

A couple of examples will illustrate the importance of salt content on the microbial ecology and ripening of cheese. First, let's once again consider Emmental or Swiss-type cheeses, which rely upon the bacterium *Propionibacterium freudenreichii* ssp. *shermanii* to produce carbon dioxide (necessary to form the eyes) and propionic and acetic acids (necessary for typical Swiss-like flavor). This organism is strongly inhibited at brine concentrations greater than about 2.0 to 2.5 percent salt, which typically correspond to salt contents in Swiss-type cheeses of around 0.8 to 1.0 percent. Thus it is not surprising that the salt content of Swiss-type cheeses typically falls in the range of around 0.4 to 0.8 percent. Cheese with greater than 1.0 percent salt content is likely to develop few if any eyes and to lack typical Swiss flavor, due to strong salt inhibition of *Propionibacterium*. Unfortunately, low salt content also opens the door to the growth of clostridial spore-forming bacteria, such as *Clostridium tyrobutyricum,* which may occur as contaminants in milk when equipment is not cleaned properly or when grass silage is fed to the cows. If allowed to grow in cheese, these spore formers may produce large amounts of carbon dioxide and hydrogen gas, sometimes accompanied by obnoxious flavor and aroma compounds. Consequently, so-called late gas blowing by clostridial bacteria is a constant threat to low-salt cheeses such as Emmental; it is essential to keep the spores out of the milk in the first place. For this reason, the use of grass silage in milk production is banned in some regions of Europe where Alpine cheeses are produced.

Cheddar cheese, which typically has a salt content ranging from around 1.5 to 1.8 percent, provides another example of the critical role of salt in establishing the microbial ecology of the cheese. In order for typical Cheddar cheese flavor to develop normally during ripening, the starter bacteria must remain alive and metabolically active in the cheese during the first month or two following manufacture and then progressively die off. If the salt content is too high, the starter bacteria will not be active enough during the critical period when they are needed to kick-start the cascading series of reactions that lead to Cheddar cheese flavor. The result will be slow and incomplete flavor development. On the other hand, if the salt content is too low, the starter culture will reach very large populations during the first two months and then continue to survive rather than dying off. Failure of the starter to die off after the first couple of months also interrupts the series of reactions that give rise to Cheddar cheese flavor, as we will examine in more detail in the next section on enzymatic changes. The bottom line is that salt content in Cheddar cheese strongly influences the survival, activity, and death rate of the starter bacteria during ripening, which in turn impact the complex sequence of chemical reactions that ultimately result in typical Cheddar cheese flavor.

One final observation about the importance of salt content to the microbial ecology of cheese can be drawn from another experience of my undergraduate students. During one Cheddar cheese-making exercise some years ago everything proceeded flawlessly almost to the end. However, the students inadvertently added too little salt to the milled curds, and the resulting cheese ended up with just under 1.0 percent salt, instead of the target level of 1.6 to 1.8 percent. The final cheese also turned out to be abnormally high in moisture because less whey was expelled during salting and pressing due to the small amount of salt added. The higher moisture content (and therefore higher residual lactose) in turn resulted in an abnormally low initial pH. Thus, unlike in the earlier example, where the salt content of the students' Cheddar cheese was low and the initial pH was high (which led to the development of Swiss-type characteristics), this cheese was low in salt, low in pH, and high in moisture. Upon ripening, the cheese did not develop Swiss-type characteristics because the low pH (less than 5.0) suppressed the growth of *Propionibacterium*. However, noticeable slits developed in the body of the cheese due to gas production. Furthermore, a detectable butyric acid fermentation off-flavor was present, which was strong evidence that clostridial spores, which are often present in milk and cheese but normally inhibited by the salt content in Cheddar, had gained a foothold in this low-salt cheese and caused the defects in flavor and texture. Again, the underlying message is that the microbial ecology of a ripening cheese is complex and can be inadvertently shifted in undesirable directions if the salt content and pH (and moisture content) are not carefully controlled.

Effect on Enzymatic Potential/Proteolysis

The enzymatic reactions that contribute to cheese ripening take place in the water phase of the cheese. The amount of salt that is dissolved in the water phase affects enzymatic activity in various ways. One example that has been studied extensively and is particularly well characterized is the complex role that salt plays in establishing the optimum rate and pattern of protein breakdown in Cheddar cheese. Controlled proteolysis is essential for proper flavor and texture development. The stepwise sequence of protein breakdown in Cheddar cheese is illustrated schematically in figure 6.2. Salt plays a critical role in controlling this complex proteolytic cascade, and if the salt content is too high or too low, proteolysis—and, therefore, flavor and texture development—cannot proceed optimally, as the following comparisons will illustrate.

Proteolysis in Cheddar Cheese: Normal Salt Content

The first step in the cascading sequence of Cheddar cheeese proteolysis is initiated by rennet enzymes (for example, chymosin) that carry over from the milk to the cheese (see figure 6.2, step 1). Chymosin attacks casein molecules that form the structural matrix of cheese, cutting them into large fragments called peptides. In Cheddar cheese with normal salt content (around 1.5 to 1.8 percent salt), chymosin selectively breaks down alpha-caseins at a moderate rate, which contributes to a gradual desirable change in texture. In contrast, chymosin hardly touches the beta-casein. This is fortunate, because the peptides that are produced from the breakdown of beta-casein tend to be quite bitter and can cause bitterness in the cheese. The large peptides produced by the action of chymosin on alpha-caseins are next broken down into smaller peptides by proteolytic enzymes located in the cell walls of the starter culture bacteria (see figure 6.2, step 2). Some of the small peptides that are produced at this step have a bitter taste and will cause the cheese to become bitter if they are allowed to accumulate. Fortunately, this does not usually occur in Cheddar cheese with normal salt content because the salt causes the starter bacteria to die off progressively after a couple of months of ripening. When starter bacteria die, their cells burst open and release various proteolytic enzymes into the water phase of the cheese. These enzymes, no longer trapped inside the bacterial cells, then attack and break down the small peptides (including bitter peptides) into very small peptides and free amino acids that are not bitter (figure 6.2, step 3). Finally, the relatively few surviving starter bacteria, as well as a growing population of nonstarter bacteria, then transform the very small peptides and free amino acids into flavor compounds that contribute to Cheddar cheese flavor. Clearly, this proteolytic cascade is quite complex, and there are many things can go wrong enzymatically and microbiologically along the way.

Proteolysis in Cheddar Cheese: Low Salt Content

Cheddar cheese with abnormally low salt content is often characterized by defects associated with proteolysis gone awry, including weak and pasty texture, bitterness, and lack of typical Cheddar cheese flavor. Why? Because salt directly affects the entire proteolytic cascade shown described in figure 6.2. For example, when the salt content is low, chymosin becomes overly active against alpha-caseins and, therefore, proteolysis occurs too quickly

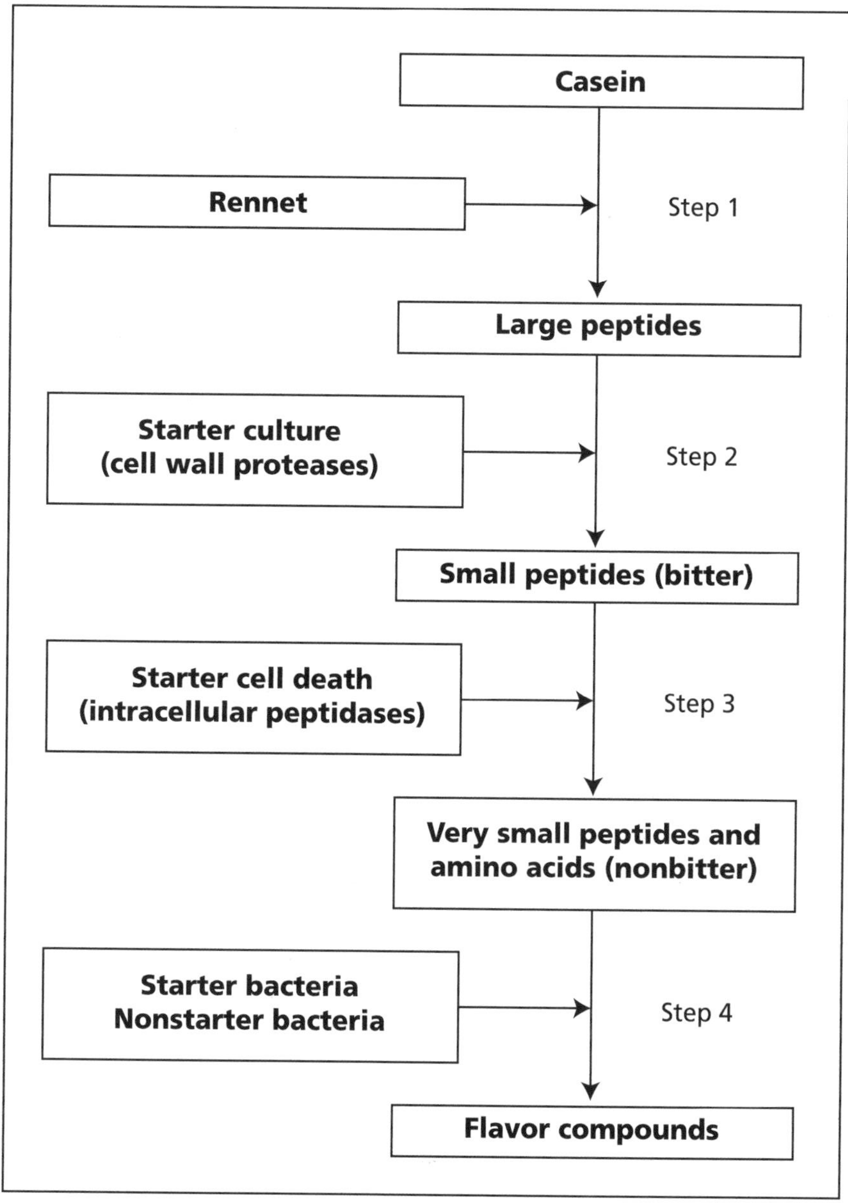

Figure 6.2. The breakdown of protein in Cheddar cheese occurs as a cascading sequence. First, casein is broken down by rennet into several large fragments, or peptides. The starter-culture bacteria, which possess protein-degrading enzymes, or proteases, in their cell walls, then degrade the large peptides into smaller peptides. Some of these peptides are bitter and will cause the cheese to become bitter if they accumulate to high levels. After about two months of aging the starter bacteria begin to die off and their cells burst open and release peptidase enzymes that degrade small peptides into very small peptides and amino acids. Finally, starter and nonstarter bacteria participate in the conversion of amino acids into flavor compounds.

(figure 6.2, step 1). This results in excessive weakening of the cheese structure and a greater incidence of weak and pasty texture defects. Furthermore, chymosin is much less selective in a low-salt environment and thus readily attacks beta-casein to form bitter peptides, thereby adding to the pool of starter-produced bitter peptides and increasing the chances for bitter defects. To make matters worse, low salt content also enables the starter bacteria to attain higher populations and survive longer. The net effect is to increase the production of bitter peptides (figure 6.2, step 2) and decrease the conversion of bitter to nonbitter peptides by delaying the death and lysis of the starter bacteria (figure 6.2, step 3). Finally, the reduced conversion of small peptides to very small peptides and amino acids due to delayed starter die-off (figure 6.2, step 3) reduces the pool of precursors that are converted into flavor compounds (figure 6.2, step 4), thereby contributing to reduced flavor development.

Proteolysis in Cheddar Cheese: High Salt Content

Whereas Cheddar cheese with low salt content suffers from excessive proteolysis by rennet enzymes, cheese with high salt content is characterized by too little proteolysis. High salt content strongly inhibits rennet activity; thus the first step in the proteolytic cascade (figure 6.2, step 1) proceeds slowly, thereby slowing the entire proteolytic cascade to a crawl. Furthermore, the high-salt environment causes the starter to die off rapidly, further disrupting the stepwise proteolytic chain of events represented in steps 2, 3, and 4. The end result is abnormally slow development of both texture and flavor.

MOISTURE CONTENT

Moisture or water content represents still another critical parameter that governs cheese identity and quality. As we saw in chapter 4, many of the technological practices during cheesemaking are designed to control the expulsion of whey from the curd, with the goal of attaining a specific target moisture content in the final cheese. All cheeses must fall within a fairly narrow moisture range immediately after manufacture in order to ripen normally and develop typical flavor and texture. Why is water content so critical? Because microorganisms, like people, require water for their survival. Water is also necessary for enzymes to function. The greater the amount of water that is available to microorganisms and enzymes, the greater the enzymatic activity and microbiological growth, all else being equal. When a cheese contains too little water, enzymatic reactions that are essential to flavor and texture development may proceed too slowly or not at all, and microorganisms that contribute to ripening may be unable to grow and remain metabolically active. Consequently, the cheese may age slowly and never fully develop its typical flavor and texture. On the other hand, too much water favors excessive enzymatic activity and excessive microbiological growth that would normally be kept in check. The resulting cheese may ripen too quickly and develop defects in flavor and texture due to excessive proteolysis, lipolysis, and abnormal fermentations. Thus along with the pH and salt contents, the initial moisture content of the cheese shapes the microbiological and enzymatic changes that occur during ripening. Successful cheesemakers instinctively strive to control the moisture content in their cheeses.

It's important to recognize that some of the water in cheese is not available to support microbiological growth and enzymatic activity because cheese contains various water-binding components that tie up water molecules and render them inaccessible. For example, dissolved substances such as sodium chloride compete for water molecules and reduce the amount of available water. The higher the salt content, the lower the amount of available moisture, all else being equal. Consequently, two cheeses that contain the same total moisture content and are otherwise similar will differ in the amount of available moisture if they have different salt contents. For example, if two Cheddar cheeses contain 37 percent moisture but one contains 1.2 percent salt and the other 1.8 percent, the cheese with less salt will possess more available water and will age more quickly, despite the cheeses' identical moisture content. Moisture and salt can be measured fairly easily in cheese, even at the farmstead level, as will be discussed in chapter 8. From these two measurements, a parameter called salt-in-moisture can be calculated as follows:

Salt-in-moisture = (% salt in cheese ÷ % moisture in cheese) x 100%

Salt-in-moisture, which can be thought of as the brine concentration of the water phase of the cheese, provides a better indication of the amount of available moisture than does the total moisture content. Thus you can go a long way toward gaining control over the amount of available water in your cheese by optimizing its salt-in-moisture content. In the case of Cheddar, the optimum salt-in-moisture content has been determined through research to fall within the range of about 4.0 to 6.0 percent. For many other, less well-studied cheeses, the optimum range may not be known, in which case you will need to develop your own target values based on experience. This requires some effort, but it will pay off in the long run. We will consider how to develop compositional targets for salt-in-moisture in chapter 8.

Casein also has a strong ability to bind water and render it unavailable to microorganisms and enzymes. Therefore, the higher the casein content of cheese, the lower the available moisture, all else being equal. Casein in cheese is inversely related to fat content: When the fat content of the cheese increases, the casein content automatically decreases. This is typically what happens during autumn, when the fat content of the milk increases more quickly than the casein content (see chapter 3, figures 3.7 and 3.9), resulting in cheese with higher fat and lower casein levels. Less casein in the cheese means less bound water and, therefore, more available water and a "wetter" cheese. For this reason, cheese produced in fall (higher in fat and lower in casein) generally has more available moisture and behaves as a "wetter" cheese than one produced in summer (higher in casein and lower in fat). This has implications for cheesemaking, the nature of which will depend on the type of cheese produced. For example, Cheddar cheesemakers often intentionally strive to produce a slightly drier cheese in autumn than in summer to compensate for the higher fat content and greater availability of the moisture in fall (due to the lower casein content). Cheddar cheesemakers who do not adjust the moisture content downward during autumn may run the risk of producing cheese that is too "wet" and cannot ripen optimally. In contrast, blue cheese requires abundant available moisture to support the growth of the *Penicillium* blue mold. During summer, when available moisture is lower because the casein content of the cheese is higher, makers of blue cheese sometimes intentionally strive to produce a slightly higher-moisture cheese than in autumn. These cheesemakers run the risk of producing an excessively "dry" cheese during summer that does not support the growth of the *Penicillium* blue mold if the moisture content is not adjusted upward.

In summary, your target moisture content may need to be different at different times of year (for instance, autumn versus summer) in order to compensate for seasonal changes in the availability of moisture within your cheese. Moisture availability changes with season because the casein and fat contents of your milk and cheese follow seasonal patterns of change. We will examine the issue of composition control in more detail in chapter 8. The basic message at this juncture is that moisture content is very important to cheese quality, and that the ideal moisture target may change as the composition of the milk and cheese changes, due to season, lactation, and other factors.

IMPLICATIONS FOR SAFETY

As noted earlier, the chemical environment within a cheese becomes more hostile to microbial growth, and the range of microorganisms that survive and proliferate becomes increasingly limited, as: (1) the pH decreases, (2) the salt content increases, and (3) the available moisture decreases. Conversely, the chemical environment becomes more hospitable and the door is opened to a much wider range of microbiological growth, including the growth of pathogens (organisms that cause foodborne illness), as (1) the pH increases, (2) the salt content decreases, and (3) the available moisture increases. Ripening time also influences the survival of pathogens in cheese. In general, the longer a cheese is ripened, the less likely it is that pathogens will survive in the cheese and cause foodborne illness. Consequently, cheeses vary greatly in their vulnerability to pathogens, depending on their pH, salt and moisture contents, and ripening times. Soft cheeses such as the bloomy-rind and smear-ripened types that are relatively high in moisture (around 50 percent), have short ripening times, and attain high pH values during ripening (around 7.0) are especially vulnerable to pathogens. On the other hand, very hard cheeses, such as Parmigiano-Reggiano, that contain low moisture (around 30 to 35 percent), high salt (around 2.5 to 4 percent), and moderate pH (around 5.4), as well as require long aging (one to two years), carry a much lower, if not negligible risk. Current U.S. regulations reduce risk by requiring pasteurization of all milk used to make fresh cheeses that are aged for less than 60 days after manufacture, whereas cheeses aged longer than 60 days may be produced from either raw or pasteurized milk. However, it must be stressed that the appropriate level of safety in any cheese, whether made from raw or pasturized milk, can only be achieved through strict adherence to high standards of hygeine and sanitation. Sanitation, hygiene, and safety aspects are the focus of chapter 7. The Vermont Cheese Council Code of Best Practices, available through the Vermont Cheese Council, is another good sorce of information in this area. The pasteurization issue will be considered in detail in chapter 9.

FINAL THOUGHTS

At this point you may feel overwhelmed with the complexity of cheese chemistry and microbiology. Gaining control over cheesemaking and cheese ripening may seem hopelessly complicated. Don't be discouraged. There are a few steps that most cheesemakers can take to help prevent problems before they occur and correct problems quickly when they do strike. These steps, which include routine measurement of pH at key stages during cheesemaking, and development of target ranges for salt and moisture contents, are presented in chapter 8.

Todd Jay Pritchard, Ph.D.

Ensuring Safety and Quality I: Hazard Analysis Critical Control Point and the Cheesemaking Process

7

Developed in the 1960s by the National Aeronautics and Space Administration (NASA) in response to the need for a biologically safe food source for manned space flights, Hazard Analysis Critical Control Point (HACCP) is a systematic evaluation of the manufacture of a food product, from selection of raw ingredients through to and including shipping. The emphasis of HACCP is to identify and control potential hazards so that real-time decisions can be made to ensure a safer end product. In short, HACCP is a detailed risk analysis of a process. By addressing the conditions or situations in which pathogenic organisms may persist, we can also address many of the same conditions that allow for the survival and proliferation of organisms responsible for quality problems.

The production of safe, high-quality products should be the primary goal of the artisanal cheese producer. HACCP is a dynamic system that can be, and should be, adapted to each individual cheesemaking process. While many "HACCP in a box" plans are available, in reality no two plans are the same. Quite often it is the nuances of a process that aid in the development of the flavor and texture of a particular product. You, the cheesemaker, are the most knowledgeable person with regard to the production of your specific cheese(s). This intimate knowledge of the process is what will make an HACCP plan a useful tool. Development of the plan forces you to more completely understand the process, so as to be able to identify what could potentially go wrong. And really, who is better able to act as the quality and safety control person for your product than you?

It is important to note that HACCP represents only the tip of the iceberg. There are many prerequisite programs that must be in place before you undertake the task of developing and implementing an HACCP plan. These programs will be the basis of many of the decisions during the development of the hazard analysis step.

PREREQUISITE PROGRAMS

It has often been said that "cleanliness is next to godliness." Nowhere is this maxim more true than in the cheesemaking arena. Cleaning and sanitation will aid in preventing phage problems, and, equally as important, they will minimize the potential for postprocessing contamination of the product. Even the use of pasteurized milk and an HACCP plan will not ensure a microbiologically safe cheese if there is postprocessing contamination from dirty or unsanitary equipment and storage areas.

Cleaning and sanitation do not happen by accident. They require forethought and effort on the part of the producer. Your procedures for cleaning and sanitizing should be written down in the form of Standard Sanitation Operating Procedures (SSOPs). While it is not necessary to write procedures for every piece of equipment, it is important that those pieces that are different from others are addressed individually. For example, it may be possible to write a general cleaning and sanitizing procedure to address surfaces of vats, tables, and cutting knives, but it would be important to write a separate SSOP for pumps.

SSOPs should include each of the steps utilized in the process. These steps include disassembly of equipment, prerinsing, application of cleaner, type of cleaner used, type of cleaning process used (clean in place, or CIP, versus clean out of place, or COP), rinsing, inspection, application of sanitizing agent, rinsing of sanitizing agent, and how and where the equipment is dried. SSOPs also are a means of documenting the cleanliness of the equipment. Before cheesemaking, a preoperational evaluation of each piece of equipment to be used should be conducted and documented. Equipment failing to meet cleanliness standards should be recleaned and documented as clean and ready for use. Similarly, operational SSOPs should be documented during production. Operational SSOPs can include an evaluation of employee health, proper handwashing, maintaining rubbish, controlling condensation on overhead piping, and adherence to Good Manufacturing Practices.

A second prerequisite program that should be put in place is the development of written Good Manufacturing Practices (GMPs). Having both a documented set of GMPs and an employee handbook that addresses the "whys" of the GMPs will aid the cheesemaker greatly. A properly written HACCP plan will typically utilize the GMPs as control measures. GMPs should be written that address the design of the manufacturing environment. This may include the use of proper materials for floors, walls, and ceilings; proper lighting; ventilation; and means of handling condensation. GMPs should also be written that address proper attire in the processing plant, including clothing (uniform), footwear, hair/beard nets, jewelry, and proper hand maintenance. Good personal hygiene practices are part of GMPs, as well. These may include issues such as personal cleanliness, proper handwashing, and appropriate bathroom behavior. Limiting access to the processing facility, upkeep of the physical property, storage of ingredients, and a policy regarding sick workers in production should be addressed. A more complete list of GMPs can be found in Title 21, Chapter 1, Part 110 of the U.S. Code of Federal Regulations (http://www.access.gpo.gov/nara/cfr/waisidx_02/21cfr110_02.html).

Other prerequisite programs include an understanding of microbiology and the factors that suppress or promote the growth of organisms. This includes an understanding of the effects that temperature, water activity, atmospheric conditions of storage, and acid production have on the growth of unwanted microbes. Any general food microbiology book will include an overview of these factors and how they affect the growth of organisms. Most cheesemakers have an understanding of these factors and how to use them to their advantage. For example, the production of a particular cheese may require a defined humidity and temperature of storage areas in order to promote proper rind culture development and cheese ripening. Similarly, producers wishing to minimize the growth of unwanted surface molds may vacuum-package their product to remove oxygen.

Good agricultural practices may also be utilized as prerequisite programs. These practices include the proper use of antibiotics, animal health, proper acid production in ensiled feeds, proper feeding practices, manure-handling practices, and equipment upkeep. Any failure in these practices may lead to hazards in the cheesemilk. For instance, milk can easily become contaminated during harvest if proper udder hygiene is not practiced. Milking machines and pipelines that are not properly cleaned and sanitized, or that have milk stone/biofilms, can also lead to postharvest contamination of the milk. (*Milk stone* is a film consisting of precipitated minerals and organic matter from milk that can harbor microorganisms.) The rapid cooling and subsequent cold storage of milk in the bulk tank is beneficial in limiting the growth potential for contaminating pathogenic bacteria.

Failure to segregate the milk from animals being treated with antibiotics for mastitis may result in contaminated cheesemilk. The presence of antibiotics in the milk can lead to serious health effects for people who are allergic to the antibiotic, and may also retard the starter culture added to the cheesemilk.

Studies of silage have shown that those silages that are not fermented properly (and thus have improper acid levels) and show signs of mold growth have an increased incidence of *Listeria* contamination. Constant vigilance of herd health is also beneficial; animals shedding pathogenic organisms in their milk due to such diseases as salmonellosis or listeriosis can lead to safety issues in the finished cheese. Similarly, while not a safety-related issue, the feeding of silage can increase the possibility of late blowing in some cheeses.

THE SEVEN PRINCIPLES OF HACCP

Once the prerequisite programs have been documented and put into action, the development of an HACCP plan can begin. HACCP is based on seven principles: (1) development of a hazard analysis,

(2) identification of critical control points (CCPs) in the process, (3) identification of critical limits for the CCPs, (4) identification of monitoring procedures for the CCPs, (5) record keeping for the CCPs, (6) identification of corrective actions, and (7) verification of the process. Each of these steps has a number of projects that must be accomplished in order for your plan to be complete.

Step One: Hazard Analysis

Step one is the development of a hazard analysis. It is crucial that this step be complete and thorough. Before beginning the actual task of developing the hazard analysis, it is important to gather those individuals who have the best knowledge of the process and have them work on this process together. Individuals on this HACCP team might include the owner of the operation, the sanitation supervisor, the production supervisor, the warehouse personnel, the farm manager (in the case of farmstead operations), and sales personnel. All members of this group should share their personal expertise relative to the overall production of the product. In some cases this "group" may be the same person (in other words, you). If in fact that is the case, it may be advisable to contact the Cooperative Extension office associated with the nearest land-grant university to identify an individual with a knowledge of food safety and cheese production to aid in your HACCP plan development process.

If a company makes several products under similar processes, it may be possible to group the products together. If a second product is made whose production process is different from the others, then a separate HACCP plan should be developed for that product. For example, a company that makes a number of cultured cream products from pasteurized milk may group them together, since the products all have the same general steps and control points (that is, pasteurization and acid development). On the other hand, if a company is producing both an Italian-style and a Cheddar cheese, then—even though they both are cultured milk products—the means of controlling issues are different enough that they would each have a separate HACCP plan.

After the number of HACCP plans needed has been determined, a product summary page should be developed for each type of product made. This page should include the name and address of the company, the name of the owner, the name of the product, the shelf life of the product, the means by which it will be maintained during storage, distribution and display at the point of sales (refrigeration, for instance), the intended audience, and any labeling information on the package.

A flow diagram of the process should then be developed. Identify each step in the process and place a box around it to indicate that it is a separate step. It is during this initial phase that having many people in the HACCP group is most advantageous, as it will cut down on the likelihood of missing a step. Flow diagrams should be complete, including everything from receiving and storage of raw ingredients through aging and shipping of the finished

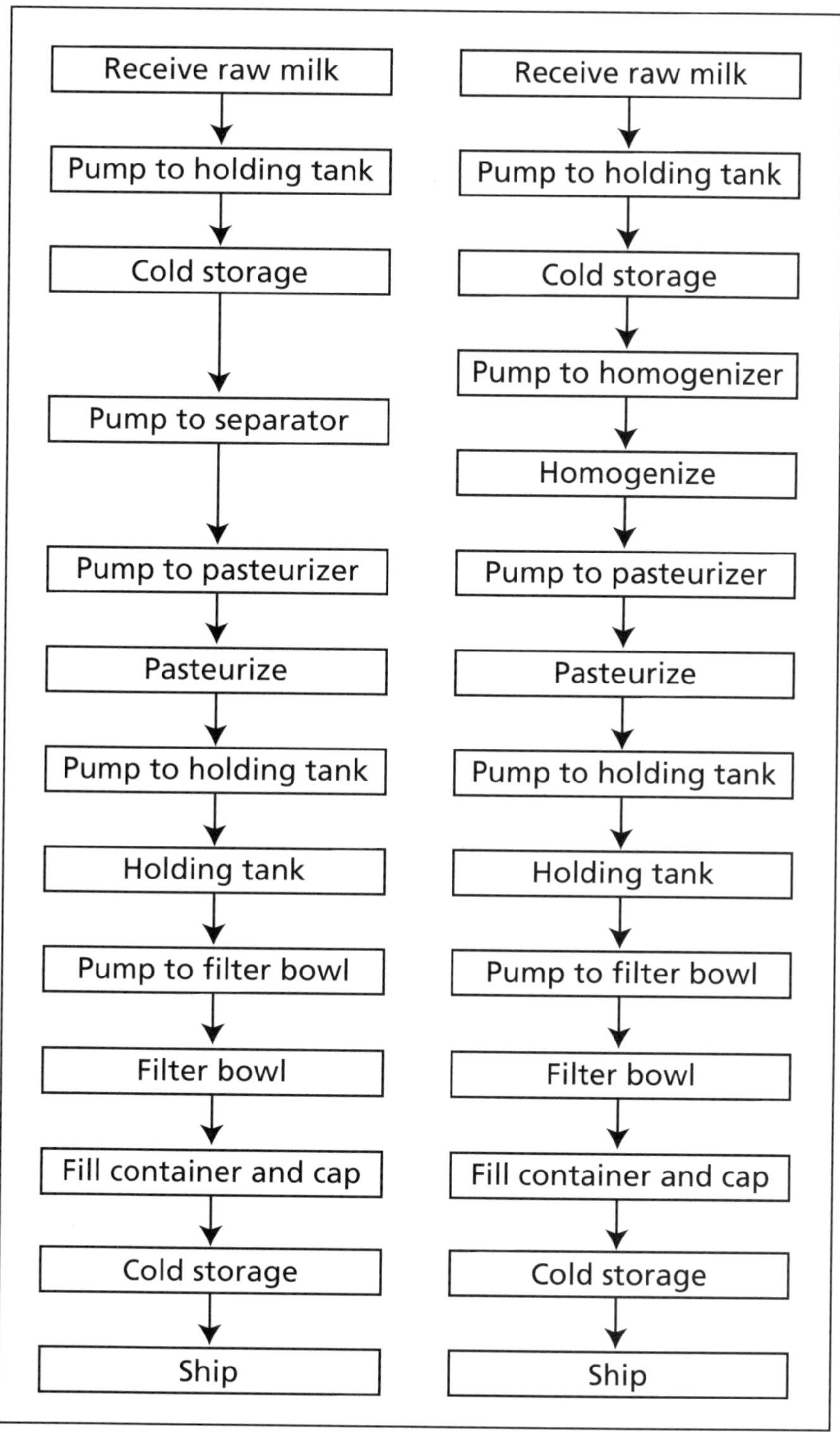

Figure 7.1. Flow diagrams for pasteurized skim milk (left) and whole milk (right).

product. They should accurately reflect the process being used. They can and should, however, be changed if the process is changed.

Note that in figure 7.1 the two processes, while quite similar, are not identical. The whole milk is not separated and is homogenized, whereas the skim milk is separated but not homogenized. Be specific in the development of your own flow diagram. For example, a different fluid milk processor packaging skim milk might actually separate the milk after pasteurization while it is still warm. Thus the process, while containing the same overall steps, would not be similar. This second scenario would have an increased risk of postprocessing contamination due to a failure of SSOPs.

Each of the steps identified in the flow diagram will need to be addressed with respect to the possibility of *each* of three types of hazards that may occur: physical, chemical, and biological. (Antibiotics are a hazard unto themselves, and should be addressed at the time of milk receiving.) Physical hazards include such items as jewelry, hair, twigs, stones in spices, pits, metal or plastic from packaging materials, glass, pens, buttons, nuts/bolts from machinery, or any other object that might make its way into the product. Chemical hazards include cleaning and sanitizing agents, vitamins used for fortifying milk, pesticides, rodenticides, and non-food-grade lubricants used in the facility. The term *biological hazards* typically refers to the presence of pathogenic (disease-causing) bacteria. These organisms may be present in the raw milk, on the skin or clothing of personnel, on the surface of processing equipment, on flies, dust, animals, and manure, and/or in the processing environment itself.

The particular hazard should be identified and an explanation given as to what is being done in the facility to prevent it from occurring. If there is more than one control measure in place, then both control measures should be documented. In the case of receiving milk you might identify the possibility of antibiotic residues in the incoming cheesemilk as a potential hazard. Cite the preventive measure(s) in place and describe when and where they will be performed. In the case of antibiotics you may have a number of different control measures in place. If a single farm is the sole supplier of the milk and it has a no-antibiotics policy in place for its animals, then this documented practice would be the preventive measure. If, however, the cheesemilk comes from farms where there is no such policy, then the control measure should involve the use of an antibiotic-residue-detection system that is performed on each tankload of milk arriving at the facility. In many instances the control measure will be prerequisite programs that are already in place. Chemical residues from cleaners and sanitizing agents are typically addressed in SSOPs, as is the cleanliness and sanitary nature of the surfaces used during production. Similarly, GMPs are the control measures for physical contamination of the product during production. Biological contamination from improperly cleaned and sanitized equipment is addressed by using proper, documented SSOPs. Biological contamination of the product by personnel during production and subsequent handling of product is addressed in GMPs.

Step Two: Identification of Critical Control Points

Once the hazard analysis step has been completed, you may notice that there are many points along the process in which some sort of control can be exerted. In some cases a failure to control something at one point in the process is not critical—the hazard will be prevented, reduced, or eliminated at a later step. In other instances, though, steps will be identified where there is nothing farther along in the process to prevent, reduce, or eliminate the hazard. In this event the consumer is the next to come in contact with the hazard, and the point is considered a *critical control point.* A general means of distinguishing a critical control point from a control point is to answer the following question: Is there a step farther along in the process where the hazard will be prevented, reduced, or eliminated? If there is, then the step is probably a control point, but not a critical one. When in doubt, it is better to have an extra critical control point or two versus too few critical control points. Identify each of the critical control points on the flow diagram and in the hazard analysis with the letters *CCP* and a number designation. These steps will receive extra attention during the manufacture of the product.

Step Three: Setting Critical Limits

For every CCP identified during the hazard analysis step, you will need to establish a critical limit. These critical limits will be used to determine that the system is under control and, therefore, working at its best to minimize the chance of safety problems in the product. The critical limits should be based on scientific analysis of the specific issue being addressed. They should be measurable via an instrument or standard test. Critical limits may include heating cheesemilk to a specific temperature and holding it there for a designated amount of time (pasteurization), a pH value, or, in the case of hard cheeses, the water activity of the product. For example, it is well documented that pasteurization of raw milk will eliminate pathogenic bacteria. The conditions of pasteurization have been developed to ensure the safety of the product leaving the pasteurizer. These conditions include a requirement that every particle of the milk achieve a specified temperature for a specified amount of time. Heating the raw milk to a lower temperature or keeping it there for a shorter time than prescribed for the type of pasteurization being performed (vat versus HTST versus UHT) may not afford a reasonable level of safety.

If there is a heating step in the process whose time–temperature parameters can be documented and shown to meet or exceed those of pasteurization, then it can be used as a critical control point with regard to the elimination of pathogens. It is important that the process be validated by a process authority with knowledge of microbial inactivation of pathogens. Once it has been validated, it is possible to use this alternative process as a critical control point.

Step Four: Developing Procedures for the Monitoring of Critical Limits

Monitoring of critical limits is an active

event in which the process is evaluated in real time. A number of points must be addressed when developing the procedure for monitoring critical limits.

The monitoring process should state *how* the critical limit will be evaluated. In the case of cheese production, if a critical control point were to be identified as the development of acid from an active starter culture, then the "how" of the monitoring could include either a specified titratable acidity (TA) or pH measurement, which must be obtained. In either case the test should be identified and the calibration of the test noted (for example, "the cheese-milk will be evaluated by titration against a standardized 0.1 N solution of NaOH"). The value chosen should be supported with data. Quite often the exact value of interest will be one that has been determined from past production. Documented historical data that can be correlated to a positive end product is especially valuable. The monitoring process also needs to address the frequency of testing, where in the process the critical limit will be monitored, and, finally, who will evaluate the critical limit.

Monitoring can be a done via automated equipment such as continuous recording devices on pasteurizers, or by properly trained individuals in the processing environment who perform a test or take a reading with an instrument. If at all possible, more than one person should be properly trained in the monitoring procedure, so that if the person who normally performs the duty is not available, a second person can monitor the critical limit. Regardless of how the monitoring is done, it must be recorded in order to be valid.

In the example of antibiotics, a critical limit monitoring description might be written as follows: "Each load of milk will be evaluated for the presence of antibiotics before it is allowed into the facility. The milk will be evaluated by receiving personnel using [insert the name of a specific properly validated antibiotic test method]." If these fictitious cheesemakers were then going to change from their established antibiotic-residue test to a different antibiotic-residue test from another manufacturer, then they should revise the HACCP plan to note the name of the new test being used.

Step Five: Record Keeping

HACCP development and decision making are driven by data. It is imperative that the data be recorded. Putting the data on paper make them real and certifiable. Record keeping should include the data obtained during the monitoring of CCPs, verification activities, and SSOP information. Should a safety-related issue with a product occur, these records become a written history of what went on with that particular lot at the time it was produced. It is a means of showing due diligence and demonstrating that the process was kept in control with regard to scientifically valid measures.

It is very important that the recording of data happen as close to real time as possible. Information should not be written on scraps of paper or committed to memory; it needs to be recorded on forms developed for the purpose of record keeping. Data should accurately reflect the readings taken and should not be entered as "dry data." (Dry data is a form of automatic response that does not reflect what was done or evaluated at the time noted on the forms.) Assume, for the sake of example, that because of an issue with a late milk delivery, production is running late, and that historical data have shown that the cleaning and sanitizing crew always perform tasks accurately and completely. Recording an "okay" for all the data points in a preoperational SSOP checklist without actually checking each piece of equipment or surface would in effect be entering dry data. The entering of dry or false data onto record forms is both unethical and illegal. Actions such as these will not only bring the whole process into question, but may in fact invalidate even the best HACCP plan.

Step Six: Corrective Actions

Failures will happen from time to time, and it is from these failures that we learn about the process and how to better manage it. If a particular critical limit is found to fail on a more-than-seldom basis, however, it may be worth reevaluating the effectiveness of the HACCP plan. In those instances when a process fails to meet or exceed the designated critical limit, you must document this failure and follow up by enacting corrective actions. The results of such actions are fourfold: The corrective action should (1) bring the situation back into control (within critical limits), (2) identify the reason for the deviation in the process, (3) identify changes that will be enacted to ensure that the critical limit is kept under control in the future, and (4) verify that measures have been taken to ensure that no product potentially injurious to health is allowed into commerce. If corrective actions are required, they must be documented on a corrective-actions form. This form should address the four points noted above. A properly working, in-control HACCP plan should not require the writing of corrective actions. If a company is writing corrective actions, then it may be time to reevaluate the HACCP plan to determine if the process needs modification. Changes to the plan must be documented in writing and added to the most current HACCP plan. An HACCP plan must accurately reflect the actual process. If a company is making a product by some means other than what is documented in the HACCP plan—even if it is found to be "safe"—then it is not in compliance with the plan and may be cited by regulatory agents.

Step Seven: Verification

Verification must address three different areas of concern:

1. Verification of CCP monitoring records must be performed, and includes a direct observation of the record-keeping forms to ensure that the CCPs were monitored on *at least* the frequency noted in the HACCP plan, and that the data are complete (including information on who performed the task, the result obtained, time of testing, date of testing, and so forth).

2. Verification of monitoring activities by a second individual including the time, date, and name of monitor must be performed.
3. The final verification is the direct observation of monitoring equipment/supply calibration records to ensure they are properly calibrated. This may include reviewing thermometer calibration records, pasteurizer certification records, lot numbers, certification of the strength of NaOH used in titration, and in some cases scale certification records.

THE CHALLENGES OF HACCP

HACCP represents an interesting challenge for the cheesemaker. Short of pasteurization of the cheesemilk and then production of the cheese in a totally sterile environment, there is no guarantee that any cheese is without risk. Even cheeses made from pasteurized milk have been responsible for foodborne illnesses when either the processors have failed to keep the environment clean and sanitary or personnel have not followed GMPs. The use of HACCP in cheese production is complicated by the fact that many of the parameters we can test during the production of a cheese (pH, titratable acidity, temperature) do not represent conditions that will *eliminate* pathogens. In many cases there is no magic number above or below which pathogens will no longer be present. The best a cheesemaker can do is to use certain measurable values to gauge whether the process is progressing in a proper fashion or is meeting governmental regulations.

Development and adaptation of HACCP by small cheese manufacturers has a financial cost associated with both the required monitoring and verification activities, and the work associated with record keeping. While a simple TA setup is relatively inexpensive, the cost associated with certifiable pH meters and temperature probes can be quite high. In many cases the cheesemaker is also responsible for milking, cleaning, sanitation, packaging, shipping, and marketing. Clearly such a person could easily be overwhelmed by the daily record-keeping aspect of HACCP. Without proper documentation, however, even the best-developed and -implemented HACCP plan is of limited, if any, value.

Even in the face of the above-noted shortcomings, cheesemakers can still identify a few areas where it is critical that they have some indication of what is occurring. Often a number of processes collectively add to the development of a cheese with intrinsic qualities that inhibit the growth of pathogenic bacteria. In some instances the combined effect of the processes can even be lethal to pathogenic bacteria. Some of these processes include steps in the production of a cheese that address the following points.

Antibiotic-Residue Issues

This issue must be addressed at the point of receiving milk. There is no step farther down the stream of production that will address it; the only way to eliminate it is to prevent it from the start. If a cheesemaker does not have direct control over the use of antibiotics in the animals that produce the cheesemilk, then this step must be monitored at the point of receiving. And even if you have control over antibiotic use, it is still a good practice to perform a test on the milk as a way to document that there were no antibiotic residues in it. A momentary lapse in judgment that results in the milk from the udder of an antibiotic-treated animal accidentally being added to the bulk tank can result in disaster if it is not identified in time. Failure to identify this hazard can result in the production of adulterated cheese that cannot be sold yet costs the producer in the form of labor and storage.

Heat Inactivation of Pathogens

Safe cheeses are those devoid of pathogenic bacteria that could cause illness or even death in those who eat them. Milk can easily become contaminated with pathogenic bacteria via manure, silage, workers, and/or improperly sanitized machinery; in some instances pathogens are also shed directly into the milk by the animal itself. The best way to prevent pathogenic organisms from becoming a health and safety issue is to prevent them from getting into the milk in the first place. This is not always practical or possible, however, so the alternative is to somehow kill them if they have contaminated the milk. One way to do this is through the application of heat of sufficient temperature to kill the organisms.

The use of pasteurization is one means of eliminating pathogenic bacteria, which may be in the cheesemilk up through the point of actually going through the pasteurizer proper. Pasteurization parameters have been established to ensure a level of public safety by eliminating the most heat-resistant human pathogens thought to on occasion be present in raw milk. There is nothing magical or mythical about pasteurization. The organisms do not know they are experiencing pasteurization; rather, the biochemicals of which they're composed are responding to the heat. The organisms are killed as a result of critical proteins being denatured and the destruction of the cell membrane. In some instances the combined effect of the heating steps in the production of a cheese may supply heat energy equal to, or exceeding, pasteurization. If a heat step can be shown to eliminate pathogenic bacteria to the level obtained during pasteurization, then it would be reasonable to consider the step as a critical control point for the elimination of pathogens in the cheesemilk.

An example of such a heating step might be the time–temperature parameters of the stretching step in the production of Italian cheeses such as mozzarella. By following the temperature of the cheese curd over the time of exposure to the hot water, you may be able to show that the step would achieve sufficient temperatures to kill human pathogens. Similarly, a cheese product that requires a high-temperature cooking step for a sustained amount of time in order to reach a desired moisture content or textural consistency may be an effective heat treatment.

The effective heat-kill of a process can be evaluated by the collection of time–temperature parameters, which a process authority can then use to determine the effective "D-value" of the process. The fact that one company has shown that a heating step it performs is effective at reaching pasteurization equivalence does not automatically validate a similar process at a second company. The temperature and/or heating time may differ significantly from company to company. Once a process has been validated, it is important that the time–temperature parameters reached during production meet or exceed what has been validated. A change in the temperature or time of exposure will require a new validation to ensure that the proposed process change is of sufficient lethality. Pasteurization or its equivalent is not a cure-all. Heat treatment will not prevent pathogens from contaminating the milk after pasteurization or contaminating the finished cheese. This fact highlights the need for a company to have documented and implemented SSOPs in place as a prerequisite program.

Evaluation of Starter-Culture Activity

The chemical changes produced in cheesemilk from the activity of starter culture are discussed in other chapters within this book. With regard to HACCP, the presence of an active starter culture is a safety issue. Starter cultures aid in developing a level of safety in cheesemilk by outcompeting potentially contaminating and pathogenic organisms for the nutrients available in the milk. Starter cultures are typically added at levels far exceeding those of any contaminating organisms. They also produce large amounts of lactic acid, which not only aids in the formation of the curd but also works to lower the pH of the cheesemilk, thereby slowing the growth rate of non-acid-tolerant pathogenic contaminants. As the concentration of acids build within the cheesemilk/curd, the potential growth rate of contaminating pathogens within the milk decreases.

The activity of the starter culture can be measured via either pH or TA. It is possible to use changes in either measurement as a means to evaluate the activity of the starter culture. Ideally, we would have some indication early on in the cheesemaking process that the starter is viable and active. However, even an active starter culture does not absolutely guarantee that pathogenic bacteria will not grow. Instead it is an indicator that the conditions are such that, if the pathogenic bacteria were to be present, they would have a reduced possibility of growing to high numbers. Apparently small differences in acid production can have big safety implications. In one outbreak of salmonellosis associated with Cheddar cheese, it was found that the pH of the uncontaminated cheese was 5.4, while the pH of the contaminated cheese was 5.6. It was suspected that a slow starter culture was the cause of this difference.

Aging

Aging is important in the development of textural and flavor characteristics of cheeses. These issues are addressed in other chapters within this book. While proper flavor and textural development are very important to the cheesemaker, they are not issues that need to be addressed by HACCP.

However, the issue of added safety due to aging is an issue that an HACCP plan would address. At present government regulations require the aging of raw-milk cheeses for at least 60 days, for safety reasons. This requirement was originally based on the belief that coliform bacteria are a good indicator of the possible presence of other pathogenic bacteria. It was thought that, if a cheese was aged under conditions that would eliminate the coliform bacteria, then any salmonella that might be present would also be eliminated, making the cheese safe for human consumption. However, we know that this is not always the case. There are organisms that die more rapidly than 60 days, and others that survive longer. There is no magic number of days of aging that will ensure a completely pathogen-free cheese. The amount of time in which a pathogen can survive in a given cheese depends on a number of factors. These can include the level of contamination by the organism, the activity of the starter culture, the manufacturing process itself, the moisture and salt contents of the cheese, the point in the process where the contaminant enters the cheese, the strain of the organism, and the acid tolerance of the organism. While aging is beneficial as a means of reducing pathogens, it should not be relied upon by the cheesemaker as an infallible cure-all for the presence of pathogenic bacteria. Raw-milk cheese producers would be well served if they did not identify aging as a critical control point, but rather as a condition of the raw-milk cheese identity.

FINAL THOUGHTS

There is no doubt that the production of cheese can be a very rewarding, almost spiritual experience. The production of safe cheeses of a consistently superior quality should not, however, be mystical. The application of the scientifically based principles behind HACCP is clearly beneficial to all cheesemakers. The time taken to develop a hazard analysis and to identify areas of special interest in a manufacturing process is time well spent, if for no other reason than gaining a better understanding of the principles behind the process of cheesemaking.

Ensuring Safety and Quality II: Controlling the Initial Chemical Composition

8

There are three major challenges that every cheesemaker must effectively master in order to produce high-quality cheese day in and day out. The first challenge is to implement an effective quality assurance program based on the HACCP principles described in chapter 7. The third challenge, which is specific to aged cheeses, is to provide the environmental, technological, and artisanal conditions that will transform the bland, newly made curd into the exquisite cheese that you seek to bring to market. Ripening and affinage will be touched on in chapter 10. That leaves the second challenge, the topic of this chapter, which is to produce a cheese that possesses the correct initial chemical composition. Getting the composition right applies to all cheeses but is especially critical for aged cheeses, because the initial composition determines whether the newly made cheese has the potential to ripen along the desired pathway.

In chapter 6 we considered three compositional parameters that strongly influence ripening behavior: the initial pH (which goes hand in hand with the calcium phosphate content), and the moisture and salt contents. If you fail to hit the targets for these three aspects of composition, the ball game is probably over, regardless of what takes place thereafter, because cheese with abnormal composition is predisposed to ripen abnormally. With respect to cheese composition, then, there are two questions that should be of concern to every cheesemaker:

1. What are the correct compositional targets for your cheese?
2. How do you know whether or not you're hitting those targets on a regular basis?

Over the years I have observed that many farmstead cheesemakers experience problems because they do not realize the importance of hitting key compositional targets and have no way of knowing whether they are hitting the targets on a regular basis. The objective of this chapter is to introduce some basic tools that can be used to gain control over the initial chemical composition of your cheeses.

ESTABLISHING A TARGET ACIDITY SCHEDULE

Gaining control over initial cheese composition begins with gaining control over key parameters during cheesemaking. As touched on in chapter 5, times and temperatures at each step in the cheesemaking process should be specified, and the acid development by the starter culture should follow a defined schedule. By controlling the conditions of time, temperature, and acidity from one vat to the next, you can eliminate much of the variation in moisture content and initial pH that can cause undesirable fluctuations in quality and compromise safety.

The first step in gaining control over acidity development is to learn how to measure acidity, either as titratable acidity (TA) or pH (see chapter 4). Titratable acidity works well with liquid samples (milk and whey, for instance), but it is not easily adapted to measuring solid curd samples during cheesemaking. Therefore, titratable acidity is most effective when used for cheeses that produce a steady stream of whey that can be collected and measured throughout manufacture (such as Cheddar). Titratable acidity is less useful with cheeses that develop most of their acidity during pressing, after most of the whey has been expelled (Swiss-type cheeses, for example). In contrast, pH measurements can be readily performed on both liquid (milk and whey) and solid (curd, cheese) samples, thus making pH the method of choice for many cheeses.

Regardless of whether you measure pH or TA during cheesemaking, it is necessary to develop target acidity values at key stages during manufacture to use as benchmarks for evaluating starter performance. In other words, it isn't very useful to measure acidity unless you know what the acidity values should be at critical stages of the process. Some popular cheeses such as Cheddar and mozzarella have well-known schedules for optimum acidity that have been determined through extensive scientific research. For many other cheeses, especially artisanal cheeses, only general guidelines for acidity development may be available, in which case you will need to create your own acidity benchmarks that are specific for your cheese.

The spreadsheet shown in table 8.1 provides an example of an optimum acidity schedule for the manufacture of Cheddar cheese made with traditional bulk starter. The target values for pH and TA at various stages during manufacture were determined through scientific research that was carried out in the 1940s (Wilson et al., 1945; Lochry et al., 1951; Price and Calbert, 1951). The spreadsheet also includes examples of abnormally slow and abnormally fast acid schedules for purposes of comparison. The data in table 8.1 are represented graphically in figure 8.1. In these examples all three vats (optimum, fast, and slow) were drained at the same time (starting at three hours after adding the

Mfg Stage	Time (min)	pH Optimum	pH Slow	pH Fast	TA Optimum	TA Slow	TA Fast
add starter	0.0E+01	6.6	6.6	6.6	0.16	0.16	0.16
	30	6.6	6.6	6.55	0.16	0.16	0.165
add rennet	60	6.55	6.6	6.5	0.165	0.16	0.17
cutting	90	6.5	6.55	6.4	0.12	0.1	0.14
	120	6.45	6.53	6.3	0.125	0.1	0.15
	150	6.35	6.5	6.2	0.13	0.105	0.16
	180	6.25	6.45	6.05	0.135	0.105	0.17
draining	210	6.15	6.35	5.9	0.14	0.11	0.18
	240	5.95	6.15	5.65	0.22	0.16	0.3
	270	5.7	5.95	5.45	0.3	0.2	0.4
milling—fast	290			5.35			0.48
	300	5.5	5.75		0.4	0.27	
milling—optimum	330	5.35	5.6		0.5	0.37	
	360		5.5			0.41	
milling—slow	410		5.35			0.52	

Table 8.1. Spreadsheet containing examples of optimum, fast, and slow acidity schedules, as measured by pH and titratable acidity, for the manufacture of Cheddar cheese. In this example all three vats (optimum, fast, slow) were drained starting at three hours after starter addition and milled at pH 5.45 (curd pH). Titratable acidity values are for whey throughout cheesemaking. The pH values are for whey through the end of draining and for curd thereafter.

starter culture) and milled at the same curd pH (5.45). Examination of figure 8.1 reveals that the fast and slow vats differed from the optimum vat in two major respects. First, the acidity of the whey at at the start of draining differed substantially among the three vats (slow = pH 6.45; optimum = pH 6.25; fast = pH 6.05). Second, the total manufacturing time (the time from starter addition to milling) also differed substantially (slow = 375 minutes; optimum = 330 minutes; fast = 290 minutes).

These differences in draining acidity and total manufacturing time have important implications for cheese quality. Draining the slow vat at high whey pH (6.45) would result in greater retention of calcium phosphate in the final cheese and, therefore, a higher initial pH. Conversely, draining the fast vat at low whey pH (6.05) would result in less calcium phosphate in the final cheese and a lower initial pH. Furthermore, the longer manufacturing time of the slow vat (375 minutes) would provide more time for syneresis and thus favor cheese with a lower initial moisture content and less residual lactose (due to less whey retention). The combination of less residual lactose and more calcium phosphate in the cheese produced from the slow vat would give rise to an abnormally high initial pH. In contrast, the short manufacturing time of the fast vat

(290 minutes) would provide less time for syneresis and thus favor cheese with a higher initial moisture content and more residual lactose. The combination of more lactose and less calcium phosphate in the cheese produced from the fast vat would give rise to an abnormally low initial pH. In summary, the three different acidity schedules represented in figure 8.1 would produce three very different cheeses. The slow vat would be abnormally low in moisture and abnormally high in pH, while the fast vat would be just the opposite. Neither would be expected to ripen normally or develop optimum quality.

The acidity schedules represented in figure 8.1 were generated from measurements that were taken every 30 minutes throughout cheesemaking. Farmstead cheesemakers may find it difficult to measure acidity at such frequent intervals and may soon become discouraged with the idea of routine acidity determination. Fortunately, it usually isn't necessary to take measurements this frequently in order to gain valuable information. Generally speaking, most of the essential information can be acquired by measuring the acidity at a few key stages during cheesemaking. For example, the key points for acidity measurement in Cheddar cheesemaking are as follows: the starting milk; the milk immediately after the starter culture is added, if bulk starter is used; the whey immediately after cutting; the whey at the beginning of draining; and the whey or the curd at milling. (The pH of the curd will typically be about 0.1 pH unit lower than that of the whey.) The graphs shown in figure 8.2 were generated using only these acidity measurements. Almost the same diagnostic information can be obtained from these acidity measurements as from measurements made every 30 minutes. Thus although it is always desirable to take as many pH measurements as possible to provide the most accurate picture of acidity development, the essential information can often be gleaned from a few key measurements.

What should you do if you don't know what the optimum acidity schedule looks like for the type of cheese you make? You will have to establish your own acidity benchmarks based on empirical experience. To do this, you will need to decide what are the critical stages during cheesemaking at which acidity should be measured, and whether to measure pH or TA. As noted previously, pH measurement is preferred for most cheeses because pH can be measured on both liquid whey and solid curd samples. It is worth noting that another advantage of pH over TA measurement is that the target values for pH during cheesemaking are not affected by changes in milk composition. In other words, once you have determined the optimum pH values at various stages of manufacture for your cheese, those targets remain fixed regardless of the composition of your cheesemilk. In contrast, the target values for TA can shift with changes in the solids content, specifically the casein content, of your milk, because casein micelles are rich in weak acids (such as phosphoric) that are measured by TA. For example, fresh milk with high protein content may have a TA of 0.18 percent (expressed as lactic acid), whereas the TA of low-protein milk may only be

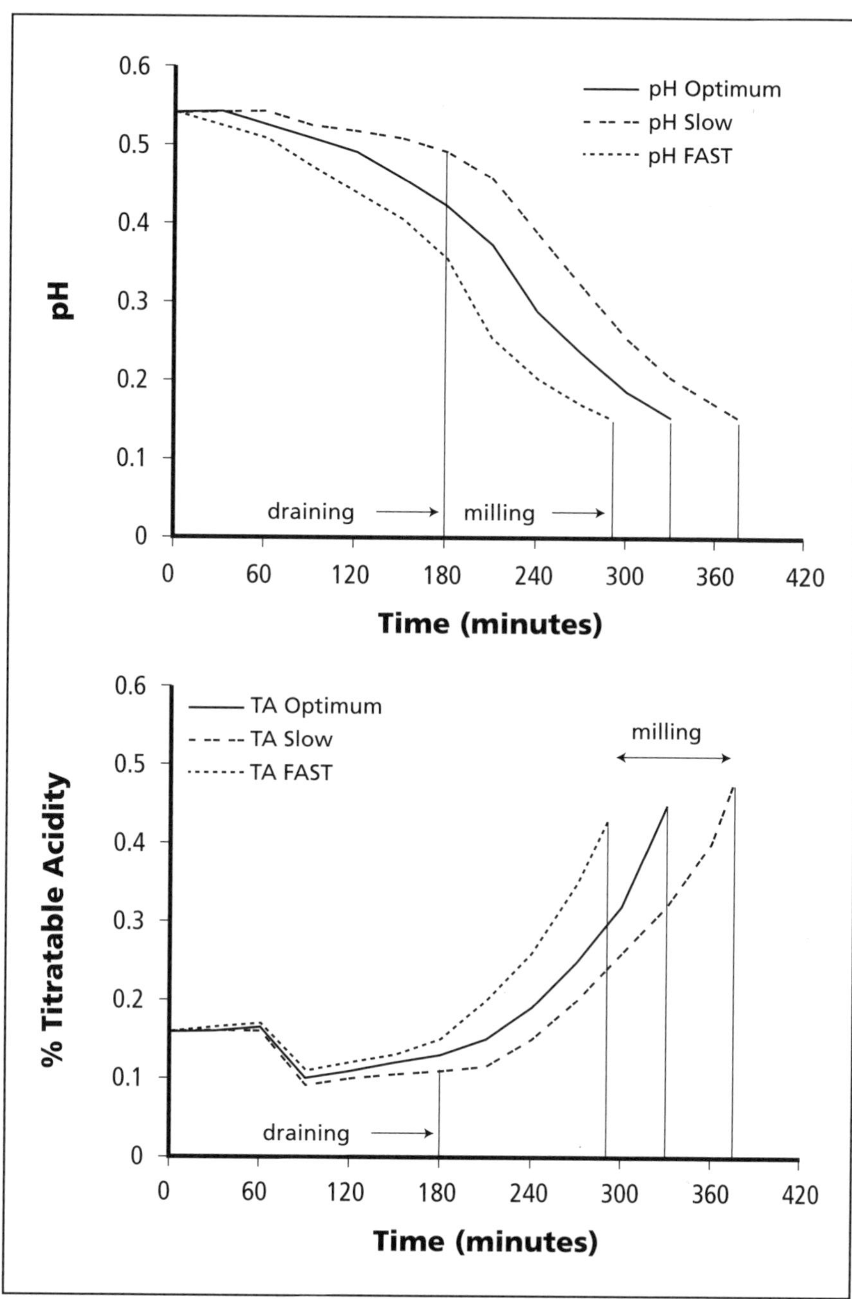

Figure 8.1. Examples of optimum, fast, and slow acidity schedules, as measured by pH (top) and titratable acidity (bottom), for the manufacture of Cheddar cheese. In this example all three vats (optimum, fast, slow) were drained starting at three hours after starter addition and milled at pH 5.45 (curd pH). Titratable acidity values are for whey throughout cheesemaking. The pH values are for whey through the end of draining and for curd thereafter.

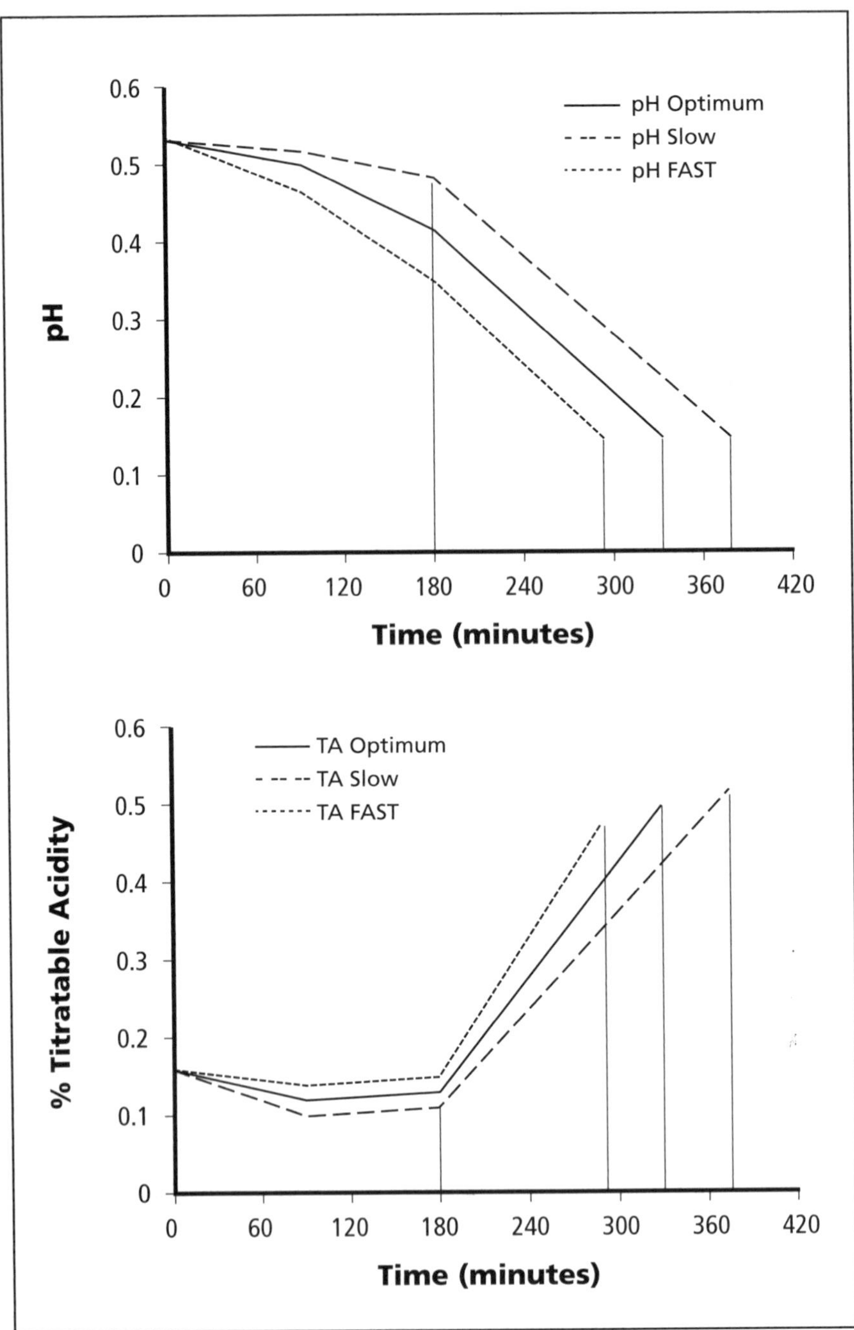

Figure 8.2. Examples of optimum, fast, and slow acidity schedules, as measured by pH (top) and titratable acidity (bottom), for the manufacture of Cheddar cheese. In this example all three vats (optimum, fast, slow) were drained starting at three hours after starter addition and milled at pH 5.45 (curd pH). Measurements were made after starter addition and at cutting, draining, and milling.

0.14 percent. Thus the high-protein milk starts out with a higher TA value than the low-protein milk. Furthermore, the targets for TA at any given stage in cheesemaking will be higher for the high-protein milk (due to its higher initial TA and greater amount of casein micelles, which absorb hydrogen ions during cheesemaking) than for the low-protein milk. On the other hand, the pH targets would be the same for both milks.

Acidity measurements should generally be taken of the milk immediately after starter addition, the whey immediately after cutting, and the whey at the start of dipping/draining. For bloomy-rind, blue mold, smear-ripened, and washed-rind cheeses, the pH of the curd, or of the whey as it flows off the draining racks, should also be measured once or twice at specified times during draining/molding (for example, after a certain number of turns). The final pH measurement should be taken on the cheese the next day. For cheeses that are pressed immediately after dipping/draining (such as Swiss and hard Italian types), it may not be practical to take any pH measurements during pressing. The final pH measurement should be made upon completion of pressing the next day.

Once you have decided at what points to measure acidity, you should take those measurements routinely on every vat of cheese and then track each vat and take note of the final quality of the cheese at the end of ripening. Over time you will build up a database of acidity schedules versus ultimate cheese quality, from which you can develop a profile of the optimum acidity development that correlates with superior-quality cheese. This profile then becomes the basis for the benchmarks that you will use to evaluate starter performance from one vat to the next. This may seem like a lot of work, but once you have established a target acidity schedule you will possess a powerful management tool.

In addition to building a database of acidity schedules and cheese quality, I recommend that you concurrently measure the initial salt and moisture contents of your cheeses as discussed below. This will allow you to develop a more complete profile of your optimum cheese that includes targets for initial salt and moisture contents along with acidity development.

ACIDITY TESTING AS A MANAGEMENT TOOL

Assuming that you know the optimum acidity schedule for your cheese and that you routinely measure acidity at key stages during cheesemaking, there are two different ways you can use this information to make management decisions. First, you can use it to make *online* manufacturing adjustments (that is, as the cheese is being made) in an effort to salvage what might otherwise become a bad batch of cheese. For example, according the data in figure 8.2, it was evident by the time of cutting that the acidity of the fast vat was developing more quickly than desired. When confronted with this situation, a seasoned maker of Cheddar cheese might consider taking steps to slow down the starter culture and promote whey expulsion to limit the damage from runaway acid development. You might, for instance, cook to a slightly higher temperature in an attempt to slow down the starter and drive more moisture out of the curd. Stirring may be continued during draining to further help with whey expulsion. If the acidity continues to develop rapidly during cheddaring, you might consider cheddaring at a higher-than-normal temperature, turning the curd slabs more frequently, and piling them less, again to try to slow down the starter and encourage whey expulsion. These online adjustments may help to prevent the making of a high-moisture, high-acid, and poor-quality cheese. Conversely, if the vat shows evidence of slow acidification early in manufacture, you might perform cooking and cheddaring at lower-than-usual temperatures, turn the curd slabs less frequently, and pile them higher to stimulate the starter culture and reduce the expulsion of whey.

Second, you can use acidity data to monitor changes in the acidity schedule that may occur gradually over time, so that appropriate adjustments can be made to bring the acid development back on target before it strays so far as to negatively affect the quality of your cheese. For example, the pH changes during manufacture may gradually slow down (as evidenced by an increase in total manufacturing time) over the course of several weeks at certain times of the year due to increasing levels of protein in the cheesemilk. (Remember, casein micelles absorb hydrogen ions during cheesemaking and release calcium in return. Therefore, the more casein in the cheesemilk, the more hydrogen ions are absorbed, and thus the more lactic acid must be produced during cheesemaking in order to achieve the target levels for acidity.) In this situation you might decide to increase the amount of starter added to the next vat or increase the ripening time to speed up the acidity development and bring it back on target. Conversely, when the protein content of the milk decreases, the pH changes during manufacture will tend to speed up (as evidenced by a decrease in total manufacturing time), and you might decide to cut back on the amount of starter or the ripening time to slow down the acid development and get it back on target. Of course, if you're not aware that the acidity schedule is changing, you will not know that it needs to be adjusted—hence the importance of routine measurement of acidity. Other factors that may cause the acidity schedule to slow down include a buildup of bacteriophage in the cheesemaking room, an increase in mastitis in the herd, and the onset of late lactation. The take-home message is that gradual changes in acidity schedule must be counteracted before they become large enough to adversely affect cheese quality.

An extreme example of how the acidity schedule may change over time is illustrated in figure 8.3. These data are from a study conducted in Ireland on the effect of late-lactation milk on the manufacture and quality of mozzarella cheese (Lucey et al., 1991). Mozzarella cheese was made once weekly for four weeks (October 23 to November 14) using milk from a spring-calving herd of cows that were approaching the end of their lactation cycle. For purposes of comparison, a vat

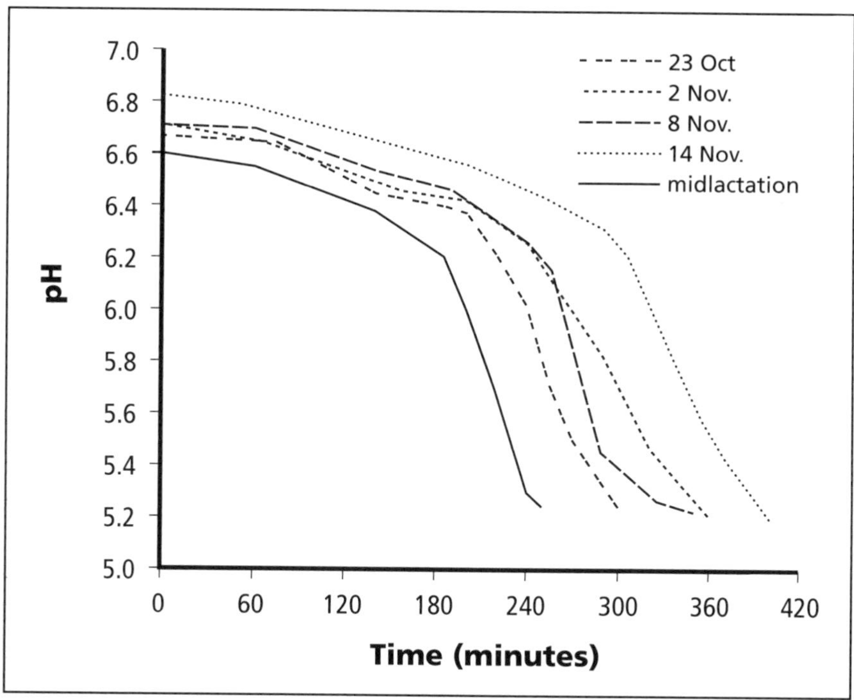

Figure 8.3. Acidity schedules of four vats of mozzarella cheese made weekly between October 23 and November 14 from milk obtained from a seasonal herd of cows that were approaching the end of their lactation cycles. Cheeses also were made concurrently from milk obtained from a different herd in midlactation. The average total manufacturing time for cheeses made from midlactation milk was 250 minutes. In contrast, the total manufacturing times for cheeses made from late-lactation milk increased from 300 minutes on October 23 to 400 minutes on November 14 due to the progressive inhibition of the starter culture. (From Lucey et al., 1991.)

of cheese was also made each week using milk from a different herd of cows that were in midlactation. The cheeses made from the midlactation milk had consistent acidity development over the four-week period. The average acidity values for the four vats made from midlactation milk are shown in figure 8.3, along with the acidity values for the four vats of cheese made from the late-lactation milk over the same time period. Two conclusions are obvious. First, all four vats made from late-lactation milk showed much slower acidity development (therefore longer manufacturing times) than the midlactation vats. Furthermore, the acidity development of the late-lactation vats became progressively slower as autumn progressed. Consequently, the total manufacturing time increased from 255 minutes on October 23 to 400 minutes on November 14 due to starter inhibition. As expected, the quality of the cheese made from the late-lactation milk became progressively worse with each passing week. The extreme changes shown in figure 8.3 were due to the Irish practice of producing milk seasonally, coupled with their complete reliance on pasture feeding. Most American farmstead cheesemakers will probably never experience changes during lactation as extreme as those in Ireland because our management practices and conditions are different, but all farmstead cheesemakers can expect their acidity schedules to drift from time to time. The bottom line is that all cheesemakers should routinely monitor acidity and make adjustments when necessary to maintain consistent starter performance.

ESTABLISHING TARGETS FOR INITIAL COMPOSITION

Occasionally I receive urgent phone calls from farmstead cheesemakers who are experiencing quality problems with their cheeses and need help. Quality problems can result from a variety of factors, and identifying the specific cause can sometimes be like searching for the proverbial needle in the haystack. For example, the cheese may have become contaminated with undesirable microorganism(s) (including coliform, clostridium, or psychrotrophic bacteria) due to a lapse in sanitation or an unanticipated change in environmental conditions. The acidification schedule during cheesemaking may have changed due to a number of different factors. The initial cheese composition may have become abnormal for a variety of reasons. The conditions during ripening (temperature, humidity, and the like) may have changed and caused the problem. Where do you begin? Inevitably, my conversation with the distressed cheesemaker turns to two vital diagnostic questions:

1. Are you consistently producing cheese according to the optimum acidity schedule, or has the acidity schedule drifted from the target values?
2. Are you consistently producing cheese with the correct initial composition (pH, salt, moisture), or has the composition shifted from the target values?

Unfortunately, most farmstead cheesemakers draw a blank at this point, which means that we are starting at square one. Perhaps the solution to the cheesemaker's dilemma simply involves getting the acidity schedule and/or the initial composition back on target, which generally can be accomplished fairly easily by adjusting the manufacturing conditions. However, if we do not know the targets for acidity and composition, we cannot easily make the correct diagnosis and formulate a remedy to get back on track. Consequently, precious time will be lost, and time is of the essence when problems strike. On the other hand, if we can rule out incorrect acidity development or initial composition as causes of the problem, then we can focus on other possible sources, such as microbiological contamination or environmental conditions during ripening and affinage that may have caused the problem. Most problems can be diagnosed and corrected much more quickly if the cheesemaker has taken the time up front to establish the optimum acidity schedule and initial composition targets.

In the previous section we considered the importance of establishing a target acidity schedule and hitting that target routinely. Let's now turn our attention to developing targets for initial composition. As we learned in chapter 6, the moisture content, salt content, and initial pH strongly influence cheese ripening and quality. Furthermore, these parameters can be measured relatively easily and at relatively low cost, making them feasible for use by most farmstead cheesemakers.

Methods for Sampling Cheese

The first step in testing for initial cheese composition is to obtain a sample of the cheese. Ideally you want a sample representative of the entire batch of cheese produced from the original vat of milk. This is easier said than done, though, because composition will vary to a greater or lesser extent from one cheese to the next within a batch, and also within a single cheese, particularly if the cheese has been brine-salted or dry-salted at the surface. Thus as a practical matter you will never be able to obtain a perfect measurement of the overall cheese composition. Nevertheless, if you employ sound sampling and analysis techniques you will be able to obtain approximate measurements that are far superior to having no measurements at all, and that can be used to make sound management decisions.

If you produce very small cheeses such as Camembert, you can afford to use an entire cheese for testing, which provides the best measurement of the average composition. For larger cheeses, you will probably want to obtain samples in the least destructive manner possible, so that the remainder of the block or wheel can be ripened and sold. Sampling is a relatively simple task for cheeses such as Cheddar that are dry-salted before pressing because such cheeses are reasonably uniform in composition. Perhaps the most practical and least destructive method for sampling is by means of a cheese trier (figure 8.4). Stainless-steel triers of various lengths (4.3 to 11.8 inches/11 to 30 cm, depending on the size of the cheese to be sampled) can be purchased from dairy supply companies. Ideally, the trier should be long enough to extend from the sampling surface to the center of the cheese. It should be kept meticulously clean. The trier should be sterilized or sanitized by immersing it in boiling water or a sanitizer solution, and air-dried before each use to limit the introduction of mold contamination into the shaft that is produced in the interior of the cheese during sampling. The trier should be inserted into the cheese until it reaches the approximate center of the block or wheel, rotated through one complete turn, and then carefully withdrawn so that an unbroken core of the desired length is removed. A second core should be obtained by inserting the trier into the surface opposite the one from which the first core was removed (see figure 8.5). It is important that the cores extend the entire length from the surface to the center of the cheese, because cheese composition may vary with distance from the surface. For very large blocks of cheese, additional core samples may be obtained according to the sampling plans shown in figure 8.5 to obtain a more

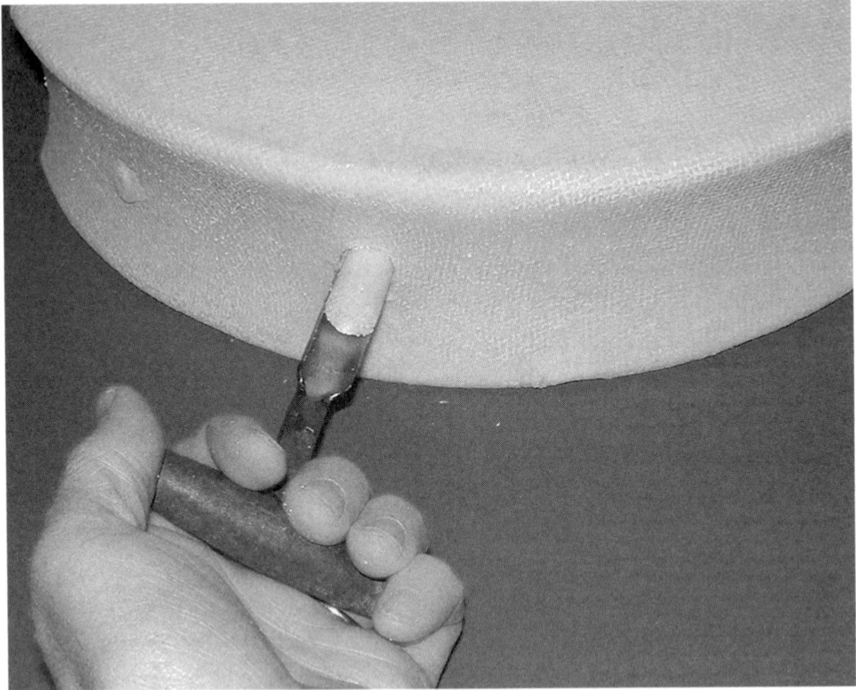

Figure 8.4. The cheese trier is perhaps the most practical and least destructive method for sampling cheese.

accurate estimate of the overall composition. The top ½ inch/1.3 cm of each core should be cut off and used to plug the hole left by the trier to minimize mold growth and moisture loss. The plug should be smeared with a sealing compound, inserted into the hole, and then smeared again at the surface once the plug is in place to create an airtight seal. Sealing compound can be obtained from dairy supply companies or prepared by heating a 1:1 mixture of paraffin wax and beeswax together or a mixture of 60 percent white petroleum jelly with 40 percent paraffin wax to obtain a spreadable jell (IDF, 1980; Kosikowski and Mistry, 1997).

Cheeses that are brine-salted and/or dry-salted at the surface pose a much greater sampling challenge because such cheeses generally contain large, systematic gradients in composition. Specifically, the salt content is highest at the surface and decreases progressively with increasing depth, whereas the moisture content follows the opposite trend. Under these circumstances, core samples obtained with a cheese trier will overrepresent the lower-salt, higher-moisture interior of the cheese and underrepresent the higher-salt, lower-moisture exterior. Therefore, a more representative and accurate sampling plan is to remove a sector or piece of the cheese according to the plans shown in figure 8.6. Unfortunately, these sampling plans are far more destructive to the cheese than obtaining core samples, and

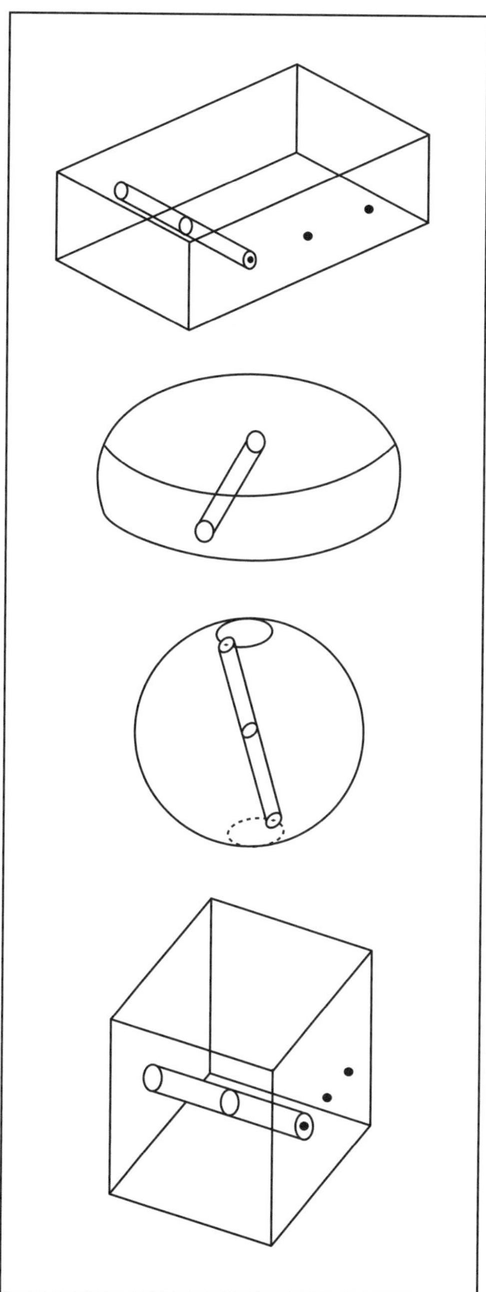

Figure 8.5. Sampling plans for cheeses of various sizes and shapes by means of a trier. (Adapted from International Dairy Federation. 1980. "Milk and Milk Products—Guide to Sampling Techniques." *Provisional International IDF Standard* 50A. IDF, Brussels.)

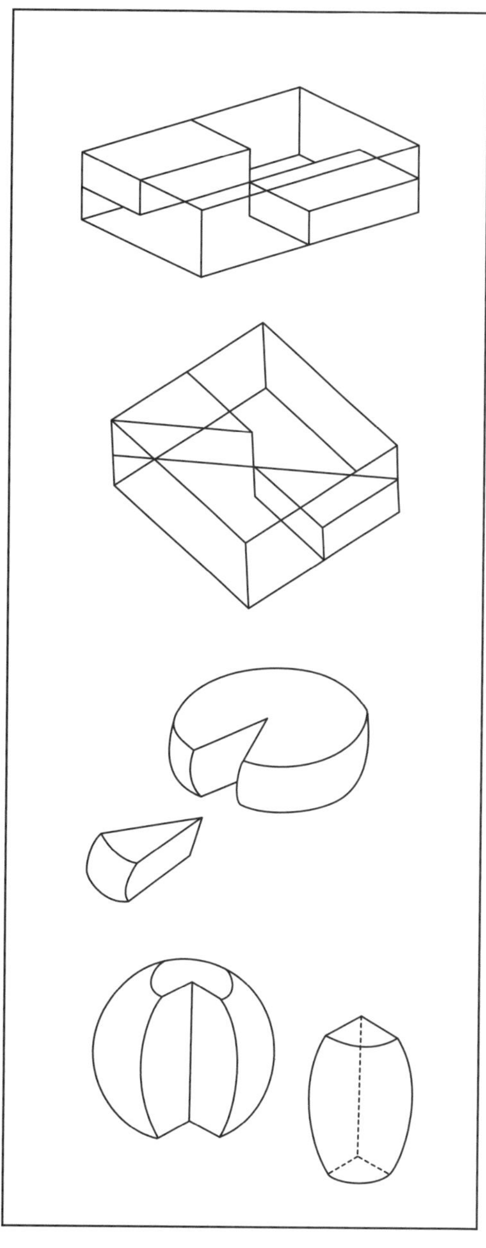

Figure 8.6. Sampling plans for cheeses of various sizes and shapes by cutting a sector. This method is particularly appropriate for brine-salted and dry-salted cheeses. (Adapted from International Dairy Federation. 1980. "Milk and Milk Products—Guide to Sampling Techniques." *Provisional International IDF Standard* 50A. IDF, Brussels.)

some farmstead cheesemakers may not be willing or able to sacrifice an entire cheese, or a large portion thereof, in order to obtain a representative sample for composition testing. If you fall into this camp, don't despair. You can still obtain useful, albeit imperfect, approximations of cheese composition by obtaining core samples (it is especially important that each core spans the entire distance from surface to center of the cheese) according to the plans shown in figure 8.5. The bottom line is that core sampling of brine- and dry-salted cheeses for composition testing is far superior to no composition testing at all.

Sampling for initial composition should be performed on a specified date—for example, at seven days after manufacture (for brine-salted cheeses, seven days after the cheese is removed from the brine). If you use core samples to test brine-salted cheeses, it is especially important to perform the sampling at a fixed time after manufacture because composition gradients (salt and moisture contents) within the cheese change continuously, which may affect the composition measurement obtained from the core samples.

Cheese will immediately begin to lose moisture when exposed to the atmosphere. Therefore, the core samples (at least two) from the block or wheel should be placed immediately in a tightly sealed plastic bag (such as Whirl-Pak) or wrapped tightly in aluminum foil to prevent moisture loss. The samples should be held in refrigerated storage (40°F/4°C or lower) and, ideally, analyzed for composition within 24 hours. If necessary, properly sealed samples can be stored cold for several days before analysis. However, if samples develop mold at any time before analysis, they have been held too long and should not be used for testing. Just before analysis, the cores should be cut into small pieces with a knife, combined in a blender jar, and grated at high speed in a household blender to produce a finely ground sample of cheese particles. The ground cheese sample should be mixed thoroughly and then immediately placed in a tightly sealed airtight plastic bag or a universal milk sample vial and refrigerated if not analyzed immediately. Ground cheese particles rapidly lose moisture to the atmosphere due to their large surface area, so you must work quickly during cutting, blending, and mixing to avoid moisture loss. Also, avoid any open headspace in the plastic bag or sample vial above the cheese sample. Finally, finely ground cheese tends to develop mold very quickly; analyses should be performed within 24 hours whenever possible.

Moisture Analysis

The moisture content of cheese can be measured by several different methods. Moisture-testing instruments that are based on infrared or halogen drying give rapid and relatively inexpensive results, provided they are calibrated and operated properly. The infrared and halogen drying instruments currently start at around $2,000 to $3,000. Other, more sophisticated instruments that are based on microwave drying or near-infrared absorption are available, but they are considerably more expensive.

The least expensive way to test for moisture, and perhaps the most practical for farmstead cheesemakers, is by traditional oven drying using a gravity convection or mechanical convection oven. This analysis is conducted by accurately weighing a finely ground sample of cheese into a dry, disposable aluminum weighing dish, placing the dish containing cheese into a 212°F/100°C oven for 24 hours (during which time the moisture is driven off from the cheese), and then cooling the sample and reweighing to determine the amount of moisture in the original cheese sample. To conduct this test you will need a balance that can weigh to at least 0.01 gram. A suitable digital electronic balance (0.01 g) can currently be obtained for $300 and up. (A balance is a good investment because it is also needed for salt testing, and can be used for general-purpose weighing of small quantities, such as direct-set starter culture.) You will also need a laboratory oven capable of maintaining a temperature of 212°F. There are two types of ovens available: the gravity convection oven and the mechanical convection or forced-draft oven. The mechanical convection oven gives more accurate and precise moisture measurements than the gravity convection oven because it contains a fan that circulates the air inside the oven and thus maintains a more uniform temperature throughout. In contrast, gravity convection ovens do not provide for air circulation within the oven other than the convection currents that occur naturally during heating. Consequently, the temperature within the oven can vary by several degrees depending on the exact location, which results in less reliable moisture test results. Mechanical convection ovens start at around $1,500, whereas gravity convection ovens can be purchased for about $500 and up. Finally, you will need a desiccator, which is a sealed vessel (preferably plastic) containing a moisture-absorbent material such as calcium sulfate that maintains a very dry atmosphere. The desiccator is used to cool sample dishes in a dry atmosphere. The procedure for moisture analysis by oven-drying is as follows:

1. Dry a suitable number of disposable aluminum weighing dishes in the oven at 212°F/100°C for at least one hour and then cool in a sealed desiccator for at least 30 minutes. Once dried, the dishes should be stored in the desiccator until use and handled with metal tongs to prevent transfer of moisture from your skin to the dish.
2. Weigh two empty aluminum weighing dishes to at least 0.01 gram for each cheese to perform duplicate analyses. (You should always analyze each cheese in duplicate and take the average of the two test results as your reading.) Add 2 to 3 grams of finely ground cheese to each dish and reweigh. Subtract the weight of the empty dish to obtain the wet weight of the cheese sample.
3. Place the aluminum dishes containing cheese samples in the 212°F/100°C oven for 24 hours, plus or minus one hour.
4. Remove the dishes from the oven and cool in a desiccator for at least 30 minutes.
5. Reweigh the dish plus dried cheese. Subtract the weight of the empty dish to obtain the dry weight of the cheese sample.

6. Calculate the total solids and moisture contents of the cheese samples as follows:

$$\% \text{ total solids} = \frac{\text{dry weight of cheese}}{\text{wet weight of cheese}} \times 100\%$$

$$\% \text{ moisture} = 100 - \% \text{ total solids}$$

Salt Analysis

The salt content of most cheeses can be measured easily and inexpensively using titrator strips for chloride such as the Quantab test strip. The chloride titrator consists of a graduated plastic strip that is impregnated with silver ions. The bottom of the strip is placed into a water extract of the cheese sample. The extract containing chloride ions from the cheese sample then diffuses by capillary action into the strip, and the chloride ions in the extract react with silver ions in the strip to form silver chloride, which causes the strip to change color from orange to white. The greater the concentration of chloride ions in the extract, the greater the reaction, and the higher the color change from orange to white progresses up the graduated strip. The final height of the color reaction is correlated with the chloride content, and therefore salt content, of the cheese sample. The procedure for salt analysis by the chloride titrator method is as follows:

1. Weigh 10.00 g of finely ground cheese into a clean blender jar.
2. Add 90 ml of boiling water (chloride-free) to the blender jar containing cheese.
3. Blend the sample plus water at high speed in a blender for at least 30 seconds to extract the chloride from the cheese. Ideally, the cheese particles should disperse completely during blending, but this will depend on the type of cheese. Cheeses that fail to disperse and remain as particles or congeal into a melted mass should be blended for an additional 60 seconds.

   If the cheese still fails to disperse, the following procedure should be tried. Weigh 10.00 g of grated cheese into a 250 ml glass beaker and add 90 ml water (chloride-free) at room temperature. Cover the beaker tightly with aluminum foil to prevent evaporation, and heat the contents on a hot plate to boiling. Stir the hot liquid to disperse the cheese.
4. Cool the hot water extract to room temperature. Keep the container covered tightly during cooling to prevent evaporation.
5. Fold a qualitative-grade filter paper into a cone and place the cone directly into the water extract.
6. Place a high-range (300 to 6,000 ppm Cl^-) Quantab test strip into the filtrate that collects at the bottom of the filter paper cone and allow the reaction to proceed to completion, at which time the band at the top of the strip turns from orange to purple.
7. Read the titrator scale at the leading edge of the white front and convert the reading to percent NaCl using the conversion table supplied with the test strips. Multiply the result by 10 (to account for the dilution) to obtain percentage NaCl in the cheese.

As noted earlier, if you do not know what the initial moisture and salt contents of your cheese should be, you can develop target ranges at the same time that you develop your targets for acidity development. That is, along with acidity measurements you should take moisture and salt measurements routinely on every vat of cheese and then track each vat and take note of cheese quality at the end of ripening. In this way you can build up a database of acidity schedules and salt and moisture contents versus ultimate cheese quality and develop a profile of the optimum acidity schedule and initial composition. Again, this may seem like a lot of work, but once you have established your targets you will possess a powerful management and diagnostic tool that will make your life easier in the long run.

Composition Testing as a Management Tool

Ideally, composition testing should be performed on every vat of cheese for purposes of routine surveillance. However, this is not practical for most farmstead cheesemakers. Fortunately, less frequent testing (say, weekly) can still provide a valuable assessment of whether you are consistently hitting the composition targets. The data in figures 8.7 through 8.9 illustrate how weekly composition testing can be used to advise manufacturing adjustments aimed at maintaining cheese composition within the optimum ranges for moisture and salt contents. The data are from a study of cow's-milk Cheddar cheese produced by a Vermont farmstead cheesemaker who was switching from year-round to seasonal milk and cheese production. We expected that milk composition would vary more widely across season under the new seasonal and largely pasture-based approach to milk production, and we wanted to evaluate the effect of that variation on the composition and quality of the resulting cheese. The variation in fat and protein contents of the milk produced during this study were discussed previously in chapter 3 (see figure 3.7).

Weekly moisture values for cheeses produced between June 1 and December 21 are shown in figure 8.7. We knew from the research literature and through previous experience that the optimum target for initial moisture content for this rindless, long-aged (more than one year) Cheddar cheese was about 35 to 36 percent, represented by the dashed lines in figure 8.7. It is evident that moisture content followed an increasing trend as the season progressed; consequently, many of the cheeses exceeded the target range from late summer onward. Elevated moisture content is a common problem that seasonal cheesemakers encounter toward the end of lactation in late autumn. Therefore, the cheesemaker in this study took deliberate action during autumn to produce a lower-moisture cheese. These efforts were only partly successful; the moisture values crept up and remained on the high side from September onward.

The weekly values for cheese salt content are shown in figure 8.8. Again, we knew from the research literature and through previous experience that the initial salt content should fall within the range of about 1.5 to 1.8 percent, represented by the dashed lines in figure 8.8, to produce the best-quality aged Cheddar. The data in figure 8.8 reveal that the

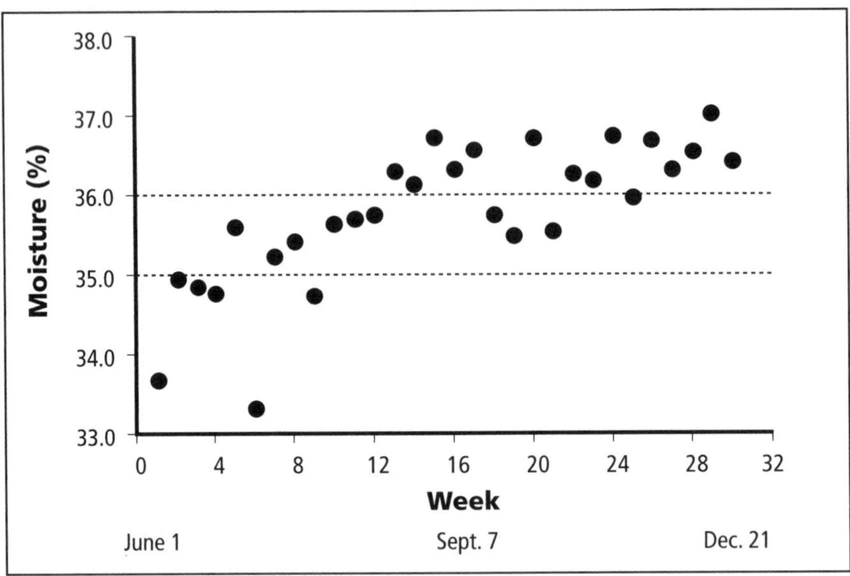

Figure 8.7. Seasonal variation in the moisture content of Cheddar cheese produced from the milk of a herd of Brown Swiss cows at Shelburne Farms in Shelburne, Vermont. The entire herd commenced milk production in spring and was dried off at the end of autumn. The dashed lines indicate the target range for optimum moisture content for aged Cheddar cheese. (Source: Dixon, 1999.)

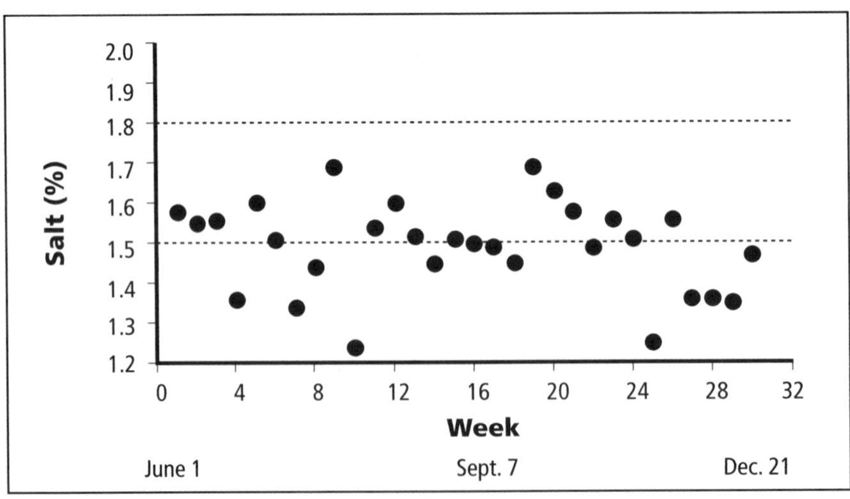

Figure 8.8. Seasonal variation in the salt content of Cheddar cheese produced from the milk of Shelburne Farms' herd of Brown Swiss cows. The entire herd commenced milk production in spring and was dried off at the end of autumn. The dashed lines indicate the target range for optimum salt content for aged Cheddar cheese. (Source: Dixon, 1999.)

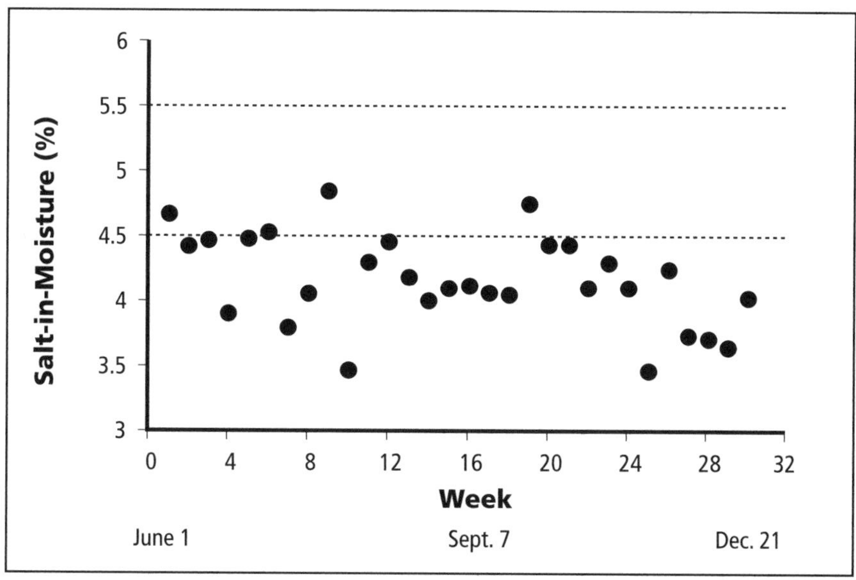

Figure 8.9. Seasonal variation in the salt-in-moisture content of Cheddar cheese produced from the milk of Shelburne Farms' herd of Brown Swiss cows. The entire herd commenced milk production in spring and was dried off at the end of autumn. The dashed lines indicate the target range for optimum salt-in-moisture content for aged Cheddar cheese. (Source: Dixon, 1999.)

majority of cheeses fell either near or below the lower limit of the target range. Thus overall these seasonally produced Cheddar cheeses tended to be on the low side for salt content throughout the cheesemaking season and on the high side for moisture content during the second half of the season. Hence the cheeses strayed significantly from their optimum targets for initial composition, thereby decreasing their probability of consistently attaining the highest quality.

As discussed in chapter 6, the data for moisture and salt contents can be combined mathematically by dividing the percent salt by the percent moisture to give a parameter known as salt-in-moisture. Salt-in-moisture, which is basically the brine concentration of the water phase in the cheese, is one of the most useful parameters for optimizing initial cheese composition. By optimizing the salt-in-moisture content, you will tend to automatically optimize both salt and moisture contents simultaneously. Thus you can go a long way toward gaining control over initial cheese composition by optimizing the salt-in-moisture content for the particular cheese type you make. In the case of aged Cheddar cheese, the optimum salt-in-moisture content has been determined through research over the years to fall within the range of about 4.5 to 5.5 percent.

The salt-in-moisture values for the cheeses are shown in figure 8.9, with the optimum range represented by the dashed lines. Clearly most of the cheeses fell below the target range, signaling to the cheesemaker that the salting rate should be increased, especially during the second half of the cheesemaking season. Increasing the salting rate would have simultaneously increased the uptake of salt by and expulsion of whey from the curd during salting, resulting in a higher-salt, lower-moisture cheese with a higher salt-in-moisture content. Unfortunately, the test results from this study were not available at the time of cheesemaking; therefore, the cheesemaker did not know that the cheeses were falling below the optimum range for salt-in-moisture. It would have been a simple manufacturing adjustment to increase the salting rate, had the cheesemaker known to do so.

In summary, the Cheddar cheeses represented in figures 8.7 through 8.9 were generally lower in salt and higher in moisture than their optimum ranges throughout much of the season. This could have been easily corrected if the cheesemaker had been aware of the salt-in-moisture data in figure 8.9. By week eight it would have been evident that salt-in-moisture was hovering at or below the lower limit for the optimum range. Alerted to this, the cheesemaker could then have increased the addition of salt to the curd in subsequent vats, which would have increased the salt-in-moisture content by simultaneously decreasing the moisture and increasing the salt contents. By keeping the salt-in-moisture at around 5 percent—the middle of the optimum range—the cheesemaker would have automatically produced a cheese better suited for the long aging process to follow. Ultimately, better-quality cheese would likely have been produced. In the same manner, we can go a long way toward optimizing the initial cheese composition and ultimate quality of almost any type of cheese by optimizing its initial salt-in-moisture content.

CHAPTER 8 REFERENCES

Dixon, P. 1999. "The Effect of Seasonal Milk Production on Cheddar Cheese Composition, Quality and Yield." M.S. thesis, University of Vermont, Burlington.

International Dairy Federation. 1980. "Milk and Milk Products—Guide to Sampling Techniques." *Provisional International IDF Standard* 50A. IDF, Brussels.

Kosikowski, F. V., and V. V. Mistry. 1997. *Cheese and Femented Milk Foods*, Vol. 1: *Origins and Principles*. F. V. Kosikowski, LLC, Great Falls, Va.

Lochry, H. R., G. P. Sanders, J. P. Malkames, and H. E. Walters. 1951. "Making American Cheddar Cheese of Uniformly Good Quality from Pasteurized Milk." USDA Circular 880.

Lucey, J. A., P. S. Kindstedt, and P. F. Fox. 1991. "Seasonality: Its Impact on the Production of Good Quality Mozzarella Cheese." *Irish Journal of Agricultural and Food Research* 30: 41–48.

Price, W. V., and H. E. Calbert. 1951. "Cheddar Cheese from Pasteurized Milk." University of Wisconsin Bulletin 464.

Wilson, H. L., A. A. Hall, and L. A. Rogers. 1945. "The Manufacture of Cheddar Cheese from Pasteurized Milk." *Journal of Dairy Science* 28: 187.

Catherine W. Donnelly, Ph.D.

The Pasteurization Dilemma

9

As American consumers express increased demand for specialty cheeses, especially those produced via centuries-old European traditions, an inevitable debate has ensued concerning the merits of raw-milk cheesemaking. Cheesemaking evolved centuries ago as a way of preserving raw milk through a fermentative process. Initially through selection of the beneficial natural flora in milk, and later through the addition of defined beneficial organisms as starter cultures, cheese is a form of milk that is processed for preservation and safety. However, cheeses can become contaminated with harmful pathogens as a result of their presence in the raw milk used for cheesemaking and subsequent survival during the cheesemaking process. Alternatively, bacterial pathogens can contaminate cheese through postprocessing contamination if sanitation and other measures during manufacture are not sufficient to prevent recontamination. The characteristics of the specific cheese variety will determine the potential for growth and survival of microbial pathogens. Ripened soft cheeses present a higher risk for growth and survival of pathogens because there are no barriers to prevent pathogen growth. In comparison, in aged hard cheeses, a combination of factors including pH, salt content, and water activity (the amount of available moisture) interact to make these cheeses microbiologically safe.

While certain European countries permit the manufacture and sale of soft ripened, semisoft, and hard, aged raw-milk cheeses, the United States restricts raw-milk cheesemaking and importation to those cheeses that are aged for 60 days or longer. Cheeses included in this category are principally the aged hard cheeses including Cheddar, Swiss, and Italian hard cheeses such as Parmesan and Romano, as well as a variety of soft and semisoft cheeses. The Code of Federal Regulations (21 CFR, Part 133), lists specific requirements pertaining to cheeses by category.

Today the raw-milk cheese debate is intensifying, as challenges are being made to the microbiological safety merits associated with the 60-day rule. There is general confusion surrounding the scientific basis for permitting raw-milk cheese manufacture, particularly related to aged hard cheeses and the chemical and compositional characteristics that make these cheeses safe. In an attempt to provide clarification on this scientifically complex and frequently emotional issue, we will review in this chapter the principles that are designed to ensure the safe manufacture of cheeses. The role of pasteurization will be discussed, along with examples of where pasteurization is needed to ensure cheese safety, and where aged raw-milk cheese can be safely manufactured in the absence of pasteurization. The pasteurization dilemma is therefore a complex issue, one with profound implications for the future of global trade, public health, and artisan cheesemaking. Translated into practical application, however, this chapter is designed to provide an overview of the safety implications concerning raw-milk cheese manufacture and will provide advice to cheesemakers deciding whether to make raw-milk cheese.

WHAT IS PASTEURIZATION?

Pasteurization is the heat treatment of milk and is designed to destroy disease-producing microorganisms that have public health significance. The concept of pasteurization was pioneered by the famous French scientist Louis Pasteur (1822–1895), who discovered in the 1860s that subjecting grape juice to a mild heat treatment could eliminate spoilage organisms and ensure the production of wine of consistent high quality. This concept was later employed as a public health intervention, and has had a profound impact upon the safety of dairy products. The use of pasteurization to ensure the safety of milk and dairy products is perhaps the most significant public health achievement of the last century. Prior to the advent of milk pasteurization, serious illnesses, including typhoid fever, scarlet fever, diphtheria, tuberculosis, and brucellosis, were associated with raw milk consumption. We might then ask: If pasteurization is so effective at ensuring the safety of dairy products, why is mandatory pasteurization not required for manufacture of all cheeses?

The U.S. Food and Drug Administration (FDA) regulates milk and dairy products produced in and imported into the United States. European cheesemakers are governed by EU directives, which permit the manufacture of raw-milk cheeses, but U.S. regulations are very different. Current regulations governing the use of raw, heat-treated, and pasteurized milk for cheesemaking were promulgated in 1949 (U.S. FDA, 1950; 21 CFR, Part 133). Cheesemakers have two options to ensure the safety of their cheese: They can pasteurize milk destined for cheesemaking, or they can hold their cheese at a temperature of not less than 35°F/1.7°C for a minimum of 60 days (the so-called 60-day rule). Pasteurization of milk for cheesemaking is performed using regulations contained in the Pasteurized Milk Ordinance (PMO). The PMO specifies that each particle of milk will be subjected to heat treatments, which include high-temperature, short-time or holding (vat) pasteurization. Cheesemakers who produce cheeses made from pasteurized milk require capital investment in equipment that meets the mandates of the PMO. Pasteurizer operators must be licensed, and must submit to a comprehensive inspection process conducted by state and federal regulators. The choice of whether to employ pasteurization or to age cheeses for 60 days or longer involves a number of considerations, which include food safety implications, the desired quality and sensory characteristics of the cheese, yield losses (which come as a result of heat treatment of milk proteins), the cost associated with capital investment in pasteurization equipment, and concerns about consistency of milk quality.

PATHOGENS OF CONCERN IN RAW MILK

Raw milk can serve as a source of harmful bacterial pathogens. *Salmonella, Listeria monocytogenes, Staphylococcus aureus,* and enteropathogenic *Escherichia coli* are associated with raw milk, and these are clearly the pathogens that pose the greatest risk to the safety of aged raw-milk cheese. *E. coli* 0157:H7 is a very serious pathogen that can readily contaminate raw milk on the farm. *E. coli* 0157:H7 was first characterized in 1982 as a result of outbreaks in North America. More than 70 cases of *E. coli* 0157:H7 infection, characterized by bloody diarrhea, hemolytic uremic syndrome (HUS), and kidney failure, have been traced to the consumption of raw milk (Borczyk et al., 1987; Martin et al., 1986; Bleem, 1994), with a few additional cases in England linked to yogurt (Morgan et al., 1993). Cattle are thought to be the primary source of this important human pathogen, and ground beef is the food most frequently linked to human illness outbreaks. A study of *E. coli* transmission on four Wisconsin dairy farms identified contaminated animal drinking water as the most probable source of infection of animals and a potential control point to eliminate this pathogen. Intermittent shedding of this pathogen by cattle suggests reinoculation from an environmental source rather than colonization of the pathogen. When the 60-day aging rule was promulgated, *E. coli* 0157:H7 did not exist. Therefore, it is reasonable to examine whether current regulations provide public health protection for this important bacterial pathogen. Cheesemakers who manufacture raw-milk cheeses should be aware of this important human pathogen and its potential consequences in cheesemaking.

Salmonella enterica serovars Enteritidis, Typhimurium, and Dublin have been associated with foodborne disease outbreaks involving raw milk and milk products (Cody et al., 1999; De Valk et al., 2000; Maguire et al., 1992; Villar et al., 1999). *S. enterica* serovar Dublin is present in dairy cattle and was identified as the most invasive of the *Salmonella* bacteria for humans in studies conducted in Denmark (Lester et al., 1995).

Salmonella can be regularly isolated from raw milk. Wells et al. (2001) examined recovery of *Salmonella* from fecal samples obtained from dairy cows in 91 herds from 19 U.S. states. *Salmonella* spp. were recovered from 5.4 percent of the samples. Recovery rates from cows on farms with less than 100 animals were much lower (0.6 percent) than those from farms with more than 100 cows, where recovery rates were 8.8 percent. The incidence of *Salmonella* in milk would be expected to occur at a much lower frequency than in fecal samples. Most farmstead cheesemakers maintain small dairy herds, where lower *Salmonella* frequencies would be expected.

Salmonella typhimurium definitive-type (DT) 104 emerged in the United Kingdom as an important source of human infection in the late 1980s (Threlfall et al., 1996). Subsequent outbreaks of human illness traced to dairy sources were reported in Vermont (Friedman et al., 1998), Nebraska, California (Cody et al., 1999), and Washington State (Villar et al., 1999). This organism possesses resistance to multiple antibiotics, making it an organism of concern for cheesemakers. Two outbreaks of *S. typhimurium* DT104 infection were recently linked to consumption of Mexican-style soft cheese manufactured from raw milk (Cody et al., 1999; Villar et al., 1999).

Extremely low levels of *Listeria monocytogenes* (1.0 *Listeria*/ml) exist in commercial bulk tank raw milk. *Listeria* is eliminated by pasteurization; thus any contamination of processed dairy products results from postpasteurization contamination from the dairy plant environment. *Listeria* can be found within this environment in places such as floors in coolers, floor drains, freezers, and processing rooms (particularly entrances); in cases and case washers, floor mats and footbaths, and conveyor belts (Klausner and Donnelly, 1991). *Listeria* are able to form biofilms that protect them from cleaning and sanitizing agents. Pritchard et al. (1994) found that farmstead cheesemaking operations had a significantly higher incidence of *Listeria* contamination than those without an on-site dairy farm. This information suggests the increased need for attention to cleaning and sanitation practices in order to control *Listeria* contamination in farmstead facilities. Arimi et al. (1997) demonstrated the link between on-farm sources of *Listeria* contamination (dairy cattle, raw milk, and silage) and subsequent contamination of dairy-processing environments. These findings demonstrate the importance of farm-based Hazard Analysis and Critical Control Points (HACCP) programs for controlling *Listeria* (see chapter 7). This work also demonstrated that aggressive cleaning and sanitation is necessary, because *Listeria* can persist in processing environments for a number of years.

Abou-Eleinin et al. (2000) analyzed 450 goat's-milk samples obtained from the bulk tanks of 39 goat farms for *Listeria* over a one-year period. Milk samples from 46 percent of the farms tested positive for *Listeria* at least once during the yearlong study. Isolation rates of *Listeria* were markedly higher during winter (14.3 percent) and spring (10.4 percent) compared with autumn (5.3 percent) and summer (0.9 percent). Similar trends have been previously reported for cow's milk. Farmstead cheesemakers should be aware of the role of silage feeding and seasonal onset of listeriosis, particularly in goats, which show enhanced sensitivity to this illness.

MILK QUALITY

The quality of raw milk used for cheesemaking is perhaps the most important consideration when producing raw-milk cheeses. European cheesemakers pay great attention to raw-milk quality, knowing that this will in turn dictate cheese quality. Raw-milk quality is assessed through an analysis of bacterial numbers and somatic cell counts (SCCs). When low, these indicators generally indicate high-quality milk, but as numbers of bacteria and somatic cells increase, the potential for contamination of milk and cheese with pathogens also increases. It is very important for the cheesemaker to have a program in place that provides regular monitoring and control of bacteria and somatic cell counts in milk. In addition to potential safety concerns, as raw-milk bacteria and SCCs increase, cheese quality and cheese yield may decrease. Raw-milk quality decreases during refrigerated storage; therefore, utilization of milk as soon as possible for cheesemaking protects cheese quality. In artisan cheesemaking, if milk is produced on the farm, the reduction in elapsed time from milking to cheesemaking ensures the manufacture of high-quality cheese. Immediate manufacture of milk into cheese without cooling reduces the opportunity for the growth of undesirable bacteria. Conversely, when milk is cooled and held in a bulk tank, the potential for growth of psychrotrophic (cold-loving) pathogens and other bacteria is increased. Cheesemakers should be aware of how raw milk treatment and storage can impact cheese quality and consistency.

The European Community Directives 92/46 and 92/47 contain regulations for the production and marketing of raw milk, heat-treated milk, and milk-based products. These regulations establish hygienic standards for raw-milk collection and transportation that focus on issues such as temperature, sanitation, and microbiological standards, enabling production of raw milk of the highest possible quality. Raw cow's milk must meet certain quality standards—for example, a standard plate count at 86°F/30°C of less than 100,000 cfu/ml and somatic cell counts less than or equal to 400,000 per ml of milk. To meet these and other established standards, EU countries employ HACCP principles in the production of fluid dairy products. This involves identification of sites to be monitored and evaluated to ensure that products are produced under the correct conditions, as well as the development of critical limits established by valid and verifiable parameters. In the case of fluid milk products, many processors have identified length of shelf life as a critical limit. Shelf life is influenced by a number of factors, including cleaning and sanitizing of pipelines and milking equipment, condition of the raw milk used to make the product, and storage temperature. Post-pasteurization contamination of milk is problematic if the processing/packaging environment is not maintained. Some regulations, such as those of the EU, have established microbiological limits at the sell-by date for cheeses and other products. With respect to regulations governing the use of raw milk for cheesemaking, limits have been established for *Staphylococcus aureus* in raw milk. Finished cheeses must meet specific hygienic standards, in which case the presence of *S. aureus* and *Escherichia coli* indicate poor hygiene. U.S. cheesemakers may benefit from the adoption of some of the EU directives.

HEAT TREATMENT OF MILK

Milk contains compounds (including lactoferrin, lysozyme, and lactoperoxidase) that are inhibitory to the growth of some pathogens. However, these inhibitors are sensitive to heat and may be destroyed during pasteurization. Pitt et al. (2000) demonstrated that the growth of raw milk pathogens, including *Staphylococcus aureus, Salmonella enteritidis,* and *Listeria monocytogenes,* was reduced in raw milk held at 99°F/37°C for 72 hours, compared with growth observed in pasteurized milk. Further research is needed to understand the impact of natural inhibitor systems in raw milk, which help to control growth of pathogenic bacteria during cheesemaking. For instance, the lactoperoxidase system is a naturally occurring inhibitory system in raw milk and contains three components: lactoperoxidase, thiocyanate, and hydrogen peroxide. All three components are required for inhibitory effects. Gram-negative psychrotrophic organisms, such as pseudomonads, are inhibited by this system. Bovine milk typically contains sufficient lactoperoxidase to inhibit pathogens, but quantities of thiocyanate and hydrogen peroxide can be variable. Pitt et al. hypothesized that the inhibitory effect of raw milk in their study was due to activation of the lactoperoxidase system by hydrogen peroxide–producing lactic acid bacteria naturally present in the raw milk that grew at 99°F/37°C. Thus pasteurization may partially inactivate the lactoperoxidase in milk, facilitating growth of pathogens in cheese during and after cheesemaking.

Cheeses made from milk that has been given a subpasteurization heat treatment (or *thermization*) are technically classified as raw-milk cheeses. This process can be beneficial when milk has to be transported and stored under refrigeration, or when there will be a time delay prior to cheese manufacture. The use of thermization may help to reduce the growth of psychrotrophic bacteria that cause quality defects in cheese, but may also damage natural inhibitor systems in milk. Much of the milk used in the United States for aged raw-milk cheesemaking is subjected to some form of heat treatment, generally thermization. As a rule this treatment consists of heat treatment at 131°F/55°C for a period ranging from 2 to 16 seconds. While frequently used to improve cheese consistency, the impact of subpasteurization heat treatment, combined with the interactive effects of salt and pH during subsequent ripening on pathogens such as *Listeria, Salmonella,* and *Escherichia coli,* has not been well explored.

The pathogens *Salmonella, Listeria monocytogenes, Staphylococcus aureus,* and enteropathogenic *Escherichia coli* pose the greatest risk to the safety of cheese (Johnson et al., 1990a; DeBuyser et al., 2001; Leuschner and Boughtflower, 2002). Epidemiological investigations conducted in France reveal that most cases of reported illness linked to soft and semisoft cheeses are due to *S. aureus*. If active lactic acid starter cultures are used, *S. aureus* is usually a low-risk pathogen because it is a poor competitor with other organisms (Johnson et al., 1990a). However, *S. aureus* may grow to high levels in cheeses where active starter-cultures are not used, thereby presenting a risk for toxin production. Factors that contribute to the microbiological safety of cheese include milk quality, starter-culture or native lactic acid bacteria growth during cheesemaking, pH control, salt, control of aging conditions, and chemical changes that occur in cheese during aging (Johnson et al., 1990c). Other technologies (for example, the use of starter cultures that produce substances inhibitory to pathogens) may provide opportunities to add more barriers to the growth of bacterial pathogens. It is particularly important for makers of raw-milk cheese to have a documented and systematic approach to ensure product safety, complete with record keeping.

Growth of microbial pathogens in cheese is dictated by external (extrinsic) and internal (intrinsic) parameters. Important intrinsic parameters include moisture content, pH and acidity, nutrient content, redox potential, presence of antimicrobial compounds (either those occurring naturally or those added as food preservatives, such as nitrite), and the presence of competitive microflora (ICMSF, 1986). All these factors dictate the potential for bacterial pathogens to grow, persist, or decline in cheeses. Extrinsic parameters include factors such as the type of packaging/packaging atmosphere, time and temperature of storage and holding conditions, processing steps, product history, and traditional use. The interaction of these factors dictates the potential for microbial growth in cheese.

Depending on the cheese variety, intrinsic parameters such as pH may serve to enhance or inhibit the growth of bacterial pathogens. Ryser and Marth (1987a) studied the behavior of *Listeria monocytogenes* in Camembert cheese. The high moisture content and neutral pH of this surface-ripened cheese facilitate growth and survival of pathogens such as *Listeria*. Growth of *Listeria* in Camembert was found to parallel the increase in cheese pH during ripening and reached extremely high populations that could cause human illness. This contrasts with blue cheese, where *Listeria* failed to grow and decreased in number during 56 days of storage (Papageorgiou and Marth, 1989). *Penicillium roqueforti,* which is inoculated during cheesemaking, may produce bacteriocins against *L. monocytogenes*. In hard cheese varieties such as Colby and Cheddar, *L. monocytogenes* populations decrease during aging, with survival strongly influenced by the moisture content and the pH (Ryser and Marth, 1987b; Yousef and Marth, 1990). Cheeses such as Camembert and feta have nearly identical composition in terms of moisture content, water activity, salt-in-water percentage, and ripening temperature. Fully ripened Camembert has a pH of 7.5, however, while feta's pH of 4.4 prevents *Listeria* growth.

CHEESES MADE FROM RAW MILK

In the United States and other parts of the world, the manufacture of cheese from raw milk is a topic that is being revisited from the perspective of microbiological safety. Pasteurization of milk prior to cheesemaking is but one step that may reduce the risk of the presence of pathogenic bacteria in cheese. Current U.S. regulations governing the use of raw, heat-treated, and pasteurized milk for cheesemaking were promulgated in 1949 (U.S. FDA, 1950; (21 CFR, Part 133). One of two options can be selected by cheesemakers to ensure the safety of cheese: Pasteurize milk destined for cheesemaking, or hold cheese at a temperature of not less than 35°F/1.7°C for a minimum of 60 days. Recent research has shown that *Salmonella typhimurium, Escherichia coli* 0157:H7, and *Listeria monocytogenes* can survive well beyond the mandatory 60-day holding period in Cheddar cheese prepared from pasteurized milk (Ryser and Marth, 1987a; Reitsma and Henning, 1996). In a referral to the National Advisory Committee on Microbiological Criteria for Foods in April 1997, the FDA asked if a revision of policy requiring a minimum 60-day aging period for raw-milk hard cheeses was necessary. The FDA expressed concern that 60 days may be insufficient to provide an adequate level of public health protection, citing numerous studies and outbreak investigations documenting the presence of *Listeria, Salmonella,* and *E. coli* 0157:H7 in raw milk. Of particular concern was the report by Reitsma and Henning detailing survival of *E. coli* 0157:H7 in aged Cheddar cheese. The FDA did note, however, that there was "limited epidemiological evidence that foodborne illness results from consumption of raw-milk hard cheeses that have been aged for 60 days." Groups outside the U.S. have also recently expressed concern about the safety of raw-milk cheeses. The Institute of Food Science and Technology (IFST, 2000) in the U.K. issued a position statement drawing attention to the potential public health hazards posed by pathogenic bacteria in cheeses made from raw milk. The IFST indicates that these hazards apply particularly to soft and semisoft cheeses. Codex Alimentarius is presently recommending a "combination of control measures" (including pasteurization) to achieve the appropriate level of public health protection (Groves, 1998). The National Academy of Sciences recently recommended establishment of process criteria in lieu of mandatory pasteurization and labeling of cheeses made from raw milk at retail.

When outbreaks of human illness associated with consumption of aged raw-milk cheese are reviewed, it is clear that in the majority of instances factors other than the use of raw milk contributed to pathogens being present in cheese (Donnelly, 2001). Further, in challenge studies examining the fate of pathogens in aged cheese, confounding factors can also explain the appearance of pathogens following 60 days of aging. Such confounding parameters in actual outbreaks or challenge studies involve the use of pasteurized versus raw milk in cheesemaking trials, inadequate development of acidity during cheesemaking, low salt levels, contamination by ill employees during manufacturing, temperature abuse of milk designed for cheesemaking, and environmental contamination during cheesemaking.

PREVIOUS REVIEWS ON THE SAFETY OF RAW-MILK CHEESES

Two comprehensive reviews have been published regarding outbreaks of human illness linked to cheese consumption. Johnson et al. (1990b) conducted a comprehensive review of the epidemiological literature during the 40-year period between 1948 and 1988. Only six outbreaks of illness transmitted by cheese produced in the United States were identified. Postpasteurization contamination of cheese was the primary cause of these outbreaks. Improper pasteurization equipment and/or procedures were implicated in only one outbreak each in the United States and Canada, and use of raw milk was a factor in one outbreak in each of these countries. No outbreaks were linked to hard Italian cheese varieties such as Parmesan, Romano, and provolone. In rare instances Swiss and Cheddar cheeses were linked to food-poisoning outbreaks. Factors other than pasteurization cited by Johnson et al. (1990b) as contributors to cheese safety include milk quality and management, lactic starter management, pH, salt, controlled aging conditions, and natural inhibitory substances in raw milk.

Altekruse et al. (1998) reviewed all cheese-associated outbreaks reported to the Centers for Disease Control and Prevention (CDC) from 1973 through 1992. These authors noted how infrequently large, cheese-associated outbreaks were reported during the period, and suggested that improvements in cheesemaking methods and process control have resulted in cheese being a safer product. There were 32 cheese-associated outbreaks, 11 of which were attributed to contamination at the farm, during manufacturing, or during processing. Of the 11 outbreaks attributed to contamination prior to distribution, 5 were associated with Mexican-style soft cheese versus only 1 outbreak that was linked to Cheddar cheese. It is notable that no outbreaks reported to the CDC from 1973 through 1992 were from raw-milk cheese that was aged for a minimum of 60 days.

Outbreaks Involving Cheddar Cheese

In 1976 seven lots of Cheddar cheese manufactured from pasteurized milk were contaminated with *Salmonella heidelberg* and were responsible for 339 confirmed cases of illness and an additional 28,000 to 36,000 cases of illness (Fontaine et al., 1980). The cheese had been aged for less than 60 days, and improper pasteurization was cited as the cause of this outbreak. Follow-up with the first few patients led epidemiologists to suspect that cheese eaten in Mexican-style restaurants as the vehicle of infection. Seven lots of Cheddar cheese produced from pasteurized milk by a Kansas manufacturer and purchased from a single Denver distributor were identified as the potential sources of contamination. The epidemic began in July in two widely separated Colorado cities: Denver and Pueblo. Levels of *S. heidelberg* in these cheeses were estimated to be 0.36 to 1.8 per 100 g. The pH of the contaminated cheese was 5.6, which may have been a factor in this outbreak. Poor manufacturing practices coupled with inadequate control programs at the cheese plant were cited as causative factors. The Kansas State Health Department had recorded numerous instances of noncompliance with Good Manufacturing Practices. The Kansas Board of Agriculture required that raw milk contain less than three million organisms per ml, and the grade B or surplus grade A milk used at the plant greatly exceeded this standard. In the production of cheese, raw milk was stored for one to three days in an unrefrigerated holding tank prior to pasteurization.

A large Canadian outbreak of salmonellosis linked to consumption of Cheddar cheese was reported in four Canadian Atlantic provinces (Newfoundland, New Brunswick, Prince Edward Island, and Nova Scotia) between January and July 1984. This outbreak proved to be the largest single epidemic of salmonellosis ever to occur in Canada, involving more than 2,700 cases of illness (Bezanson et al., 1985; Johnson et al., 1990b). Production of the cheese, which was manufactured from either pasteurized (165°F/73.8°C for 16 seconds) or heat-treated (152°/66.7°C for 16 seconds) milk, was traced to a single plant on Prince Edward Island. Testing of the raw-milk supply identified two cows in separate herds, one that shed *Salmonella typhimurium* and the other, *S. heidelberg*. Levels of *Salmonella* in the cheese were low, ranging from 0.36 to 9.3 per 100 g. The pH of the cheese ranged from 4.97 to 5.40, consistent with normal Cheddar, which has a pH range of 5.0 to 5.5. *S. typhimurium* phage type 10 was found to survive in Cheddar cheese for up to eight months of storage at 40°F/4°C. The authors compared *Salmonella* recovery as a function of whether mild Cheddar cheese was manufactured from heat-treated versus pasteurized milk. Tested samples of mild Cheddar manufactured from heat-treated milk were found to contain *Salmonella* at levels ranging from 0.36 to 9.3 MPN/100g. However, four lots of mild Cheddar manufactured from pasteurized milk also contained *Salmonella* at low levels. Certain lots of cheese contained *Staphylococcus aureus* at high levels (greater than 10^5 per g), indicating poor starter activity or contamination through handling. This outbreak illustrates that pasteurization of cheesemilk does not ensure safety of mild Cheddar cheese. An evaluation of the pasteurization process, described by Johnson et al. (1990b), indicated that the employee in charge of the process manually overrode the electronic controls, which shut down the pasteurizer while milk continued to flow through the unit and into the vat. The pasteurizer was shut down after filling three vats and later restarted to fill the next three-vat series. The first and third vats of each three-vat sequence tested positive for *Salmonella*, except for the first vat of the day. The middle vat of each three-vat series consistently tested negative. This pattern only occurred when raw milk that included milk from the cow shedding *S. typhimurium* was used. Bezanson et al. subsequently subjected outbreak strains to genetic analysis and revealed that two genetically distinct organisms were involved in this outbreak. These studies revealed the existence of a double infection, indicating that the incriminated cheese likely had two sources of contamination. *S. typhimurium* phage type 10 subgroup I strains were identified among cultures from raw milk and cattle associated with the incriminated dairy. *S. typhimurium* phage type 10 subgroup I and II strains were recovered from individuals employed at the dairy, along with their family members. These strains were also present in cheese curd samples obtained from the plant, as well as from a consumer pack obtained from a distributor. Cheese plant workers from whom both subgroup I and II strains were cultured were involved in the production and or packaging of Cheddar cheese, raising questions about the possibility of contamination of the cheese by ill workers. *Salmonella* was confirmed in a cheese trim bucket. Plant inspections revealed that employees used their bare hands to transfer cheese to a forming machine, and an employee tested positive for *S. typhimurium*. It is likely that this incriminated cheese was also responsible for an outbreak of illness reported at the same time in Ontario linked to *S. typhimurium* phage type 10 biotype 4 (D'Aoust et al., 1985).

Four outbreaks occurring in the late 1990s were reported in the U.K., although detailed epidemiologic data on these outbreaks are lacking. An outbreak of *Escherichia coli* 0157:H7 (phage type 8, Verotoxin gene 2) infection involving 22 cases was reported in Scotland in 1994. This outbreak was associated with the consumption of raw-milk cheese (Anonymous, 1997a). A December 1996 outbreak of *Salmonella gold-coast* that occurred in England and Wales was linked to consumption of a brand of mild, colored Cheddar cheese produced in August and September 1996 in Somerset, England. Phosphatase tests and examination of recording chart records from the pasteurizer indicated that pasteurization had failed at the plant on several occasions (Anonymous, 1997b). An outbreak of infection caused by *E. coli* 0157:H7 (phage type 21/28 VT2) was reported in 1999 in northeast England (Anonymous, 1999a, 1999b). The vehicle of infection was Cotherstone cheese, a raw-milk cheese manufactured in small quantities and distributed to specialty cheese shops in England. Samples from the dairy herd, slurry, and environmental samples from the cheese-manufacturing facilities tested negative for *E. coli* 0157:H7. In March 1999 a large outbreak of infection was reported in England and Wales due to consumption of contaminated milk from a single dairy.

An outbreak of *Escherichia coli* 0157:H7 infection was reported that was linked to consumption of fresh cheese curd (held for less than 60 days) from a dairy plant in Wisconsin (Durch et al., 2000). Nineteen of 55 laboratory-confirmed patients had purchased cheese curds from an unrefrigerated display at the cheese plant. To be legal, cheese curds must be manufactured from pasteurized milk. Vats of raw-milk Cheddar cheese were inadvertently used to make fresh curds, which were incorrectly labeled as "pasteurized" Cheddar cheese curd.

A comprehensive risk assessment would consider, among other factors, the degree to which the consuming population is exposed to risks associated with consumption of aged raw-milk cheeses. Cheddar cheese is produced worldwide and is therefore considered an important variety of hard cheese. The U.S. Department of Agriculture, National Agricultural Statistics Service, reports that Cheddar cheese was the most popular variety of cheese produced and consumed in the United States in 1999. Given that a large amount of this cheese is produced from raw or heat-treated milk, the high degree of exposure (consumption) of this product, coupled with the low incidence of disease outbreaks, attests to the safety of aged cheese made from raw and heat-treated milk. These outbreaks serve to illustrate the process controls necessary to ensure the safety of cheeses, and demonstrate the shortcomings of use of mandatory pasteurization.

Challenge Studies

Reitsma and Henning (1996) examined the survival of *Escherichia coli* 0157:H7 during the manufacture and ripening of Cheddar cheese. *E. coli* 0157:H7 was inoculated into pasteurized milk prior to cheesemaking. The organism sharply decreased in numbers over the 158-day testing period. Treatment 1 (1,000 cfu/ml) showed a 2-log CFU/g reduction after 60 days of ripening; however, *E. coli* 0157:H7 was still present even after 158 days of ripening, when viable cells were detected. Treatment 2 (1 cfu/g) showed a reduction to less than 1 cfu/g in 60 days, with no viable *E. coli* 0157:H7 detected at 158 days. As the authors state, "The results of this study cannot predict the behavior of heat-injured cells which could result from the pasteurization of naturally contaminating *E. coli*." Further, the low salt-in-moisture content (SMP) and absence of natural inhibitors present in raw milk create an artificially protective environment for *E. coli* 0157:H7 in pasteurized milk. The SMP determines the water activity, which in turn dictates the potential for growth of a microorganism in the cheese environment. The SMP in this study ranged from 2.75 to 3.76 percent with a mean of 3.25 percent, whereas in normal Cheddar the average SMP ranges from 5 to 5.5 percent. The low SMP could have affected the results of this study. Sodium chloride is an important inhibitor of microbial growth in cheese. The major roles of sodium chloride in Cheddar cheese are to check lactic acid fermentation after an optimum peak has been attained; reduce moisture through syneresis of the curd; suppress the growth of spoilage microorganisms; and create physical changes in cheese proteins that influence cheese texture, protein solubility, and protein conformation (Fox et al., 2000). There are no state or federal standards for the amount of salt added to Cheddar cheese, and variations in salt content from 0.8 to 2 percent are common. The minimum moisture content (adjusted with NaCl) necessary for growth of *E. coli* is 0.950 (Fennema, 1985) Further, most raw milk receives some heat treatment, albeit at a subpasteurization level. The combination of heat, salt, and natural inhibitors could provide barriers to survival of *E. coli* 0157:H7. It is likely that use of pasteurized milk for cheesemaking provided *E. coli* 0157:H7 with a more protective environment than raw milk. The authors state, "The low number of outbreaks seems to indicate that pathogens in cheese are not a major problem."

Teo and Schlesser (2000) examined survival of three groups of bacteria in raw-milk Cheddar cheese during cheesemaking and ripening: naturally occurring coliforms, a streptomycin-resistant strain of *Escherichia coli* K12 (ATCC 35695), and *E. coli* 0157:H7. Populations of naturally occurring coliforms present at levels of approximately 10^5 cfu/ml experienced a 1-log reduction after 60 days of aging at 45°F/7°C, and a further 3- to 4-log reduction after 180 days. In contrast, *E. coli* K12 populations exhibited a reduction of less than 1 log during 60 days of aging, and only a 1- to 2-log reduction by 90 days. Similar results were recorded with a five-strain cocktail of *E. coli* 0157:H7, where populations declined by 1 log following 60 days at 45°F, and by 1 to 2 logs following 90 days at this same temperature. A number of questions are raised by this study. The coliform levels used are extremely high, and such levels would raise concerns about raw-milk quality. The FDA has set standards for enterotoxigenic *E. coli* and *E. coli* in cheese at levels of 10^3 and 10^4 cells/g, respectively. The cheese produced by Teo and Schlesser greatly exceeded these standards.

Studies by Ryser and Marth (1987a, 1987b, 1987c) examined the fate of *Listeria monocytogenes* during the manufacture of Cheddar, Camembert, and brick cheese. Rapid growth to populations of $5x10^7$cfu/ml is observed in Camembert cheese, in which the pH normally increases during ripening, thereby creating a favorable growth environment for *Listeria* (1987a). In contrast, *Listeria* populations show a marked decrease during ripening of Cheddar cheese. Current U.S. regulations call for cheese made from raw or subpasteurized milk to be ripened at 35°F/1.7°C for at least 60 days prior to sale. Ryser and Marth (1987b) have shown that aging alone will not ensure the production of *Listeria*-free Cheddar cheese. However, the greatest threat posed to the safety of cheese is due to postprocessing environmental contamination from *Listeria.* While outbreaks of illness have resulted from the presence of *L. monocytogenes* in soft ripened and Hispanic-style cheeses (Linnan et al., 1988), no outbreaks of listeriosis have been reported as a result of *Listeria* surviving in cheese aged for a minimum of 60 days. Genigeorgis et al. (1991) evaluated the ability of 24 types of market cheeses to support growth of *L. monocytogenes.* Cheeses able to support growth included soft Hispanic-type cheeses, ricotta, Teleme, Brie, Camembert, and cottage cheeses (pH range 4.9 to 7.7). Cheeses not supporting growth, and which resulted in gradual death of *L. monocytogenes*, included Cotija, cream, blue, Monterey Jack, Swiss, Cheddar,

Colby, string, provolone, Muenster, feta, and Kasseri (pH range 4.3 to 5.6). A correlation was observed between growth of *Listeria* in cheeses having a pH of greater than 5.5, and in cheeses that were manufactured without a starter culture.

Approximately 80 percent of the cheeses made in Switzerland are manufactured from raw milk. However, the term *raw-milk cheese* as applied to Swiss cheese is a misnomer because Swiss cheese receives an extensive heat treatment during its manufacture. Bachman and Spahr (1995) assessed the safety of Swiss hard and semihard cheeses made from raw milk. These authors inoculated *Aeromonas hydrophila, Campylobacter jejuni, Escherichia coli, Listeria monocytogenes, Pseudomonas aeruginosa, Salmonella* spp., *S. aureus,* and *Yersinia enterocolitica* to raw milk at levels ranging from 10^4 to 10^6 cfu/ml for the manufacture of hard (Swiss-type) and semihard (Tilsit-type) cheese. In the hard cheeses, no detection of pathogens beyond one day was recorded. This was attributed to the curd-cooking temperature of 127.4°F/53°C for 45 minutes and 107.6°F/42°C for 15 minutes for Swiss hard and semihard cheeses. Further, the rapid decrease of the redox potential of Swiss cheese is likely to impart additional inhibitory effects. Pathogens were found to survive longer in the semihard cheese than in the hard cheese. After 90 days of aging at 52 to 54°F/11 to 13°C, when ripening was complete, all pathogens except *Listeria* were below detectable limits. *Listeria* survived but did not grow in the interior of the cheese, though they grew well on the cheese surface. Thus manufacturing parameters used in the production of semihard cheese inhibit, but do not kill, *Listeria*. Based upon these studies, the Swiss dairy industry has adopted a *Listeria*-monitoring program for cheese and other dairy products. Spahr and Schafroth (2001), in studies examining the fate of *Mycobacterium avium* subsp. *paratuberculosis,* recorded pH values associated with Swiss hard and semihard cheese manufacture. After 24 hours, cheeses manufactured under these curd-cooking conditions reach pH values of 5.3 in hard cheese and 5.2 in semihard cheese, and these pH conditions remain for 10 days for hard cheese and 25 days for semihard cheese. Further, the rapid decrease of the redox potential of Swiss cheese likely imparts additional inhibitory effects. The combined effects of active antimicrobial enzyme systems in raw milk, coupled with antagonistic effects of starter cultures, fast acidification, inhibitory effects of lactic acid, and high curd-cooking temperatures, render a microbiologically safe hard cheese when produced under Good Manufacturing Practices.

Pellegrino and Resmini (2001) examined the safety of the Italian hard cheeses (Grana Padano and Parmigiano-Reggiano). The authors noted several parameters associated with these cheeses that contribute to their microbiological safety: cooking of cheese curd to temperatures between 127 and 133°F/53 and 56°C for 15 to 20 minutes, with a total holding time of up to 85 minutes at these temperatures; molding of the cheese, whereby it is held at temperatures of 126°F/52°C and 133°F/56°C for at least 10 hours at pH 5.0; brine-salting of the cheese, which lowers the moisture content (A_W) to 0.9; and extended ripening for periods of 9 months (Grana Padano) to 12 months (Parmigiano-Reggiano), which promotes a further decrease in the moisture content to levels inhibitory for growth of bacterial pathogens. Pellegrino and Resmini also demonstrated the high-temperature/low-pH conditions occurring within Grana cheeses, which they described as "self-pasteurization," and which result in the inactivation of alkaline phosphatase, except within the outermost 1¼- to 1¾-inch/3 to 4 cm layer. In this layer however, the SMP ranges between 8 and 24 percent in the ripened cheese and the moisture content is close to 0.8. *Staphylococcus aureus,* which is more tolerant of low moisture than other pathogens, cannot survive below an A_W of 0.86 and can produce toxins only above 0.90.

Panari et al. (2001) examined the fate of pathogens during the production and ripening of Parmigiano-Reggiano cheese. *Escherichia coli, Salmonella typhimurium, Staphylococcus aureus,* and *Listeria monocytogenes* were inoculated to raw milk at levels ranging between 10^4 and 10^6 cfu/ml. None of the inoculated pathogens was detected 24 hours after cheesemaking, confirming that the cheesemaking conditions of Italian Grana cheeses do not support pathogen growth or survival. These results are consistent with those obtained by Yousef and Marth (1990), who reported a rapid decline of *L. monocytogenes* from initial levels of 10^4 to 10^5/ml in Parmesan cheese to undetectable levels within 14 to 112 days of ripening. These authors attributed the decline of *L. monocytogenes* viability in Parmesan cheese to the following parameters: addition of lipase for flavor development, heat treatment of the curd, and reduction in moisture content during ripening. Battistotti (1995), in an analysis of more than 100 samples of mature Italian Grana cheeses, failed to detect *Salmonella, S. aureus, L. monocytogenes,* coliforms, or enterococci, further confirming the microbiological safety of hard Italian cheeses.

Most studies that have shown survival of pathogens have been based on the use of pasteurized milk rather than raw milk in the experimental design, and may therefore overestimate survival during 60 days of aging. The Institute of Food Science and Technology has stated that the total health risk to the consumer is less from cheese made from pasteurized milk than from cheese of similar composition made from unpasteurized milk (IFST, 2000). Alternative hypotheses could be offered, including consideration that the use of raw milk provides protective effects from pathogens in milk and that postpasteurization environmental contamination poses a far greater threat to the safety of cheese. As a result, use of pasteurized milk in cheesemaking may create an environment that provides for optimum growth of pathogens, whereas in raw milk the normal flora and natural inhibitors provide a margin of control over pathogen growth. In fact, a study conducted by Rudolf and Scherer (2001) showed a higher incidence of *Listeria monocytogenes* in cheeses made from pasteurized milk (8 percent) than in cheese made from raw milk (4.8 percent). Phage-typing of isolates revealed persistent *Listeria* contamination within dairy plant environments for periods of weeks to several months, and documented cross-contamination within the plant environment as a significant factor associated with contamination of cheeses.

The recommendation for mandatory pasteurization may ultimately lead to use of milk of inferior quality for cheesemaking. Pathogens harbored in this inferior-quality milk can be transported to a processing facility and become established as environmental pathogens. A wiser strategy may involve routine testing of incoming lots of raw milk and working with producers when infected animals are identified, to allow treatment and confinement of animals to control infectious disease. There is no evidence in the literature to support the view that cheese made from raw milk in which pathogens are not present is a dangerous food. Thus raw-milk screening, coupled with use of Good Manufacturing Practices to control environmental contamination during cheesemaking, may be the most effective control strategy to improve the safety of aged cheeses. The U.S. Food and Drug Administration has recently stated that "a review of the literature relating to the potential for growth of pathogens in hard cheeses that are aged for at least 60 days shows that such growth is not likely to occur because of the combined effect of decreased pH, decreased water activity, and possibly other factors inherent to these cheeses" (Anonymous, 1999d). Although survival during aging is possible, the FDA cited a considerable body of evidence showing that certain cheeses do not support the growth of pathogens during the aging process and subsequent storage.

Growth and Survival of Bacterial Pathogens in Soft and Semisoft Cheeses

Legitimate concerns can be raised regarding the safety of soft and semisoft cheeses manufactured from raw milk, as well as high-moisture, low-salt aged cheeses. An outbreak of foodborne listeriosis linked to cheese was reported by Bille and coworkers (1992). This outbreak occurred in Vaud, Switzerland, and was linked to consumption of Vacherin Mont d'Or cheese. A total of 122 cases occurring during the period from 1983 through 1987 were reported. The normal rate of listeriosis in Switzerland is 5 to 10 cases per million persons. During the outbreak period, the rate of listeriosis rose to 50 per million. Sixteen cases were reported in 1983, 24 in 1984, 13 in 1985, 28 in 1986, and 41 in 1987. A mortality rate of 28 percent was associated with these cases. Of the clinical isolates available from the epidemic period, 111 of 120 (93 percent) were serotype 4b of two unique phage types, and 85 percent of these strains matched the epidemic phage types isolated from Vacherin Mont d'Or cheese.

Listeria monocytogenes in Mexican-style cheese has been responsible for two major outbreaks of foodborne disease in the United States. Mexican-style cheeses comprise a range of cheese products including *queso blanco, quesco fresco, panela ranchero, queso de hoja,* and soft Hispanic cheese (Bolton and Frank, 1999). These cheeses do not have a standard of identity. Most are formulated by coagulation using rennet and may have added organic acids (citric, acetic, and lactic); usually lactic starter cultures are not used (Bolton and Frank, 1999). The first link between cheese consumption and an outbreak of listeriosis was reported in California in 1985. Jalisco-brand Mexican-style cheese was implicated as the source of the outbreak (Linnan et al., 1988). A total of 142 cases involving 93 pregnant women or their offspring and 49 nonpregnant immunocompromised adults were documented in Los Angeles County. Forty-eight deaths were recorded, yielding a mortality rate of 33.8 percent. The majority of affected individuals (62 percent) were pregnant Hispanic women. An additional 160 cases occurred in other parts of California, but the study reported by Linnan et al. was limited to Los Angeles County. In this outbreak the cheese was most likely manufactured from a combination of raw and pasteurized milk, and the plant that made it was found to harbor *Listeria* as an environmental contaminant. The epidemic strain in this outbreak was a serotype 4b, and this serotype was recovered from unopened packages of *queso fresco* and Cotija Mexican-style cheese.

An outbreak of listeriosis associated with homemade Mexican-style fresh soft cheese occurred in North Carolina between October 2000 and January 2001 (Boggs et al., 2001). The outbreak involved 12 cases: 10 pregnant women, 1 postpartum female, and a 70-year-old immunocompromised male. The women reported symptoms of fever, chills, headache, abdominal cramps, and vomiting. The cheese implicated in the outbreak was purchased from door-to-door vendors. *Listeria monocytogenes* isolates obtained from nine patients, three cheese samples from two stores, one cheese sample from a patient's home, and one raw-milk sample from a dairy all had indistinguishable patterns in PFGEs (a type of DNA testing), indicating a common link. It is important to note that the manufacturing conditions in this outbreak would not be those encountered in a licensed, inspected commercial cheese-processing facility.

Microbiological surveys of raw milk conducted in the United States have shown the presence of *Listeria monocytogenes* in 1.6 to 7 percent of tested samples. This incidence is similar to Canada (1.3 to 5.4 percent of samples) and Western European raw milks (2.5 to 6.0 percent). In the recently released Health and Human Services (HHS) and USDA *Listeria* risk assessment and *Listeria* action plan, the USDA and FDA advise pregnant women, older adults, and people with weakened immune systems that "Cheeses that may be eaten include hard cheeses, semisoft cheeses such as Mozzarella, pasteurized processed cheeses such as slices and spreads, cream cheese, and cottage cheese." However, people belonging to these risk groups are advised, "Do not drink raw (unpasteurized) milk or eat foods that contain unpasteurized milk."

There are particular varieties of soft

and semisoft uncooked cheeses that can be legally manufactured in the United States from raw milk, provided that they are aged for 60 days (21 CFR, Part 133). These cheeses may pose safety concerns if cheese composition and processing parameters are not carefully controlled. Examples of high-risk cheeses include those with bloomy rinds, along with some of the washed-rind cheeses and semisoft tommes.

In the final analysis, the aged hard cheese varieties pose little risk from a food safety standpoint. However, those washed-rind and bloomy-rind varieties with variable moisture and pH content may present food safety concerns that will not be corrected through 60 days of aging.

IMPROVEMENT IN CHEESE SAFETY AND FUTURE NEEDS

Utilization of more sensitive methods for the detection of pathogens existing at low levels in Cheddar and aged raw-milk cheeses could do much to ensure cheese safety. Altekruse et al. (1998) stated, "Because of inherent problems of statistical sampling of foods for microbial pathogens (ICMSF, 1986), end-point testing may not assure the safety of cheese. These problems increase when organisms are present in small numbers below the test sensitivity or when there is intermittent contamination and the tested specimens do not contain pathogens." Raw-ingredient testing—screening of the raw-milk supply—may overcome these shortcomings.

In recent years cheese and cheese products have been recalled due to the presence of pathogenic bacteria such as *Salmonella, Listeria monocytogenes,* and *Escherichia coli.* In some instances, cheeses, both domestic and imported, have been linked to outbreaks of human illness. In November 1998 the Food and Drug Administration issued the Domestic and Imported Cheese and Cheese Products Food Compliance Program. The objectives of this program are for the FDA to conduct inspections of domestic cheese firms; to examine samples of imported and domestic cheese for microbiological contamination, the presence of phosphatase, and filth; and to take appropriate regulatory action when violations are encountered. Target pathogens for analysis include *L. monocytogenes, Salmonella, E. coli,* enterotoxigenic (ETEC) *E. coli,* enterohemorrhagic *E. coli* (0157:H7), and *Staphylococcus aureus.* Under this initiative, direct seizure or detention of cheese based on the presence of *L. monocytogenes* is authorized. It should be noted that ETEC analysis is only performed if *E. coli* is present at 10^4 cfu/g. A review of the FDA Product Recalls, Alerts and Warnings Archive (http://www.fda.gov/oc/po/firmrecalls/archive.html) for the calendar years 1999, 2000, and 2001 revealed several recalls due to the presence of *L. monocytogenes* in cheese, one recall involving *E. coli* contamination of blue and Gorgonzola cheeses, and one recall involving *Salmonella* contamination of Mexican white cheese. The strain of *E. coli* identified was not 0157:H7. *Listeria* contamination appears to be a function of postprocessing contamination. It is unknown whether aged cheeses made from raw milk during this period were the subject of a recall.

Future research in a number of areas is suggested to improve the safety of cheeses made from raw milk. The impact of pasteurization of milk on the microbial ecology of cheeses aged for more than 60 days deserves full examination. Mandatory pasteurization of milk may increase the susceptibility of cheese to growth of pathogens introduced via postprocessing contamination. The potential for survival of *Salmonella typhimurium* DT104 and other antibiotic-resistant strains of *S. newport* in raw milk and through raw-milk cheesemaking requires examination. Such pathogens did not exist at the time the 60-day aging rule was promulgated. Also crucial are improved microbiological methods for raw-milk screening and aged raw-milk cheese analysis that are both rapid and sensitive.

The contributions of microbial injury to the interactive effects of salt, pH, and mild heat in suppression of growth of *Listeria, Escherichia coli,* and *Salmonella* should be explored. Do acid-adapted cultures of these microbial species show enhanced ability to persist in aged raw-milk cheese by withstanding salt, moisture content, and mild heat conditions encountered during aged raw-milk cheesemaking? Finally, consistent with our colleagues in Europe, establishment of microbiological criteria for raw milk destined for aged cheesemaking is needed, including setting tolerance limits for coliforms, *E. coli,* enterotoxigenic *E. coli,* enterohemorrhagic *E. coli* (0157:H7), *Salmonella, L. monocytogenes,* and *Staphylococcus aureus.* This, coupled with development of risk-reduction procedures and practices at both the primary production level (milk screening) and the cheese production level will undoubtedly lead to improvements in the safety of aged raw-milk cheese.

Aged hard cheeses made from raw milk are microbiologically safe when manufactured under conditions that use milk-screening procedures, GMPs, and HACCP. Soft and semisoft cheeses aged for 60 days have characteristics that greatly increase the potential for pathogens. Careful investigation of the safety of aged raw-milk cheeses may indicate that raw milk provides protective effects from pathogens in milk, and that environmental contamination poses a far greater threat to cheese safety. This issue deserves the benefit of full study, careful evaluation of published research information, and new research to fully assess all potential risks and benefits.

CHAPTER 9 REFERENCES

Abou-Eleinin, A.-A. M., E. T. Ryser, and C. W. Donnelly. 2000. "Incidence and Seasonal Variation of Listeria Species in Bulk Tank Goat's Milk." *Journal of Food Protection* 63: 1208–1213.

Altekruse, S. F., B. B. Timbo, J. C. Mowbray, N. H. Bean, and M. E. Potter. 1998. "Cheese-Associated Outbreaks of Human Illness in the United States, 1973–1992: Sanitary Manufacturing Practices Protect Consumers." *Journal of Food Protection* 61: 1405–1407.

Anonymous. 1997a. "Vero Cytotoxin Producing *Escherichia coli* 0157." *Communicable Disease Report* 7: 409, 412.

———. 1997b. "*Salmonella gold-coast* and Cheddar Cheese: Update." *Communicable Disease Report* 7: 93, 96.

———. 1999a. "*Escherichia coli* 0157 Associated with Eating Unpasteurized Cheese." *Communicable Disease Report* 9: 113, 116.

———. 1999b. "*Escherichia coli* 0157:H7 Associated with Eating Unpasteurized Cheese: Update." *Communicable Disease Report* 9: 131, 134.

Arimi, S.M., Ryser, Pritchard, and Donnelly. 1997. "Diversity of *Listeria* Ribotypes Recovered from Dairy Cattle, Silage and Dairy Processing Environments." 60: 811–816.

Bachmann, H.P., and Spahr. 1995. "The Fate of Potentially Pathogenic Bacteria in Swiss Hard and Semihard Cheeses Made from Raw Milk." *Journal of Dairy Science* 78: 476–483.

Battistotti, B. 1995). "Carratteristiche microbiche e presenza di attivita da fosfatasi alcalina." In *Grana Padano: un formaggio di qualità*. Vol. 2. *Consorzio per la Tutela del Formaggio Grana Padano*. Desenzano, Italy: 37–47.

Bezanson, G.S., R. Khakhria, D. Duck, and H. Lior. 1985. "Molecular Analysis Confirms Food Source and Simultaneous Involvement of Two Distinct but Related Groups of *Salmonella typhimurium* Bacteriophage Type 10 in a Major Interprovincial *Salmonella* Outbreak." *Appl. Env. Microbiol.* 50: 1279–1284.

Bille, J., D. Nocera, E. Bannerman, and F. Ischer. 1992. "Molecular Typing of *Listeria monocytogenes* in Relation with the Swiss Outbreak of Listeriosis." *Proc. XI. Intern. Symp. on Problems of Listeriosis,* Copenhagen, Denmark, May 11–14, pp. 195–196.

Bleem, A. 1994. "*Escherichia coli* 0157:H7 in Raw Milk: A Review." *Animal Health Insight*, Spring/Summer. Fort Collins, Colo: USDA-APHIS: VS Centers for Epidemiology and Public Health.

Boggs, J.D., R.E. Whitman, L.M. Hale, R.P. Briscoe, et al. 2001. "Outbreak of Listeriosis Associated with Homemade Mexican-Style Cheese—North Carolina, October 2000–January 2001." *MMWR* 50(26): 560–562.

Bolton, L.F., and J.F. Frank. 1999 "Defining the Growth/No-Growth Interface for *Listeria monocytogenes* in Mexican-Style Cheese Based on Salt, pH, and Moisture Content." J. Food Prot. 62: 601–609

Borczyk, A.A., M.A. Karmali, H. Lior, and L.M.C. Duncan. 1987. "Bovine Reservoir for Verotoxin-Producing *Escherichia coli* 0157:H7." *Lancet* i:98–99.

Cody, S.H., S.L. Abbott, A.A. Marfin, B. Schulz, P. Wagner, K. Robbins, J.C. Mohle-Boetani, and D.J. Vugia. 1999. "Two Outbreaks of Multidrug-Resistant *Salmonella* Serotype Typhimurium DT104 Infections Linked to Raw Milk Cheese in Northern California." *JAMA* 281,1805–1810.

D'Aoust, J.-Y., D.W. Warburton, and A.M. Sewell. 1985. "*Salmonella typhimurium* Phage-Type 10 from Cheddar Cheese Implicated in a Major Canadian Foodborne Outbreak." 48: 1062–1066.

DeBuyser, M.L., B. Dufour, M. Maire, and V. Lafarge. 2001. "Implications of Milk and Milk Products in Foodborne Diseases in France and in Different Industrialized Countries." *International Journal of Food Microbiology* 67: 1-17.

De Valk, H., E. Delarocque-Astagneau, G. Colomb, S. Pie, E. Goddard, V. Vaillant, S. Haeghebaert, P. H. Bouvet, F. Grimont, P. Grimont, and J. C. Desenclos. 2000. "A Community-Wide Outbreak of *Salmonella enterica* Serotype Typhimurium Infection Associated with Eating a Raw Milk Soft Cheese in France." *Epidemiology and Infection* 124: 1–7.

Donnelly, C. W. 2001. "Factors Associated with Hygienic Control and Quality of Cheeses Prepared from Raw Milk: A Review." *Bulletin of the International Dairy Federation* 369: 16–27.

Durch, J., T. Ringhand, K. Manner, M. Barnett, M. Proctor, S. Ahrabi-Fard, J. Davis, and D. Boxrud. 2000. "Outbreak of *Escherichia coli* 0157:H7 Infection Associated with Eating Fresh Cheese Curds Wisconsin, June 1998." *Morbidity and Mortality Weekly Report* 49(40) (Oct. 13): 911–913.

Fennema, O. R., ed. 1985. *Food Chemistry*, 2nd ed. Marcel Dekker, Inc., New York.

Fontaine, R. E., M. L. Cohen, W. T. Martin, and T. M. Vernon. 1980. "Epidemic Salmonellosis from Cheddar Cheese: Surveillance and Prevention." *American Journal of Epidemiology* 1: 247–253.

Fox, P. F., T. P. Guinee, T. M. Cogan, and P. L. H. McSweeney. 2000. *Fundamentals of Cheese Science*. Aspen Publishers, Inc., Gaithersburg, Md.

Friedman, C. R., R. C. Brady, M. J. Celotti, et al. 1998. "An Outbreak of Multidrug-Resistant *Salmonella* Serotype Typhimurium Definitive Type 104 (DT104) Infections in Humans and Cattle in Vermont." *Program and Abstracts of the International Conference on Emerging Infectious Diseases*, March 8–11, Atlanta, Ga.

Genigeorgis, C., M. Carniciu, D. Dutulescu, and T. B. Farver. 1991. "Growth and Survival of *Listeria monocytogenes* in Market Cheeses Stored at 4 to 30°C." *Journal of Food Protection* 54: 662–668.

Groves, D. 1998. "Codex and Its Potential Impact." *Cheese Reporter* 123(17): 4.

Hedberg, C. W., J. A. Korlath, J.-Y. D'Aoust, K. E. White, W. L. Schell, M. R. Miller, D. N. Cameron, K. L. MacDonald, and M. T. Osterholm. 1992. "A Multistate Outbreak of *Salmonella javiana* and *Salmonella oranienburg* Infections Due to Consumption of Contaminated Cheese." *Journal of the American Medical Association* 268: 3203–3207.

Institute of Food Science and Technology. 2000. "Position Statement on Food Safety and Cheese." http://www.ifst.org/hottop15.htm.

International Commission on Microbiological Specifications for Foods. 1986. *Microorganisms in Foods. 2. Sampling for Microbiological Analysis: Principles and Specific Applications*, 2nd ed. University of Toronto Press, Toronto.

Johnson, E. A., J. H. Nelson, and M. Johnson. 1990a. "Microbiological Safety of Cheese Made from Heat-Treated Milk. Part I. Executive Summary, Introduction and History." *Journal of Food Protection* 53: 441–518.

———. 1990b. "Microbiological Safety of Cheese Made from Heat-Treated Milk. Part II. Microbiology." *Journal of Food Protection* 53: 441–518.

———. 1990c. "Microbiological Safety of Cheese Made from Heat-Treated Milk. Part III. Technology, Discussion, Recommendations, Bibliography." *Journal of Food Protection* 53: 519–540.

Klausner, R. B., and C. W. Donnelly. 1991. "Environmental Sources of *Listeria* and *Yersinia* in Vermont Dairy Plants." *Journal of Food Protection* 54: 607–611.

Lester, A., B. G. Bruun, P. Husum, H. J. Kolmos, B. B. Nielsen, J. H. Scheibel, N. Skovgaard, and F. Thune-Stephensen. 1995. "*Salmonella dublin*." *Ugeskr Laeger* 2: 20–24.

Leuschner, R. G. K., and M. P. Boughtflower. 2002. "Laboratory-Scale Preparation of Soft-Cheese Artificially Contaminated with Low Levels of *Escherichia coli* 0157, *Listeria monocytogenes*, and *Salmonella enterica* serovars Typhimurium, Enteritidis and Dublin." *Journal of Food Protection* 65: 508–514.

Linnan, M. J., L. Mascola, X. D. Lou, V. Goulet, S. May, C. Salminen, D.W. Hird, M. L. Yonekura, P. Hayes, R. Weaver, A. Audurier, B. D. Plikaytis, S. L. Fannin, A. Kleks, and C. V. Broome. 1988. "Epidemic Listeriosis Associated with Mexican-Style Cheese." *New England Journal of Medicine* 319: 823–828.

Maguire, H., J. Cowden, M. Jacob, B. Rowe, D. Roberts, J. Bruce, and E. Mitchell. 1992. "An Outbreak of *Salmonella dublin* Infection in England and Wales Associated with a Soft Unpasteurized Cow's-Milk Cheese." *Epidemiology and Infection* 109: 389–396.

Martin, M. L., L. D. Shipman, J. G. Wells, M. E. Potter, K. Hedberg, I. K. Wachsmuth, R. V. Tauxe, J. P. Davis, J. Arnoldi, and J. Tilleli. 1986. "Isolation of *Escherichia coli* from Dairy Cattle Associated with Cases of Hemolytic Uremic Syndrome." *Lancet* ii: 1043–1044.

Morgan, D., C. P. Newman, D. N. Hutchinson, A. M. Walker, B. Rowe, and F. Majod. 1993. "Verotoxin-Producing *Escherichia coli* 0157 Associated with Consumption of Yoghurt." *Epidemiology and Infection* 111: 181–183.

Panari, G., S. Perini, R. Guidetti, M. Pecorari, G. Merialdi, and A. Albertini. 2001. "Study of the Behavoir of Potentially Pathogenic Bacteria during the Manufacturing of Parmigiano-Reggiano Cheese." *Scienza e Tecnica Lattiero-Casearia* 52: 13-22.

Papageorgiou, D. K., and E. H. Marth. 1989. "Fate of *Listeria monocytogenes* during the Manufacture and Ripening of Blue Cheese." *Journal of Food Protection* 52: 459–465.

Pellegrino, L., and P. Resmini. 2001. "Cheesemaking Conditions and Compositional Characteristics Supporting the Safety of Raw Milk Cheese Italian Grana." *Scienza e Tecnica Lattiero-Casearia 52:* 105-114.

Pitt, W. M., T. J. Harden, and R. R. Hull. 2000. "Investigation of the Antimicrobial Activity of Raw Milk against Several Foodborne Pathogens." *Milchwissenschaft* 55(5): 249–252.

Pritchard, T. J., C. M. Beliveau, K. J. Flanders, and C. W. Donnelly. 1994. "Increased Incidence of *Listeria* Species in Dairy Processing Plants Having Adjacent Farm Facilities." *Journal of Food Protection* 57: 770–775.

Reitsma, C. J., and D. R. Henning. 1996. "Survival of Enterohemorrhagic *Escherichia coli* 0157:H7 during the Manufacture and Curing of Cheddar Cheese." *Journal of Food Protection* 59: 460–464.

Rudolf, M., and S. Scherer. 2001. "High Incidence of *Listeria monocytogenes* in European Red Smear Cheese." *International Journal of Food Microbiology* 63(1–2): 91–98.

Ryser, E. T., and E. H. Marth. 1987a. "Fate of *L. monocytogenes* during Manufacture and Ripening of Camembert Cheese." *Journal of Food Protection* 50: 372–378.

———. 1987b. "Behavior of *Listeria monocytogenes* during the Manufacture and Ripening of Cheddar Cheese." *Journal of Food Protection* 50: 7–13.

———. 1987c. "Behavior of *Listeria monocytogenes* during Manufacture and Ripening of Brick Cheese." *Journal of Dairy Science* 72: 838–853.

Spahr, U., and K. Schafroth. 2001. "Fate of *Mycobacterium avium* subsp. *paratuberculosis* in Swiss Hard and Semihard Cheese Manufactured from Raw Milk." *Applied and Environmental Microbiology* 67: 4199–4205.

Teo, A., and J. Schlesser. 2000. "Survival of Naturally Occurring *Escherichia coli* and a Streptomycin-Resistant Strain of *E. coli* K12 (ATCC 35695) during the Aging Period of Hard Cheeses Made from Raw Milk." *Journal of Dairy Science* 83 (Suppl. 1): 109.

Teo, A., J. E. Schlesser, K. Madsen, and R. Gerdes. 2000. "Survival of Naturally Occurring Coliforms." *Journal of Dairy Science* 83 (Suppl. 1): 109.

Threlfall, E. J., A. J. Frost, L. R. Ward, and B. Rowe. 1996. "Increasing Spectrum of Resistance in Multiresistant *Salmonella typhimurium*." *Lancet* 347: 1053–1054.

U.S. Food and Drug Administration. 1950. "Part 19—Cheeses; Processed Cheeses; Cheese Foods; Cheese Spreads, and Related Foods: Definition and Standards of Identity [Docket no. FDC-46]. Final Rule." *Federal Register* (Aug. 24): 5656–5690.

Villar, R. G., M. D. Macek, S. Simons, P. S. Hayes, M. J. Goldoft, J. H. Lewis, L. L. Rowan, D. Hursh, M. Patnode, and P. S. Mead. 1999. "Investigation of Multidrug-Resistant *Salmonella* Serotype Typhimurium DT104 Infections Linked to Raw Milk Cheese in Washington State." *Journal of the American Medical Association* 281(19): 1811–1816.

Wells, S. J., P. J. Fedorka-Cray, D. A. Dargatz, K. Ferris, and A. Green. 2001. "Fecal Shedding of *Salmonella* spp. by Dairy Cows on Farm and at Cull Cow Markets." *Journal of Food Protection* 64: 3–11.

Yousef, A. E., and E. H. Marth. 1990. "Fate of *Listeria monocytogenes* during the Manufacture and Ripening of Parmesan Cheese." *Journal of Dairy Science* 73: 3351–3356.

Peter H. Dixon

The Art of Cheesemaking

10

Cheesemaking as an art can be thought of in several ways. On the surface cheesemaking seems to fit the definition of an art. Traditionally it has been a nonscientific branch of learning, However, in many places we have to go back more than 100 years to revisit the times when cheesemaking perpetuated itself solely through a system of techniques handed down from generation to generation rather than through advances in science and engineering. Milk was ripened and curdled, curds were drained and perhaps pressed into a shape, and this was eaten fresh or was aged until a specific flavor developed. Cheesemakers facilitated the process and used their intuition and knowledge of their craft, which was learned by practical experience rather than by study. Although cheesemaking remains, for the most part, a natural process, it is difficult to view it as nonscientific in this day and age. In fact, it would be rare to find cheese being made without the use of some scientific advancement such as standardized-strength rennet or freeze-dried starter culture prepared in a laboratory.

The phrase *artisanal cheese* comes from the sense of the cheesemakers carrying on the work of their forebears and following traditional methods. There is a point at which cheesemaking can no longer be thought of as artisanal and cheese turns into a manufactured food product. Manufacturing implies that the milk is made into cheese by means of a large-scale, mechanized industrial process. Even though "natural" cheese is made this way, it is hard to find the artistry in it. Advances in science and engineering have literally taken the process out of the hands of cheesemakers by automating the activities that define it.

Therefore, the challenge in defining the art and craft of cheesemaking and artisanal cheese is in determining where to draw the line between art and science. All artists and craftspeople would agree that they follow a creative process when they work. There are forces greater and more powerful than the artist, which serve to guide the artist toward completing a piece. There is some external motivation being channeled through the artist. In cheesemaking this force, which resides in the milk and the environment, has directed cheesemakers to adapt to changing situations and created cheeses that embody the character of specific regions. These cheeses continue to be made by traditional recipes that have developed through a combination of factors: the social culture of the farmers, the soil, the plants available for feeding the animals, the type and breed of livestock, the climate, and the productivity of the region. The initial process of shaping the recipes is highly creative, involves many external forces, and stretches out over generations. In replicating this cheese, subsequent generations of artisan cheesemakers are still following a creative process. They are bound closely to nature and must modify their techniques because their environment effects changes in the composition and quality of the milk and the conditions that influence the making and aging of the cheese. Much as painters reside in the landscape they paint, cheesemakers are a part of their local agricultural landscape. Either they are farmers themselves or members of families that have their own livestock and make cheese on their farms, or they work in small-scale cooperative creameries where local milk is turned into cheeses. They have an intuitive knowledge of the properties of the milk, which springs forth and provides the substance for their labors. Pierre Androuët (1973) sums up this sense of cheese as a product of the terroir and the artisan cheesemaker working as a part of the regional environment:

> Every region has its mysteries, over which no technology, no chemistry have yet prevailed. . . . Vegetation, climate, rainfall, nature of the subsoil, breed of animal, all contribute towards making a cheese into a unique, inimitable product.

Artisanal cheese exemplifies the creative spirit in nature. When scientific advancements are used to standardize the process, then cheesemaking loses a part of the system that defines it as an art. Artisanal cheeses are individualized products; the color, appearance, texture, and flavor of a certain type of cheese all change during the year that it is made. In the same way that the set of six mugs our neighborhood potter made for us are slightly different in form and appearance, my wheels of cheese are different in size and coloring of the rinds. I believe that it is precisely this quality that distinguishes artisanal cheese from its industrial, mass-produced counterpart.

At the core of the art of cheesemaking is the main ingredient, the milk itself, which contains the life force. The steps that a cheesemaker follows to turn milk into cheese have a profound effect on the essence of the cheese. The fresher the milk and the less it is manipulated before the souring begins, the more the cheese will represent its terroir. When milk is standardized in terms of its bacteriological content, chemical composition, and color, it is possible to produce cheese with a considerable degree of uniformity. It becomes possible to make decent versions of regionally distinctive cheeses anywhere in the world. The role of science in cheesemaking has been to facilitate this process, which has led to industrialization. For the successful mass production of cheese, standardization of ingredients and finished product is critical. Scientists' efforts have been focused on developing processes compatible with the latest advances in engineering, which have also served to alter some traditional methods of cheesemaking in order to better fit into the manufacturing process. Industrialization hasn't necessarily been a bad thing for artisan cheesemakers, who have benefited from scientific advancements including standardized rennet, defined-strain starter cultures, and acidity testing, which can improve the quality of their cheese. I intend to explore this concept shortly. I will also outline in this chapter the practices that are essential to understanding the art of cheesemaking. First, however, it is important to understand how science has enhanced artisanal cheesemaking.

For an artisanal business to succeed, the product must be unique and consistently well made, and there must be a market for it. Therefore, artisan cheesemakers adhere to the traditional methods of their craft to bring forth the nuances in flavor that are generated through the intimate connection with the seasons and the environment. The finest cheese may vary, but it should vary within a certain standard if it is to be commercially marketable. Some artisan cheesemakers benefit from following traditions that produce these results, but most of us are relatively new at the game. For the less experienced cheesemakers, then, traditional methods should be supported by scientific principles to the extent necessary to make consistently high-quality cheese. It is important to note that many of the traditional artisan cheesemakers have strong support from the scientific community in their distinctive agricultural regions. The melding of craft and science is used to strengthen the activity on which their livelihood is based.

A cheese such as Cheddar, which was once exclusively made by artisan cheesemakers in Great Britain, has largely turned into the product of an industrial process, though the craft of making Cheddar is still alive. Wheels of Cheddar sealed in cloth bandages, which represent the fruit of an artisan cheesemaker's labor, are still being made. In reading about the history of cheesemaking, we learns that 150 years ago the farm-made Cheddars were more variable in quality because cheesemakers differed in attitude and aptitude—that is, some were better at their craft than others. This could be attributed to many factors, most notably attention to cleanliness during milking and cheesemaking; construction of dairies, creameries, and cheese stores; and systems of cheesemaking. In the case of Cheddar, quality was improved by using methods based on scientific principles—such as the cheddaring process, hygiene, and temperature control during making and aging—that were developed by Joseph Harding in England from the 1850s onward.

Joseph Harding dedicated many years to improving the standard of quality for

British cheese. He used scientific principles to develop methods for making cheese that did away with some of the guesswork and exorcised the mysticism of certain traditional methods that produced haphazard results. In this way he was able to demonstrate that some "traditional" practices led to poor quality and also showed how to make significant and consistent improvements by following new practices based on an understanding of dairy science. At first cheesemakers were skeptical of his methods, but the string of blue ribbons collected by his family for their Cheddar cheeses proved him the wiser, and several of his daughters went on to consult and work for other cheese businesses in Great Britain and the United States (Cheke, 1959).

This is the appropriate way for artisan cheesemakers to use science. It is now common practice to integrate scientific principles with traditional cheesemaking practices to better understand how cheese of the highest quality standard is made. This, in turn, enables dairying regions to maintain and develop viable economic enterprises that are centered on artisanal cheesemaking. The key is to produce cheese with a high level of quality, on which a reputation can be built, thereby ensuring marketability over the long term. As a cheesemaker myself—I make 20,000 pounds/9,000 kg of cheese a year for sale throughout New England—I need an approach that will reduce variability and build a reputation for quality. Therefore, I rely on science to enhance the art of cheesemaking. I use standardized rennet and pure starter cultures made in laboratories, and I test acidity regularly during the cheesemaking process. The rest of what I do is based on my knowledge of the craft, which has been built up over only 20 years.

ARTISANAL CHEESEMAKING

The craft of cheesemaking is arranged over a set of activities that are based on fundamental principles of food preparation. Fermentation of the milk sugar into lactic acid, manipulation of curds and whey, and salt preservation are used to dehydrate the milk into cheese. The type of fermentation, method of salting, and degree of dehydration are channeled into the eight basic steps cheesemakers use to create the plethora of cheese varieties. To fully explore the practical aspects of the craft, it is best to take a walk through the cheesemaking process and discuss how the techniques are adapted to account for changes in the milk composition, environment, and seasonality. Since excellent, detailed descriptions of each step have been provided in already chapter 5, this section will be more of a practicum in artisanal cheesemaking. Please refer to the previous chapter to fill in any gaps.

USING STARTER CULTURE AND RENNET

Cheesemakers need to know the specific type, amount, and correct use of starter culture for each kind of cheese they want to make. I have successfully used some of the recipes in various cheesemaking books. These recipes, along with an understanding of starter-culture properties gleaned from reading this book, should be enough to point you toward making good batches of cheese. In recipes, the types and amounts of starter are often given in specific detail. Before actually making a batch of cheese, though, it is important to interpret the recipe to fit your own conditions. I find that many first attempts at cheesemaking produce acid cheeses that are too dry and crumbly and don't ripen in the expected time frame. They stay tangy and monodimensional and never develop the desired flavor. I have made a lot of these cheeses myself, especially when trying to make a new variety. There are many types of starter cultures available now, including cocktails of thermophilic and mesophilic bacteria. It is always a good idea to talk with the culture supplier about the properties of these starters and which cheeses they are most suitable for. When creating your own "originals," or cheeses that are similar to obscure traditional varieties, there is often very little information available to guide you in selecting appropriate starter cultures.

When I decide to make a new kind of cheese for the first time, I think about it for a long while before I attempt it. In the process of envisioning the end result, I start with a wedge of cheese or a photograph and description, and ask myself some questions:

- Does it have a rind and, if so, what is the rind composition: color, thickness, texture, and visible microflora?
- How do I describe the texture: degree of openness, round gas holes, mechanical openings, closely knit, creamy, coarse, or flaky?
- What is the body like: soft, semisoft, semihard, hard, elastic, or crumbly?
- How ripe is the cheese; at what stage of development is it?
- What characterizes the flavor: buttery, nutty, piquant, and so forth?

The answers to these questions help me to choose the type and amount of starter culture to use in making a similar cheese. Next, I attempt to find a recipe for this type of cheese. It will give me a starting point. There are a few things to know about recipes:

- Either pasteurized or raw milk is used.
- Starter may or may not be used (if it is used, the type of starter may or may not be specified).
- Color and calcium chloride may be added.
- The milk will be ripened for some amount of time before the rennet is added.
- Surface-ripening cultures may be used to give a specific appearance to the rind and influence the flavor of the paste (interior).

Then I consider whether I am going to use pasteurized or raw milk. For cheeses that are aged 60 days or more, a recipe will often mention that raw milk is used. Farmstead cheesemakers do not often pasteurize their milk for these types. In fact, you can't replace the diversity of bacteria destroyed by pasteurization with a starter culture. Pasteurization also adds expense to producing these longer-aged cheeses.

Pasteurized milk requires more starter culture than raw milk to complete its fermentation into any type of cheese because the lactic bacteria in the milk are destroyed by pasteurization. If the same amount of starter used for pasteurized-milk cheese is used to make raw-milk cheese, the resulting cheeses will tend to be too acidic and chalky and won't ripen well; they stay hard, and flavor development is very slow. This is due to the later growth of the raw-milk bacteria (they begin 12 to 24 hours after warming the milk), which, combined with a large number of starter bacteria, produces more lactic acid than desired.

> As a general rule of thumb, if you adapt a recipe from pasteurized milk to raw milk, use one-quarter to one-half as much culture as indicated as a starting point for developing your recipe.

With a smaller amount of starter culture, the bacteria will grow at a slower rate during draining, but the acid production should remain steady. The raw-milk bacteria will grow later on in the cheesemaking process, and the cheese will have sufficient lactic acid for preservation, but it will retain the characteristics you are looking for: softer texture, more complex flavor, and proper rind development.

In the extreme case, when rapid acidification occurs because too much starter is used, the cheese is dry and hard directly after draining the whey. This happened to me once when I tried a new mesophilic aromatic culture in making Brie from pasteurized milk. I was searching for a solution to my problem of making cheeses that were too firm and not ripening fast enough. The technical representative who worked for the manufacturer of my starter cultures recommended a new culture. So I made the switch to the new culture and added the recommended amount. During curd draining and knitting, the whey acidity shot up like a rocket. By the end of the day the cheeses were drained to the point of feeling like bricks! In making the Brie, the curds were not cooked and the draining was done in plastic forms at ambient temperatures. That was a powerful demonstration of the bacteria's ability to produce lactic acid, which caused curds to contract and expel whey.

The next time I made cheese, I used half as much of the starter, but that was not enough. The next morning, after the normal draining time was finished, the cheeses were not firm enough to take out of the forms for salting. I removed the wheels and salted them anyway (I wasn't as patient a cheesemaker back then); they soon lost their perfect 9-inch/23 cm diameter and straight-sided shapes, and they softened up much faster during aging than my Brie usually did. I liked the cheese very much, and a French visitor told me that it was similar in form and taste to the farmstead Brie she normally buys at her local farmer's market. However, it wasn't consistent with our normal production because the texture was more elastic at a young age. (I still remember my father's reaction when he saw the batch!) I wanted to be somewhere in between the two extremes. Eventually, when I figured out how much to use, the new culture worked very well. This experience left me with many things to ponder: the selection of the starter bacteria based on their requirements for growth, the specific amount needed for the cheesemaking process, and what goes into producing a cheese that meets my expectations.

As lactic acid develops during the fermentation, calcium is leached out of the curds and runs out with the whey. Calcium is important in maintaining the elasticity of the cheese body. If calcium is running out too fast, then a dry, crumbly, acidic cheese is made. These characteristics aren't always apparent after the draining is complete; they can show up later during aging. Calcium also acts as a buffer against lactic acid production. For any type of cheese, a requisite amount of calcium must be retained in the curds after draining (and sometimes pressing) before cheeses are cooled, brined, or dry-salted. The level of calcium is determined by the rate at which the starter bacteria convert lactose into lactic acid. If the acid develops quickly, the cheeses will lose calcium and elasticity. In choosing the amount of starter to add, you are in effect trying to control the rate of acid production so that the proper amount of calcium is retained. Also keep in mind that different types of starter cultures are more or less sensitive to changes in salt content and temperature. This emphasizes the necessity of working with your culture supplier's technical representatives to learn the properties of your starters, as well as learning from your own trials. Make sure to keep records of your experiments.

TRANSLATING RECIPES USING DIRECT VAT SET AND BULK STARTERS

The manufacturer's recommendations concerning the amount of direct vat set (DVS) starter to use are based on a quantity called a unit (the *U* on the package stands for "units").

> One unit is the amount of starter that will turn a specific quantity of milk into lactic curd (without the addition of rennet) at a specific temperature in a certain amount of time.

For example, 2U of a specific DVS culture that I sometimes use will turn 227 pounds/100 liters of milk into lactic curd (pH 4.5) at 72°F/22°C in 15 hours. So the unit can be thought of as a "unit of strength" or "unit of acidification." With a different DVS starter series that I also use, 1U (one unit) will inoculate 50 pounds/22.7 kg of milk. This is equivalent to adding ½ pound/0.23 kg of a traditional bulk starter to 50 pounds of milk or, put another way, to adding 1 percent starter culture by weight. They each have the strength to make a lactic curd from 50 pounds of milk in 15 hours at 72°F.

This does not mean that the starter's only use is to make lactic curd. This amount of starter is used to make other cheeses and, in general, is the amount used in making cheeses from pasteurized milk and others, such as Cheddar, from raw milk when a fast fermentation is desired. You have to choose the amount of starter to reach the appropriate pH (acidity level) for the cheese in a specific time. For example, when 1U of a DVS culture that is equivalent in strength to ½ pound/0.23 kg bulk mesophilic lactic culture is added to 50 pounds/22.7 kg of milk: for Cheddar, it should take 5 to 6 hours to reach pH 5.3; for Brie, 12 hours to reach pH 4.8; and for feta, 20 hours to reach pH 4.6. The differences in the recipes account for the variation in the rate of acid production. Cooking the curds for Cheddar, for example, causes the starter bacteria to grow faster and produce sufficient acid in a shorter amount of time.

Bulk culture is easy to measure by volume, but to accurately measure the DVS culture it is best to weigh it. The weight of the starter in the packages varies by the lot number, so the amount you are using may change if you start a new package from a different lot (you can see the lot numbers on the packages). Remember that each gram of the DVS starter contains 10^{11} bacteria, which is a powerful amount. Because of this,

> it is best to measure the weight of 1U of starter, calculate the number of units needed to make your cheese, and multiply this number by the weight of 1U to calculate the weight of the starter you are going to use.

Example:
Assume that you have 350 pounds of milk for Cheddar, which will make one 35- to 40-pound wheel. You seek to use 1U of a specific DVS culture for each 50 pounds of milk. You have a 20U package of this DVS culture, which weighs 12.0 grams. How much starter (in grams) should you add to the 350 pounds of cheesemilk?

1. Pour the contents into a dry sterile container.
2. Weigh the bag; this will be the same for the 20U bags from other lots of starter.
3. Subtract the weight of the bag (for instance, 5 grams).
4. The weight of 20U starter is 12 - 5 = 7 grams. 1U starter weighs 0.35 gram (7 grams ÷ 20U = 0.35 gram).
5. The number of units needed: 350 pounds milk ÷ 50 pounds milk/U = 7U.
6. The weight of starter needed is 7U x 0.35 grams/U = 2.45 grams.
7. Therefore, add 2.45 grams of the DVS culture to the vat and stir it in.

The DVS starter has revolutionized cheesemaking practice. I know very few farmstead cheesemakers who make bulk starters and even fewer who generate a natural starter from their own milk. The majority open foil bags of DVS starters to commence cheesemaking. It makes life easier when you don't have to prepare your own starter and worry about maintaining consistency. When you propagate your own starters from commercial mother cultures or raw milk, you are adding another variable in the cheesemaking process that needs to be controlled. Natural starters made from raw milk are inherently wild and can vary in their rate of acidification and gas production during the year. Bulk starters made from commercial cultures can be continuously propagated as long as they maintain consistent acid and gas production. The longer the period of time that these bulk starters are propagated, the more wild strains of bacteria they can contain. Activity (rate of lactic acid and carbon dioxide production) may vary and must be strictly monitored to make consistent quality cheese. With the DVS starters, storage conditions and shelf life are the main concerns. I started making cheese before the advent of DVS starter technology, when making bulk starters was a necessity. I continue to do so out of habit. I'm not advocating the use of either bulk or DVS; the choice is yours to make.

> Compared with a bulk starter, the DVS starter requires an additional 30 minutes to ripen the milk before adding rennet.

The starter bacteria's role in cheesemaking is to act as a competitor against the bad (spoilage) bacteria in milk. The starter bacteria's job is to gain the upper hand, thereby arresting the growth of the bad guys and creating conditions for their own optimum growth. Bulk starter bacteria are ready to work the moment you add them to the warm milk in the vat; the bacteria have grown up in milk and are ready to plunge into action. The DVS starter bacteria, on the other hand, are still asleep. They need to wake up and get through the morning routine before they can enter the competition.

ADDING STARTER TO MILK

There are two different options for using DVS starter cultures; both can save some of the 30-minute lag time:

1. For raw-milk cheese, the starter can be added to the milk at 80°F/27°C during heating up to the setting temperature, which is usually 86 to 92°F/30 to 33°C. By putting the bacteria in earlier you also have a better chance of inhibiting spoilage bacteria—many bacteria begin to grow when the milk reaches 65°F/18°C.
2. As you start filling the vat, put 1 quart/liter of the milk into a Mason jar and heat it quickly to 90°F/32°C. Add the starter to this milk and mix it in. Keep the jar in a water bath at 90°F. At this point, start measuring the ripening time before adding rennet. The starter bacteria will grow to the proper strength in the quart of milk as well as they would in the full vat at 80 to 90°F/27 to 32°C. When the milk in the vat reaches 86 to 92°F/30 to 33°C, add the quart of starter to the vat. In this way, you can save the amount of time it takes to heat your milk up to the setting temperature. In many cases the rennet can be added directly after mixing in the starter. It is wise to mix the starter in for five minutes before adding rennet to ensure equal distribution.

Here are a few other tips on using starter that I have learned from experience:

- It is common to increase the amount of starter used to make cheese from late-lactation milk by 25 to 50 percent to maintain same rate of acid production. This is because there is some inhibition of starter in milk with high somatic cell count (SCC), which can be higher during late lactation; also, levels of vitamins, which bacteria need to grow, are lower when animals switch over to eating stored forages.

- The setting temperature can be changed if the cheese room doesn't have a constant temperature (climate control). In cooler times of year the milk is curdled at a higher temperature, so that there is enough heat in the curds during draining. This allows the bacteria to grow and produce acid at the appropriate rate for curds to drain well, which is especially important in cheeses made from uncooked curds. The opposite is true in hot weather when the milk is set at a lower temperature so that the curds do not drain too fast later on. An example is for feta where starter is added at 96°F/36°C in cool weather and 84°F/29°C in hot weather, when the optimum temperature in the recipe is 90°F/32°C.
- Since the starter bacteria are anaerobic, they grow better in deep vats of milk. Also, if you are working with a small quantity of milk in the vat, make sure that you maintain the optimum temperature during ripening—shallow vats of milk tend to cool down quickly. You can heat the milk in the vat until the rennet is added, but remember that, if the vat sides are hot, the milk will curdle and firm more quickly in that area of the vat.
- After the rennet is added to the milk, it should be stirred in for a period of time relative to the size of the vat being used. This can be anywhere from 30 seconds for a pot of milk to five minutes for a 3,000-gallon vat. The point is to distribute the rennet evenly throughout the milk. The swirling milk should then be slowed down so that it comes to rest as soon as possible. Spend another 30 to 60 seconds using a flat-bladed tool, such as the stirring paddle, to "break" the motion of the milk.
- In a pot or a kettle, the milk can be stirred up and down to mix in the rennet. The milk will come to rest sooner in this way than if it is stirred in a circular motion. As the milk begins to curdle, any motion will result in cracks and pockets of whey in the coagulum. When it is time to cut the curds there will be an uneven consistency throughout, which leads to uneven-sized curd particles. This can make a cheese with a swirled texture or one with areas of poorly drained curd, which create bleached, acid pockets in the cheese.

CUTTING THE CURDS

Cutting the coagulated milk into pieces is the first major step that separates the substances desired for cheese from the nonessential portion, which is the whey (unless ricotta cheese is being made). At this step, two decisions must be made that profoundly influence the characteristics of the finished cheese: (1) the length of time from adding rennet to beginning to cut the curds; and (2) the size of the curd particles.

Soon after I began making Brie and Camembert I had the pleasure of learning the secrets to these cheeses from fourth-generation cheesemakers on Ile de France, where Brie has been made for centuries. When determining the time to wait before cutting the curd, their method differed from my earlier training of waiting for a "clean break." After adding rennet, the French cheesemakers hovered around the vat waiting for the time when the milk began to curdle. I could actually see the curdling take place. As I moved a sanitized flat blade up and down in the milk, I watched the thickening of the milk, followed by the appearance of small grains. In the case of making the French cheeses, curdling took place in 12 to 15 minutes. The cheesemakers used a formula to calculate the cutting time, which was based on this curdling time or, as they called it, flocculation time. They multiplied the flocculation time by a factor of 6, which made the total time we waited from adding rennet to cutting equal to 72 to 90 minutes. I never knew why they did this.

I stopped making these cheeses in 1989. Several years later, after having made a variety of sheep's-, goat's-, and cow's-milk cheeses, I had forgotten about the French formula and was always waiting for the clean break of the curd to decide when to cut the coagulum. It always seemed as if I needed a magic touch to figure this out; one person's time to cut was another's time to wait five minutes. I was working on a project at Vermont Shepherd during the summer of 2000 when a French technician named Jacky Mege came to instruct the different Vermont Shepherd cheesemakers in the methods of making Pyrenees sheep cheese, which is the model for Vermont Shepherd Cheese. When it came time to determine when the curd was ready to cut, Jacky used the formula method! Armed with a metal spatula and his watch, he waited patiently by the vat until he could see the grains of curd forming on the surface as flocculation occurred. He multiplied this time of 10 minutes by 3 to get 30 minutes of waiting from adding rennet to cutting the curd.

My curiosity was piqued, so I asked him about the logic behind the method, which proved sound enough that I began to use the formula in all my cheesemaking. The underlying principle is that there are two phases in curd formation (as discussed in chapter 5):

1. **The enzymatic phase,** where the rennet enzymes cleave the kappa-casein on the surface of the casein particles (micelles), thereby exposing the remaining portion to calcium ions. When approximately 80 percent of the kappa-casein is cleaved, the next phase begins.
2. **The aggregation phase.** Here the micelles start to stick together, with calcium acting as the glue. As this phase continues, more casein micelles are connected by calcium, which entangles water, fat, whey proteins, and minerals in a lattice structure, thereby forming the curd.

The flocculation point parallels the start of the aggregation phase, which depends on the levels of casein and ionic calcium in the milk. Since these levels change during the year, the formula method accounts for these changes. I believe that the cheesemaking process is more uniform when this method is used.

The two important parts of this method are: (1) timing the flocculation point, and (2) choosing a multiplication factor to obtain a curd that, after it is cut, has the correct properties for the specific type of cheese you are making. So how do we decide on the correct factor—should it be 2, 3, 4, or what? The answer Jacky gave came in the form of another explanation.

During the aggregation phase, water becomes entrapped in the casein–calcium lattice structure. First, water is entrapped in a layer in direct contact with casein. This first-layer water is tightly occluded and resists expulsion during curd cutting. Therefore, the longer the aggregation continues, the more the curd resists whey drainage. On the other hand, curd from a short aggregation period releases whey readily when it is cut. This can be easily demonstrated by making a Swiss-type and a Brie-type cheese, which have short and long times of waiting before cutting, respectively. In Swiss cheesemaking, the curd is continuously harped until the curd particles are the size of rice grains, and there is a lot of whey in the vat after 15 minutes. By the time the curds are cooked and the curd mass is lowered into the press form, there is very little whey left to press out. The Brie cheese curd is cut vertically into 1-inch/2.5 cm ribbons with a saber and left to rest for 15 minutes. A small amount of whey comes out and is removed from the top of the curd. A saucer-shaped perforated disk called a *pelle* is used to transfer ½-inch/1.3 cm slices of curd into the forms. The whey drains from the curd, without pressing, for several hours in a warm room before the desired moisture content is achieved.

Factor	Cheese type
2, 2.5	Swiss, Alpine, and Grana
3, 3.5	Cheddar, (Hard British) Scandinavian, Dutch, Tomme, Mozzarella and Provolone
4	Feta, Blue
5, 6	Soft-ripened, smear-ripened (soft to semi-soft paste)

Table 10.1. Suggested factors to be multiplied by flocculation time in order to determine the cutting time for selected cheeses.

To obtain curd for Swiss cheese, a factor of 2 or 2.5 is used, while the factor for Brie is 6. In essence, you can influence the rate of whey drainage from the curd by the factor you choose. The values listed in table 10.1 seem to work well enough for me for choosing the multiplication factor.

There are exceptions to this method of choosing factors. Temperature also influences the flocculation time, which is why I use a factor of 3 for both soft (fresh) mozzarella and pizza mozzarella. The soft mozzarella curd is renneted at 98 to 100°F/37 to 38°C; it flocculates in 5 to 6 minutes and must be cut in 15 to 18 minutes, or else the curd sticks to the harp wires and creates an imperfect cut. The pizza mozzarella curd, like provolone, is renneted at 90°F/32°C, while the curd flocculates in 10 to 12 minutes and is cut 30 to 36 minutes after adding rennet.

Aged goat cheeses are made from a hybrid lactic–rennet curd. Cutting, which is actually performed by ladling the curds into forms, commences when the curd has developed sufficient acidity (pH 4.5, or 0.45 percent titratable acidity). These curds drain very slowly, like those for Brie, indicating the large amount of water retained in the curd, which is entrapped during the 15- to 36-hour setting time. In this case the acidity is the important consideration. If the acidity has not developed enough, the curds will not drain uniformly, leaving a skin on the outside with a mushy interior.

The second decision relates to the curd particle size, which ranges from scoops taken with a ladle to rice grains cut by vigorous action of a curd harp. For any type of cheese, larger curd particles will make higher-moisture, softer cheeses. Remember that acidity also plays a role in whey removal and cheese moisture content. Even though Cheddar and Swiss cheeses have approximately the same moisture content, Cheddar curd is cut into pea-sized particles, whereas Swiss curd is cut into rice-sized grains. However, Cheddar curds develop more acidity prior to pressing; the larger curd size prevents the cheese from becoming too dry by the time it is hooped and pressed. The Swiss-cheese curds are relatively sweet and must be very small to release as much whey as possible during cooking before they are gathered and pressed into a shape. Table 10.2 includes some typical choices for curd size.

Cheese type	Curd particle size
Swiss, Alpine and Grana	rice grains
Hard British, Provolone	small peas
Tomme, Feta, Scandinavian, Dutch	larger peas to hazelnuts
Soft to Semisoft (soft-ripened and smeared)	walnuts or ladle-sized

Table 10.2. Suggested cut sizes for selected cheeses.

WORKING AND FIRMING THE CURDS

There is an old cheesemaker's adage: *The cheese is made in the vat.* This points to the importance of the treatment of the curds prior to draining whey. For many cheeses most of the whey is removed by cooking and stirring the curds in the vat, and the decision on when to stop this action has a strong influence on the final moisture content of the cheese. This is one step that the cheesemaker needs to have under strict control. The moisture content of the cheese strongly influences how the cheese will age, and it is important to keep moisture content in a specific range that yields cheese that, in turn, develops the right flavor at the right time. Of course, this is where cheese grading comes in: to separate the good from the not-so-good, and to determine which cheeses have the potential for long aging and which must be sold young. However, training yourself to sense when the curds are ready to be drained is a worthwhile endeavor. This is also the hardest part of cheesemaking to teach.

The acidity of the whey can be measured to indicate if it is time to drain, but for most cheeses the artisan's intuition is needed. Cheesemakers have to acquire a sense of the "grip" or texture and density of the curds to decide when to stop cooking. This is done in a couple of different ways.

Figure 10.1. Margaret Morris demonstrates the "grip" of the curd while making Gouda cheese. (Photo by Peter Dixon.)

Both methods begin with you collecting some curds using a sanitized utensil such as a perforated ladle.

1. Gently or firmly squeeze the curds (free of whey) in the palm of your hand to check for springiness, and even rub the cake of squeezed curds between both hands to determine how well they separate into individual curd grains again. (Discard the curds; do not return them to the vat.)
2. Let a thin layer of curds settle on the underside of the fingers of one hand as you hold them tightly together. Hold them at an angle so that the whey can drain off, and then turn your hand over to find out the degree to which the curds will stick to your fingers. Usually you want the curds to be permanently attached to fingers held upside down.

Some of the best parts of cheese recipes discuss how the grip of the curds is determined. It is a good idea to read up on this subject.

Since the bacteria are growing and converting lactose into lactic acid during this time, it is important to think about the relationship between their rate of growth and the firming of the curds. As acidity increases, curds are shrinking and expelling whey. Heating and stirring the curds is also causing whey expulsion. The trick is to have curds firmed to the right moisture content with the proper amount of acid developed by the time they are ready to leave the vat. In making some cheeses, such as Cheddar, the conditions during cooking encourage both these things to happen rapidly because a mesophilic culture is used and the bacteria are growing at close to their optimum temperature. In other cheeses, like Swiss, acid develops slowly due to the small amount of starter used and higher cooking temperatures, which inhibit the rapid growth of the thermophilic bacteria. In feta and soft (fresh) mozzarella the curds are stirred for a short time, usually 10 to 30 minutes, without any additional heating; the point is to firm the curds only by stirring, and the increase in acidity is negligible. Here are a few points to consider when cooking curds:

- If the acidity is developing too quickly, the cooking temperature can be raised to slow down the bacteria (for instance, cooking at 103 to 104°F/39 to 40°C for mesophiles, and at 125 to 135 °F/52 to 57°C for thermophiles).
- If acidity is increasing too slowly, the temperature can be lowered a couple of degrees and the cooking time drawn out longer.
- It is best to be at approximately the same acidity from one batch to another when it is time to drain whey. However, adjustments can be made later on if your senses are telling you that the curds are firm enough but the acidity is either too high or too low. If the acidity is rising slowly, curds can be piled and left to ripen longer before pressing, or wheels of cheese can be kept on the press longer before brining to allow acidity to increase. If the acidity is increasing too quickly, curds can be salted earlier or wheels can be cooled down after pressing to slow the acid development. (I have seen cheesemakers in Armenia run cold water over the cheese about halfway through the pressing to mitigate rapid acid development, which was caused by the acid milk they received in the morning.)
- With a mixed culture of thermophilic and mesophilic bacteria, higher temperatures (up to 110°F/43°C) can be used to inhibit the growth of coliform bacteria when making tomme-style cheeses.

A natural addition to this discussion is how curd firming is influenced by the composition of the milk. This will lead into the next section on seasonal milk production, milk composition, and cheese quality. *The cheese is made in the vat* applies here again. Indeed, the moisture content of any cheese that isn't made from hand ladling curds from a smooth, uncut vat of curd is best controlled by the techniques used when cutting, stirring, and cooking the curds. By the time of pressing, it is too late to remove a significant amount of moisture; this step is mainly used to form curds into a distinct shape. How can the moisture be controlled if the composition of the milk is changing dramatically, as is so often the case in seasonal herds and flocks? Table 10.3 may help guide you in deciding how and when to change your techniques during cooking or firming the curds in the whey. The information in this table pertains to making a slightly cooked-curd and pressed cow's-milk cheese, such as a tomme, with a moisture content of approximately 45 percent, and assumes that the milk is of good quality and not

Stage of lactation (days in milk)	Milk total solids	Curd size at cutting	Cooking time (min)	Cooking temp. (F/C)
Early: 0–60 DIM	medium–high	average	average: 20	98–99/36.7–37.2
Middle: 60–240	low–medium	smaller	longest: 20–30	99–101/37.2–38.3
Late: 240–300	highest	larger	shortest: 10–15	97–98/36.1–36.7

Table 10.3. Examples of adjustments that can be made in the manufacture of tomme-style cheese as the season progresses, to compensate for lactational changes in milk chemistry.

altered by late-lactation effects that would cause problems in making cheese (see Seasonal Dairying and Cheesemaking, page 214). None of this is set in stone; you can adapt your technique according to your own perception of changes in the composition of your milk.

> The point is to change your techniques so that your cheese maintains its characteristic quality, with subtle variations in flavor and uniformity in texture and body characteristics.

Air temperature has a significant effect on curd draining and acidification rates. Without a controlled air temperature, which is normally the case in farmstead operations, you will notice differences in the rate of whey drainage from your hoops of curds. This is especially true for cheeses that drain for a long time at ambient temperatures, because the curds will have a longer time to cool down from the initial hooping temperature. Cheeses that drain optimally at 70°F/21°C will lose too little whey at 60°F/16°C and too much at 80°F/27°C, thereby causing variation in cheese moisture content. The lactic bacteria produce acid, which stimulates whey drainage. Their growth rate is also affected by temperature, so that, in addition to changes in moisture content, the final acidity (pH) of cheeses will change depending on the ambient temperature of the day. Low ambient temperature is of particular concern because the combined effects of slower acid development by the starter and greater moisture retention increase the risk of microbiological problems and foodborne illness. This combination should be avoided at all costs. Does this mean that we should all install climate control systems? Not necessarily, in my opinion. As long as we can move our cheeses to cooler places sooner on hot days and later on cool days *in such a way as to optimize draining and acidification,* we can provide manual control. It's a matter of learning to adapt to whatever Mother Nature sends our way.

PRESSING: FORMING THE SHAPE OF THE CHEESE

The last bit of whey is squeezed out and the characteristic shape of the cheese is made by pressing. The amount of pressure applied and the time the cheese is under the press vary considerably, depending on the cheese you are making. Cheddar and other milled-curd cheeses take the most amount of pressure to squeeze all the separate curds back together after they are salted. In these cheeses it is important to keep the curds around 90°F/32°C during the mellowing period between salting and pressing to prevent the fat from solidifying on the outside of the curds. This creates cheeses that are poorly knit together, with visible seam lines between the curds. Recipes list pressure amounts in pounds per square inch (psi) or kg/m^3—both helpful figures for hydraulic and pneumatic presses, but they don't give you much to go on for lever-type presses. The best way to figure it out is to apply enough pressure to compress the curds sufficiently so the cheese rind is smooth (no nooks and crannies on the cheese surface) without having the fat squeezed out, which gives the cheese a greasy surface. Of course, this is a trial-and-error exercise.

In other types of cheese, the lactic fermentation continues during pressing, and generally speaking it is important to keep the cheese room warm so the proper amount of acidity is attained in the curd before it is brined. Suprisingly, it does not require very much pressure to form large wheels of Alpine-style and Grana cheeses. I remember seeing some 100-pound/45 g wheels of Swiss being pressed under sections of railroad rails that were sitting on top of the forms. During dipping, the curds for these cheeses are gathered under the whey by slipping a coarse cheesecloth underneath and raising them out in one mass. After a short draining period, the curd cake is left in one piece or divided before it is placed into the hoops, and the hot curds are easily pressed into wheels. For any cooked-curd cheese, it is important to work quickly while dipping the curds into their forms to prevent excessive cooling. If the curds lose heat, it is difficult to press them into shapes with smooth rinds.

For pressing smaller (2- to 5-pound/0.9 to 2.3 kg) wheels, such as tomme and Gouda, a gallon jug filled with water, sand, or gravel and set on top of the follower is perfectly adequate. It takes about three to four hours to press the cheeses. Barbell weights also make very good press weights because of their low center of gravity, which prevents the cheeses from getting cockeyed if the taller jug-type weight slips off-center. One of my favorite things is seeing the different press weights cheesemakers have created out of simple materials.

Cheesecloth is essential for making well-drained wheels with smooth rinds. This is because the cloth acts as a wick for the whey, allowing it to leave the curd through the holes in the forms. Use cheesecloth to prevent mechanical openings in the rind from forming during pressing. This point can be illustrated by way of a contrast: Blue cheese curds are not pressed, and drain in open-ended forms without any cheesecloth lining to give the cheese an open texture inside and on the surface. In contrast, the open texture in pressed-curd cheeses comes more from pockets of carbon dioxide gas between the curds, which are produced by bacteria in raw milk and specific starter cultures.

The cheesecloth sometimes sticks to cheeses during pressing because the acidity is rising and the curds are hot. To prevent sticking, it is good practice to remove the cloth after pressing for one hour and soak it in saturated brine before putting it back over the cheese and returning it to the press. If a coarse cloth is used initially, it can be changed to a smoother cloth after one hour so that the rind will also be smooth instead of grainy. The coarse cloths are very tough and long lasting, facilitate better whey drainage, and are helpful in making larger wheels.

If too much pressure is applied, the cheesecloth will be pressed far into the rind and will be difficult to remove. However, the cloth is deliberately pressed into the rinds of clothbound cheeses such as Cheddar and Cheshire. After first pressing, the cheeses are dipped in scalding hot water, encased in two layers of fine greased cheesecloth, and pressed again for a day to bind the cloth onto the rind. This gives the cheeses a protective coating that can be cleaned during aging. Some cheesemakers practice scalding on a regular basis to close up the rinds of other types of cheeses that are not going to be clothbound.

Muslin cheesecloth is ideal for pressing rinded cheeses that are going to be brined or clothbound. It leaves few wrinkles. The nylon wraps for lining block forms work well but are not suitable for rounds and smaller cheeses—they leave too many wrinkles, which become areas for tenacious molds to grow and are hard to keep clean. This may not be problem if you are going to wax the cheese, anyway. Turn the cheeses in their forms two or three times during pressing to make the shapes more symmetrical.

It takes at least four hours to press semihard and hard varieties of cheese. Make sure that you control acid development during pressing so that the cheese is pressed enough. In making Gouda, if the acid is running ahead of the pressing, the cheeses must removed from the press early and brined according to the degree of acidity. This will create the proper texture, but the resulting cheeses may be higher in moisture because of a shorter pressing time. The balance between acidity and moisture content is a key to making cheese with the right body, texture, and flavor when aging is finished. Higher-moisture cheeses will age faster, and you should make note of any batches that do not follow the usual pattern.

SEASONAL DAIRYING AND CHEESEMAKING

Seasonal dairying follows the natural cycles of growth, decline, and dormancy, starting with lactating animals giving birth to their young in spring. At this time the warmth is returning to the earth and pasture plants yawn, shrug off the cold of winter, and begin to grow. By June all the young have been weaned and their mothers are approaching their peak in milk production, which generally coincides with lush pasture growth. Summer rolls along, bringing periods of rain and sometimes drought that affect the growth and nutritional quality of pasture plants.

Typically, in the northeastern United States, there is a period of rapid plant growth in late spring to early summer, followed by a phase in midsummer when drier conditions prevail, which slows down plant growth. If drought sets in, there is little for grazing animals to eat, and less hay is made by farmers because they have to skip a cutting and wait for the rain. The rains usually come in late summer, and warm weather in autumn can lead to an extended period of pasture growth and grazing. In late November plants are again dormant and animals are finishing out their lactations by consuming stored forages; then it is nice to reflect on the entire year of dairying and feel comfortable or worried about next year's prospects.

For those farmers and cheesemakers with seasonal herds, December is usually the final month of milking cows and goats, whereas the sheep dairy season ends in October. These seasonal end points are due to the length of the natural lactation of the particular animal; cows and does may give milk for 300 days and ewes for 180 days after parturition, respectively. We can discuss this lactation period regardless of when parturition occurs, but this discussion is focused on farm operations where the entire herd or flock is spring-birthing. A reverse-season approach is used with cows and goats where birthing occurs in fall so that the lactation ends in summer, to free up the farmer's time for crop production. At the end of lactation comes the dry period, providing the lactating animals a rest before the next birthing cycle. The following section is relative to either form of seasonal dairying, as long as the entire herd or flock is following the natural length of a lactation together. The major difference is that, with spring-birthing systems, the focus is on pasture grazing as the nutrient source.

Two aspects of seasonal milk production are important to the farmstead cheesemaker: (1) the change in milk composition during the year, and (2) the quality of the milk for cheesemaking in late lactation, which dictates when is the best time to stop.

Milk composition is affected by many factors: breed, age, animal individuality, diet, stage of lactation, environment, and health. Breed will determine the average total solids (protein, fat, lactose, and minerals) content of the milk. For instance, Jersey cows have the highest fat levels relative to protein and overall higher total solids; Brown Swiss have fat levels closer to protein and higher total solids; and Holsteins have fat levels closer to protein and lower total solids. The first lactation generally produces the lowest total solids relative to later ones. All farmstead cheesemakers are aware of individual animal differences and want animals that produce the greatest amount of fat and protein over their lactations because this yields more cheese. Let's take a look at the remaining four factors and discover how they contribute to some important changes in seasonally produced milk and cheese.

Factors Affecting Milk and Cheese Quality

Two different ways of managing seasonal dairy farms are widely used:

1. Rotational grazing within the environs of the farm, with animals being milked and fed varying amounts of concentrates

Figure 10.2. A *bachilo* (sheep farmstead cheesemaking station) on Bistra Mountain in western Macedonia.

(or none at all on grass-based dairy farms) in the barn or milking shed, where milk may be stored under refrigeration before being made into cheese.

2. Traditional migration (transhumance) to alpine pastures, where animals graze freely, are milked in sheds or outdoors, and cheese is made after every milking.

The traditional method is practiced throughout the Mediterranean region and in the European Alps. In the Mediterranean this practice is essential, because the climate is very dry during the grazing season and the best pastures are at higher elevations. Sheep and goats are the milking animals of choice. In the Pyrenees, on Corsica, and in the mountains of the Balkan peninsula, farmers and cheesemakers generally live and work in simple huts without electricity from May until October (see figure 10.1). In the European Alps small herds of cows graze on high-elevation pastures where milking is done and cheese is made. The various plants consumed by the lactating animals contribute directly to the unique flavors of the cheeses. Because plant growth occurs in cycles and is dependent on the weather, the animals' diet changes during the grazing season and, along with it, so does the cheese flavor.

The same relationship among plant species, quality, and cheese flavor exists on North American farms where rotational grazing is practiced. Although our regulations prevent farmers and cheesemakers from milking and making cheese out in the open, the animals still get the majority, if not all, of their diet from grazing on fresh pastures. Regional cheese flavor comes from the specific plants that inhabit the pastures of the Pyrenees or the Swiss Alps or southern Vermont, for example, but the quality of the diet animals get from these pastures is under the control of Mother Nature.

The diet quality or nutritional plane of the animals is very important and needs to be maintained at a sufficient level to ensure good-quality milk production for cheese, particularly in late lactation (more on this later). The superior vitamin content of milk produced when animals are on good-quality pastures is beneficial to the growth and activity of microorganisms essential for cheesemaking and aging (Van Slyke and Price, 1979). When animals are on lush spring and summer pastures, the milk is full of flavor compounds, minerals, and vitamins, and the flavor of spring and summer cheese seems more delicate and complex. In periods of drought animals can actually experience some degree of starvation from the effects of heat, lack of water, and scarcity of food; milk production drops off, and cheeses may be firmer and less creamy. Flavor may be diminished because of limited plant growth.

In late autumn, when milking animals are in late lactation, milkfat and protein (and cheese yields) reach peak levels. In this period a cheese's complexity of flavor is diminished but it is still creamy and rich, and the body is softer. When the milking animals go off pasture and consume stored forage, the cheese color gradually becomes more pale. It is clear that the cheese's sensory attributes (body, texture, and flavor) are heavily influenced by diet, but even during a growing season, with the best conditions for pasture growth (high diet quality), there will still be significant changes in the levels of milkfat and protein, which are entirely due to stage of lactation. The variation in these milk constituents is imparted directly into the cheese, thereby altering its composition, which affects the cheese body (how firm or soft the cheese is). It can be a real challenge to cheesemakers to cope with large changes in milk composition because it is hard to control cheese moisture content.

Environment and Health

Farmstead cheese houses are generally very open to the environment. The changes in types and levels of microorganisms that inhabit the surroundings add another level of influence and variation to cheese flavor, as well as another level of risk from environmental pathogens. Variation in cheese flavor is very pronounced in farmstead cheese made from milk of grazing animals, particularly if the milk is raw. There is a direct transfer into the milk of microorganisms from the entire farm environment, whose levels are unchanged by heat treatments. These microorganisms release a multitude of enzymes into the cheese during aging that create texture and flavor. The less desirable microbes, especially from the barnyard, proliferate during dry and dusty or wet and muddy conditions around the farm and can cause defects in the cheese's sensory attributes, such as unclean flavor and gassy texture. Animal health is another factor that affects milk and cheese quality. When animals in the milking string become diseased, namely with subclinical or clinical mastitis, the bacterial and somatic cell count loads in milk become elevated; later on during aging, this transfers to the cheese undesirable qualities such as bitterness and rancidity.

Late Lactation

Late-lactation milk has been identified as having poor cheesemaking qualities. In Ireland and New Zealand all milk used for cheesemaking is produced seasonally by grazing animals. Studies there have shown that substantial changes can occur in the milk; these cause problems during cheesemaking when the animals are in late lactation (more than 240 days in milk) and receive poor nutrition (their diet consists only of the plants they eat off pasture at the end of the growing season). Specifically, poor-quality late-lactation milk for cheesemaking resulted in soft curd formation, poor whey drainage, and slow acidification, which in turn led to the production of high-moisture Cheddar and mozzarella. Cheeses having moisture contents above their normal targeted range are undesirable because they age too fast and in the wrong way, yielding soft body, pasty texture, and bitter and rancid off-flavors. Farm cheesemakers who are striving to produce good-quality cheese, while still allowing for nuances in flavor during an entire lactation, have to pay strict attention to controlling the moisture content in order to maintain the identity of each specific type of cheese they make, as discussed in chapters 6 and 8. Milk quality can be improved if stored forages and concentrates are fed to replace pasture in decline. The idea is to maintain an adequate plane of nutrition throughout lactation so as not to disrupt the mineral balance of the milk.

The susceptibility of lactating animals to mastitis is high in late lactation. In the small herds and flocks that most farmstead cheesemakers have, one sick animal can elevate the somatic cell count of the entire milk supply, while also contributing some undesirable bacteria to the mix. High-SCC milk is more alkaline (with a pH greater than 6.8) and will inhibit the growth of natural milk and starter bacteria such that the fermentation of lactose to lactic acid is slowed. Increasing the amount of starter can help to overcome this problem, and more starter is typically used in late lactation to produce the same amount of acidity in the cheese. Cheese yields are inversely related to SCC, decreasing proportionately as SCC increases above 100,000/ml for cow's milk. The best approach is to cull out any animals that develop subclinical mastitis (detected with a California or Wisconsin Mastitis Test). If the farmer manages the herd or flock by providing a good-quality diet and controlling udder health, the cheesemaking season should go the full 180 days (for sheep) or 300 days (for cows and goats). Using this management strategy, Cheddar cheese was made throughout the entire lactation at Shelburne Farms in Shelburne, Vermont, in 1995 when the entire herd of 90 Brown Swiss cows was spring-calving.

Remember to look for the telltale signs of problematic late-lactation milk:

- High pH: greater than 6.8.
- High SCC: greater than 500,000 for individual cows, and greater than 250,000 for bulk tanks.

- Slower starter activity.
- Very long curdling times and soft curd formation.
- Poor whey drainage and cheese with excess moisture.

The benefit of using good-quality late-lactation milk for cheese is in the increased yield. For example, the yield of Cheddar cheese from Shelburne Farms' seasonal herd during 1995 is shown in chapter 3, figure 3.8. Every 0.1 percent increase in milk protein increased Cheddar cheese yield by 0.14 percent.

Practical Cheesemaking during Lactation

Aside from the sensory qualities of cheese, what changes take place in the cheese vat during the 6 to 10 months of lactation? As the milkfat and protein contents vary (see chapter 3, figure 3.7), so does the cheese composition (see chapter 8, figure 8.7). The trick is to allow for flavor variation (seasonal effect) in the cheese without experiencing large changes in the moisture content. It is very helpful to have some sense of the variation in milk total solids. Monthly milk composition testing will certainly give you direct information about the changes in milkfat and protein levels. As the total solids vary, cheesemakers will notice the following changes: (1) the curd sets up firmer or softer after adding rennet, (2) curds firm up faster or slower after cutting, (3) whey drains faster or slower from the curds, (4) the amount of fat lost in the whey varies, and (5) the finished cheeses are firmer or softer.

SALTING AND BRINING CHEESE

Brining is the means by which most rinded cheeses are salted. Soft ripened cheeses can also be brined, but for a very short time due to their small size. In the brining process a thin rind forms from dehydration, which is caused by the salt concentrating itself around the outer layer of the cheese. During the days following brining the salt diffuses throughout the cheese so that the salt content becomes uniform, usually 1.0 to 1.5 percent. The main reasons for salting cheese are to slow down acid production by lactic bacteria, to retard spoilage by inhibiting the growth of contaminants, and to produce flavor. Anyone who has tasted low-salt cheese knows how important the last reason is.

Brine Composition and Quality

Cheese brines should be nearly saturated salt solutions (that is, around 24 percent). Important characteristics of salt brines such as brine concentration, temperature, calcium concentration, and pH are discussed in chapter 4. This fresh brine recipe works well for me:

For every 10 pounds/4.54 kg brine at pH 5.2, mix together:

- 3 pounds/1.36 kg salt
- 8 pounds/3.63 kg (1 gallon) water
- 1 tablespoon calcium chloride (30 percent solution), or 5 grams dry CaCl powder
- 1 teaspoon white vinegar (5 percent acetic acid), or 1 ml lactic acid

After the brine has been made, it is very important to maintain the quality. The real key for maintaining brines is keeping the temperature around 50°F/10°C. This is usually done by keeping the brine tank in the aging room (cellar). So when you design your cheese cellar, make sure to have a space for the brine tank and shelving to put the cheese on to dry before it is moved to the actual aging area. The temperature of most cheese aging cellars is 45 to 55°F/7 to 13°C, so it works very well to combine brining and aging in the same space. It is also important to skim cheese particles from the brine surface and wipe down the sides of the tank above the brine to prevent contamination from yeast and molds. Always keep the brine at a constant strength (for example, around 24 percent salt) so that the cheeses are absorbing the same amount of salt while they are in the brine. The effects of acidity (as measured by pH), calcium content, and temperature of the brine on the cheese are summarized in table 10.4.

In a near-saturated brine a time of four hours per pound of cheese renders the appropriate salt content for many cheese types. However, the shape of the cheese influences this rule, and it's important to adapt it somewhat. For example, a cheese with a thickness of 3 to 4 inches/7.5 to 10 cm can be brined for three to four hours per 1 pound. But a 2-inch/5 cm cheese will only need two hours per pound to acquire the same salt content.

> A general rule for brining is to brine for one hour per pound/0.45 kg per 1-inch/2.5 cm thickness of the cheese.

Of course, some cheeses benefit from being saltier, including blues, feta, and Romano; the taste isn't quite right without being slightly salty. So suit yourself (that is, your customers), but remember to adjust brining time according to weight, shape, and temperature.

I recommended that brine temperature not exceed 55°F/13°C, but I have seen brining done at warmer temperatures in the Balkans, where it is hot during the cheesemaking season. Even in cellars where there is no refrigeration the temperature is usually above 70°F/21°C. In this case it is a good idea to make fresh brines every week. Eventually enough whey and solid residues will leave the cheeses so that

pH	Calcium content	Rind character	Temp. F/C	Effect on cheese
>Cheese	<Cheese	Soft, pasty, slimy	>55 / >12.8	Whey drainage out of cheese Fast salt uptake
=Cheese	=Cheese	Firm, thin skin	45-55 / 7.2–12.8	Ideal, consistent salt uptake and cheese salt content
<Cheese	>Cheese	Hard, tough as cow horn	<45 / 7.2	Slow salt uptake

Table 10.4. Summary of the effects of acidity (pH), calcium content, and temperature of the brine on the characteristics of the cheese.

the brine will have a high protein content and will be able to support the growth of microbes. The quality of the brine can be checked by doing the titratable acidity of a 9 ml sample of brine. Readings higher than 40 percent acidity indicate that it is time to make a new brine. Brines kept at 45 to 55°F/7 to 13°C are usually changed every six months to a year.

Brining Technique

The temperature of the cheese should be the same as that of the brine before the cheese is actually placed in the brine. This creates uniform salt absorption at the desired rate. It also prevents blocks and wheels from losing their shape if they are placed closely together on their sides. Some cheesemaking procedures, such as those for Gouda, Swiss, and feta, involve brining cheeses directly after pressing, when they are still warm. In this case it is very important to place the cheeses in the brine flat in one layer only, so that they retain their shape as they cool down while floating independently. This is actually a good idea for all cheeses—warm *or* cold—because if they are packed in tightly on their sides or in more than one layer, there will always be places where the cheeses are touching each other, thereby inhibiting salt absorption. Later on, during aging, there may be quality problems such as gas blowing on one side of a cheese because there wasn't enough salt to check microbial growth. This is why brine tanks are so big and shallow. You can use the packing method in smaller brine tanks, but you'll have to turn the cheeses a few times during the brining period to prevent poor salt absorption. Dry salt should always be spread on the exposed surfaces of cheese in the brine. Turn the cheeses once a day while they are in the brine; if you pack them in tightly, turn them more frequently. A well-brined cheese should have formed a thin rind around it by the time you take it out, and the rind should remain fairly smooth during aging.

Pickled cheeses such as feta depart from the above techniques because they are aged in brine-filled containers. Usually blocks are brined for 18 to 24 hours in a saturated brine. Then three to four layers of cheese blocks are packed into a can, with the pickling brine (8 to 12 percent salt) poured in after. The blocks have already absorbed a lot of salt and formed a rind from being in the saturated brine; the pickling brine eventually works its way around all the blocks during aging. Traditional feta made from raw milk typically has a 5 percent salt content and has gone from 62 to 52 percent moisture content after aging for a few months.

SOME NOTES ON AGING CHEESE

I'll wrap up this chapter with a few notes on the final steps of cheesemaking, aging and affinage. Artisanal cheesemaking often entails making do with what is at hand—that is, using common materials and your own labor or working on the cheap to construct facilities. Nevertheless, it goes without saying that your facilities and practices in the aging cellar or cave

Figure 10.3. Cheeses made by Peter Dixion ripen in the aging cellar at Westminster Dairy. (Photo by Peter Dixon.)

must conform to applicable regulatory standards, just as they must in the cheese room and milking parlor.

Recently, when I set out to build a cheese cellar, the beginnings of it already existed in the foundation of the building, which housed the cheese room. It was a much bigger space than I needed. My challenge was to put a room into the cellar that would have the right conditions for aging the cheeses I wanted to make. Since I wanted flexibility to age a variety of cheeses, I opted for the following design, which works well for some types of cheese but not so well for others. The cellar is naturally humid because it is 7 feet/2.1 m underground and made from poured concrete. It is directly underneath the cheese room, and a dumbwaiter is used to move the cheeses up and down. After creating the space by using two of the foundation walls and setting up two more walls with interlocking insulated panels from an old cooler, I needed to provide air circulation and cooling.

The cellar is cooled by radiation from ice water flowing through a loop of 1-inch/2.5 cm copper pipe, which is suspended around the upper perimeter of the cellar (where the walls meet the ceiling), because heat rises and cold air sinks. The cooling pipe is connected to a 500-gallon ice builder. A 5-horsepower compressor pumps refrigerant through pipes across metal plates suspended in the ice builder tank. The water in the tank can be maintained at close to freezing temperatures. Air circulation is created by a window fan, which hangs in one corner of the cellar. A dumbwaiter shaft leading upstairs provides exhaust for the airflow. The present setup can't keep the room cold enough (below 60°F/16°C) in summer. I plan to put in some sections of pipe with radiating fins to provide better cooling. I know of other people who have had good success with using low-velocity refrigeration units in their cellars, coolers, and caves to keep the temperature in the appropriate range. The refrigeration company you work with needs to know that this is the same kind of refrigeration used in florist shops to store cut flowers and in butcher shops to hang meat.

The conditions in the cellar change during the course of the year. The humidity fluctuates and, since there is some flooding in spring, the relative humidity can get quite high (better than 95 percent), which is perfect for Camembert, Brie, and smear-ripened cheeses. Sometimes I leave the door open to the outer part of the cellar during the day to dry it out a bit. The outside humidity affects the cellar humidity, but it never gets very dry (less than 85 percent relative humidity). In the dead of winter, when it is too dry, I have poured water on the floor. The concrete soaks it up gradually like a sponge, which seems to increase the humidity. I do this when the smear-ripened cheeses are getting too dry and the smear is not growing very well. The temperature ranges from 44 to 62°F/7 to 17°C (winter to summer), which seems like a lot, but I can work with the situation for most of the cheeses I make. I cannot make Camembert if the temperature goes above 55°F/13°C, because the outside paste near the rind ripens too fast.

I find that the smear-ripened cheeses are stronger in flavor during the warm period. They age much more slowly and stay mild longer when the temperature dips below 52°F/11°C. The washed-rind cheeses are easy to take care of. As long as the pH isn't too low before brining, they take care of themselves. I turn the wheels once a week and smear the sticky paste around. This yeasty coating persists for about one month and gives way to the reddish growth of *Brevibacterium linens.* If it gets too dry in the cellar, I may dip my hands into a 5 percent brine and wash the rinds twice a week to maintain the smear, but this is a rare occurrence. It is always a good idea to use sanitized gloves when handling smear-ripened cheeses.

The hard Alpine types do very well; the rinds get some yeasts and *Brevibacterium linens* on them and are not extremely high in density. It makes sense that the aging process goes faster in summer and slower in winter. I make more hard cheese in fall, and these wheels age through the cold winter period to be ready for sale in late spring or early summer. I turn and care for the rinds once a week.

There has been a problem in aging cheeses with really tough, hard rinds such as Grana and aged provolone (picante). The yeast growth during periods of high humidity keeps the dry, tough rinds from forming. These cheeses are better off in a drier environment.

My experience with making a natural-rind, aged provolone has been the following. The provolone has a lower pH (around 5.0), and blue mold tends to proliferate on the rind. I was spending a lot of time scrubbing it off. My routine was to clean the rinds twice a week and rub in a liberal amount of olive oil, which darkened the rind and added a flavor component. I gave up doing this for two reasons:

too much time cleaning rinds, and no way to justify the time with a higher cheese price. Provolone is one of those cheeses that is simply associated with a lower price—even the aged, piquant Italian cheese. However, I have been able to make a few salami-shaped cheeses that hang in the drier part of the cellar where the temperature gets up to 68°F/20°C in summer. These cheeses are hard bodied and sharp and more than one year old. My current method for most of the provolone is to dry the rinds in a large refrigerator as they sit on racks for complete air circulation. After two weeks of this the cheeses acquire a uniform yellow color; then I wax them. This provolone is a deli-style cheese with a higher moisture content, which can be sold after 60 days.

I made several 40- to 65-pound/18 to 30 kg wheels of Grana cheese over one winter. In spring it was very humid in the cellar, and the rinds began to get too soft and covered with a sticky paste of yeasts and bacteria. Rot spots began to appear. I moved the cheeses onto shelves in the main cellar, and the rinds dried out enough so that I could scrape off some of the microbial buildup to reveal the hard, smooth rind again. The mites began to get to this cheese when it was 8 to 10 months old, and it had excellent flavor. I am making and aging as much as possible now to get an inventory ready for next year.

In spring, before the temperature exceeded 55°F/13°C, I aged a few batches of Brie- and Camembert-type cheeses in the cellar. The first batch had toad skin; after that, I stopped putting *Geotrichum* in the spray for inoculating the cheese. I believed that there was sufficient *Geotrichum* in the cellar environment, and spraying with white molds was adequate. The subsequent batches ripened very well during the two weeks they were in the cellar. After the bloomy rind was complete, I moved the cheeses to a cool, dry spot in the outer cellar for a few hours, then wrapped them and moved them to a 50°F/10°C refrigerator for a month before sale.

I guess the lesson from all this is that it is possible, with some ingenuity, to age different styles of cheese in the same cellar. It is also very challenging and may involve more risk than you are willing to accept. I definitely see the need for a second, drier cellar—say, one with 80 to 85 percent relative humidity and a temperature around 60°F/16°C, which would be best for the harder Italian cheeses such as provolone, Asiago, Romano, and Parmesan. Completing the picture for aging and storing my cheeses is a standard walk-in cooler with conventional refrigeration (big ventilation fans) that can be used for storing the fresh cheeses and staging orders of cheeses for delivery. This cooler should maintain temperatures of 34 to 38°F/1 to 3°C and have maximum ventilation to distribute the cold air.

FINAL THOUGHTS

In closing this chapter, it is necessary to review the preceding information by taking a last look at the nature of artisanal cheesemaking. To do this, I pose the question: How can cheesemaking be defined in terms of the outcome of the process—

in other words, by the cheese itself? Given two different approaches to making a certain type of cheese, there may be two distinct outcomes in the quality of the final product. For example, there is industrial Parmesan and then there is Parmigiano-Reggiano. In this and many other cases, the authentic artisanal version has been duplicated by a factory counterpart, which comes as close as possible to the real thing, given the constraints of industrial processing. We have only to compare various artisanal cheeses and their industrial versions side by side to identify the characteristics of the artisanal cheese: a range of flavor, from full and robust to delicate and complex; earthy, natural rinds inhabited by a diversity of microflora; and subtle changes in texture due to variation in the levels of gas-producing bacteria from the raw milk.

There is definitely more risk in making artisanal cheeses because of the higher proportion of cheese that does not meet the standard of excellence. The brain trust of dairy science is assisting in reducing the amount of substandard-quality cheese by conducting research and providing technical information to traditional artisanal cheesemakers. This work is being done in France, Italy, Spain, Switzerland, and other countries where the tradition of farmstead and artisanal cheesemaking is embedded in the culture. However, it is important to remember that cheesemaking began as a handcraft and that cheesemakers create products that can be appreciated, like any work of art, by people using all their senses. The melding of science and art in the craft of cheesemaking is a good thing so long as the traditions that define the craft are not stripped away to make way for modern "improvements" and changes to the artisanal process.

CHAPTER 10 REFERENCES

Androuët, P. 1973. *Guide du Fromage: The Complete Encylopedia of French Cheese.* Harper's Magazine Press, New York.

Cheke, V. 1959. *The Story of Cheesemaking in Britain.* Routledge & Kegan Paul, London.

Van Slyke, L. L., and W. V. Price. 1979. *Cheese.* Ridgeview Publishing Co., Atascadero, Calif.

Allison Hooper

The Business of Farmstead Cheesemaking

11

You have read 10 chapters about cheese technology and are just now getting to the business and marketing plan. This chapter should not be considered an afterthought, however. In fact, reading this before you make cheese will hopefully save you some headaches later on.

Bob Reese and I started Vermont Butter & Cheese Company almost 20 years ago and have been selling cheese ever since. We are no experts. We have, however, learned some lessons along the way—and if given the chance to do it all again, *we* might have given more thought to this chapter before we made our first cheese. You can buy other books that cover cost accounting and marketing. In this chapter, though, I share a few of our personal experiences in our company, in the hope that some of our mistakes and successes will be relevant to your situation.

As for my disclaimers, I milked many goats in the early days of the company and have made farmstead cheese. I have worked on several farms but have not owned one. We are not farmers and cannot speak from first-hand experience about the challenges of producing milk in addition to making and marketing cheese. Every farmstead model is different, both from the point of view of the asset base and the goals of the farmer/cheese-maker. The information in this chapter is purely anecdotal and may differ greatly from that of our colleagues.

A LOT OF HUMILITY IS A GOOD THING

This chapter also presumes that the farmstead cheese business needs to make money. If you do not need to make money and have a lot to spend to get set up, you do not need to do as much planning and homework. If you do not need to sell cheese to support yourself or your family, your decisions may be easier and certainly less risky.

At Vermont Butter & Cheese Company, we had to make money the day we started. We began with $1,000 each and have grown the business with debt financing ever since. Owning a farm was not an option because we did not have the credit or the collateral to purchase one. This is an important point because each decision was based on an analysis of risk. How big a mistake could we afford to make? There were many cheeses we would have liked to make in the early days and still would like to make today. Early on, those cheeses were not an option. Not only did we not have the cash to store aging cheeses, but we also did not have the expertise in cheese technology to make long-hold cheeses of a consistently high-enough quality to warrant the pricing required at retail.

It is important for relatively new cheesemakers to show humility for what has taken the Europeans generations to achieve. Select a business model and a product mix that is doable—not *easy*, that is, but rather consistent with your resources and access to knowledge. With lemons we made lemonade. We decided to make fresh goat cheese. It was relatively easy for someone without a cheese technology background. It was relatively easy to duplicate. Most importantly, it created cash in the business.

Your farmstead cheese business has an origin and it has a vision. These two ideas will provide clarity for all the planning in between. First the origin:

As crime novel authors concede, "Once you've got motive, opportunity and weapon are easy." Motive is the passion from which you define the core values of your farmstead business. For each of us there was an event, or even a series of serendipitous accidents, in our lives that shaped our business idea. Why are you doing this in the first place? Enjoying a good cheese with a good wine is romantic. Making cheese every day is not. It's a lot of hard work for a long time. You need to identify the initial passion that will keep you going.

The story of our company's founding dates back to a special awards dinner in 1984, when a chef in Vermont wanted goat cheese. Bob Reese supplied the chef with this cheese, which he had asked me to make expressly for the dinner. Hence the serendipitous events that brought us together to form our partnership. Really, though, both of our passions to sustain the business went much deeper, to earlier events in both our lives. For Bob, he was developing his expertise in the challenges of distributing lamb and vegetables in southern Vermont. That combined with his penchant for numbers set him trolling for a unique dairy business idea. For me, farming and cheesemaking internships in France during college were infectious, and the French food culture left an everlasting imprint on me.

That moment at the awards dinner would never have taken place had both Bob and I not had a strong desire to do this. It was earlier events in our lives that set the stage, not the dinner itself. And so, when times get tough in the business, or our sense of purpose feels muddled, by revisiting the past we occasionally get a clearer perspective about the future.

Think about formative events and identify your motive. Your own story need not be profound or complicated, yet you will tell it over and over. Make it true.

WHAT IS THE VISION?

In 1984 Bob and I were dangerously naive. We knew very little about what we had gotten ourselves into. We hadn't a clue as to how to imagine our business in five years. There were no models or benchmarks, though we did have some fundamental parameters. Bob was married with a new baby and a home. Our $2,000 capital infusion would not buy us a farm. Our business model was a creamery that would buy milk from farmers. We wanted to make French-style cheeses that were not being made in the United States at the time. The business grew organically despite our lack of planning.

A farmstead is different. This business is also your home. Your five-year plan will depend on your financial needs. There is a difference between making money from the cheese and making enough money to earn a living. If you calculate the total pounds of cheese you will need to sell to earn a living, your operation may look very different from what you had imagined. You *can* sell 10,000 pounds/4,500 kg of cheese per year and make a profit. But is that enough? It is probably safe to say that farmers do not farm for the money. Nevertheless, imagine what your financial needs will be in 5 and 10 years. How many pounds of cheese does that represent? What does your farm look like? Depending on your location, a farm may not be an ideal place for manufacturing. Do you have coolers and Dumpsters? Employee parking? Are trucks entering to pick up cheese? What about tourists? Do you want the public to visit every weekend?

These questions are not posed to discourage you, but rather encourage you to get into the business with your eyes open. Once you know your magic volume number, you will be better prepared to consider your sales and distribution strategy.

DOING SOME HOMEWORK

Twenty years ago a little market research would have told Bob and me that making and selling goat cheese was quixotic. It was. There wasn't a history of goat cheese sales in the United States, much less a market for esoteric products such as crème fraîche and mascarpone. Twenty years ago the American specialty and farmstead cheese "industry" was virtually nonexistent. The market was far more forgiving than it is today. This lack of market development helped us as we muddled through a decade of figuring out a product mix and sales strategy.

As our industry matures and we cheesemakers expose chefs and consumers to different cheeses and how they are made, they become more discriminating. As cheesemakers, we are expected to deliver a higher-quality cheese, a memorable story, and a competitive marketing strategy.

At Vermont Butter & Cheese Company we blindly started to make cheese without having made one trip to a retailer or had a single discussion with a chef. In those days it worked out. However, I would not recommend approaching a cheesemaking venture with the same lack of planning and analysis. It is certainly valuable to visit cheesemakers in Europe. At the same time, it is imperative to carefully analyze the cheese outlets where you hope to sell your cheese. Find out which cheese sells and why.

WHAT CHEESE WILL YOU MAKE?

You have done your primary market research and have selected a cheese. Now you need to research the technology and do some preliminary calculations based on your milk cost, expected cheese yield, and holding time to see if this endeavor is at all feasible. If it looks promising and fits into your financial goals, you need to thoroughly research the process to determine what equipment you will need and the amount of storage space you will require for the optimum aging period.

Research your cheese before you build your plant. The better you understand the cheese technology, the fewer costly mistakes you will make. A good cheese from a well-managed operation uses equipment and space that is adapted to the specific technology of that cheese. For example, a lactic curd cheese production facility is different from a pressed-curd operation. Each cheese will require not only different equipment but also a different organization of the work. Time is money, and how you manage it in the cheese plant is crucial to your bottom line.

Bob and I visited a tiny Reblochon plant in the Alps. The plant was owned by 20 farmers milking about 20 cows each. They all lived within a mile or two of the plant and delivered their milk twice a day. The plant made more than 500,000 cheeses per year. There were two employees in cheesemaking and aging and a few part-time personnel to wrap the wheels.

We were both impressed by the efficiency of this operation. These were artisan cheesemakers, yet their respect for the precise technology allowed them to produce a high-quality cheese in a very small space. Their time was managed to the minute. The lesson for us was that the better we understood our cheese technology, the more control we would have over our cheesemaking process, and hence the more likely we would be able to generate income from the operation.

CONTROL EQUALS PROFIT

Control is key and is often misconstrued when we talk about the "art" of cheesemaking. You need control to make a good cheese, and you need it to operate your business profitably. Know your cost. Once you know your cost, you can price your cheese and decide on a strategy for making money. I have spoken with farmstead cheesemakers who separate their cheese business from the farm business. This is a good idea, because the more you can create meaningful cost centers, the better you will identify your cost drivers and have the ability to control them.

What is cost? Every expense associated with making, marketing, and shipping a pound of cheese. There will likely be costs that you cannot control on the farm. You cannot control the cost of grain or electricity. And you cannot control the weather. Be conservative and try to build in enough margin to sell the milk profitably. If you do not separate the two businesses, you may blame a bad haying season for the poor profitability of your cheese sales, when in fact the bottom line may have had more to do with the high cost of shipping to one customer.

Cost Drivers We Have Discovered That You May Want to Consider

Too Many Cheeses

If you find yourself in a hole, stop digging.

The fewer products you make, the better your chances of realizing a profit from operations. We all fall into the trap of having an insatiable appetite for developing new cheeses. Such creativity is what drives our businesses in the first place. Be careful. The decision to make a number of cheeses should have more to do with your sales and distribution strategy and your plant capacity than your ego.

We have made a lot of different products over the years and have decided to discontinue some of them for one reason or another. Our biggest lesson was a goat's-milk Fontina-style cheese. This was a washed-rind cheese. We made it because we loved washed rinds and we wanted the challenge of making a good one. It was a good one, and it had a great following. As our business grew, however, we realized that we could not do everything. The Fontina was a departure from the technology of our lactic curd cheeses. The only thing that they had in common was the raw materials. We simply could not afford to invest in both of these cheeses as the business grew. And most importantly given our limited resources, we could not produce both cheeses well.

Unless your cheeses share the same equipment and similar technology, try to curb your appetite for product development. It is better to be expert at fewer cheeses.

Distribution

This is typically the category where we all lose money. The reality of the small company is that the cost of moving cheese is high, and since it falls at the end of the process, we tend to forget about it until the time comes when we need to ship cheese. A good distribution cost strategy is key. I recommend that you either have your customer pay for the shipping and make that cost explicit on the invoice or build your shipping cost into the price of the product. Distribution is usually the difference between making money and losing money on a customer-by-customer basis.

Shrinkage

Milk is the largest cost of your product and should not exceed 50 percent of your cost of sales. Keeping track of the yield on the milk is the difference between making and losing money. You know that the yield changes seasonally with the changing composition of the milk. If you are using organic milk, goat's milk, or sheep's milk, the milk cost per pound of cheese is particularly high. The smallest yield change will greatly change your cost. If you are making a fresh cheese, the seasonal changes are more dramatic. A fresh goat cheese yield can be as high as 18 percent and as low as 14 percent. This change in yield will result in cost change of as much as $0.56 per pound. This is a lot, so pay close attention to your cheese technology and milk quality in order to maximize milk yield. You will need to consider seasonal changes in milk composition when pricing your cheese.

If you are making a rennet-type pressed cheese, the seasonal yield differences on the milk will not be as large. If, however, you are planning to make a natural-rind cheese, you can expect to lose several percentage points in yield during the aging. Be sure to take this shrinkage into consideration early in your planning. Aging cheese is costly in both labor and shrink.

If you are making a natural-rind cheese, a large portion of your cost of goods will be in the aging of the cheese. You want to try to avoid long hours of damage control in the aging room. Most of your cheese aging problems can be avoided in the cheesemaking process. Making sure that the moisture, pH, and salt are standardized in the vat will enable you to balance the aging conditions accordingly. If you put cheeses with varying composition into the storage room, you will spend a lot of time rescuing cheeses that are not adapted to the aging conditions of the room. A lack of control over the process will produce a greater variance of quality at the end of the aging period. Throwing away cheeses that do not meet your quality standards creates a huge cost to your business.

HACCP and Quality Control

HACCP is not a cost driver but rather a "shrink saver." A good HACCP plan will save you from discarding a lot of cheese over the years. One size of HACCP plan does not fit all, however. Your HACCP plan is unique to your operation. It is based on your cheese technology and your cheese plant. It will not guarantee protection from a product-liability lawsuit, but it helps to mitigate risk. HACCP is crucial to the success of a farmstead cheese operation for several marketing reasons:

- HACCP forces cheesemakers to standardize their procedure and their cheese. Note that I am not suggesting you standardize your milk. You are a farmstead producer. The artisan cheesemaker who respects the cheese technology every day can take pride in making a consistently high-quality cheese. And a consistent cheese is a salable cheese.
- HACCP gives you valuable institutional memory when it is time for you to hire an employee or two. If your procedure is in your head only, you are not helping yourself or your bottom line. Anyone who works for you should be able to make your cheese exactly the way you want it made.
- HACCP gives you the historical data so that when something goes wrong in

the cheesemaking or aging process—and it will—you can research what happened and make any needed adjustments or corrections.

- HACCP gives those who want to help you some important information about your cheese. Paul Kindstedt has been ready to help American cheesemakers who come to him with problems. Yet without information about the cheese and the process, we cannot identify our target or intelligently seek someone else's assistance. If you don't like your cheese and you want to change it, you need to know what you are doing today in order to change your technology tomorrow.

Collect the Money

Cash is king. You can lose money on paper for years, but when you run out of cash you are done for. You cannot afford to finance your customers' businesses. You may be selling to the best restaurants and retailers, but if they do not pay on time, you cannot sell to them. Reducing your collection days from 40 to 30 will make a big difference in your ability to finance your aging cheese inventory.

MARKETING AND COMMUNICATIONS

By now you have already given a lot of thought to marketing and communications. You have identified your motive for having a farmstead cheese, visited some of your target retailers, talked with chefs, or scoped out a local farmer's market. You have made some assumptions about the market opportunity for the cheese that you have researched. Now you need to answer the next set of questions, which will help to define your market position. Each of these questions should be answerable in a sound bite. If you can't answer these questions clearly and concisely, your customers surely will not be able to articulate what you do.

Who Am I? What Do I Do?

The first two questions should be relatively easy, unless you have a lot of different profit centers on the farm. If you have a store, you are also a retailer. If you make maple syrup, you are a sugarmaker. If you have an inn or bed-and-breakfast, you are in the hospitality business. Identifying your first activity will help to prioritize your activities and allocate scarce human and financial resources. For example, if your primary activity is indeed an inn, and this is your primary source of income, then you may not want to build a cheese warehouse to age cheese from 50 cows on the property.

At Vermont Butter & Cheese Company we are cheese manufacturers. We are not a tourist destination. We do not distribute our own cheese and therefore do not own a truck. We do not have a retail store. Anytime we can define an activity as a separate business we usually won't consider it. At the end of the day, we think that manufacturing cheese and taking care of our customers is all-consuming; losing that focus is too risky.

How Am I Different?

Be ready to give the answer. List the three most distinguishing facts or benefits of your enterprise. They could be anything from your farm to your cheese to you. Are you adding value to a chef's menu? Are you appealing to the social consciousness of your customers because they think they're saving your farm? Are you saving the retailer time? Is your cheese better understood than one with a French name?

Put yourself in the position of your customers and assume that they know nothing. Why should they buy? Then put yourself in the place of your customers and assume that they know a lot. Again, why should they buy? Will they buy because they know you personally and see you at the farmer's market every Saturday? If they live in Manhattan, will they pick up your cheese from a case full of 500 other cheeses? If yes, is it because it looks good or contains truffles, or because the clerk behind the counter recommends it? As you consider the distinguishing benefits, who will buy, and why, you will realize how very small we are as cheesemakers in the larger marketplace. The farther from your farm you sell, the more strategic you need to be in finding your voice on restaurant menus and in cheese cases. Once you know why customers choose your cheese, you can duplicate those kinds of purchases.

Who Cares?

Who is your target market? Sure, anyone who loves to eat good cheese. That group is too big. Focus on a subset of it and make your message resonate. To whom are you talking? Chefs? Neighbors at the farmer's market? Busloads of tourists? The cheese buyer at the retail chain? The more specific you are about your target customer, the more you can customize your message.

SWOT Analysis

This four-step exercise should be a short one and very much from your gut. You need to assess your Strengths, Weaknesses, Opportunities, and Threats. Here is a quick analysis of a typical farmstead cheese enterprise:

1. **Strength.** The cheese is unique because the milk comes from one herd. By definition it cannot be duplicated by a competitor. Farmstead cheeses have a positive image of purity, sustainable farming practices, and special attention to care and quality of the milk and cheese.
2. **Weakness.** A farmstead is usually too small to have the resources to hire expertise in the areas of sales, cheese technology, quality control, and financial management. The owner-operator serves in all these functions out of necessity. The cost of producing and distributing a farmstead cheese is high. You do not have a lot of cheese to amortize your overhead cost. Nor do you have the weight to amortize the cost of shipping the cheese. Since the business is at your home, it is difficult to develop a succession plan or retirement strategy.

3. **Opportunity.** Your target customers are increasingly concerned about the origin of their food and are actively looking for cheeses that are hormone-free, are GMO-free, and have a level of traceability. The advent of the cheese course as an important source of protein in our diet has increased demand for high-quality, flavorful cheeses. The target customers are typically well educated and affluent; their food decisions are lifestyle decisions.
4. **Threat.** Farmstead cheesemaking is a passion and an albatross. Farming, making cheese, and marketing are all-consuming. There are no days off, and burnout threatens the long-term health of the business. If you are making a raw-milk cheese, pending laws regarding mandatory pasteurization threaten to eliminate an important point of difference in the marketplace for farmstead cheeses.

The real purpose of the SWOT analysis is to create a strategy to emphasize the strengths and opportunities while at the same time minimizing the risks by keeping the threats in mind and improving on the weaknesses.

An Effective Marketing Strategy Is Focused on Achievable Results

You now have points of difference, benefits, strengths, and target customers. Now you need a strategy and focus. For some of us, focus has taken several decades to learn. If you can learn it early, you will spare yourself wasted money and headaches. You will also achieve your goals faster. The fewer priorities you have, the more likely it is that you will succeed. For example, if you decide to start your business by making 5 different cheeses that you will sell in 10 major markets, you are not likely to implement any one of those priorities particularly well. Don't try to conquer the entire U.S. market at once.

Tell Your Story

Everyone has one. Remember, these are those formative events that drove you to making cheese in the first place. You may think they are insignificant because it is *your* life. Yet your story makes your business personal, real, and memorable for your customers.

Clarity and Repetition

As a rule, the wider your distribution, the clearer your message needs to be. Remember that consumers and chefs in Denver do not know you if you're making cheese in Vermont. We must not assume that the public knows anything about farming or cheesemaking, or even the term *farmstead*. We must assume that they know nothing about what you do. You are making a shift in communication from speaking across the table at the farmer's market where your clients see you every week, ask about your children, and are sophisticated about farm products and rural living. In a larger metropolitan market things are different. Sure, there are more people with a greater willingness to spend more money for a pound of cheese. There is, however, a huge challenge in overcoming the competition for those customers' attention.

Yours is a small business in a large marketplace. You have a limited opportunity to communicate one idea to your customers. You have your distinguishing benefits. These are the attributes that you will repeat over and over. Repetition and clarity will help you increase awareness of your farmstead business.

Good Editorial Testimony Is Your Best and Most Affordable Advertising

The feature story in the *New York Times* food section is believed by many to be the Holy Grail for launching a marketing campaign for any food product. The reach and credibility of such an article is huge. Getting the article may take some strategy, or it could be dumb luck. The main objective is to be able to take advantage of the increased awareness and demand for your cheese.

Be prepared for the "Big PR Hit." Everyone likes to have their ego stroked and see their name and photo in the paper. Yet the story does you little good if you are not prepared to fill the orders when the phone starts ringing. Remember that the object is to increase sales of your cheese and justify the high price. The article can and should be leveraged in all your promotional materials.

The power and influence of a major daily paper should not be underestimated. You are likely to get only one chance at that story. The initial bump from the story will last until the next week's feature story. Make sure that you take the time to consider whether you are ready for the increased business. Ask yourself whether you have the inventory of cheese. Is *all* the cheese good and ready to ship? How will you get it to your customers? Know all this before the article runs. If you like the article, the cost of reprinting it is a sound investment, and it can be used in your brochure. Testimonials from the media, top chefs, or retailers build credibility and should be used wherever possible.

Good relations with the media take time to build. Be patient. The key to a good relationship is to provide the media with meaningful and useful information in a timely manner. A writer will often call with a question and need the answer that day. You are expected to drop everything and find the answer, send information, testimonials, photos, and recipes. If you have some of those things together before they call, you will appear to have your act together.

Make sure your press release is newsworthy. Give a writer a reason to write the story. Do not blast-fax a press release that has obviously been sent to a long media list. It is best to target a few key media contacts and nurture the relationship. Make them feel like they are special and have an exclusive scoop on your story.

SALES AND DISTRIBUTION

There are several ways to accomplish sales. Each method has its advantages and disadvantages. Early in the business most of us devise a distribution strategy by accident that works for the moment. We need to think ahead about the possibilities of outgrowing our initial strategy and make sure that we plan for the future. You need to consider building a hierarchy of pricing to accommodate various distribution options.

At Vermont Butter & Cheese Company we started in 1985 to buy goat's milk from two farms, and had more cheese than we could sell to the three potential retail stores and five chefs in Vermont. At the time the market was limited locally, and it was difficult to justify driving around the state with a few pounds of goat cheese. Our products are perishable and do not tolerate warm UPS trucks and FedEx terminals. The cost of shipping directly to chefs and retailers was too high. We found regional distributors and have followed that strategy ever since.

Mail Order Direct to Consumers

The ability to service a request for your cheese from anywhere in the country or world is a good thing. Food writers will often ask whether consumers will be able to buy your cheese once they read about it in a national consumer publication. You ought to be able to ship the cheese even if it is not a focus of your marketing plan.

Direct consumers are loyal customers. They should be stored in a database for future new-product sales, holiday offerings, and good consumer feedback. They will keep you honest and let you know when something is wrong as well as when something is right.

If you are doing mail-order cheese, consider the true cost of getting your customers' attention as well as the cost of shipping. Consumers often want a different combination of cheeses from what you are offering on your brochure or Web site. If you are having to spend a lot of time on the phone responding to special requests, the cost of the transaction is going up. Consider also the amount of time it takes to pack a special order and hope it is correct. You hope that the box is large enough and that you or an employee have taken care to pack the parcel so it will stay cold and not be crushed. Be sure to capture all these costs. You have a captive audience, and they need to pay for special treatment.

At the beginning you will have plenty of room and probably time to pack 5 or 10 direct-mail parcels of cheese per day. How will your day, space, and balance sheet look when you have 50 boxes per day? Do you have the space to store the boxes ready to be shipped? Do the gross sales cover the cost of hiring a person to fill the orders and pick the cheese? Can your Web site generate 50 orders per week without the additional marketing costs of search engines and targeted PR? Most importantly, have you built in enough profit margin now that it is becoming a larger part of your business?

Farmer's Markets

Farmer's markets are a wonderful place to start selling cheese. Unless you have a market in a nearby city, you won't sell high volumes of cheese at the farmer's market.

You will, however, receive productive feedback and good primary market research for your cheeses. You will also develop loyal customers who will buy your cheese no matter what. Charge your customers at least what they would pay at a retail store. Even if you do not have any retail customers to start, research the appropriate markup so that when you do have retail customers, you will not undercut them.

The larger marketplace is going to hold you to a higher standard. You will need packaging, labels, and shipping cartons. These are all items to add to your cost.

Direct Wholesale versus Distributors

Selling directly to retailers and chefs is a good step from the farmer's market. The advantages are that you have an opportunity to develop your packaging so that it will endure the wear and tear of the retail case. Some retail cases are less forgiving than others. You need to put your cheese to the test and simulate exactly what happens in the distribution chain. Send a box to yourself and see how warm the cheese is when it arrives. Wrap it in cellophane and see if it rots. Don't wrap it and see how long it takes to dry out. Remember that the conditions and attention in retail are not the same as in your cozy cheese cave. What about the label and the name of the cheese? If the customer can remember the name, you have won the battle.

Some retailers prefer to buy direct because they can develop a relationship with you, the vendor. This is a good thing when the bad things happen. And they will. If you have a shortage of cheese or if your cheese is not consistent in quality, you can speak to them directly. This is invaluable. Chances are your retailer friends will be supportive and counsel you on your marketing challenges. If you are having a problem and they don't know you, they will probably buy a different cheese. Do not give your wholesale customers better pricing than a distributor would. It costs you to give them that special level of service. You may also want to have a distributor service those customers down the road. It will be difficult to transition your wholesale customers to buy from a distributor if the price just went up.

The challenges of selling direct to retailers include the high cost of shipping and keeping cheese cold, and providing the administrative support required to call for orders, invoice the customer, and collect the money. There is a cost associated with all these points, and your pricing needs to reflect that. I often hear small cheesemakers say that they sell direct to retailers and chefs because they can make more money. If you consider the cost from the initial phone call to getting the shipment out the door to getting paid on time, you might not be making more money.

Distributors

Distibutors are not marketers or manufacturer's representatives. You should not count on them to light up the market with your cheese. They move cheese and other products and collect the money for you. Once you have established your product mix and have the confidence to fill a larger order, distributors can simplify your life. If, however, your cheese is inconsistent and does not have adequate marketing support, you may find yourself lost selling through a distributor. It is recommended that if you want to work through a distributor, you need to have enough profit margin built into your direct wholesale pricing; make room for the distributor without compromising your own profit margin. Remember that you are going to save on some costs. You do not need to hire a person to call each individual chef and retailer or collect the money. You do not need to pack a lot of individual boxes filled with shavings and ice packs. You do, however, need to anticipate their ordering cycle and make sure that your cheese shipments are absolutely foolproof. Leave nothing left to interpretation. Distributors have many products and do not have the time to baby your cheese. A well-made cheese should be capable of being shipped through the distributor without a problem. If your cheese is having a problem you may need to rethink the packaging, the ordering cycle, or even the cheesemaking procedure.

Customer Service

All your customers, whether they are chefs or distributors, want to feel like they are your only customer. Take care of them even if it costs from time to time. Having a reputation for being responsive will go a long way as you grow your business. It is important that your customers be able to contact you.

BUSINESS PLANNING

You can spend hours and hours running spreadsheets, and as soon as you start the business something different will happen. Just because reality is different from your plan, however, that is no excuse not to plan. The following models are just one way to view your business. It is recommended that you plan conservatively and run numbers for your best- and worst-case scenarios.

If this is the part that you want to read later or you typically promise yourself to balance your checkbook next month, it's advisable to get help from someone who loves numbers. It is worth it to know that someone is looking after the cash in the business if it is not going to be you. Yes, indeed, you need to understand cost and how to manipulate the numbers. You cannot afford to get behind or cut corners when it comes to analyzing the financial health of your enterprise. The following spreadsheet (table 11.1) is an example of the kind of business plan we do in our company. We try to have all the parameters on the spreadsheet and run as many "what ifs" as we can imagine. This preliminary planning tool may have little to do with reality, but you need to start with a set of numbers that can be changed easily. This business plan depicts a set of assumptions based on a cow's-milk cheese operation that is paying \$0.22 per pound for milk. The cheese is a small washed-rind wheel. The 10 percent yield on the milk is intentionally conservative.

Note the price per pound for cheese of \$6.00. This is the price of the cheese from the farm to a distributor. Regardless of

Item Descripton	Basis	# Grass Fed Cows in Herd 10	20	30	50	100
Weekly Production:						
# Grass Fed Cows in Herd		10	20	30	50	100
Milk Production/ Cow/Day	35	350	700	1,050	1,750	3,500
# Vats/Week	500 Gal Processor	6	6	6	6	6
Cheese — lbs.	10% Yield	210	420	630	1,050	2,100
# Wheels/Week	12 oz. Wheels	280	560	840	1,400	2,800
# Wheel/ Inventory	Min. 60 Days Turnover	2,380	4,760	7,140	11,900	23,800
Annual Data:						
Milk — lbs.	Cow Milk	105,000	210,000	315,000	525,000	1,050,000
Milk — gallons		12,209	24,419	36,628	61,047	122,093
Cheese — lbs.		10,500	21,000	31,500	52,500	105,000
Whey — gallons		10,988	21,977	32,965	54,942	109,884
Income Data:						
$ Revenue — Cheese	$6.00 lb.	$63,000	$126,000	$189,000	$315,000	$630,000
Total Cheese Sales		$63,000	$126,000	$189,000	$315,000	$630,000
Engineering Costs:						
Materials — Cow	$2.20 lb.	$23,100	$46,200	$69,300	$115,500	$231,000
Labor	$0.50 lb	$5,250	$10,500	$15,750	$26,250	$52,500
Factory Overhead	Fixed Costs @ $1,000/Mo.	$12,000	$12,000	$12,000	$12,000	$12,000
Total Manufacturing Costs		$40,350	$68,700	$97,050	$153,750	$295,500
Gross Profit		**$22,650**	**$57,000**	**$91,950**	**$161,250**	**$334,500**
Gross Profit %		35.95%	45.48%	48.65%	51.19%	53.10%
Material Cost/lb.		$2.20	$2.20	$2.20	$2.20	$2.20
Labor Cost/lb.		$0.50	$0.50	$0.50	$0.50	$0.50
Factory Overhead/lb.		$1.14	$0.57	$0.38	$0.23	$0.11
Total Cost/lb.		$3.84	$3.27	$3.08	$2.93	$2.81
Project Data:						
Building	$0					
Equipment	$0					
Preoperating Exp.	$0					
Improvements	$0					
Total	$0					
Lease:						
Debt Service & ROI	(IRR = 9%)	$0	$0	$0	$0	$0
Operating Income		**$22,650**	**$57,300**	**$91,950**	**$161,250**	**$334,500**

Table 11.1. Example of a business plan for a farmstead cheese company.

the option of selling through a distributor, direct wholesales to the retailer or chef, or direct to consumers, the pricing should reflect a healthy gross profit margin to the distributor. If this cheese were sold to a retailer, the wholesale price would be $7.20 per pound. The distributor usually works with a 20 percent markup. The price to the consumer at the store will be $14.40. The retailer typically doubles the price on the store shelf.

Note also the increase in profit margin as the number of cows increases. You may not want to milk 30 cows, but it will have a profound effect on your profit margin to amortize your overhead cost over more cows.

Income Analysis

The following three spreadsheets show an evolution of detailed income statements. The first is an actual set of numbers by a farmstead cheesemaker. The second and third statements have been rearranged and augmented to illustrate a different way of analyzing the business.

The first three-month income statement (table 11.2) was generously shared by a dairy farmer in Vermont. The farm is making 400 to 800 pounds of cheese per week, which represents about one-third of the herd's production. The cheese plant pays the farm $15.00/cwt. The remaining two-thirds of the production is sold to a cooperative for $11.25/cwt before trucking, fees, and promotion.

Assumptions

The net profit is high. We need to remember that the farmer has not paid himself in this income statement, and he is only paying the farm $15/cwt for the milk. For a farm that has been in business less than 10 years, this is a financially healthy operation. There are two indicators for some promising trends. The first

	Mo. 1	Mo. 2	Mo. 3	Total	% Sales
Cheese sales	9.501	11,486	13,06	34,693	100%
Milk purchases @ 15/lb.	3,500	4,000	3,000	10,500	30%
Gross profit	6,001	7,486	10,706	24,193	69%
Expenses:					
Cheese expenses	435	625	3,251	4,311	12%
Maintenance		108		108	0.30%
Advertising	56	114	313	483	1.30%
Interest	286	100	100	300	0.86%
Payroll	286	1,080	770	2,136	6.10%
Professional services	450	263	1,367	2,080	5.90%
Shipping	361	266	1,367	1,944	5.60%
Total expenses	1,688	2,556	6,314	10,558	30.40%
Net profit	4,313	4,930	4,392	13,635	39%

Table 11.2. An example of an income statement from a farmstead cheesemaker in Vermont.

is that the milk cost is only 30 percent of sales. The second is that the debt service is very low. The farm has obviously made some modest investments in setting up the creamery. By keeping this overhead cost low, this farmer will have more operating income and be able to weather future problems that may arise.

In the next income statement (table 11.3), we have rearranged the numbers to better illustrate the true cost of production.

As you can see, we have not changed any numbers or added any costs to the chart of accounts. We have moved all cost that relates to the actual production of a pound of cheese above the cost of goods sold. This rearranging has reduced the gross profit margin from the first spreadsheet from 60 percent to 45 percent. This is a more realistic view of the amount of revenue needed to cover the operating expenses. It includes all the fixed overhead cost. It is important to include as much cost related to the making of cheese in the cost of goods as possible.

The third income statement (table 11.4) is fictitious. We have added a number of cost items that should be tracked on a monthly basis. We also think that the third set of numbers is arranged in a way that gives the farmer a more conservative analysis of the health of the business.

Item	Month 1	Month 2	Month 3	3 Month Total	3 Month Average	% Sales
Cheese sales	$9,501	$11,486	$13,706	$34,693	$11,564	100.00%
Manufacturing Costs:						
Milk*	$3,500	$4,000	$3,000	$10,500	$3,500	30.27%
Cheese expenses	$435	$625	$3,251	$4,311	$1,437	12.43%
Maintenance		$108		$108	$36	0.31%
Payroll	$286	$1,080	$770	$2,136	$12	6.16%
Shipping	$361	$266	$1,367	$1,994	$665	5.75%
Total cost of goods sold	$4,582	$6,079	$8,388	$19,049	$6,350	54.91%
Gross profit	$4,919	$5,407	$5,318	$15,644	$5,215	45.09%
Operating Expenses:						
Advertising	$56	$114	$313	$483	$161	1.39%
Professional services	$450	$263	$513	$1,226	$409	3.53%
Interest	$100	$100	$300	$300	$100	0.86%
Total operating expenses	$606	$47	$926	$670	$670	5.79%
Total manufacturing costs	$5,188	$6,556	$9,314	$7,019	$7,019	60.70%
Profit before taxes & depreciation	$4,313	$4,930	$4,392	$13,635	$4,545	39.30%
Break-even sales				$1,335		

Notes: *$15 cwt.

Table 11.3. An example of an income statement from a farmstead cheesemaker in Vermont that has been revised to emphasize the true cost of production. (See table 11.2 for the original income statement.)

Item	Month 1	Month 2	Month 3	3 Month Total	3 Month Average	% Sales	$Cost /LB
Cheese sales	$9,501	$11,486	$13,706	$34,693	$11,564	100.00%	
Chese lbs. (10% yield)	$2,333	$2,666	$2,000	$6999	$2,333		
Avg. price/lb.	$4.07	$4.31	$6.85	$4.96	$4.96		$4.96
Manufacturing Costs:							
Milk ($20 cwt.)	$4,666	$5,332	$4,000	$13,998	$4,666	40.35%	
Packaging (5% sales)	$475	$574	$685	$1,735	$578	5.00%	
Cheesemaking supplies/ingredients	$50	$50	$50	$150	$50	0.43%	
Total Materials					**$5,294**	**45.78%**	
Payroll (1 part-time)	$950	$1,149	$1,371	$3,469	$1,156	10.00%	
Employee benefits	$200	$200	$200	$600	$200	1.73%	
Total Labor					**$1,356**	**11.73%**	**$0.58**
Chemical cleaning supplies	$100	$100	$100	$300	$100	0.86%	
Lab services - milk testing (2x/month)	$30	$30	$30	$90	$30	0.26%	
Quality assurance - Cheese testing	$50	$50	$50	$150	$50	0.43%	
Quality assurance - environmental testing		$300		$300	$100	0.86%	
Payroll taxes	$87	$106	$126	$319	$106	0.92%	
Insurance	$200	$200	$200	$600	$200	1.73%	
Maintenance	$100	$100	$100	$300	$100	0.86%	
Utilities—fuel & electrical	$200	$200	$200	$600	$200	1.73%	
Whey management ($0.02/cheese lb.)	$47	$53	$40	$140	$47	0.40%	
Shipping	$361	$266	$137	$1,994	$665	5.75%	
Total Overhead					**$1,598**	**13.82%**	**$0.68**
Total cost of goods sold	$7,516	$8,710	$8,519	$24,745	$8,248	71.33%	$3.54
Gross profit	$1,985	$2,776	$5,187	$9,948	$3,316	28.67%	$1.42
Operating Expenses:							
Advertising	$100	$100	$100	$300	$100	0.86%	
Professional services	$450	$263	$513	$1,226	$409	3.53%	
Telephone	$100	$100	$100	$300	$100	0.86%	
Interest	$100	$100	$100	$300	$100	0.86%	
Total operating expenses	$750	$563	$813	$2,126	$709	6.13%	
Total manufacturing costs	$8,266	$9,273	$9,332	$26,871	$8,957	77.45%	
Profit before taxes & depreciation	$1,235	$2,213	$4,374	$7,822	$2,607	22.55%	
Break-even sales					$3,760		

Notes: Break-even sales = fixed costs (factory overhead)/% contribution margin

% contribution margin =

1) Variable sales price/unit – variable costs/unit (materials & labor) = $ contribution margin

2) $ contribution margin/varible sales price/unit = % contribution margin

Table 11.4. A fictitious income statement that has been arranged to represent a more conservative analysis of the health of the farmstead cheese business.

You will note that the profit before taxes is significantly lower in the third statement. Note that we have increased the cost of milk to the farm. You may want to show more profit on the farm where you have more assets to depreciate. We also wanted to increase the cost of milk in the event that you are thinking about purchasing milk from a farmer other than yourself. You will need to build in some profit for the farmer.

You may be able to bury some of these costs early in the business. For example, insurance may be paid by the farm, or whey handling may be negligible. As you grow, however, some of these costs will be more apparent, so it is not a bad idea to be looking at them at the beginning.

The three income statements have the same general numbers yet show a discrepancy in profitability. In fact, they look like different businesses with different break-even points.

How much cheese does this farmer need to sell in order to break even? This is an important question to answer early on because it will tell you how aggressive your sales plan needs to be, as well as how much working capital you will need to borrow until you break even and start making a profit. The farmer in the first model needs to sell only $1,335 per month to break even. In the third, he needs to sell $3,760. Remember that the cost of milk is higher in the third model. This has lowered the profit margin and increased the need to sell more pounds of cheese to stay in business. There are more costs included in the second model. The gross profit margin is only 28 percent. The smaller the operation, the larger the gross profit margin needed. A farmstead operation should operate at about a 40 percent gross profit. This is a difficult goal. The total material costs and labor are usually high as a percentage of sales. The place to save is in the fixed overhead.

The lesson here is that it is better to have all your costs in front of you and be able to separate the fixed from the variable costs. If you want to remain small, you need to keep your fixed costs as low as possible. You may be able to borrow a lot of money from the bank for a "showplace" building. But you will need to pay for it with every wheel of cheese.

FINAL THOUGHTS

This chapter touches on a few of the important considerations of your marketing plan as well as your financial plan. There are several main areas that you need to make a priority as a small operator:

1. **Sound financial management of the business.** If you do not like to do it or don't have any particular expertise, hire it out. You already wear too many hats in your business, what with being an expert in milk production and in cheese production. You need to do your own marketing because your customers want to get to know you. Find someone to take care of the finances.
2. **Maintain the quality of your cheese.** You are too small to sell anything less than terrific. You do not have a household brand name; you only have your reputation for impeccable quality. When you

are starved for cash, it is tempting to sell cheese that has defects. Resist the temptation. When defects become the standard, your business is on a slippery slope.

3. **Customer service is everything.** Being on a tractor all summer long is not an excuse for your customers' inability to contact you. They don't care. They adore you for being on the tractor, but they still want service. You will not keep your good customers unless you devise a system by which they can leave messages, fax orders, and get an answer from you.
4. **Do a lot of planning before you start.** It is a luxury you will never have again once you start your business.

Cindy Major

Putting It All Together: The Vermont Shepherd Story

12

THE HISTORY OF VERMONT SHEPHERD

Vermont Shepherd, owned by David and Cindy Major, is located on a sheep dairy in Westminster West, Vermont. Vermont Shepherd is a cheese business that produces 40,000 pounds/18,160 kg of cheese annually. Of its total cheese production, 20,000 pounds/9,080 kg is a farmhouse sheep's-milk cheese called Vermont Shepherd. Another 20,000 pounds is made at a neighboring cow dairy by the Vermont Shepherd staff. The two cow's-milk cheeses, Timson and Putney Tomme, are then brought to the cheese cave at the Majors' sheep dairy, where all the cheeses ripen together. Vermont Shepherd markets its cheeses throughout the United States to specialty food stores and restaurants. Over the years Vermont Shepherd has received many awards and has been featured in national food magazines and newspapers.

The following is Cindy Major's account of how she and David started Vermont Shepherd, what led them to make the cheeses they make today, how they learned to make their cheeses, how they market their cheeses, and some of the challenges and successes they have encountered over the years.

Milking Sheep?

In 1983, when David and I started farming, we really didn't know what we were doing. We were raising sheep for lamb and wool on David's family's farm in Westminster West, Vermont. David's family had 60 sheep, all meat breeds, Cheviots and Dorsets. We worked off-farm jobs and tended the sheep in the late afternoons and on weekends. Though we really loved the work, the farm couldn't turn a profit, despite the fact that we had virtually no overhead. All the land, barns, tractors, and sheep were owned by David's

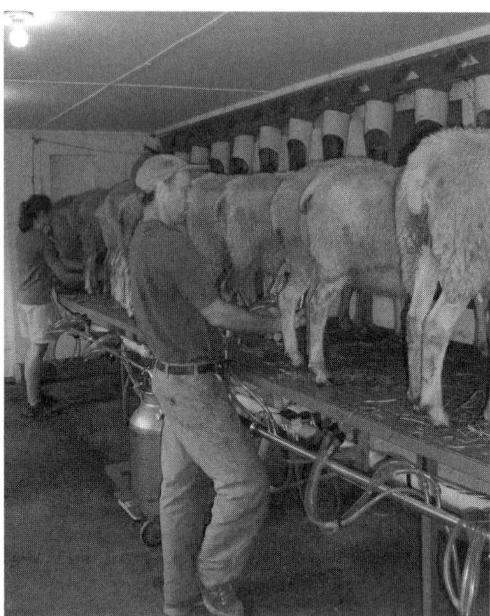

Figure 12.1. David Major and Bec Whitcomb milking the Vermont Shepherd flock during summer 2003.

parents and were available to us at no cost. One day my father said to us, "Why don't you try milking your sheep and making cheese?" That was a pretty strange idea. We had never heard of milking sheep or sheep's-milk cheese. It made sense to my father; after all, he was the co-owner of his family's business, Elmhurst Milk and Cream Co. in Queens, New York. The dairy business was familiar territory to him, and to me, too, by matter of heritage. Eventually that history helped me feel comfortable with the idea of working with dairy products, and together David and I had a lot of support from both of our families.

So that's how our cheese adventure started. Our early years of dairying were pretty rocky. In 1987, with the help of Olivia Mills, a British sheep dairy farmer, cheesemaker, and author of *Practical Sheep Dairying*, a how-to guide, we were put in touch with a man from Burlington, Vermont, named John Finlay. John was starting to make sheep's-milk yogurt on a commercial scale. He had rented a dairy processing room at the University of Vermont and was gathering together a group of farmers interested in supplying him with milk. There were about six of us at the time. Through his knowledge and enthusiasm, we were able to set up a licensed milking parlor within the year. Since there were no commercial sheep-milking stanchions available in the United States, John urged us to begin manufacturing them for ourselves and for others, as well. He even did the legwork needed so we could purchase the patent on a trouble-free, cost-effective sheep- and goat-milking stanchion. We still make these stanchions today to sell to sheep and goat dairies.

In spring 1988 we began milking our flock, freezing the milk, and driving full freezer loads to Burlington every other week. But by July we had decided to quit milking; it was tremendously hard work for very little milk, and, besides, David and I had our wedding date planned. We were going to get married in the beginning of July. We had plans to take a 10-day honeymoon and wouldn't be able to milk. John gallantly volunteered to move into our house and milk while we were away. We weren't allowed to stop!

Beginning to Make Cheese

We continued selling frozen milk to John for a year or two, and then it became clear that his sheep yogurt business was struggling. John was having trouble paying us farmers, and it seemed that it was just a matter of time before he would go out of business. So there we were, with a licensed sheep-milking parlor and a flock of sheep that we had begun selecting for milk production. We decided to try our hand at cheesemaking. We hired our neighbor, Peter Dixon, to help us develop some cheeses. Peter had made cheese for his family's business, Guilford Cheese Company, which had just gone out of business. Peter's experience at the time was mostly in Camembert and Brie production. Peter agreed to help us develop some recipes and oversee our cheese production. It happened that a local boarding school had set up its own small licensed dairy to make cheese and yogurt for the school's students. The Putney School offered to rent us its dairy processing room. In spring 1990 David, Peter, and I began making cheese.

Figure 12.2. Roberto Gautier, David Major, and Cindy Major pressing Vermont Shepherd Cheeses, June 2003.

Making cheese at the Putney School was a bit chaotic, to put it mildly. At that time we were trying to develop three cheeses in the hope that at least one of them would prove successful. We chose to make a blue cheese, a Gouda, and a feta. We continued to freeze our sheep's milk because we had been told that freezing sheep's milk would not harm its properties in any way. Since we were renting the Putney School's cheese room by the day, this made a lot of sense. We froze the milk in long, cylindrical tubes, and the night before we made cheese, we would load the frozen bags into the back of our truck so they would thaw slightly overnight. The next morning we drove the milk to the Putney School, sanitized all the milk bags, and poured the milk into the cheese vat. It was a highly complicated procedure, but we were all determined to make it work. Unfortunately, our blue cheeses never turned blue, our waxed Goudas became moldy almost immediately, and the feta was either too salty or too mushy from lack of salt. Through trial-and-error marketing at the Brattleboro Farmer's Market, we discovered that the cheese that was selling best was the blue cheese that wasn't blue. The next year we tried to develop a hard cheese with a natural rind that wasn't blue. We tried making them small and tried making them large. We worked to perfect this cheese for two full milking seasons and ended up throwing almost all these cheeses away. They were dry, salty, and flavorless. My job was to sell them. So I took the cheeses to one of New York City's premier gourmet food stores, Dean & DeLuca, and offered my samples to Steve Jenkins, who was then the cheese buyer. Steve tasted the cheeses, spat them out, and told me they were horrible and to never come back to his store with cheeses as bad as those. He knew I could do better. I was devastated and walked up West Broadway and burst into tears. When I returned home to Vermont I told David that we had to either quit milking and making cheese or go to Europe and learn traditional cheesemaking methods. We decided to give our dream one last chance.

A Trip to France

Neither David nor I speak any language other than English, and this was a big obstacle for our research trip to a foreign country. We knew that there were a lot of sheep's-milk cheeses made abroad, especially in Spain, Portugal, Italy, Greece, Turkey, and France. As it happened, a young woman who worked for us in summer 1992, Calysta Drake, was part French and part American. I called Calysta and asked if she could spend her college winter break helping us research farmhouse sheep cheese production in France. She was excited about the idea, and we started making plans to meet in Marseilles, a few hours from her family's home in Provence.

More than 400 varieties of cheese are made in France, and a good number are made from sheep's milk. We were still in the dark about where to go, whom to visit, and which variety of cheese to learn how to make. I decided to write to Patrick Rance, a British cheese shop owner and author of two well-respected cheese books, including *The French Cheese Book,* one of my favorite books on French cheeses. I explained our situation to Mr. Rance, telling him that we wanted to learn some traditional techniques for making aged sheep's-milk cheese and wondered where he thought the best places to visit might be. He wrote back and said, "Go to the Pyrenees. You will find what you are looking for there." One of the great things about *The French Cheese Book* is that Mr. Rance lists the names and addresses of cheesemakers from all over France. We then wrote letters to many of the farmers listed in the Pyrenees index. We sent photos of ourselves, our sheep, and our farm and told the farmers when we planned to be visiting their area, adding that we hoped to meet them and would call when we arrived in France. The next step was to figure out exactly what it was we wanted to learn and come up with a list of questions. We arrived at the Marseilles airport with our two small children, ages 18 months and four years, a lot of poor-quality sheep's-milk cheese, and a spiral notebook full of questions.

Our trip to France in the winter of 1993 was probably the most exciting time in the development of our cheese business. Looking back, both David and I feel we learned more in two weeks in the Pyrenees than we had in three years of trial-and-error experimentation.

As it turned out, the farmers we wrote to were very willing to meet with us. The sheep farms in the Pyrenees were quite a bit like our own; they all had about 200 sheep and the same amount of acreage as our own farm. Some of the French cheesemakers had farms where their traditional Bearn or Basque sheep cheeses had been made for generations, while others were fairly new to the enterprise. They all shared a common goal: to make the best cheese possible using the traditional methods. The French farmers also introduced us to the concept of terroir.

We made cheese with many of these cheesemakers. Those who were relative newcomers to the craft were part of a traditional cheese revival much like what is happening here in the United States today. We saw cheese being made in metal cauldrons over propane burners on the floor, and we made cheese in state-of-the-art stainless-steel cheese vats. All the cheesemakers we visited used the same recipe and were making the same type of cheese, Fromage de Ossau in the Bearn region and Etorki in the Basque region. The French farmers assured us that if we grazed the sheep on the fields that were in the pictures we showed them of our farm and followed their directions, our cheese would be wonderful. It was an exciting time.

Figure 12.3. Cindy Major and Ferdinand Pujalet, Lys, France, February 1993.

Voilà!

When we returned to Vermont in late February, we decided to discontinue renting the Putney School cheese room and begin using our own space. This way we would have more control over the final outcome of our product. A big lesson we learned in the Pyrenees was to use fresh milk only—freezing milk was out of the question! With fresh milk we would need to make cheese at least three times a week to keep the milk from spoiling. We had a lot to do to get ready for the next cheese season. We needed to convert our cheese vat so it would reach the temperatures needed for our new "recipe." We also had to acquire some new equipment, including a cheese press, cheese molds, and a cooling unit that could provide the aging temperatures and humidity our new cheeses would need. And then, in the beginning of March, it was time for the sheep to have their lambs. By early April we were ready to start cheese production.

We started making cheese three times a week and adapted the French recipe and techniques to the needs and constraints of our own facility. We diligently followed our French mentors' directions. After three and a half months, we decided it was time to try the cheeses. I picked out the ugliest, grayest, most pitted-looking wheel and cut it open. I was prepared for disappointment, since all our earlier attempts were so unsuccessful. I was shocked at the richness of flavor and smooth, supple texture. The cheese tasted sweet and delicate, with an amazing, slightly mushroomy flavor. We knew we had finally created what we had been working toward! The next week we entered a wheel of our cheese in the distinguished American Cheese Society contest and were awed when we received the award for Best Farmhouse Cheese in the Uited States. All of a sudden we had a desirable product, and buyers from all over the country wanted to carry our farmstead sheep cheese.

Teaching Farmers and Growing Our Business

Over the next few years we continued milking the sheep and making cheese. Since our Vermont Shepherd Cheese is only made during the Vermont grazing season, it is only available for six or seven months of the year. Every spring our cheese would sell out, and every spring our customers would cry for more. At this point we came to a major crossroads. We asked ourselves some very hard questions about the future of our business. In the end we decided to build our volume by teaching other Vermont sheep farmers how to milk their sheep and how to make our cheese. We based our idea on a traditional model we observed while in the Pyrenees. In the Pyrenees and in the Jura region of France where Comté is made, and in Switzerland where Gruyère is made, it is common for cheesemakers to make the same type of cheese and then sell their cheeses to an affineur (French for "cheese ripener"). The cheeses are then marketed from the affineur's cheese cave. This model was attractive to us because it afforded us a way to increase the quantity of Vermont Shepherd without turning our farm into a "factory farm." It was extremely important to us that our farming practices be gentle to the earth and healthy for our animals. We wanted to make sure that our cheeses were made from sheep grazing on pastures, not from animals kept inside barns all year long and fed grain and hay produced hundreds of miles away. We also knew that many area farmers were interested in the type of work we were doing and were looking for new opportunities. We decided to give the European cheese cave model a try here in Vermont. Early on in the planning stages, a French affineur said to me, "What you are trying to do is very difficult; here in France we have a tradition of this, everyone knows what we are supposed to do." We were determined, however, to make this model work here in the United States, though it was a huge undertaking.

We ended up working closely with The Vermont Land Trust and the Vermont Department of Agriculture to secure funding to establish a Sheep Dairy Center. The center oversaw teaching prospective farmers the skills of sheep dairying and cheesemaking. We consulted with the stu-

Figure 12.4. Vermont Shepherd producers attending a workshop given by Jacky Mege in summer 2000. Back row, left to right: Bruce Clement, Neil Urie, an anonymous intern, David Major, Jacky Mege, Mark Fischer, Mike Ghia. Middle row: Ellen Clement, Rebecca Nixon (French translator), Bob Works, Ann Works, Gari Fischer, Margo Ghia. Front row: Gus Dixon, Peter Dixon (cheese consultant), Cindy Major, and Chet.

dents not only about the agricultural and cheesemaking aspects of their operations, but also in the actual setup of their facilities. It was our hope that once these dairies were set up, they would provide us with high-quality sheep cheese that we could then add to our own stock and sell as part of our Vermont Shepherd line. This model is quite similar to the Vermont maple syrup industry. The syrup is made at many sugarhouses around the state, then graded and sold as Vermont Maple Syrup.

Between 1997 and 2000 we worked with eight farm families from around the state of Vermont and into neighboring New Hampshire, and at the same time we were running our own farm and cheese operation and raising our two young children. It was an intensive undertaking. After a couple of years all the new farmers were up and going. Immediately we had all sorts of quality issues: The cheeses were too wet or too dry, too acid, too salty, too funny-looking. Despite many more hours of input from David, myself, and the dairy science program of the University of Vermont, we still felt we had to do more to give the farmers the support they needed to succeed. As a group of sheep dairy farmers, we decided to bring in a technical sheep cheese expert from the Pyrenees region of France. We worked with several of the Vermont Shepherd Cheese producers on proposing a SARE (Sustainable Agriculture Research and Education) grant to bring Jacky Mege, a Pyrenees cheese technician, here to Vermont. The grant funding was received and all eight of us farmer-cheesemakers hosted Mr. Mege. We all learned a great deal.

Despite a huge amount of effort on our part and on the farmer-producers' parts, many of the farmers we worked with decided to discontinue sending cheese to the Vermont Shepherd Cheese Cave. Perhaps the volume of cheese they produced was not enough to make the enterprise economically worthwhile, or perhaps the producers ultimately wanted to make their own individual products and market them under their own labels. In any case, the model of working with many sheep dairies slowly fell apart. We continue today to work with two other producers on a much smaller scale.

Building a Cheese Cave

As our own cheese production increased we quickly realized that it was just a matter of time before we would run out of cheese-ripening space. We had been using an 8-by-14-foot/2.4-by-4.3-meter

Figure 12.5. Cindy Major and Bianca Fernandez brushing cheeses inside the Vermont Shepherd Cheese Cave.

walk-in cooler with metro shelving for ripening our Vermont Shepherd Cheeses. We were also using the cheesemaking room to pack our cheeses for shipping, and our home for office space. It was becoming an uncomfortable and ineffective way to run a cheese business. We needed a lot more space. We decided to build an underground artificial "cheese cave" on a hillside a few hundred feet from our cheesemaking room. The new cave would serve as ripening space for 50,000 pounds/22,700 kg of cheese and would provide us with much-needed office and shipping space. We knew of no other cheese caves here in the United States, so yet again we decided to go to Europe to learn how caves are built. We visited caves in France and Switzerland and observed how humidity and temperatures were controlled, how shelving was constructed, and so on. When we came back we had a much better idea how to construct our own cave. In the end we decided to build a cave using connecting concrete culverts. These culverts are buried 4 to 6 feet/1.2 to 1.8 m underground in a cross-type configuration with two long "wings."

Figure 12.6. Vermont Shepherd now sells three cheeses: a sheep cheese, Vermont Shepherd, and two cow's-milk cheeses, Putney Tomme and Timson.

Growing by Adding Cow's-Milk Cheeses

As our cheese markets continued to grow, and as it became clear that we would not be able to increase volume substantially by working with other sheep farmers, we decided to begin making two varieties of cow's-milk cheeses. We again hired Peter Dixon to help us develop the new cheeses.

We knew we wanted to make natural-rind, unpasteurized, aged cow's-milk cheeses, ones that would complement our Vermont Shepherd. In the end we decided to develop a brushed-rind cow's-milk cheese similar to Tomme de Savoie and a washed-rind cow's-milk cheese similar to Taleggio. As with any new product, it took many months of trial-and-error experimentation to perfect the final cheeses. The process takes especially long with aged cheeses because of the need to wait for many months to know the final outcome. In the end it was two years before we finally settled on some recipes and techniques that worked best for our cave and farm. We now sell three cheeses: our sheep cheese, Vermont Shepherd, and our two cow's-milk cheeses, Putney Tomme and Timson.

VERMONT SHEPHERD TODAY

A lot has changed since David and I started our sheep dairy back in the mid-1980s. We now have three full-time employees and three part-timers. Our flock has grown from 60 meat sheep to more than 200 dairy sheep. Our farm has grown as well, from 40 to 250 acres/16 to 101 hectares. We now sell to more than 200 specialty food stores and restaurants around the United States and host an active Web site that receives orders on a regular basis. Our lives are full (and a little crazy) with farming, cheesemaking, and running our cheese business.

FREQUENTLY ASKED QUESTIONS

How did we decide what type of cheese to make?
Right from the start we narrowed down our options, mostly with my father's advice. My father ran a large dairy processing business for 40 years and has had an enormous amount of experience marketing dairy products. He told us to avoid making fresh cheeses. He said that since we live in a rural area, far from any markets, we would struggle with marketing fresh cheeses that spoiled quickly. That made a lot of sense. We chose three varieties to start: blue cheese, feta, and Gouda. After experimenting with these three varieties we quickly stopped making the feta since it is virtually impossible to ship via UPS or FedEx; it needs to be stored in buckets of liquid salt brine, and the extra liquid makes shipping cumbersome and expensive. We also discontinued the blue cheese because we had so much trouble getting it to develop blue veins. It was a year or so into cheesemaking before we came to the conclusion that it was essential that we make a specialty product, not a commodity product. We decided to focus our efforts on a natural-rind, aged cheese that would have a long shelf life.

How did we learn to make cheese?
Learning to make cheese is a multifaceted, long-term undertaking. We learned in many ways, and each way contributed to where our cheese company stands today. In fact, we're still learning. Every year we work to improve on the previous year's production through refining our procedures. The key elements of our learning have been trial and error, traveling, working with consultants, conferences and workshops, and learning from our employees.

Trial and Error

There is no doubt that trial-and-error cheese development is incredibly time consuming, not to mention frustrating enough to bring just about anyone to tears. Unfortunately, it is really the only way to learn how to make cheese. As any cheesemaker knows, when starting a new product, expect to throw away hundreds if not thousands of pounds of poor-quality cheese. Only through the arduous process of learning what they *don't* want to create can cheesemakers really come to understand what it is they want to create. Our first three years learning to make cheese were just that: learning the basics of curd and whey and acidity and aging. If we hadn't had a good grasp of the process and how cheese is made, and if our cheeses hadn't turned out as badly as they did, we wouldn't have known what questions to ask to get us to where we are today.

Traveling

Traveling has played a major role in the development of our cheese. In the United States there are very few specialty cheeses made, and the technical resources are growing but still very limited. Through visiting cheese operations around the United States and abroad, David and I have been able to broaden our perspective on the specialty cheese industry. The American Cheese Society has proved to be a great resource for this—cheese tours are built into the end of its annual conferences.

In 1995, after we had established our Vermont Shepherd Cheese, I knew I had a lot more to learn about cheese rinds and was able to set up a monthlong internship at Neal's Yard Dairy in London, where many varieties of natural-rind cheeses are matured and marketed. I learned about brushing cheese rinds, caring for cheese boards, and how to keep a cheese aging room humid by simply running cold water on the floor a few times a day. I also learned how to put together beautiful cheese displays. A few years later we went to France and Switzerland to learn more about building cheese caves. We discovered that whitewash is an ideal coating for a cave's walls since mold and bacteria are unable to grow on whitewashed walls. We saw how the Swiss caves use kilns to dry their wooden boards; we observed cheese-cleaning machines in action, a robot that turned and brushed cheese, and a mechanical machine that did the same thing but with human assistance. David is in the process right now of inventing a cheese-cleaning machine for our own cave here in Vermont. We also learned the ins and outs of each cave's business structure. Traveling is expensive and time consuming, but if you're really clear about the information you're looking to learn and ask specific questions, it can be invaluable.

Consultants

I love consultants and am also extremely wary of them. The idea that someone can come and show you how to set up your operation and teach you how to make wonderful cheese is fabulous. Consultants appear to be the easy answer. They're not. A cheese consultant is spending your money and has no financial risk if the products he or she is helping you to develop do not come out as you had hoped. Consultants have been helpful to us in the beginning phases of cheese development. After the first batch or two is made, however, it is important for the cheesemaker to take on the responsibility of tweaking the recipe and techniques. Otherwise the process can be incredibly slow and expensive.

Our work with Peter Dixon, a cheese consultant and cheesemaker, is a good example of how a consultant can get a cheesemaker started. Peter helped us with the start-up phases of all three of our cheeses. When we first starting to make cheese, we knew absolutely nothing about the process. As I've mentioned, we wanted to develop a blue cheese, a Gouda, and feta. At the time Peter knew very little about these types of cheeses, as his primary experience was with Camembert. He came up with recipes that worked, the cheese we made resembled the ones we were aiming for, but there was a lot of reworking we needed to do to have the cheeses come out exactly as we wanted them to. Peter, and most consultants, are talented at setting up the trial phase of product development. It is the cheesemaker's role to identify the errors and guide the process along.

One very successful experience we had with a consultant was with Pyrenees cheese technician Jacky Mege. The two weeks that he spent consulting with us were exceptionally valuable because we asked him to address some very specific concerns: to help us eliminate a grainy texture in the cheese, eliminate gas holes, and increase production efficiency. As a group we had set up his visit so he could work one-on-one with each producer, and we set up times for him to present two workshops. The other reason his visit was so valuable was that his area of expertise was related to our specific type of cheese. Mr. Mege works with around 100 producers of sheep cheese and is trained in the technical issues it involves.

We have also worked extensively with Dr. Paul Kindstedt and the University of Vermont. Dr. Kindstedt has assisted us one-on-one, has set up workshops for our group of Vermont Shepherd producers, and has also offered classes in the UVM cheesemaking facility. Through many hours spent with Paul, we have learned a great deal about the scientific aspect of cheesemaking. One of the most important pieces of information we learned from Paul is an understanding of when acid begins to develop in our cheeses. This information has helped us choose the best intervals for monitoring acid development. Dr. Kindstedt also helped us develop production record sheets. In our earlier years of cheesemaking we kept extensive records on every batch we made. This was extremely time consuming, and we really didn't know why we were going through all the trouble. Dr. Kindstedt helped us simplify our record keeping and explained how the records could be used as a tool to increase the quality of our cheeses.

Conferences and Workshops

Every year the American Cheese Society holds a conference, and almost every year we attend. Held in different regions of the United States, these conferences offer cheesemakers and others in the cheese industry a way to exchange ideas and information about the world of cheesemaking. Each conference is usually three to four days long and includes a cheesemakers' day, which includes technical workshops on specific topics such as cheese rinds, fresh cheese, cheese aging, and so on. During the main part of the conference, presentations are geared to both cheesemakers and others in the industry—wholesalers and chefs, food writers, dairy scientists, and more. Topics might include marketing, industry concerns, specific cheese types, and tastings of cheeses from various regions. We have attended many regional workshops on food safety and HACCP (Hazard Analysis Critical Control Points) programs, which have helped us develop a food safety program. This program has given us substantial credibility for the occasional surprise FDA inspection.

Learning from Employees

We have been extremely fortunate to have worked with so many amazing, dedicated people over the past 15 years. Our employees have played a significant role in shaping where Vermont Shepherd is today. The day-to-day input we receive from our staff is invaluable. Everyone who has worked here has made a difference in the growth of Vermont Shepherd, but three employees really stand out as having made a huge impact on the development of our cheese business. In summer 1992 we hired a young woman named Calysta Drake, then a sophomore at Harvard University. She worked for us that summer, helping with milking, cheesemaking, and haying. It was at the end of that cheesemaking season that we decided to go to the French Pyrenees to learn some new cheese recipes and techniques. Since neither David nor I speaks French, we asked Calysta if she would join us and translate. If it weren't for Calysta's amazing gift of connecting with people and her comfort with both our family and the French culture, our trip to France never would have been as successful as it was.

Another employee who had a huge impact on the development of Vermont Shepherd was Beth Carlson, who worked with us from 1996 to 1999. Beth and I met in 1995 in London, when I was working as an intern at Neal's Yard Dairy. She was in charge of the ripening room at Neal's Yard and cared for dozens of varieties of natural-rind cheeses: clothbound cheddars, Cheshires, Stiltons, washed-rind cheeses, bloomy-rind cheeses, and more. She had immersed herself in cheese ripening and was learning everything she could about the process. Beth eventually had to leave Neal's Yard Dairy because her work visa expired; she started working for us a few months later. She had a strong background not only in cheese ripening but also in cheese retailing, because she had worked at Zingerman's Delicatessen in Ann Arbor, Michigan, an award-winning deli that carries specialty foods from around the globe. She taught us a great deal about how to manage the cheese in our cave, and her background in retailing helped us shape our marketing approach. Many of the ripening procedures and marketing techniques we use today were ones that we developed with Beth.

In 2000 we hired Charlie Parant to work as our cave manager. Charlie had experience in cheesemaking and photography, and his passion for cheese led him to spend many hours tweaking our cow's-milk cheese recipes. He reworked them so well that they are now winning awards and have a strong retail following. Charlie's background in photography has been extremely helpful to us, as well. We have been able to take most of our own publicity photos for our brochure and Web site, thanks to his expertise.

MARKETING

Believe it or not, we have never developed a comprehensive marketing plan, and to this day have a minimal promotion budget, yet we manage to sell all the cheeses we produce. I believe part of our success is due to the fact that our products are high quality, unique, made in a beautiful location, and have a great story connected to them. We can't help but think that some of our success with marketing is due to pure luck and timing. When we started making our Vermont Shepherd Cheese back in 1993, there were only three other sheep dairies in the entire United States. We were the first sheep dairy in New England, and the food and agricultural media were interested in what we were doing and wrote about us often. These stories reached thousands of potential customers and helped establish our business.

Web Site

A few years ago my sister-in-law, Sarah McCoullough, offered to put together a Web site. This site has been up and running for five years now, and every year it becomes a larger part of our cheese marketing. We offer holiday specials on the site and also use it to announce the start of the Vermont Shepherd Cheese season as well as our open houses.

Open Houses

We offer four open houses every year. These are terrific promotions and a lot of fun. During the open houses we open our cheese cave and cheese house (where the cheese is made) to the public; we also have a few sheep for guests to look at, offer cheese tastings, and explain how our cheeses are made and ripened. These events are great advertising for our products because the public can really see what happens here, and this often generates a lot of excitement.

Staying Connected to Buyers

I like to visit our wholesale customers whenever I can. I think good personal communication is important for both the buyer and the seller. Relationships are an important part of our business.

Entering Contests

We enter cheese contests—both domestic and international—whenever the opportunity arises, usually two or three times a year. Cheese awards can go a long way toward establishing credibility.

Talks, Demos, and Tastings

We have built on our marketing success by making ourselves available for public talks at all types of conferences. David often gives talks to regional and national agricultural organizations. I gear my talks toward the food world: organizations within the specialty food and dairy industry and culinary schools. I also make myself available to retail cheese buyers for staff training sessions. We like to have an active presence in our local community and demonstrate our cheeses at local food co-ops and specialty food events.

Shipping

We are a small company and have a relatively small volume of cheese. Since all our cheeses are fairly durable and all are aged more than 60 days, they ship very easily. We ship most of our cheese via UPS or FedEx. The cheeses are packed in insulation with ice packs and are sent via regular ground service in the Northeast or via air service to other parts of the United States.

FINAL THOUGHTS

Often I am asked: Would I do it all over again? It's a hard question to answer. Running a farmstead cheese business is an incredible life commitment. The responsibility is enormous. A farmstead cheesemaker has to wear many hats: farmer, cheesemaker, veterinarian, maintenance person, cleanup crew, cheese technician, marketing expert, shipping expert—the list goes on and on. The hours are very long, often 14-hour days, 7 days a week. It's virtually impossible to take time off, as both the animals and the cheese are so labor intensive.

Yet there is incredible personal satisfaction that comes from farmstead cheesemaking, as well. We are ultimately responsible for the outcome of our cheeses, and are now part of the process that the French cheesemakers in the Pyrenees described to us. We have reaped the ultimate reward. By treating our animals and land and cheese with respect, by carefully following an ancient recipe, we have been able to capture some of the flavors of our pastures in our cheeses, and these we can share with the cheese eaters of the world.

FURTHER READING

GENERAL-INTEREST WORKS ON CHEESE

Amata, F., L. Guiseppe, and D. Mormorio. 2000. *Heritage and Landscape: The Art of Traditional Cheese-Making.* Consorzio Ricerca Filiera Lattiero-Casearia, Ragusa, Sicily.

Bonilauri, F., ed. 2001. *Parmigiano Reggiano: A Symbol of Culture and Civilization.* Consorzio del Formaggio Parmigiano-Reggiano, Leonardo Arte srl, Milan.

Carroll, R., and R. Carroll. 2003. *Home Cheese Making,* 3rd ed. Workman Publishing, New York. ISBN 1580174647.

Ciletti, B. 1999. *Making Great Cheese.* Lark Books, Asheville, N.C. ISBN 1579401093.

Harbutt, J. 1999. *Cheese.* Willow Creek Press, Minocqua, Wisc. ISBN 1572232005.

Harbutt, J., and R. Denny. 2003. *The World Encyclopedia of Cheese.* Hermes House, London. ISBN 1843096714.

Jenkins, S. 1996. *Cheese Primer.* Workman Publishing, New York. ISBN 0894807625.

Masui, K., and T. Yamada. 1996. *French Cheeses.* DK Publishing Inc., New York. ISBN 0789410702.

McCalman, M., and D. Gibbons. 2002. *The Cheese Plate.* Clarkson Potter/Publishers, New York. ISBN 0609604961.

Rance, P., et al. 2002. *Cheeses of the World.* Rizzoli International Publications, New York. ISBN 0847815994.

Sardo, P., G. Piumatti, and R. Rubino, eds. 2000. *Italian Cheese.* Slow Food Arcigola Editore, Bra. ISBN 8886283989.

Sokol, S. 2001. *And That's How You Make Cheese!* Writers Club Press, San Jose, Calif. ISBN 0595177093.

Tewksbury, H. 2002. *The Cheeses of Vermont.* The Countryman Press, Woodstock, Vt. ISBN 0881505137.

Werlin, L., and M. Jacobs. 2000. *The New American Cheese.* Stewart, Tabori & Chang, New York. ISBN 1556709900.

WRITTEN FOR FARMSTEAD AND ARTISAN CHEESEMAKERS

Biss, K. 2002. *Practical Cheesemaking.* The Crowood Press Ltd., Ramsbury, Marlborough Wiltshire. ISBN 1861265530.

Le Jaouen, J.-C. 1990. *The Fabrication of Farmstead Goat Cheese,* 2nd ed. *Cheesemakers' Journal,* Ashfield, Mass. ISBN 0960740430.

Morris, M. P. 2003. *The Cheesemakers Manual.* Glengarry Cheese Making & Dairy Supply, Alexandria, Ontario. ISBN 0973236604.

Vermont Cheese Council Code of Best Practices.

WRITTEN FOR CHEESE SCIENTISTS AND CHEESEMAKERS

Fox, P. F., P. I. McSweeney, T. P. Guinee, and T. M. Cogan. 2000. *Fundamentals of Cheese Science.* Aspen Publishers, Inc., Gaithersburg, Md. ISBN 0834212609.

———, eds. 2004. *Cheese: Chemistry, Physics and Microbiology,* Vol. 1 and 2, 3rd ed. Elsevier Academic Press, London. ISBN 012263652X and 0122636538.

Kosikowski, F. V., and V. V. Mistry. 1997. *Cheese and Fermented Milk Foods,* Vol. 1 and 2, 3rd ed. F. V. Kosikowski, LLC, Westport. ISBN 0965645606.

Law, B. A., ed. 1999. *Technology of Cheesemaking.* CRC Press LLC, Boca Raton, Fl. ISBN 0849397448.

Scott, R., R. K. Robinson, and R. A. Wilby. 1998. *Cheesemaking Practice,* 3rd ed. Aspen Publishers, Inc., Gaithersburg, Md. ISBN 0853343926.

Van Slyke, L. L., and W. V. Price. 1992. *Cheese.* Ridgeview Publishing Co., Atascadero, Calif. ISBN 0917930517.

OTHER WORKS OF INTEREST

Early, R., ed. 1998. *The Technology of Dairy Products.* Blackie Academic & Professional, London. ISBN 075140344.

Roginski, H., J. W. Fuquay, and P. F. Fox, eds. 2003. *Encyclopedia of Dairy Sciences,* Vol. 1–4. Academic Press, London. ISBN 0122272358.

Walstra, P., T. J. Geurts, A. Noomen, A. Jellema, and M. A. J. S. van Boekel. 1999. *Dairy Technology.* Marcel Dekker, Inc., New York. ISBN 0585133697.

ABOUT THE CONTRIBUTORS

PAUL S. KINDSTEDT, PH.D.

Paul Kindstedt received his Ph.D. in food science from Cornell University under the mentorship of Professor Frank V. Kosikowski. He joined the University of Vermont faculty in 1986 and was promoted to the rank of full professor in 1996. Dr. Kindstedt currently teaches courses in Fermented Dairy Foods, and Cheese and Culture. His research over nearly two decades has focused primarily on the science and technology of cheeses. Dr. Kindstedt is widely regarded as an international expert on mozzarella cheese. He has published more than 100 scientific and technical articles and several book chapters. Dr. Kindstedt also has a keen interest in farmstead cheesemaking and has conducted workshops and outreach activities for farmstead cheesemakers for nearly two decades. He is currently co-director of the Vermont Institute for Artisan Cheese.

TODD J. PRITCHARD, PH.D.

Todd Pritchard grew up working on a small dairy farm that was one of the original land grants from King George of England. Today he spends his time teaching courses in food microbiology, beer making, and food-processing techniques at the University of Vermont. He also works extensively throughout Vermont with companies developing quality assurance programs such as Good Manufacturing Practices, Sanitation Standard Operating Procedures, and Hazard Analysis Critical Control Point systems.

CATHERINE W. DONNELLY, PH.D.

Catherine Donnelly is a professor of nutrition and food science at the University of Vermont. She currently serves as the associate director for the Vermont Institute for Artisan Cheese. During her tenure at the University of Vermont, she has developed a research program that investigates the foodborne role of *Listeria monocytogenes*. Widely regarded as an international expert on this bacterial pathogen, Dr. Donnelly has published numerous articles and delivered hundreds of presentations on the topic of *Listeria*. Current scholarly interests include investigation of the microbiological safety of raw-milk cheeses aged for 60 days. In 1999 the U.S. secretaries for agriculture and health and human services appointed Dr. Donnelly to the National Advisory Committee on the Microbiological Criteria for Foods. Dr. Donnelly also was appointed by the FDA commissioner to serve on the Science Advisory Board of the FDA's National Center for Toxicological Research.

Peter H. Dixon

Peter Dixon is a dairy consultant and cheesemaker from Vermont. Peter has a great deal of experience in establishing small-scale cheesemaking facilities and developing recipes and techniques. He has farmed all his life. In the late 1970s he bottled Jersey milk in glass, and then in the 1980s made French-type cheeses for six years in his family's Guilford Cheese Company, after training with fourth-generation French cheesemakers. He has bachelor's and master's degrees in animal and food sciences from the University of Vermont, where he did his thesis on the effect of seasonal milk production on farmstead Cheddar cheese composition and quality. He has worked as a cheesemaker and quality-control manager at Shelburne Farms and Vermont Butter & Cheese, after which he spent five years consulting in international development projects in Macedonia, Albania, and Armenia. Currently Peter holds workshops for farmstead cheesemakers around the United States, and works as a consultant in manufacturing and quality control of dairy products, especially cheese. He provides training and technical assistance in business establishment, including planning and cost analysis, and can help locate the proper equipment and develop recipes. His consulting jobs have included work for Vermont Shepherd, Shelburne Farms, Taylor Farm, Woodcock Farm, Cato Corner Farm, and many artisanal cheesemakers outside the northeastern United States He currently also operates The Training Center for Farmstead Milk Processing, where he teaches cheesemaking workshops every month in a licensed farmstead cheesemaking facility.

Allison Hooper

Allison Hooper is cofounder of Vermont Butter & Cheese Company. Before starting that business in 1984 with Bob Reese, she was a dairy products quality technician with the Vermont Department of Agriculture. She began her career as a cheesemaking apprentice in Brittany and Haute Alps while studying in France. Ms. Hooper has served on boards of directors for the Vermont Sustainable Jobs Fund, a state initiative fostering economic development in environmental technology, agriculture, and forestry, as well as the Vermont Fresh Network, an organization that promotes local, sustainable food distribution through farmer-to-chef partnerships. Allison and her partner, Bob Reese, were named Vermont Small Business Persons of the Year in 1996. She has worked for Land O'Lakes International Development to revitalize domestic cheesemaking in the former Yugoslav republic of Macedonia. She is the founding president of the Vermont Cheese Council. Allison lives in Brookfield, Vermont, with her husband, Don, and their three sons, Miles, Sam, and Jay.

Cynthia Major

Cindy is the cofounder and director of marketing for Vermont Shepherd LLC, 1988 to the present. Cindy and her husband, David Major, also own and operate Major Farm, home to more than 200 dairy sheep. She lives in Putney, Vermont, with David and their two teenage children.

INDEX

C

D

L

M

N

O

P

T